To The Two "J's" come sail with us!

Pat Cecil

YOU CAN'T GO

INCOGNITO

IN A

BATTLESHIP

Pat Gates
June 29, 2013

By Pat Gates

PublishAmerica

Baltimore

D1572295

First printing

ISBN: 1-59129-518-1
PUBLISHED BY PUBLISHAMERICA BOOK PUBLISHERS
www.publishamerica.com
Baltimore

Printed in the United States of America

DEDICATED TO SOME VERY SPECIAL PEOPLE

To my dearest husband, Cecil Gates, for having the vision and creativity to "dream the impossible dream"...and make it come true.

To our skipper, Bill Brockett, who charted our course so skillfully, who was always there when needed...and who taught me to have a love affair with the sea.

To our generous benefactor, Preston Avery of Land 'n Sea International, who believed in our dream and whose great financial support made the first Bicentennial dream voyage a reality.

To our last captain who did so many trips with us...Capt. Skip Crabtree, who I found on Dauphin Island south of Mobile, AL. Dear Skip...whose 200 ton license skills guided us, rescued us, brought us safely into every port, fed and burped us through miles and miles of water and four river trips.

To special friend, Frank Scott, director of Baker International, who generously donated to our USS ARIZONA when we needed rescuing from high profile mechanical troubles. His support over the years was without equal. He believed in our "mission."

To our wonderful board of directors: Harry Siler (Vice President), Gary Waldron, Lura Blindbury, Darcie Regall and Ernest Joiner (and spouses), who served our cause with enthusiasm. Their advice, financial support, and patriotic belief in what we were trying to do was a crucial factor in our success. They stood by us year after year, and their guidance was invaluable as was/is their friendship.

Without the above help and support, this book could never have been written.

THANK YOU, *dear friends.*

PREFACE

She who wants life to be a calm and tranquil ebbing and flowing of gentle undulations along the way should stay home and work in the garden.

She who can face EARLY A.M. sailings, the uncertainty of where one will place one's head on a pillow that night, the terror of 6 foot waves, the falling(s) overboard, the black and blue bruises (numerous), the need to throw a 100-foot line out to waiting, smirking (she can't do that) men in order to save a boat blown out of control in an elegant-full-of-expensive-yachts-marina—

She should go to sea.

The adventure, the mariners one meets, the ever-tightening bond with crew members, the "WE DID IT!" makes it all worthwhile. The thousands of water miles become a waterfall of memories, and this book and its pictures confirm that the funny boats had a real purpose.

The above preface verbiage is not from some famous historian. It is from an over-the-hill school teacher who had to overcome a fear of water, learn to live with three demanding (but loveable) men, penetrate the semi-closed male sea-faring circle and ended up knowing she was one of the luckiest women to ever tie up in over 200 marinas.

Pat Gates

FRIENDSHIP FLEET TRAVELS

1975   Miami, FL to New York---USS BICENTENNIAL
        Skipper Bill Brockett, Cecil and Pat

1976   New York, Hudson River, Lake Champlain, Montreal
        USS BICENTENNIAL
        Dru and Paul Stewart, Walt, Cecil and Pat

1977   Nashville to Paducah---Cumberland River
        4 ships—3 battleships, 1 aircraft carrier
        "The Nashville Navy"
        Dru and Paul Stewart, Cecil and Pat

1985   Houston/Galveston, TX to Tarpon Springs, FL.
        USS ARIZONA
        Captain Ernie and Peg, Cecil and Pat

1986   Tarpon Springs to New York
        USS ARIZONA
        Capt. Skip Crabtree, Cecil and Pat

1989   South Haven, MI to Mobile, AL
        "Hello, Dolly"
        Capt. Skip Crabtree, Cecil and Pat

1991   Hudson, MN to Dubuque, IA
        USS ARIZONA (Miss. River)
        Capt. Skip Crabtree, Cecil and Pat

1991   Honolulu, HI---Sheraton Waikiki
        USS ARIZONA (50th Anniversary-Pearl Harbor)
        Cecil and Pat

1975

Miami, FL to New York

USS BICENTENNIAL

Skipper Bill Brockett
Cecil and Pat Gates

Miami, FL to New York—1975

A BATTLESHIP IN MY BACKYARD

The lazy quiet of the late Saturday afternoon was suddenly broken! From the inside of a darting red, white and blue ship came these words: "Now hear this! This is your captain speaking. I command you to surrender or I will be forced to fire upon you. You may fire when ready, Mr. Gridley. Fire! Fire! Fire!"

Going full speed ahead, siren blaring, claxons sounding and air horn screaming, the 18-foot battleship came alongside a huge tug boat and let go with the two forward turret guns, squirting 2 jets of water fifty feet toward the starboard side of a tugboat.

Shouts of disbelief from the crew and those of other boats in the water filled the air. "Grab the camera! Hurry up on deck, Mike. Come and see this, Joe. You'll never believe! It must be radio controlled."

The hiss of the water and the slapping of the waves on the red and white hull were all that could be heard now as the battleship knifed through the sparkling waters of Biscayne Bay in Miami. Like a live thing, the ship leaped forward at full throttle under the expert guidance of her owner/builder. Churning through the turquoise sea, the little battleship, USS BICENTENNIAL, was a bright and shining creature seemingly mated to the frothy liquid that encircled her. The wind in the bay had risen, causing the 10 small American flags to stand out stiffly in the afternoon breeze. The miniature ship darted unhesitatingly in and around the behemoth ships that shared the same waters with her.

Her captain circled several cabin cruisers, weaving in and out, appearing, then disappearing from sight to the amazement of the startled boat owners. Chuckling to himself, the USS BICENTENNIAL's captain made another pass, this time at two young boys paddling a dinghy. "Surrender or I'll be forced to fire upon you," he shouted at them over the PA system. Rising to the occasion, the boys stood up. Streams of water shot out at them as the hand pump inside the battleship was activated. They clutched their hands to their hearts and hurled themselves overboard.

As the little boat wove its way in and out among the many pleasure craft, its owner finally solved the mystery of its seemingly rudderless helm. Slowly the hinged superstructure of the boat tipped upward to the glee of the onlookers. "Look, there's a man in it. It's NOT radio-controlled. Have you ever seen anything like it!" Carefully, the huge boats sidled alongside the little craft, looking down at the big friendly man sitting in one of the bucket seats.

Questions rained down on him. "Where did you get it? Did you build it? What are you going to do with it? What IS it?"

This scene and these same questions were to be repeated many times as the man and his boat were to duplicate this same "water attack" over and over for 1500 miles up America's Intracoastal Waterway (the ICW).

It all began as so many dreams do begin…with an idea, with creativity and imagination, with boyhood memories—an idea so strange as to be ridiculous. The dreamer, the creator was my husband, Cecil Gates.

It was the end of a long school day with my second graders and I was standing at the kitchen window gazing out on our circular driveway. Wondering why Cecil was so late today, I prepared dinner and waited. There he was! As he turned into the driveway, I saw that his blue pick-up truck's bed was crammed and overflowing with materials—sheets of plywood, 2x4s, pipe, cement. Happy to see him arrive, I went out to greet him. With naïve curiosity I asked him, "What are you going to build?" Unknown to me at that time, his answer was going to totally change our teachers' lives and lead us down an adventuresome path—river(s) is more like it.

"I'm going to build a battleship!" he answered—and, I might add, with a tone in his voice that asked for understanding and support.

"You're REALLY going to do it?" I asked, suddenly remembering a conversation that had taken place at Lake Almanor in northern California some two months previous.

"Yes, I may be crazy, but I want to build a battleship. I hope you understand."

Actually I should not have been overly surprised. Cecil had built me several unusual contraptions at different times. He built me a motorcycle for Mother's Day and a dune buggy for Christmas; his last project had been the purchase of a 26-foot double-ender Navy boat which had been damaged when it was dropped off a destroyer. It had a large hole in the hull. Cec repaired it with fiberglass and turned the boat into a cabin cruiser. When he was first teaching at a Los Angeles high school, he built a centrifuge to test ram jet engines that his students built. Outside his shop on the small gravel area, he and his students put up a large steel beam with a counterweight on one end and an engine on the other. Then someone lit the jet and it took off for a few seconds. The noise was supersonic and the neighbors around the school called the police. It was quite a flurry that one time and the tests were terminated. With all this background knowledge of the creativity in Cec's mind, I really wasn't overly surprised at the latest project he wanted to undertake.

But a battleship! Why? That question would be asked hundreds of times by reporters as our watery adventures took us on all the rivers of America— except the Missouri. The answer was not really difficult to find. Cecil and his brother were born and raised in Lihue, Kauai, by a civil engineer father and principal mother. A year before Pearl Harbor was bombed, his parents took the two high school boys to Honolulu as Cecil Sr.'s work location changed. I heard stories about a 16-year-old Cecil, Jr. looking out the Honolulu (Roosevelt High) study hall windows at the gray battleships coming into the harbor. He rode his bike down to the docks, looking longingly at the sailors who manned the ships. "Someday I'm going to join the Navy," he told his parents. Just one year later, on December 7, 1941, a surprise attack would come that changed Cecil's and everyone's lives forever.

In the summer of 1972, Cecil and I were building a summer cabin at Lake Almanor in the NE corner of California. We had a long vacation time, as we were both teachers with the Los Angeles City schools and had been teaching for 23 years. I was a primary teacher, Cec the head of a large Industrial Arts Dept, and both of us were in the San Fernando Valley of Southern California. That summer we had hired a young man to help us with the carpentry in the construction of our cabin. It was late afternoon and I could see both men were tired. As I climbed the ladder to the roof to take some sodas up, Bob leaned over and said to me, "You'll never guess what Cecil is going to build now!"

Cecil jumped in. "What this lake needs is a good battleship!"

"A battleship?" Bob and I laughed together. Very shortly the remark and the idea were summarily dismissed as work continued on our cabin.

The summer came to an end and the cabin was enclosed for the winter. We headed back to Southern California and the beginning of another school year. We were six weeks into the fall semester when the pick-up truck came home that memorable day. I stifled my impulse to laugh as I realized this battleship building concept meant a lot to Cecil. Instead I asked him how one begins to build a battleship. I reached back into my own experience with boats and knew that on a scale of 1 to 10, I was a minus one. One thing I did know—a hull was necessary. This concluded my in-depth knowledge of how to build a boat. From this point on, my whole life was to change. I was to become boat-oriented in a way I never dreamed possible.

Late afternoon arrival home became customary for the boat builder. Cecil haunted the model boat section of toy shops, researched Navy books in libraries, talked with any Navy personnel he could find, wrote the Library of Congress archives department for pictures, checked out books on how to fiberglass. In between all this activity, he hummed, filled yellow sheets of paper full of sketches, drew chalk outlines on the driveway and seemed quite caught up in the challenge facing him. That winter of 1972 was a busy one. Night after night, Cec would go out to the garage or to his shed where he kept his drafting equipment. By this time he had decided that the model ship must be a 40:1 scale. With the aid of an overhead projector, he had blown the original drawing up to 18 feet. This he traced onto a 2 x 20 foot sheet of butcher paper, showing the outline and silhouette of a miniature battleship.

To my surprise I learned that the hull of a ship is built upside-down. For three months he labored on the configuration of the hull. Plywood, nails, glue, bolts, fiberglass appeared in great quantities. The day my car was politely but firmly moved out of the garage to be parked outside proved to be the last time for some years that any car was parked inside. The battleship project continued to overflow.

How unsuspecting I was at the time. I had no clue we would end up with a non-profit corporation called the Friendship Fleet, Inc. which would include four 18-foot battleships, a 20-foot carrier, the 36-foot USS ARIZONA and the 23-foot RMS TITANIC. Perhaps it was just as well that this hobby-out-of-control took shape gradually.

For those readers who are not boat builders, I cannot emphasize enough how important the hull shape is. On this one design rests everything else. The stability of the boat, speed, maneuverability and that one elusive quality— grace of line—all are built upon this foundation. The most difficult part in building this battleship (other than having it upside-down for three months) was the bow. The complexity of the compound curve for a battleship took many afternoons and evenings to design. Plywood was steamed so it would bend. One huge bolt, 12 inches in length, was used to pull in the bow to give her that compound curvature.

At this time, my duties consisted of words of support and amazement, wringing of hands over design problems, supplying numerous mugs of coffee plus words of support. I well remember one late afternoon both of us were practically standing on our heads trying to see what the boat would look like right side up. A friend came quietly around the corner. "Have you two completely lost your marbles?" was his remark.. "What is THAT?" Our secret was out.

We had been very silent about this apparition beginning to take shape in our back yard. Friends who knew of Cecil's creativity and inventiveness would sometimes question us at gatherings. "What's he going to build now?" they would ask. We confided in few, timidly testing their reaction. Usually it was "He's going to build a WHAT?" It seemed easier to avoid the subject than to advertise!

Slowly the hull began to take shape. To me it looked more like a canoe, an upside-down one for sure, but recognizable as a boat. At this time Cecil decided that he would make a mold for the hull so that he could have other battleships shot up in fiberglass. This put me into temporary shock. More than one battleship? The future had many surprises for me.

Hours and hours of work went into putting the waxy substance onto the hull, but success was not to be forthcoming. The wax would not adhere, nor would the parting compound part! Despite following directions faithfully, Cec was forced to peel off his mold in small pieces. This proved to be a most discouraging time, and there were many nights he would say to me, "I'm not sure why I'm doing this—for what reason—but I feel compelled to go on with it."

Eventually all the mold material was scraped and peeled off, and the glorious day came when we turned over the hull. Even to my unskilled eye, she looked well-proportioned. Her ribs were properly spaced, her bow and stern closely resembled her "mommy" ship, the USS INDIANA. We were delighted and encouraged once again. I learned that Cecil had made a "plug" and he would now have a professional shoot up a hull mold properly so he could build more battlewagons. The delay in building was worth the time, trouble and expense, and soon Cec was ready to begin to shape the superstructure. By now it was spring of 1973. Wintery disappointments were behind us, and Cec felt a renewal of enthusiasm and expectancy to forge ahead.

Now came the flotation, the ballast and decking. Each end of the battleship was full of foam flotation. Eighty-five pounds of concrete ballast were troweled into the bottom midship of the hull. After this was completed, decking was laid and screwed in place.

Now artist's license was brought into play. Great planning was needed to adequately represent a battleship's superstructure, make it believable, yet seaworthy and capable of fitting two persons inside. Cecil's craftsmanship proved itself again, for the end result was a superstructure whose funnel gave head room for the passenger riding in the rear bucket seat. Tiny, square-shaped windows were cut in for vision and ventilation. We (I say "we" because by this time I was scooped into this weird project) had fun making radar screens and various accoutrements to hang on the ship. We searched junk yards, dumps and found parts from washing machines, cars, plumbing—whatever looked like it might make a proper shape. A vivid imagination was needed for this part, and at times it was like designing ornaments for a Christmas tree. The superstructure was partially carved out of foam, which lends itself to shaping and cutting. Large 16-inch guns mounted in turrets were made from PVC pipe. By this time we also had the top and the turrets shot up in professional molds. The forward guns had copper tubing inserted in them for water squirting purposes. The tubing was connected inside to a hand pump which was located at the right knee of the pilot. The ten five-inch guns on each side were made out of molds and also mounted in smaller turrets. Our gray lady began to look properly lethal. The day came when the superstructure was hinged to the hull. We had a battleship! We painted her—what else?—gray and put the numbers '58' on her. The miniature USS INDIANA was born.

The coup de gras was about to come. After eight months of work, disappointments, frustrations, highs and lows, questions from friends (and to those dear friends who believed in us we are ever grateful)—now was the time. Would she float? Would she turn over? Would she displace too much water and not have enough freeboard? How would she handle? How would she react in the water? As June and the end of school approached, these questions were uppermost in our minds.

THE SECRET LAUNCH

Our plans to head for our Lake Almanor cabin for the gala launching included an attempt at disguising our battleship. The trailer on which she rested was open, but we wrapped her in black plastic, hoping to drive unrecognized and unchallenged the 700-mile drive north. We left just as dawn was breaking over smoggy Los Angeles with our precious cargo obediently following along behind us. As we looked back at the black skyscraper effect we had achieved, we were not sure our elaborate attempts at deception were all that good. The result we had achieved was more like a sulking, sinister, misshapen monster rather than the camouflaged, nonchalant image we hoped to project. Such proved to be the case. For 700 miles up the highways of the state, we were waved at, pointed out, followed and obviously the object of much discussion. Cars and trucks rode our tail and rode beside our trailer for miles. When they finally passed us, they waved and gave us the thumbs up sign. Gas station attendants all chorused the same question: "What is it?" Rest stops proved to be no-rest-stops as the curious gathered around with their inquiries. Having no information or pictures with us did not help matters, and all we could was lamely describe what was enshrined behind us. Although people were astonished, they seemed very interested and supportive and wished us good luck on the forthcoming launch. One could tell that the men wished they could be there for the first launch.

Thirteen hours after starting, we chugged up the last hill and gratefully backed our black apparition into a slot among the pine trees. Hidden from the world at last! How unused to the public eye we were then and somewhat sensitive to curiosity about our yet unproven lady. The moment of truth was almost upon us. Would our offspring perform as a ship should? Or would we provide only amusement and concern from onlookers? Two more days would answer all our concerns.

The boat builder readied our USS INDIANA for her maiden voyage. In went the six HP Johnson outboard engine in the well under the back turret. In went the two 12-volt batteries on either side of the well. Hooked up to these were a siren, claxon and air horn. Our boat looked out of place under the pine trees as Cec labored to get her ready. She began to look as if she might be ready for sea duty; but was she going to be seaworthy?

We were unable to hide our gray ghost from dear neighbors, Joanne and John, plus teenagers Pete and Nancy. They made many trips over to watch our progress. Pete volunteered to put together the two kits of Kingfisher planes which would be attached to the catapults on the stern. With great interest and an outreach of understanding, the four encouraged us to proceed with our first launch. They assured us they would be with us early the next morning and that our secret would be safe overnight with them!

Two other good friends joined us in our great adventure. Ray was a captain with United Airlines and a near neighbor from San Fernando Valley days. With him came son Bob. The latter was the young man whom we had employed the previous summer and who broke the news to me that I was going to become the mother of a battleship.

There were to be eight of us altogether for the secret launch. 5:30 A.M. was to be our rendezvous time and we would head for the closest launch ramp in the hush of dawn. Spurred on by encouragement from these good friends, we faced the coming morning breathlessly. Sleep was not on our agenda that night. Restlessly, we squirmed, talked, questioned, wondered and fitfully slept. By 4 A.M. Cec was up, performing last-minute touches on his ship. D-Day had arrived. The moment of truth was upon us. Would all those months of work and creativity be for naught? Or would she make us proud? I longed for success for this wonderfully creative man of mine. As dawn came, all was in readiness and our good friends escorted us the mile to the launch ramp. All was hushed in the morning light with only an occasional squirrel to gaze in surprise or a blue jay to scream his disapproval of our invasion of his territory.

The battleship by now was uncovered and decked with flags, and we trundled our burden along twisting roads toward the lake. In this quiet resort area, no one was awake, or so we thought. As we rounded a bend in the road, we saw an early morning riser, a woman in her robe out on her deck enjoying a cup of coffee. As we slowly drove by her cabin, her mouth opened in shock, she took one long "can-it-be-real" look at us and dashed into the house— obviously to tell someone inside. Later this same woman told us that she ran in to awaken her son, who was a naval officer at Annapolis, and to tell him "a battleship just went by the house." His disbelief in her story made her wonder what she had seen. We were to experience this reaction over and over in the years to come.

We backed the trailer down the ramp and into the water. Our friends shouted encouragement and directions. We three women watch in fascination as the gray lady slowly slid into the lake. "She's floating, she's floating!" This unnecessary comment from me probably summed up our doubts and fears about this strange offspring of ours. John had a line on her nose and pulled her in close to the dock. Joanne, always equal to any occasion, brought forth a bottle of pink champagne and plastic champagne glasses with ribbons tied on them. Carefully she placed the glasses on the deck up near the bow. "May her life be long and her sailing days be smooth," was the gracious toast given by John.

"And may she please not sink," muttered Cecil beside me. The festivities over, the moment was upon us. Ray raised the hatch and Cecil climbed in. Breaking the golden morning's silence with the coughing of the engine, Cec warmed up the motor for his maiden cruise. Ray and Bob lowered the superstructure, John untied the bowline, and we gave a mighty shove. Out nosed the bow, and with a roar of her tiny motor, the battleship suddenly came to life.

Gone was her inability to move, gone was her awkwardness. It was as if she became a live thing. She sprang to life before our eyes as the captain began to put her through her paces. What a thrill he had as he was transformed into a test pilot. Sweeping in circles in front of us, gracefully weaving in and out of his self-created wakes, he made her look like the real thing. No longer was our ship earthbound, but was in the medium for which she was intended. Surely no engineer could have been happier about the launching of the *Queen Mary* than Cecil was at the launching of his battleship. After circling, speeding up, reversing and rocking her, he brought her in to the dock and the men tried to shake and capsize her. We found that a heavy man could stand on the port or starboard side of her deck and she listed only slightly. We found she needed a fairly good size turning radius and that she also responded to being put in reverse.

Next Cec gave us all rides in the rear bucket seat and we found that the stern went down a bit more with the added weight, but did not spoil the looks of her as she plowed through the water. She was amazingly stable, and I shall never forget Cecil's happiness and pride at the end of the tests when all pronounced her seaworthy, trim and worthy of the Navy name USS INDIANA. By this time, the sun was high and a crowd had begun to gather. No longer did we have to hide our creation but could confidently take her out on the now ruffled lake. The remarks were music to us. I watched from the shore as Cecil performed for the gathering crowd.. Her bow sliced through the waves perfectly. "Isn't she a beauty! Look at her go. She looks like the real thing. Did the Navy build her? Look at that bone in her nose." (Later on after many boating trips I found out that last compliment meant the bow was holding a beautiful wave as she cut through the seas.) That day Cec had hours of fun as he tooled around the lake with his invention. That night, a tired but happy battleship captain slept well.

In the next few weeks, Cecil worked the bugs out of the ship, testing, retesting, changing from a 6 HP engine to a 9.9 HP Johnson. We had no desire for a more powerful engine. It looks tacky when a battleship begins to surf and go up on plane. The well in the stern was shipping water and short circuiting the batteries, so that problem was solved by using a rubber inner tube as a gasket to keep out the splash.

We began to take our boat out for cruises to different ports on large Lake Almanor—57 miles of shoreline. The reaction was always the same. People would stream down the mountainside, children swam out to meet us, cameras were grabbed, and helping hands would always assist us in tying up. We did what Cec called "terrorizing the natives." He would circle pleasure craft, announce in sonorous tones, "This is your captain speaking. I demand you surrender or I'll be forced to fire on you." Then he shot his hand pump water cannon at them. People squealed with delight, applauded, saluted and begged for more.

One early morning when Cecil was churning out on the lake, he passed three elderly gentlemen fishing in a rowboat. As he passed them, American flags snapping in the breeze, the three men stood up, doffed their caps and placed their hands over their hearts. The battleship circled them and squirted them with a 50 ft. jet of water.

Requests to come and visit different marinas on the lake were showered on us. We were flattered. Ellie and Buck, who had a cabin on the lakefront, invited us to lunch. "But only if you come in your battleship. We'll meet you after you anchor off shore and bring you in with our canoe." We accepted this invitation, and as we rounded the bend, we found our hosts and their friends lined up along the shore waiting for us. They were wearing tri-cornered paper hats and were singing "Anchors Aweigh" off key—loudly. Since Buck did not yet have a dock where we could tie up, he came out to pick us up in his canoe. It's an accomplishment to tie up a battleship to a buoy and climb gingerly into an unbalanced canoe. We were paddled ashore as honored celebrities. Such a welcome!

As the exploits of the ship became more widely known that summer, a reporter for the local Chester paper called and wanted to do a story on our ship. Surprised and flattered, we agreed to do what we now refer to as "our thing" for the press or TV. The reporter ran a story in the weekly paper, complete with pictures. We had no idea that this was to be the first of hundreds of newspaper and magazine interviews for the next 25 years. The next surprise came when a larger city paper, *The Sacramento Bee*, assigned two women to do a feature story on us and our ship for the Sunday issue. No sooner had this been published than we had our first TV coverage. NBC's Channel 3 out of Sacramento wanted to do a feature on us for their nightly news. Again, flattered that anyone would wish to film us for TV, we made arrangements to pick up the camera crew at the local Chester airport. The photographer and soundman would fly from Sacramento to Chester the next day, a distance of some 180 miles north.

The gala TV day never had a chance to dawn. We woke to a glowering sky. The black clouds gathered on the horizon and lowered over the lake. The wind came up and the month seemed to change from mid August to early December! In vain we waited at the airport to pick up the crew. About an hour after they were to land, we received a phone call at the airport that the weather was so bad they had had to land in Chico, 70 miles away and located down on the valley floor. They were renting a car and would drive into the mountains and meet us at the lake. By the time the two NBC TV men had arrived, it was almost noon. We drove to the dock where the USS INDIANA was tied up, and we looked out over the lake. "Battleship weather," Cecil muttered...and it was for the scene was gray and unfriendly. The lake matched the sky's mood. Our friendly blue lake had turned sullen and unpredictable. The wind stirred our ship restlessly and the lake flung her waves at us standing on the dock as if to defy us to take her picture.

We were tied up at our then Home Port of Little Norway, a lovely resort on the lake, owned and operated by her friendly owner, Mac. He always made room for our little ship. Mac had made his pontoon boat available for the cameramen and Mac's son, Brett, was ready to take us out to film. Quite a crowd had gathered to witness the television debut of our battleship. Among our friends was Ray's wife, Shirley. She accompanied me on the pontoon boat along with the cameraman. Our orders were to take some 35mm slides of the crew filming Cecil. We thought this an easy assignment and away we all went. What a different feeling it was to cast off from the stable dock and be out in three-foot waves. Being on a pontoon boat made the tossing platform under us accentuate the lack of stability. Rounding the protected area of the marina, Brett headed us out into the writhing lake. The wind seemed to shriek around our ears, and spatters of rain intermittently pelted us with gay abandon as we plowed through the waves. Cecil was oblivious of our tossing about. The battleship was proving her seaworthiness by knifing through the waves just as her namesake did. The center of gravity with the concrete ballast is so low in the ship that she is surprisingly stable in tempest tossed waters. Such was not our fate on the pontoon boat. Shirley and I looked at each other and she nervously asked, "Pat, do you suppose they have lifejackets on this boat?"

Without answering I immediately began to look. Footing was impossible to find and we tossed and shook like a dog emerging from his bath. Ernie and Dick, the great camera crew, seemed unaware of the pounding of the waves. True to their profession, they got their pictures and sound while Shirley and I occasionally remembered to snap pictures. Today we laugh about it, but privately consider ourselves to be heroines to have braved the stormy waters. We were all happy to make it safely back to port and were forced to say quick goodbyes to all as the storm increased in intensity.

Cecil had planned to drive me to Sacramento that afternoon so I could catch a plane for Los Angeles where I was going to spend 36 hours with my elderly father. He was leaving on a trip to Europe and I wanted to bid him a fond farewell. Since Ernie and Dick were anxious to get their film back to the station for that night's showing, they kindly offered me a ride to Chico and a plane ride on to Sacramento. What an afternoon—rush down the mountain, turn in the rent car, hop on the Cessna, fly to the Sacramento Airport. Dick was a former Air Force pilot and I enjoyed flying with him in his one-engine four-seater. We had left the storminess of the Sierras and enjoyed flying lazily over the Sacramento Valley. Only an occasional bump reminded us of what we had left behind. On the way down they pointed out many areas they had filmed in covering numerous news stories. With fuve minutes to spare, Dick landed at the Sacramento Airport and I ran to catch my plane to L.A. The speed with which I lived that day was brought forcefully to my attention that evening. Sitting in my father's Los Angeles home in warm Southern California, miles away from the storminess of the lake, I watched our battleship plow through the morning's rough waters of Lake Almanor. The news story opened with Tom Brokaw (at that time on Channel 4 in L.A) saying, "My goodness, look at the battleship."

The phenomena of photography made our ship look like a huge battleship on the screen. Part of the clips were done in slow motion, adding to the surrealism. Dick had photographed her with nothing in the background and the ship looked gigantic. Then, as a mountain came in the viewing frame behind the boat, the boat suddenly shrunk. My father and I were thrilled to watch this first TV coverage together and I found it hard to believe that just that morning I had been cold and cowardly. Two days later I flew back to Reno where Cecil picked me up and we headed for our cabin and more battleship cruising on the now placid lake.

USS INDIANA

Interior

USS INDIANA

23

Back at the lake, Cecil had had a call to visit a port across the lake. He called next door teenager Pete to ride with him across the lake to a lovely resort called Plumas Pines. The two men were gone for several hours, and when they returned they had a hilarious story to tell me. The resort lodge had a restaurant which looks out across the water. Pacific Gas & Electric Company, a California-based power company, was entertaining quite a number of businessmen and women. Cecil and Pete arrived right at the lunch hour and they reported that the usual happened. People from all over poured out of tents, trailers and the restaurant. Those having lunch were well-dressed in city clothes and shoes. As they rushed onto the floating dock to have a close look at the ship, they weighed the dock down so heavily that it began to sink. Pete, who completely broke up while describing the scene, reported that women screamed, men grabbed their trouser legs and rolled them up, and many ended up squishing ashore with water in their shoes. We almost renamed our boat Old Docksinker.

ANCHORS "AWAY"

Late summer of 1973 we reluctantly left the blue skies and scented pines of our mountain home and began another fall semester at our schools. One evening in October the phone rang, and it was CPO Jim Smith, a recruiter for the Navy. He and some officer friends had seen our battleship on television and were calling to find out if we would help them celebrate the Navy's 199th birthday. The plan was for us to appear at one of downtown Los Angeles's small lakes within a city park. A Navy band would be there, Navy brass, city officials and TV/newspaper reporters. We were to launch the USS INDIANA with the Navy's help, take a few dignitaries for a ride and bring some publicity to the Navy for their recruiting program. This was our first real indication that the little ship might be used for something other than fun. The thought that she could bring some good, something positive to others had not occurred to us before, and we were happy to share our boat with the Navy. (Although Cecil had planned to enlist in the Navy, Pearl Harbor was bombed, his high school was closed in his senior year, his diploma was mailed to him and he was zapped in to Patton's 3rd Army. The next 20 months were spent in Europe—Battle of the Bulge, then by mistake his whole Engineer Battalion was sent from Marseilles, France to Manila, P.I. for the invasion of Japan. President Truman dropped the bomb and he finally came home; but his frustration at not having been in the Navy always stayed with him.)

The birthday arrived and we rushed home from school, picked up the truck and trailer and tried to hurry through the afternoon traffic to downtown L.A. There was CPO Smith waiting for us with the news that no launch ramp was available anywhere around the perimeter of the lake! Did that ever teach us one big lesson! ALWAYS ASK about ramp facilities! Non-boaters have no concept of logistical launching and retrieving problems. We could see the band gathering and various L.A. VIPs whose faces we recognized.

The Navy officer in charge came racing up to us. "Hurry up, get her in the water. The band's about to play 'Anchors Aweigh' and we want you in the lake for the beginning of the ceremonies!" Jim and Cecil looked at each other helplessly, and then both immediately rose to the occasion. Since the Navy is rarely without manpower for any function, he found three young seamen. The trailer was backed up to the edge of the concrete wall which circled the lake. With an assist from the three men, up and over an 18-inch high rock wall went the trailer, wheels and all, splashing into the water. Here went another first—launching boat AND trailer. The boat slid into the water and the trailer hung crazily from the hitch, tilting awkwardly, half submerged. With this ignominious beginning Cec climbed, with difficulty, into the boat and began his circling maneuvers in the lake.

Newsmen and TV cameramen swarmed over to the edge. We have since learned that newsmen always like someone who is well known to take a ride in our ships. We've had a British Ambassador in our RMS TITANIC; country singers, mayors, and CEOs all ride with one or more of our boats. Many a hapless newscaster himself has found his knees up under his chin, anxiously checking his white trousers to keep them clean for broadcast time. Some cameramen come dressed in blue jeans and are delighted to crawl in back of the pilot for a ride. However, they always seem to have a tremendous amount of photographic gear, long, long lenses and invariably swing around and hit Cec on the head. It has happened so many times that the latter has become wary and has learned to duck. The harassed cameramen, crowded in with all their equipment, always have a few wry, sometimes unprintable comments to make when they unwind and back out of the boat after shooting their footage.

This time the newsmen wanted a well-known L.A. supervisor to ride in the back bucket seat. Back to the sea wall came Cec and his boat. Being a good sport, the supervisor climbed in, business suit and all. The newsmen all leaned forward to get the best possible shot. "Start engine" Cecil directed the supervisor. (This was before we graduated to an electric starter.) This good man did his best to oblige and pulled and pulled on the starter rope. Unfortunately he was not familiar with the idiosyncracies of the motor and proceeded to flood it. "You killed my engine," I heard Cecil say to him accusingly. I winced and hoped the TV cameras would not pick up on this exchange. "Well, I haven't used one of these since I was a boy," was his plaintive answer. I could see Cecil seemed to think the engine's failure was a definite affront to his position as captain, but as I took in the whole crazy scene it suddenly became ludicrous. Here was the poor supervisor, worried that he had broken something, yet trying to smile for the newspeople. Cec was reaching around him, trying to start his flooded engine. The trailer was tilting badly, threatening to pull truck and all into the lake, the band was now playing 'Anchors Aweigh,' and the Navy brass were obviously hoping the publicity for their birthday party would not sink into the sunset.

How many times later on in our strange odyssey I would think back on many hairy, scary, awkward, disastrous launchings. No matter how many times one launches successfully, there is always another time coming when it is embarrassing, exciting, or humiliating. One cannot launch a battleship incognito. There is always a crowd gathered to watch. Thus the title to this book came to mind easily! Fortunately, the crowds of onlookers are full of good sports and a few knowledgeable boaters who come to our rescue.

With a cough the engine finally started, and with a burst of crud from the exhaust, the two men were off. As Cecil lowered the lid, I could see the poor supervisor wrapped in a haze of blue smoke, coughing for the TV cameras. I sighed a sigh of relief that the publicity needed was duly recorded for posterity and Los Angeles's nightly 6 P.M. news. We watched the coverage later with amazement.

Back to the cement obstacle came the boat, and Cec tried to line up alongside so the supervisor could crawl out without falling in the lake. The latter was obviously relieved the harrowing ride was over. Then came the "fun" part. It always happened. There was inevitably great TV and newspaper excitement, then everyone would leave and we were always left alone to dismantle, retrieve and put things back together. With the birthday party over, we still had CPO Smith and his sailors to help us. The trailer was teetering on the escarpment, but Cecil drove the boat into the trailer anyhow. Then, she was winched in. With this added weight the truck and trailer showed more signs of never wanting to leave the vicinity. Navy to the rescue! Their ingenuity should never be questioned. Using a hydraulic jack as far to the rear of the trailer as they could, they carefully lifted her wheels over the 18-inch wall. With a crash the trailer came down to earth—surprisingly all in one piece. We thanked the Navy and wearily drove home in heavy evening traffic.

In the months that followed, there were several functions to which we were invited. We always seemed to be teaching, rushing home to pick up truck, trailer and boat and roaring off to some late afternoon or weekend event. As publicity increased (see TV log), more phone calls came for appearances. We could not do them all, but we did a lot. We loaned our battleship to the Navy for several occasions: Armed Forces Day, parades, recruiting locations—any place where they were needed as an attraction.

Sometimes we went with our gray lady and sometimes the Navy carted her off in great style. We will never forget the time the Navy backed a 60-foot flat-bed truck into our driveway to pick up our ship and took it off to Riverside for the auto races. The ship looked like a guppy riding on the back of Jonah's whale. Our neighbors will not forget these happenings either.

SURPRISE PERKS

More publicity began to come in local papers and magazines. *Popular Mechanics* ran an article on us in their August, 1974 issue. Cecil had been tooling around in the Naples Canals near Long Beach, CA and the editor of *Trailer Boats* magazine slipped him a business card and asked if he could do an article on us for his publication. We did a lot of trips all over Southern California for different magazines. There was always something humorous connected with any coverage.

One superb photographer/interviewer called and asked us if we would do "our thing" so he could do a write-up for a magazine for which he was a contributor. He wanted us in a naval shipyard next to Navy ships to provide a good background for our tiny ship. Having obtained permission from the Navy to launch near their Long Beach Naval shipyard and perform in their harbor, we met one Saturday morning. It was a quiet, lovely, not windy day. Little breeze, the ramp was a long smooth one and for once, no crowds. The launch was too perfect. I should have been prepared for the excitement later on.

After we had launched Cecil safely, Ralph and I drove around to the naval part of the harbor while the battleship came around a long jetty and circled into the area where the Navy ships were tied up. We parked the car and boarded one of the cruisers. The ships were lining both sides of the harbor and were bustling with weekend reserve sailors and officers. It was apparent their day included extra sea duty, and some ships showed signs of preparing to leave their berth. Black smoke shot out from several funnels.

Having received permission to board the cruiser for good camera shots, Ralph and I positioned ourselves to await Cecil's arrival. We watched the white uniformed sailors going about their duties. No one seemed in any great hurry. A number of men were on the decks and we felt that the harbor would likely be empty of ships within the hour. Then we spotted the USS INDIANA. Coming around a bend and into the harbor in his gray ship, he blended with the ships and the water. His profile was so low that had we not been watching for him we might well have missed him. The Navy obviously was missing him!

Suddenly, all was chaos on the ship we were standing on. From our battleship's PA system we heard the familiar "Now hear this. This is your captain speaking. Surrender your ships or I'll be forced to fire on you!" The miniature ship zoomed in at 10HP speed, leaving a frothy wake behind her and throwing a perfect bow wave. Sidling up to a nearby destroyer, she unleashed her front turrets and squirted the large ship. Ralph said it was as if an excited poodle had lifted its leg on a dignified Great Dane. The quiet of the morning erupted into bedlam. Sailors left their duties, swabbies rushed for the railing, CPOs came speeding up from below, officers on the bridge saluted. We even saw one delighted captain jumping up and down before he sheepishly caught himself in the act. A sailor standing next to us remarked, "This was almost another Pearl Harbor!"

We had not counted on this reaction at all and were surprised and amused. All over the bay we could hear intercoms with authoritative voices saying, "All sailors report to your stations. Return to your station." Ralph got his pictures and we left, but not before Cecil had a wonderfully warm sendoff from the sailors. Shouts of encouragement, appreciative salutes, clapping of hands—even the toot of a cruiser's whistle capped off this rendezvous with the Navy.

That Christmas we were invited to be guests of the well-known Naples boat parade which was held on their canals that threaded through magnificent homes. We trailered to Long Beach and a fraternity brother friend helped us launch. The canal homes were ablaze with Christmas lights, the ships in the parade were beautifully lit. Cec and his friend were given a position in the parade. Off they went, and Jack's wife and I went to one of the bridges crossing over the canal to watch the procession. Soon we sighted some beautiful pleasure craft coming down the canal. Following one lovely, brilliantly lit boat was a strange apparition. It appeared to be a large raft approximately 8x14 feet. On it was an enormous fiberglass, papier-maché dragon. Cleverly rounding out this entry into the parade was a propane-fueled tongue of flame belching out of the fierce dragon's mouth. Even more interesting were the rubber suited scuba men who were propelling their serpent like creature along the waterway. Their appearance was not to be missed. Hung on each side of the raft were four botas obviously filled with wine. At least they had been full at one time. By now, half way through the parade, much of the wine was in the frogmen's interiors. Unfortunately, right behind the dragon came Cecil and his buddy, slowly propelling the INDIANA along the canal. Patt and I watched as the battleship drew alongside the dragon. The men all yelled approval. Amidst much shouting, Cecil squirted the men and their boat. As fate would have it, he landed a lucky shot and put out the dragon's flame. The yelling became louder, more serious, more toxic. Probably all in fun, the men turned on the battleship and began to rock it—seriously rock it with as much vigor as they could muster. They did fairly well and the boat sloshed from side to side, more than I had ever seen it do, but the combination of much wine, rubber suits and more boats parading down the canal saved the evening. Later, the two men said it had been somewhat scary inside, but the 85 pounds of ballast proved to make the ship quite seaworthy. The crowning glory was that Cecil won first prize in the parade—a magnificent 26-inch-tall trophy. We wondered what the dragon-men thought. Perhaps they didn't remember.

One day on my lunch hour I received a call from Cecil. Since we rarely called one another at work unless there was a real need, I hurried to the phone. "How would you like to go to the San Diego Navy Base and be a guest aboard one of their destroyers for a 100-mile trip off the California coast?" Such an unexpected invitation made my afternoon, and when we met at home I found that the Navy considered Cec to be one of their recruiters along with counselors from ROP (Regional Occupation Program). Most of the personnel going along would be high school teachers and administrators, but they also needed a few extra people to fill the quota for the tour. As a teacher I filled the bill and we happily accepted such a great invitation. Privately I thought how glad I was to be married to such an inventive man. Doors were beginning to open onto vistas I had not expected beyond my own field of primary teaching and teacher training.

The Navy weekend was a wonderful one. We were impressed with the education offered young people who joined the service. We were given a guided tour of the various schools on the San Diego Naval Base which could qualify a young person for life in the Navy and as a civilian. We ate in the CPO mess hall, then were bussed to the docks where we toured a repair ship. My vocationally-oriented mate came away with great admiration for the Navy's offerings to recent high school graduates. That night we enjoyed dinner and dancing at the Officers' Club, and the next day we put to sea. What an exciting trip on the destroyer! Nothing was off limits to visitors, and we thoroughly enjoyed prowling throughout the whole ship. Smooth sailing and sparkling seas made it a marvelous weekend and we were bussed back to Los Angeles. All of us were acutely aware of how much the services can give to youngsters in need of direction and education.

The next chapter in our gray lady's life (and ours) came when Cecil loaned his ship to be on display at an Industrial Arts show he and his department were putting on at his high school. The local paper, the *Valley News and Green Sheet*, wanted to do quite a bit of publicity to help the Industrial Arts Fair and used the battleship as part of their presentation. The photographer wanted us to trailer our boat to a small San Fernando reservoir and made arrangements for us to be allowed to do "our thing" on the lake. Motors were not allowed, but we were given permission to take a short spin. Several faithful friends showed up and we backed down a sandy, steep ramp. We all looked uneasily at the truck tires as they began tunneling south toward China. Ignoring impending disaster, Cec climbed into the ship and I was ordered to back him in and drop him into the water. By this time we were old pros at launching— or so we thought. Our procedure was for me to slowly back the trailer in to where the ship could float off the trailer. When Cecil tooted with his air horn I would go back, then slam on the brakes and into the water he would go gracefully (usually). This method worked again, but when I tried to pull the truck and trailer up and off the steep ramp, nothing happened but the sound of spinning tires.

About this time a rather grumbly lifeguard came over and told me we had no business being on the lake since motors were not allowed. I explained to him about the reporter who was taking pictures. By this time the photographer was finished and I signaled Cec to come in for a docking. I dashed to "fend him off." Those three words were to be our hysterical battle cry in the many river trips ahead in years to come. The reporter was intent on getting his story to the newspaper and left. Of course! Alone again! People with day sailors were waiting their turn for the ramp. The lifeguard was growing more irate by the minute.

Cecil finally noticed me standing there helplessly waving my hands. He did nothing to placate the lifeguard by shouting to ask him to help us. Could he please bring his 4-wheel drive truck down to rescue us and pull me out? Grudgingly the guard did so, having no other choice. We really were most grateful to him as the truck registered total obstinacy as it clung to the sandy slope. With one more mighty letting out of the 4-wheel drive's clutch, we lurched up and out. The fact that the steering wheel left an imprint in my stomach and Cecil nearly fell out of the battleship was of no concern…at least to the lifeguard. Anyhow, the ensuing publicity was good for the show, and many people came to the high school to see our ship and stayed to see the rest of the displays. The exhibit of our boat was to prove an entry into our first great water adventure.

In February, 1974, a real treat lay in store for Cec. By this time he had done many appearances for the Navy on land and in the water. A local recruiter invited Cec to be the Navy's guest at the Naval Academy in Annapolis, Maryland. What a thrill for him! On this same trip he was to travel to Washington D.C. to meet Rear Admiral Emmitt Tidd, in charge of recruiting for the USA. Again, the ROP counselors would be the nucleus of the group.

The morning he was to leave it was cold, rainy and dark at his 4:30A.M. hour of departure. I took him to the Navy recruiter's office, who in turn drove several counselors to the Long Beach Naval Air Force station. They were to take off by 9A.M. To everyone's surprise they were to fly in an old DC6. Being accustomed to jet travel, I later heard that it was fun to fly so low (9000 feet) as the scenery went by close and slowly. The two days at the Academy filled all with respect for our nation's institution which trains the fine young men privileged to be admitted. Teaching conditions were at their optimum, the cream of our country's young men (women were not permitted to attend at this time) were on display, and Cecil became an even more confirmed disciple of Navy life.

I had made plans to take two days off from teaching and had arrangements to catch an early Thursday flight from LAX to Baltimore to join Cec. Since we had a 3-day weekend coming up in that February month, I took two days of unpaid leave. It was with anticipation that I caught my plane. There were 10 passengers on the cross-country flight of the empty DC8. Landing in a snowstorm in Baltimore was a decided contrast to my sunny takeoff from L.A. I caught an airport limo to Annapolis and found Cec waiting for me at the motel. The next morning we caught a taxi for Washington D.C., where we were scheduled for a visit with RAdm. Tidd. What a great two hours we had with him and his staff. They were most interested and curious about our battleship and very supportive in their comments. I still have the Navy recruiting emblem which was pinned onto my jacket by this suave admiral. I thanked him and asked him why he didn't sing when he pinned a lady! We laughed about college pinning and singing days and together decided each of us was already "pinned" to someone else.

Since we had finished all our Navy business, we caught a flight for Miami, Florida, late that afternoon. The plane was full of chilly Washingtonians flying south for a warm weekend. What a disappointment they had as Florida was experiencing a record cold wave and we donned heavy coats for three days in this usually tropical climate. We rented a car and drove the east coast of Florida and went south to the Keys. On the afternoon of our flight home, we walked out onto a new Miami marina and had coffee at an outdoor restaurant. Beautiful ships were tied up in this marina and we had a wonderful time watching the graceful ships come and go in the harbor. As we sat there watching the tranquil scene, Cecil made the remark, "I'd love to bring my battleship to this marina and terrorize the natives!"

Could we have imagined that exactly two years from that date he would be in that marina with a boatload of TV cameramen after him? We would have given birth to another battleship—the red, white and blue USS BICENTENNIAL—and we would be hired to be "the hook" for the Miami Beach International Boat Show.

HEY MAN! DERE GO YO' BOAT!

We had been home from Florida only a few days when we had a call from a Navy friend who said he had approval to purchase three of our battleships for recruiting purposes. Capt. Max Barr, stationed in Omaha, was to fly to L.A. and check them out as he felt having three miniature Navy ships would help his recruiting efforts on the Mississippi and Missouri Rivers. Thus it was that we had three boat molds shot up and made up one full kit for Max. We delivered one completely assembled ship and two that needed to be put together. We trailered the boats to Pt. Hueneme 40 miles north of L.A. There the Navy put them in their cargo plane and flew them to Capt. Barr. It was a bizarre sight to see the small ships being loaded into the huge belly of the cargo plane. We later heard that the Seabees had done a fine job in putting the kits together. Occasionally we have Midwesterners tell us they have caught a glimpse of our ships as they cruise up and down Midwestern rivers. This event brought the first of many plaques Cecil was to eventually receive from various service oriented organizations. Our walls are full of tributes and thanks.

An invitation to be part of Seattle's hydroplane races showed up one day. Easter vacation, 1974, we headed for our Lake Almanor home and stopped briefly. Then it was on to Lake Washington for the races. This is an annual event for the Seattle people and there certainly was an air of excitement around the lake. The roar of the jet motors from the hydroplanes was deafening even from a distance. The powerful engines produced huge rooster tails of spray. We were anxious to join the crowd out on the choppy lake and searched for a good launch ramp. We finally found one we had been directed to, and a more apt description would be a slanting, muddy, rutted road which ran erratically into the lake. It was right under the floating bridge and we could hear the roar of traffic directly overhead. This was the only launch site available and we had no help this time.

A few disinterested fishermen had their backs to us while sitting on a jetty. One small boy was earnestly trying to fish from a concrete piling. Several cars parked nearby with empty trailers behind them indicated that others had daringly braved this rutted road and had apparently escaped launching their cars. Cecil backed us in as far as he could and still be able to climb onto the trailer and into the battleship. Taking off his shoes and socks, he climbed in cautiously. I backed him in, gave him a lurch and off he went. All went well and I could see him under power, so I pulled the rig out of the muck. By this time Cec had driven over to the cement where the little boy was fishing. He climbed out and I saw he had a line on the boat. I prepared to join him.

He shouted at me, "Bring my shoes and socks, please!" I yelled back that I didn't know where they were and he turned around to answer me.

Later he reported to me he felt a tugging on his pants and looked down at the little black boy fisherman."Hey man, dere go yo' boat!"

Horrified, Cecil turned back to see the boat had slipped her halter and there she went—bobbing gaily along, heading toward the middle of the lake by herself. Helplessly we watched her drift away. We debated swimming for her but the lake was cold. Then coming into view was a boat pulling a water skier. They must have been surprised for the ski boat slowed down, dumping its skier while the driver circled the runaway ship. By this time we were shouting, waving our arms to attract their attention. The skiers soon had our runaway in tow and brought her to shore for us. The usual round of questions came: "What is it? What are you going to do with it? Did you build it?" After thanking our rescuers, we prepared to get in the ship and join up with the parade of boats.

All this time our little black friend had been looking at us with disapproval. It was obvious he lived near the water and was well acquainted with boats and the proper way to handle them. As we cast off from shore, we waved at him. He waved back at us, but with very little enthusiasm. Surely he must have thought we were novices at handling a boat for his parting remark was, "Hey, Man, y'all better tie yo' line with a knot next time." Meekly we nodded and lowered the superstructure over us glad to be hidden from his critical gaze. We decided this had been one of our worst episodes yet—it is embarrassing to lose one's battleship. The next time we did this would be when we were anchored out under the Statue of Liberty in New York Harbor!

We were to be in the line of boats that was to parade around the race area in front of the stands. We felt very, very, very small as we joined the Chris Crafts, Pacemakers and Grand Banks. We found our place in the line of parade. A 40 ft. houseboat was in front of us and a 38 ft. Luers was skulking behind us. It was hard to keep up with our 10HP motor, and the whole parade had to slow down for us. The people in front of us had apparently been having a party all day on board. We found eight to ten people had lined the railing on the stern and were looking back at us gesturing, pointing and obviously discussing us. They all looked so casual, so nautical, so unconcerned. And, here we were, practically sitting in the water, being dashed about by two-foot waves. We were sloshing in their wake and we were generally uncomfortable. These were the moments when I wondered how I had become involved in situations like this. We circled the huge race area which was marked by logs that had been chained to sunken anchors. Here we found people who had tied up to the logs the night before and were in a great position to watch the hydroplanes jet their way to victory. The Navy had a small ship anchored by the reviewing stand, and we squirted it and circled to the delight of the sailors.

Late in the afternoon, we finally made our way back to the launch "ramp" and were relieved our fisherman friend had gone. Without further incident, we hauled out the battleship and deposited her safely inside her trailer home. Our only other incident that night was at the motel when we came trailering in with our miniature ship. Gone were the days of quietly checking into a motel. Cec and I got out of the truck. The usual crowd gathered around us with the same questions: "What is it? How did you build it? What are you going to do with it?" Quietly, I took my suitcase, slunk around by the back of the trailer, found our room and closed the door. *Let Cec do it this time*, I thought. I was cold and tired.

Back in Southern California and within two weeks, dear friends Gee and Deke invited us to help open the yachting season for the Newport Yacht Club. We were invited to be guests for lunch and to lead the parade of boats. We accepted with alacrity and had a delightful, surprisingly uneventful afternoon. After lunch the club's officers lined up in their splendid yachting jackets. A brief ceremony was held and a cannon was fired. We all took off. There were powerboats, sailing ships and us "kids." We joined up with six other yacht clubs and the parade of boats filled the entire harbor area of Newport Bay. Although I rode on our friend's boat, we could always spot Cecil. He always seemed to be in the center of a number of boats circling around him, shouting at him and taking dozens of pictures.

That afternoon as we were preparing to take the boat out of the water with the usual crowd gathered, Cec suddenly saw a hand come through the hordes of people. The hand gave him a business card. On the other end of the arm was the editor/publisher of *Trailer Boats* magazine. Ralph wanted to do a story on Cec and his boat. This was a prestigious magazine among boaters, and a few weeks later we met Ralph and his photographer at Marina Del Rey, a very posh yachting area. It was late afternoon, as we had been teaching all day, then trailered our rig across the city. The usual stiff afternoon ocean breeze came up. I rode with Ralph in a 20-ft. power boat and the photographer went with Cecil. We headed out beyond the breakwater. The waves were high and we wallowed heavily in the troughs as both men tried to take pictures. At this point in time my boating experience was still minimal and I knew nothing about controlling or running a boat. (Eventually I would pilot a battleship.) Nevertheless, Ralph must have thought I was experienced, for he gave me control of the boat and continued to snap pictures. That picture appeared on the front of the November, 1974 *Trailer Boats* magazine and was the one we had blown up to a 24x40-inch size for display at many boat shows. It is one of our favorite pictures and reposes on the wall of our den today. We shall always be grateful to this man, for it was his magazine story that helped us get ready for our next project.

By now Cecil was itching to have another battleship, only this one, he decided, would be different. The day he told me he was going to have a white battleship kit made, I was shocked. "White!" What would we do with a white battleship? By now we had a firm which had made the molds for the hull, deck and superstructure. Cecil asked this company to make the three parts in a white gel coat. I was skeptical but kept my own counsel. Since that time I am glad I did.

The three parts came home in the back of the pickup, and Cec began to assemble them. I had thought the gray battleship was a gray ghost, but this surely did look like a real spirit. We looked her over after all the parts were put together. My creativity and imagination have never been equal to Cecil's, and I could not imagine this ship being used for anything. I was silent as we gazed at her, not wishing to burst the bubble of pride and creativity belonging to the tall man next to me. After a few moments he spoke. "Pat, the Bicentennial year is coming up. I think I'll put some red and blue touches on this ship and we'll use her for some pre-Bicentennial events—maybe during 1976."

Immediately I could envision this rather colorless, pale lady perking up with some red on the funnel, some blue touches here and there, maybe even some gold. In the next few weeks she took shape. We added brass trim and gold paint. She sported a fierce eagle decal on her stack. We added ten 4x6-inch American flags on her mast and one larger American flag to the staff on the stern. She was beautiful. We named her—what else?—USS BICENTENNIAL. She was ready—but for what?

USS BICENTENNIAL ON LAKE ALMANOR

THE DUCKS FIND CECIL AND HIS BOAT

BOAT SHOW BIZ

By this time in our teaching careers, we were again eligible for a sabbatical leave. Rather than travel the world as we had previously done, we had been talking about seeing America from her waterways. We had read many stories about the ICW, the Intracoastal Waterway. This is a 6000-mile stretch of water which is a series of rivers and sounds. The Army Engineers connected all these, and they maintain this long waterway, continually dredging and rip-rapping. It is possible to begin in Brownsville, TX, go along the southern coast, around Florida, Miami to New York and continue up to Boston. There is a life style of boaters who live on the water, following the seasons. Many go from New York, up the Hudson River to the St. Lawrence Seaway, down the Mississippi to New Orleans or Mobile then begin to head north for the summer season. Our interest lay in going from Miami to New York, which was a 1500-mile stretch of ICW.

We had no boat on which to live, and there was nothing to rent that we could find, so we toyed with the idea of driving along the ICW, launching the battleship where we could. That seemed unsatisfactory, and our desire to go by water increased. I will never forget the evening Cecil said to me, "Let's go up the ICW with our USS BICENTENNIAL. We'll do a film of our country's history and heritage going up the waterway. Let's do it as seen through the eyes of the battleship. We'll film some history of the Revolutionary War times and bring it back to the Los Angeles schoolchildren."

As usual when confronted with some of Cec's way-out schemes, my mouth dropped open—way open. Now this idea seemed ridiculous. True, we loved the little battleship and she was a fun thing for us, but surely Cecil knew we could not eat and sleep on a mini-battlewagon. Having put in some years with this creative-minded man, I held my fire and waited to hear the end of the proposal. "Let's see if we can't hitch hike with someone or find something to help us get up the waterway. The Bicentennial years are coming up and we'll bring back something good and positive for the children." His enthusiasm was contagious. I couldn't help but be caught up with the idea.

We talked late into the night about this and the good the USS BICENTENNIAL might do for our country and how we might help participate in the celebration of our nation's 200th birthday. It seemed like the impossible dream, but we decided to pursue this fantasy of ours in the months to come.

Ralph's story in *Trailer Boats* magazine ended up doing many things for us. People along the east coast read the article, called us and said if we made the trip they wanted us to stop at their marina or at least call them from our VHF (we first contacted some of these people as we passed along the North Carolina coast). Not only did it bring attention to the trip we hoped to accomplish, but it put a spotlight on us that brought us to the attention of the public relations firm handling publicity for the upcoming Los Angeles Convention Center Boat Show. Al Franken and his firm were creative, ingenious public relations people and really knew how to capture numerous amounts of publicity for anything they represented. Their reputation was high-profile in the sporting world. Al called us and asked us if we would be "the hook" for the L.A. Boat Show. We found out what being "the hook" meant then. He laid out all the pre-publicity we would be doing—launching the BICENTENNIAL at Marina Del Rey for all the TV networks in Los Angeles, interviews by all local Southern California newspapers, radio interviews, and working the 10-day boat show at the convention center. Al felt that our boat would be a big draw for pulling people into the show. It looked like a big bite because we were teaching daily, but we decided to do this and ended up working for the Southern California Marine Association for a full week plus two weekends.

Cec had to take a half day off to fulfill the first bit of pre-publicity. He left early one A.M. for an interview on the *Ralph Story Morning Show* in the Burbank studio. He was interviewed by an enthusiastic, charming Maureen Reagan. My faculty and I watched him on the school's TV before school began that day. Another day he had to drive to a small lake outside the city limits, where the *Los Angeles Times* did a long feature story on him and his two boats, mentioning, of course, that the USS BICENTENNIAL would appear at the boat show. Another in-studio interview was conducted the day the boat show was to open and the interviewer wanted to see the guns shoot water out of the turrets. Cec put a five-gallon can of water inside the battleship, did his water-squirting interview and hurried over to the Convention Center in downtown L.A.

I was teaching and not there to help set up, but he reported he came in the back of the building and workers put our ship on a long, low dolly and wheeled him into a marvelous location. Our setting could not have been more perfect. We were placed at the very front opening of the convention center where huge doors open and escalators run up and downstairs. We were in the center of the foyer where people had to come by us to get into the main part of the boat show. Spotlights were on our sparkling boat, brass stanchions with heavy blue velvet cords surrounded us. Potted plants were in strategic places.

That Friday afternoon after teaching we drove down to the center and went to our positions behind the velvet cords. At the appropriate hour the doors were opened and the public streamed in. What a night! We stood behind those ropes and talked and talked—and talked all day Saturday and Sunday. We talked until we were hoarse. The public, we learned, is a wonderful phenomenon. No matter where one is, their interest and questions are the same. By this time we had had many public appearances and TV interviews behind us and had met thousands of people connected with our boats. The public is warm in its approval for enterprising ideas, they are generous in their praise for anything new and constructive, they approve of the struggle to make dreams come true and they applaud with enthusiasm the idea of anyone striking out on an unusual adventure.

The easels we had standing beside our boat were covered with pictures of the ships at sea. Also included was our display of the story of our hoped-for forthcoming trip. People were fascinated that we would consider going 1500 miles with an 18-foot battleship. One little girl said, "But where's the bathroom?" Several people were interested in how the turrets squirted water. Cec was happy to open the superstructure lid and show his hand pump mounted in the keel. He gave a good back and forth pull on the handle to show the interested spectators. Suddenly an arc of water shot over the onlookers' heads and a big puddle landed on the lobby carpet, spreading out into a 3 ft. diameter circle. An embarrassed Cecil had forgotten to unhook the five-gallon can of water that he had used early that morning in a television studio. Fortunately, he hit no one. Hour and after hour we fielded questions as best we could.

Our program that week consisted of teaching school, rushing home to wash and change, then a fast 45- minute freeway drive to the boat show. We found that after teaching and talking all day we would become hoarse, so we took turns spelling one another. The boat show lasted until 10 P.M. weekend nights and it was impossible to "be on" all this time. I did discover that while I was "on," many men were disappointed that Cec would not be on duty for another 30-45 minutes. However, by this time I was so immersed in battleship building and dreams that it was easy to answer their questions. They seemed somewhat mollified, although I noticed they did light up when the male part of this team came back.

This boat show turned out to be the beginning of a wonderful, long, enduring friendship of many years with Al, his firm and the Southern California Marine Association. We worked for him with various segments of our fleet seven different times. We were always treated cordially and paid well. We were never disappointed with the publicity coverage they produced, we were put up in beautiful hotels/motels, and we were treated to a food expense account and paid a stipend for our work. I learned to memorize many boat show facts, so that when I was interviewed on TV standing by one of our boats, I could give all the details needed for the publicity for the show. Our relationship became special over 20 years and I always loved to pick up the phone and hear Al say, "Hi, Pat. Has Cecil built any new boats? We've got a biggie coming up." Wow—when, what and where this next time!

On one of my relief breaks, I wandered into a part of the show I had not yet visited. Tucked back in a corner was a most intriguing looking boat. I was still a neophyte as far as knowing much about live-on craft, but this one caught my eye because it was unusual looking. It was a Land 'n Sea and had a cathedral hull. She looked like half houseboat and half cruiser. She had an eight-foot beam and was 28 ft. long. Since she did not have a deck around her port or starboard sides I knew she must have quite a bit of living space inside. I went on board and immediately fell in love with her. For a 28-foot length, she was a beauty. She slept six people comfortably, had a good size galley complete with small refrigerator. There was a four burner stove and an oven. She had a small but adequate head and shower. There were two small dining areas, one in the bow, one in the stern. Both made into double beds at night. Dual controls below and on the fly bridge were installed. Access to the stern and bow was either through the boat along the middle companionway or up and over the bridge and down the ladder on the stern. She was also trailerable. To my way of thinking she had everything.

I had been going through many live-aboard boats at the show playing my game of "if I could have this one for our trip." I had talked with salesmen about our proposed trip, and although they were interested in our venture, there was never a commitment to assist us on this trip for the publicity there might be in it for them. Even so, I could hardly wait to get back and tell Cec of my discovery.

When a slow time came around the dinner hour, I dragged him back to view the Land 'n Sea. He was as enthused as I was. We spoke with the young man who represented the company and told him of our proposed endeavor. He gave us the name of the Northern California representative and told us to contact a gentleman in the firm. I could hardly wait to get to my typewriter. For some reason I felt an impulsion to write and ask for help on this Bicentennial undertaking. But who would possibly underwrite a crazy trip such as we were proposing? Nevertheless, my letter went out to Land 'n Sea telling of our hoped-for adventure. We included in our letter our dreams of what we wanted to do for schoolchildren by bringing back the history and heritage of our country to instill a sense of patriotism in our young people. I suppose our hearts were on our sleeves in this letter, for we put a great deal of feeling into it and what we hoped to accomplish.

We sent the letter in November, 1974 and immediately became inundated at school. The holiday time is always a busy one for teachers and we had little time to think about our upcoming trip, which was to begin in Miami in March of 1975. When we did talk about it, it was with a sense of uneasiness that we were so far into a trip that thus far had no logistical support. We had both applied for our sabbatical leaves and they had been granted. Our plans were to head for Florida soon after the fall semester was over, which would be the end of January. Still, we had no idea how the USS BICENTENNIAL or the Gateses were going to go 1500 miles from Miami to New York with no boat to live on. We discussed many possibilities, but none seemed adequate. At this point in my boating experience, I had learned that "port" has four letters in it and so does "left." That way I could keep port and starboard straight. Not an auspicious or reliable boating person yet!

By this time we had completely written off hearing from Land 'n Sea. We were disappointed but we believed so strongly in what we were attempting to do that we were still sending out letters and contacting boat companies as far away as Florida. We truly wanted to reach out and touch children beyond our classroom walls and were dedicated to participating in the Bicentennial in some meaningful way. We knew the boats attracted people of all ages and description and felt we could be the symbol or the entry into young people's hearts and minds.

But, just HOW to get this trip off the ground—that was a good question….and time was running out!

OUR SHIP COMES IN

How does one describe a miracle? How does one tell about that "out-of-the-blue" happening which suddenly turns a dream into a reality? The phone rang on Sunday afternoon in mid-December. A voice on the other end of the line said, "This is Bill Brockett and I'm calling you from Land 'n Sea International in Santa Clara, California. I have your letter on my desk asking to use one of our craft for your trip up the ICW. We are going to supply you with that boat and I'm coming along as your skipper!" The pleasant voice on the other end of the line paused.

I grabbed the desk chair and tried to sit down, but got only as far as the top of the desk. My thoughts were jumbled, kaleidoscoping into one another as I tried to get a grip on what the voice had just said to me. Reason and telephone manners must have deserted me, for I well remember my inane response (screech is more like it)—"You're going to do WHAT?"

"I said," came the voice again, "we believe strongly in what you are trying to do and my firm wants to help you accomplish the job you are setting out to do."

Slowly, I began to piece it all together. My letter had been across many desks and had been sent from person to person. It finally landed on the desk of Bill Brockett, sales manager for Preston Avery, owner/builder of Land 'n Sea Craft, Int'l. As I was to learn later, Bill had been caught up with what he termed the enthusiasm and ideas in our letter. He showed the letter to Mr. Avery and urged him to back us in this endeavor. Preston Avery, a true southern gentleman and a wonderful American, gave his blessing to our request. The pieces of our jigsaw puzzle trip swiftly fell into place. Bill told us that his company would be giving us a new Land 'n Sea which he would trailer to Miami. He would meet us there and we would make plans to leave soon after his arrival. We felt that a mid-March departure would be best for this would allow us to follow spring all the way to New York.

Shortly after Bill's phone call, another call came in from Miami. A very alert public relations man, Bruce Rubin, called us. His firm was doing publicity for the large Miami Beach Boat Show, which was to be held for nine days in February, 1975. He had read about us and our battleship in *Trailer Boats* magazine and had noted we were planning to take off from Miami in mid-March. Being an enterprising young man, he picked up the phone and called us one morning just as we were leaving for school. Would we be interested in being hired to appear as "the hook" in the Miami Beach Boat Show under the same conditions as we worked the L.A. show? As I listened to him describe the Miami Beach Convention Center, I could picture this beautiful place and it sounded like a wonderful idea. That night Cec and I agreed to leave Los Angeles earlier than we had anticipated so that we could appear in the pre-publicity for the boat show. We must be ready for an event was to be staged in Biscayne Bay for the press on February 14.

We were galvanized into action. There were charts to be purchased for the trip from the U.S. Coast Guard and Geodetic Survey who maintain the ICW along with the Corps of Engineers. We must find a place to stay in Miami, for we were to be there a month before Bill arrived. We must find a renter for our home for a SEVEN-month period for we planned to stay at our Lake Almanor home upon our return in summer. Rental of the house must also include our wonderful cleaning lady of 18 years and dear dog of 11 years. All of these details piled in on us, along with trying to teach school and wind up the semester successfully. We had little time.

That month of January we corresponded quite formally with Mr. Brockett and sent him charts and a book on the ICW. We interviewed 18 people who were interested in renting our home, and we cleared out most of the home for our bachelor renter. He willingly took on all that we required of our renter—mail, cleaning lady, dog, yard—and he offered to do more. This wonderful man ended up staying and rented from us for over three years before he changed his lifestyle. He became very special to us.

We found an apartment in Miami, and Cec put the final touches on our trailer which was to completely enclose the BICENTENNIAL. We knew we could not expose her to the mud, weather and road tar of a 3100- mile trip across the US. Ah! Incognito travel at last!

Every now and then we paused to think about our undertaking and realized we had never met Mr. Avery or Mr. Brockett. We marveled at their support and their willingness to help out. We longed to meet them before we left, but this was not possible. Our soon-to-be skipper was as busy as we were trying to finish up his work.

By now, word of our trip had spread throughout many schools because of the Bicentennial committees within the school district. In quick succession came endorsement of our trip by the Bicentennial committee of the L.A. City Schools, L.A. County and the State of California. Six letters were given to us from Mayor Tom Bradley of Los Angeles to give to six mayors along the east coast. School children all over the San Fernando Valley sent us their letters for new pen pals in the same six cities. They were intrigued that a battleship was to deliver their letters to new friends. The six ports for the letters were to be Miami, FL, Charleston, SC, Williamsburg, VA, Washington D.C., Baltimore, MD, and Philadelphia, PA.

Guiding hand and dogged determination from Bill Leary, Bicentennial coordinator, could not have been better. His help and follow through from his area office was outstanding. We could not have pulled the whole thing together without him. Bill was a secondary teacher on leave to coordinate Bicentennial activities and a scholar with a brilliant mind. Thanks to him, the letters were gathered together and ready for us.

The semester drew to an end. My class tried to comprehend what I was doing. A battleship? What is a battleship? Their teacher was leaving. WHY are you leaving us? What are you going to do? What is a boat show? Will you write to us? Don't forget me! This was the hard part, saying goodbye to these little ones who were halfway through their school year. Cec felt the same way. Fine young men, halfway launched in their search for a niche in the drafting world, diffidently asked him, "Who's going to be teaching in your place? Boy, I'd like to go with you!" Feelings hidden under the mask of assumed adulthood, they shyly laid their own insecurities on their teacher. We discussed this, the trauma of leaving classrooms of youngsters dependent on us for routine, security, love and discipline. Still we felt compelled to go, to share with thousands instead of hundreds, our desire to do something for the Bicentennial.

One of the last things we did for our San Fernando Valley schools as part of Bicentennial activities was to participate in an outreach across the country with helium-filled balloons. There were 76 elementary schools in the valley with anywhere from 400-1200 students in each one. Small mimeographed slips of paper were distributed to every classroom in the valley and children were invited to write their name and address and a Bicentennial greeting. Willing Mom and Dad volunteers inserted these small slips of paper into balloons. The day of Operation Balloon lift-off, the parents came to all 76 schools and filled the balloons with helium. We all marched out to the playground with lively band music playing over the intercom. The children were excited as they had been told that someone they did not know might pick up their balloon and write back to them. It was a gala scene. Many wore red, white and blue. At a given signal, which was to be used by all 76 schools, the principal told everyone to release their balloons. Up, up, up they climbed getting smaller and smaller. We were surprised to see that some schools a few miles from us also released their balloons and we could see three sets of soaring silver dots from our playground. The children were ecstatic and there was much conversation about whether someone would find their message and send a reply. It was a great opportunity to pull out the US map, talk about wind direction (west to east) and guess where our special cargo might land. What a "balloon surprise" Cec and I were to have three months later in Virginia!

OFF AND TRAILERING

And we left…it was all a blur. We were consumed with the logistics of departure. Finding the wonderful young man who was to stay in our home, removing furniture and clothing to give him space, tying up the myriad details one does when absenting oneself from life's usual pattern for a period of seven months, correspondence with Mr. Brockett and Miami boat show people—what a flurry. It was a wrench to leave our classes, we gave at least 100 hugs to dear dog, a warm handshake and hug to dear renter. Goodbye, family. Goodbye, dear Auggie-Doggie. Goodbye, dear children. Goodbye, college daughter. Goodbye, house. What had we gotten ourselves into? What was ahead? If I had known I might not have been as excited as I was!

We looked back at the white trailer behind us. Cec had built it to hold the odd configuration of the battleship. Many thought we had a glider inside. We gave a last tuck in to our red, white and blue lady. We almost felt that she was a living thing, anxious to be released into the element in which she belonged. Somehow she had become a unique part of our life and we acquiesced to her impatience. We felt her push us out of the driveway.

It was February 6, 1975…finally OFF! And to what? Adventure, that was for sure. Miami Boat Show? What would that entail? Apartment? What would be waiting? People? Would they think these two schoolteachers crazy? Biscayne Bay? What do you want of us? Excitement, apprehension, anticipation—all these emotions flooded our minds.

First day—Victorville, Palm Springs, California, across the dry desert of Arizona to Phoenix. It was our first stop and a welcome one after our emotional send-off. The diversity of each geographical section of our country surprised us. Each area was distinctive unto itself. We loved the barrenness of the southwestern desert. We tasted the flavor of our southern neighbor, Mexico, in the dishes of chili we had in El Paso, TX. We capitulated silently to Texas being THE biggest in everything as we drove forever across this landscape. The Texans did not disappoint us in their feeling of supremacy. As we chugged along at the national speed limit of 55 mph, a giant of a car flashed by us. On its bumper was a sticker that read, "Drive 70 and freeze a Yankee."

As coincidence would have her way with us, we stumbled onto the last day of Mardi Gras in frenzied New Orleans. People, already exhausted from almost daily partying, were having their last wild fling. We prudently left our truck/trailer outside town and took a bus into the French Quarter. There we were swept up into the excitement of the Zulu Parade. What sights we did see!

Incredible costumes (or lack of), marchers twisting, bending, dancing to the jazz that only New Orleans can produce. Absolute utter chaos, gay abandon and a bit of decadence were the order of the day. Could this still be a part of the U.S. or had we lost our way? Although we enjoyed being observers of this debauchery, the noise and crowds jangled us after the peace we felt in the vast western deserts. We were ready to head eastward…then into the South!

Make no mistake about the "Southern flavor." The South is as distinct in its own way as the east or the west. We enjoyed huge stands of trees—cottonwood, gum and pine. They lined the parkways of Alabama, Georgia and Mississippi. Southern hospitality was tendered at every state border crossing by the information centers. Georgia even dispensed fresh orange juice. Then it was into the northwestern arm of Florida and a 90-degree right turn for Miami. Going from north to south in Florida seemed almost as long as going from the west coast to the east coast.

When we came into Orlando, we bought a newspaper and I read to Cec as he drove. I reached the sports section and was reading about upcoming events in Miami. My shriek rattled around in the cab and startled Cec. The truck and trailer swayed. "Listen to this. The article is talking about the boat show. It's describing a battleship that's going to be in the lobby of the convention center. It says that part of the publicity is that the USS BICENTENNIAL is going to have a mock war with a Coast Guard boat in Biscayne Bay. And the next day you're going to be out there again—they're pretending that George Washington is crossing the Delaware and you're going to attack him!"

"I'm going to do what?" said poor flabbergasted Cecil. "Read that again." We were still a day and a half away from Miami, and along with our excitement came some apprehension. "I wonder what those PR guys have in store for us," Cec muttered. "I can just imagine what they must have cooked up."

The outskirts of crowded Miami began to wrap its tentacles around us as we drove on. Large cities have a way of doing that to the unwary traveler. We were scooped into traffic but managed to find our apartment. It was lovely and a kindly landlord let us park our ship in a grassy spot. We had found our home. It was good to be off the road.

Thus began a delightful month in a cosmopolitan city. We scrubbed the ship and trailer and thousands of miles of road tar rolled off. We prepared our ship for her debut. We contacted the PR firm who was handling all the publicity and became instant friends with energetic, capable Bruce. He carefully explained the details of our first appearance. We would launch the "BI" at a public launch ramp hidden from the shoreline. Then Cec was to hurry for the shelter of the Miami City marina and lurk behind some of the docked pleasure craft. The press boat was to pick up its load of reporters and head to the outer bay. Cec was to wait until they were in Biscayne Bay and near the Coast Guard cutter. I was to ride on the press boat and take pictures of Cec as he was being filmed by the press. This proved to be how most of these forays went with the press and TV people. It seemed that I was always filming Cecil being filmed. Our pattern repeated itself often. I would caution him to "be careful." He would admonish me to "take LOTS of pictures." After all this time and so many, many launchings, our pattern continues to be the same. He shouts about pictures and I "cluck."

THE PRESS, THE COAST GUARD and GEORGE WASHINGTON

The press boat had its usual quota of seemingly bored, listless men of all descriptions and types. They sprawled about the ship in various poses, draped here and there and were casually reading the press release about our boat. Their chief topic of conversation was the morning's work where they had all covered some politician visiting the city. Their description of him left little to the imagination. I was surprised to find myself becoming somewhat unfriendly in my attitude toward them. *They should really be up by the railing looking for our boat*, I thought. By this time I was used to far more anticipation than was being evidenced around me. Here we are, about to present these guys with something offbeat and they couldn't care less. I wondered why they seemed so jaundiced. My musing was interrupted by a shout. "LOOK AT THAT! Well, I'll be a &^%#!" Expletives filled the air. My whole impression of newsmen and photographers changed right then. My analogy is likened to the policeman or fireman who becomes somewhat inured to the tragedies in their daily routine and probably have to rise above the emotion to survive their daily contact with sadness. Just so must the newsman have a "steady as you go" in their attitude toward any news. If he/she lived in a constant state of "Gee Whiz," they would be on a high all day long. I suspect any work becomes somewhat routine in its repetition.

Since this time we have spoken with and been interviewed by news people from all over the USA—from large and small towns/cities. I have found a few to be somewhat cynical from much exposure to all kinds of people, but all are intensely curious about anything new. They are rapid fire in their questioning in large metropolitan cities where they have a deadline. They will spend an inordinate amount of time with you in the small towns. They all want to know the newsman's theme of who, what, why, when and where. They can also exhibit boyishness and eagerness to do a good story when the little battleship races up to them and fires her turrets at them. These likeable men (now more women) are our friends and I understand most of them.

My reverie ended as I watched expensive camera equipment hoisted onto shoulders. Then the drama unfolded to the delight of the press, the pleasure boaters, the crowd on the shore and Bruce. Cecil came from behind a large cruiser at full speed. Clipping through the water, he headed right for the Coast Guard cutter. As the men on board the cutter saw the USS BICENTENNIAL, they stopped everything. The battleship bore down on them. "Now hear this. This is your captain speaking. Man your battle stations or I'll be forced to fire on you."

As Cecil neared the ship, he let go with the turrets, giving a good broadside to the cutter. I heard the men laugh. "Let's fix him GOOD!" they shouted. To the delight of the newsmen and to Cecil's chagrin, the Coast Guard let go with a huge fire hose and doused him with a steady stream of ocean water. I watched him dodge in and out of the jet and hoped he wasn't drenched. Later on, he told me of his plight. It was his first encounter with a large number of different news media talking to him at one time and the directions coming to him over the VHF walkie-talkie came thick and fast from Bruce and the cutter. Bruce was full of instructions about where the ship should go and what it should do for the reporters. The battleship captain had his hands full with reversing, circling, squirting water and avoiding obstacles all the while obeying orders from the squawk box. A generous Santa Clara, CA, firm loaned a marvelous Intech walkie-talkie to us and it saved us many a time from some embarrassing or dangerous fates.

When the show was over for the reporters, our press boat and the battleship headed for the marina and a windup interview. A dripping, soggy captain climbed out from his water-soaked seat and we completed the interviews. Then, we took a minute to look around at our surroundings. We had come full circle. We were tied up at a berth 50 feet away from the restaurant where we had enjoyed coffee two years ago. We were at the exact spot where Cecil had expressed his desire to be in these waters someday. What a dream come true!

The next day was the highly publicized reenactment of Washington crossing the Delaware. It took a lot of imagination to dream up this one. Instead of a cold and wintry Delaware River scene, we had balmy breezes whispering through the leaves of coco palms. Nevertheless, there was George and his party in full regalia, bravely crossing the briny deep of Biscayne Bay to an opposite shore. This time I set sail with Cec and rode in the rear bucket seat. A midget would have been more comfortable and I tried to dodge the handle of the engine as Cec steered about the bay. With my knees under my chin, I looked out toward the scene of the soon-to-be historic crossing. We had some extra time before we rendezvoused. Since it was such a lovely afternoon, we went out into the middle of the harbor and killed the engine. We casually drifted around in a huge open area enjoying the sights of the busy harbor. We were engrossed in watching one of the Bermuda bound liners getting ready to sail when we heard a loudspeaker hailing us. Turning, we saw a large tugboat slowly coming toward us. Leaning over the bow was the crew, gesturing and point at us. "Ahoy there. Are you radio-controlled?"

Cecil started the engine and we headed for the tug. As we came in closer we could see these rugged seamen laughing excitedly and obviously intrigued with the strange sight in their home waters. As we closed in, Cec squirted them with the forward guns. Delighted shouts filled the air and Cec launched into his usual attack speech. We criss-crossed in front of them several times, then killed the engine. We decided to raise the hatch and wave. Never have I seen more surprised faces. "Look, there's two people in it." Amazement is again the only word to describe the reaction. These seasoned, tough men were as excited as schoolboys and rained questions down on us.

About this time they noticed that quite a bit of oil and tar which had been drifting about in the harbor had collected on our water line. The captain of the tug sent word down that he had some special rags dipped in an extraordinary solution which would wipe our hull clean in minutes. He instructed his men to send us a batch and this they did. Down came a line and tied to it was a bunch of white square cloths which proved to be the best cleanup items we have ever used to get harbor "ooky-book" off the hull. "Ooky-book" may not be a nautical term, but it very aptly describes that which adheres to one's hull. Since this time and on the many rivers we have traveled we have found that the men who go to sea are a wonderful breed. They are the crew one finds on freighters, tugs and barges. They love our boats and are our true friends, supporters and rescuers. They are men who have seen and done everything at sea and they welcome anything that is new, different and floats—especially if it is seaworthy. We appreciated and wanted their respect. Having these men approve our funny ships has been good for our water-oriented morale!

The "crossing of the Delaware" was accomplished with little incident. The men in George's boat were highly amused at our ship darting in and out around them. George stood in the bow, one foot on the gunwale —just as in our history books—and tried to look dignified as he approached the crowd waiting for him on the shore. I couldn't help but think, *I wonder what the real George would have done if such a phantom had appeared on the Delaware back in 1776.*

TA-TA-TA-DAH!
THE GRAND OPENING!

With a lot of TV, radio and newspaper interviews behind us, we were ready for the boat show to open. What a magnificent building the convention center is. Built to house huge crowds and many displays, it surely is one of the most beautiful and adequate of centers. The day the show was to open, we drove our boat over early to the center, and workmen put her on a dolly and she was trundled into the main lobby. What a setting! This time our red/white/blue lady was placed on an elevated platform covered with royal blue cloth, and stanchions were placed around her with blue and white velvet ropes looped around the brass uprights. We were in the absolute center of the lobby where the crowd could pass on either side of us. We set up our easels of pictures showing our two battleships in the water. One easel was devoted entirely to our proposed journey up the ICW. We polished and fussed over our beauty as we readied her for the expected crowd of tens of thousands of visitors. Miami is one big boating city and we knew there were huge crowds anticipated. This was and may still be the largest boat show in the United States.

The hour was almost upon us for the opening, and we put our boat show sticker on our truck and clutched our precious passes which would admit us for the days ahead. Back to the apartment we went to change into nautical clothes and rush back for the Friday night opening. As we approached the building, we were surprised at the crowd already gathered waiting for the doors to open. The band was milling around, as were the majorettes and the boat show princesses. Excitement pervaded the tropical night air, and we felt we were a fun part of "show biz" as we used our passes to get through the crowd to our exhibit.

Miami Beach Convention Center Boat Show—Cecil

Los Angeles Convention Center Boat Show—Pat

This time we thought we knew what to expect, and we were anticipating a fun time in talking with all the interesting people we would meet in the next nine days. At least we would not be talking to a class all day before the show. Perhaps our voices would hold out.

As we took our positions behind the velvet cords, we turned and watched the crowd waiting impatiently behind the doors of the building. Then the band struck up; the many, many doors opened, the majorettes paraded in ahead of the band and we were on! The performers were showstoppers and the crowd loved it. Banners and balloons all added to the scene as the eager about-to-be-boat-owners clapped their approval of the opening number. The doormen stood aside, the band marched in and the lobby was total bedlam. The cacophony of noise, the color, the excited multitude was overwhelming. We stood in shock. In swept hordes of spectators. What a fashion show! The men wore bright peacock colored shirts and pants, the women were equally bright with their colors. We were in the tropics! The effect was a kaleidoscope of rainbow colors against the white of the walls.

We had been in a well-run, wonderful boat show in Los Angeles three months previous, but we have never experienced another boat show like the Miami Beach one. Over the years we have been hired to be "the hook" for 15 shows—all over the US. We have never seen one to equal this one in size or color.

The nine days went by so very quickly. Each day and night was different. We grew hoarse from so much talking, but the outreach from the public was astonishing. As much as one enjoys projecting a hobby, any trade show is a grueling, time-consuming job. To be "on" all day and well into the night and answer the same questions is a challenge. Again we found we had to spell one another at our lobby station. We could escape to the pressroom where there were refreshments for boat participants. Our proposed trip up the Intracoastal Waterway so interested the Miami people. Many westerners had and have no idea that this long "ditch" is in existence. But the Florida people knew, lived on it and were big into boating. Over and over we explained about our trip and told of our upcoming departure date. Many were incredulous. "You're going up the ICW in THAT?" We would explain that we had a boat to live on, we might tow the BICENTENNIAL some of the time but she would go under her own power many places, particularly when we came into ports. The Intracoastal Waterway is often referred to as "The Ditch." Sometimes it is a narrow, quiet canal, deep in the Southern bayous. It often flares out into a huge sound, like the Mississippi Sound where channel markers are miles apart. Questions were frequent and repetitive, but we never tired of the enthusiasm and interest from our visitors. We were grateful and buoyed in spirit by the wonderful acquaintances who wished us well on our forthcoming voyage.

There were so many examples of outreach to us. It was here that Intech gave us the walkie-talkies. And it was here that Johnson Outboard really came through for us. By now we were well acquainted with them because their 9.9 outboards powered both our ships. They probably appreciated the publicity we gave them but they went way beyond the call of duty in assisting us. When engines failed, they sent us new ones. They gave us many parts to engines that they thought would help us along the way. We became close friends with their fine public relations man, Bill Au Coin. He became our boat's guardian angel.

As the show ran its nine-day course, we became accustomed to the princesses who draped themselves all over various boats, including ours. The pressroom was a haven with drinks and sandwiches and fascinating conversation from behind the scenes. Even though this was not "show biz" in its strictest sense, it was near enough that we found we enjoyed being a part of it. We liked meeting the public and we learned a lot from the helpful and unusual characters who paraded by our ship. Our many grueling hours blended into a blur as we talked with the public. Visitors came with all different personalities and attitudes, but they were eager, receptive, curious kind, amazed—sometimes a few circled us repeatedly like sharks. Some spectators would come up on one side of our display, disappear, then come to the other side. They would read our giveaway literature, check out the easels, look at us quizzically and never say a word. We were questioned, scolded for our impetuosity about attempting such a trip ("You DON'T know what lies ahead of you!!") Seasoned boaters grilled us with rapid-fire questions. People surprised us by asking for our autographs. One lady told us she "just loves show biz people!" We didn't know we were in that category. Some guests wanted to buy our boat and were disappointed when told it was not for sale. One young man about 13 years of age became glued at the hip to Cec. He came to the show three times just to check out the battleship and draw it as best he could. He announced to us that he was going to build a battleship. He was not about to be dissuaded. "I WILL build one just like this," he would announce. We tried to tell him of the difficulties encountered in construction and were ignored. We wondered what he eventually did! One sweet eight-year-old boy told us he had built a model of a gray battleship "just like yours, but it doesn't look like yours anymore. It's in a drawer and it's smashed." Oh dear, said my second grade teacher's heart.

Breaks in the pressroom were a learning experience. The public relations people were always there, counting the house, juggling attendance figures, working on new press angles and guarding their catered pastrami sandwiches and liquor. Most people were considerate and courteous back there when surrounded by "goodies," but there were a few that were named "the vulture pack."

Fallout connections from the show continued to be fantastic. What "plums" dropped into our laps and how grateful we were at things which unfolded for us. Visitors from far up the east coast had come to the show and many owned marinas. They invited us to stay with them when we came into their area and insisted that they be our hosts. Teachers introduced themselves to us and made arrangements for us to deliver our special pen pal letters to the Miami children. We were helped in delivering our first letter from L.A.'s Mayor Bradley to the Miami mayor. The then Secretary of Interior Rogers Morton stood by us and wanted his picture taken with us.

A great bonus was to meet the co-editors of the famous Inland Waterway Books, *The Waterway Guide*, which covered the whole ICW territory. Jim and Liz Emmitt gave us an autographed copy of the boater's bible. One cannot function without this guide. Descriptions of how to find marinas, gas, buoys, hidden boating traps, weather warnings, and maps—it's all in their guides. We used ours daily, almost hourly.

A couple introduced themselves to us Mr. And Mrs. Lambert Gates. They told us a fascinating tale of the Gateses' history that we had never heard. There were some early seafaring Gateses who were wrecked near the Bahamas and made their way to land. The man was an actual descendant of the early Gateses, and Cecil and Lambert had a great time trying to trace the Gateses' family history back to England. They ended up by inviting us to fly to their island home in the Bahamas after the show was over.

The *coup de gras* for us was when the Good Year blimp people invited us to go up in their lighter- than-air craft. What an opportunity for us to begin filming for the schoolchildren at home. They found out we needed to get our establishing shots of Biscayne Bay and to show the entrance to the ICW. We were given free passes to ride their famous cigar-shaped vehicle. We could hardly wait for our lighter-than-air trip!

When the last night of the boat show came, we had mixed feelings of relief and regret. We had many new friends among the dealers, exhibitors and public relations people. We would be indebted to dozens of them for so many thoughtful acts of help in numerous forms—boating gifts, charts, advice, invitations. Intech Marine of Santa Clara, CA, installed our walkie-talkies free of charge, then gave us a large VHF unit for the escort boat and the two small units for the battleship. We would be able to keep track of Cecil and the BICENTENNIAL. Johnson Outboard flew down a brand new 9.9 HP motor for the battleship and a letter which entitled us to Johnson repair service all along the 1500-mile waterway. They also sent beautiful, weatherproof Johnson jackets, caps and pullover shirts. We felt quite resplendent in our finery. The clothes proved to be not only decorative, but functional, too— and needed.

The Navy had their local recruiting officer deliver a *carte blanche* letter from our friend, Vice Admiral Emmitt H. Tidd. He was in charge of recruiting for the whole US. This cordial letter allowed us entrance into the Navy ports of Mayport (Jacksonville, FL), Charleston, SC, Norfolk, VA, Philadelphia, PA, and Washington, D.C. Another newfound friend, Ret. Col. Joe Schaeffer, was a member of the Miami Yacht Club. He obtained permission for us to launch our escort boat and the battleship from the private ramp of their club. How grateful we were for all this assistance.

By this time it was the end of February and we were to set sail from Miami in two weeks. We had been in touch with Bill Brockett by phone and he assured us he was still coming with a new boat for our trip. Again, we wondered who our mysterious skipper would be. He sounded enthusiastic on the phone and ready to go; but not having met him made us wonder who this gentleman could be with whom we would live the next three to four months.

The two weeks before Bill's arrival were spent enjoying the tourist attractions of southern Florida. We were glad to pack up the boat in her trailer, become anonymous and let her and us have a rest. We visited all the tourist spots we could find—Parrot Jungle, Everglades—and attended parties new friends had invited us to. We were introduced as "the couple that had the battleship at the boat show." Or sometimes it would be "the people who own that funny little submarine that tried to sink the Coast Guard and George Washington." We found it odd and a bit amusing that we were considered semi-celebrities. We had shifted from unknown schoolteacher roles to having a semi-high profile, at least in Florida. After exploring the Keys, watching the alligators, meeting the Mayor and schoolchildren, we drove to the ICW and looked out at it from the shore. Shortly we would meet Bill, and the three of us would become a part of that privileged group of boat adventurers.

A-BLIMPING WE DID GO

We drove out to the grassy field where the blimp was tethered to the ground. The day was perfect, even though a light breeze was blowing. The blimp was anchored with ropes but tugged at her moorings as if she longed to join the pre-historic-looking pelicans. Our pilot joined us as the four of us who were to be passengers clambered the few steps up and into the comfortable gondola which could hold six passengers. It takes a crew of 17 to keep the Mayflower flying. What an uncluttered instrument panel compared to an airliner. Two small wheels were on either side of the blimp's pilot. We learned that he controlled the ascent or descent by spinning the wheels. It looked like a cumbersome operation with ropes to pull and a few mysterious gadgets to push.

We were up and away without a bump. The only way we knew we were airborne was by the upward thrust of the nose and the muffled noise of the motor. Ascending slowly was a fantastic sight and such a contrast to the takeoff of a jet. As we climbed into the indigo sky, we were struck with the beauty of the landscape below. Biscayne Bay glittered and shimmered in turquoise hues. The white of the Miami Beach sand outlined the blue-green waters picture framing the bay. The soaring white hotels along the people-strewn beaches were etched into the skyline. Their high-rise tops looked impressive and we marveled at their number. The open sea lay beyond the breakwater, an undisturbed, beckoning playmate.

The captain interrupted our viewing. "Look." He pointed below. "There is the beginning of the ICW." We looked and there was Miami's entrance to "The Ditch." We could see the entrance from the sea, a narrow opening in the breakwater. We traced with our eyes the path of the canal as it went from the openness of the bay into the slim canyons between the white buildings. Cecil filmed this for the beginning of our 16 mm film for children on the west coast. Like a dark ribbon of green we could see, in the distance, the canal disappearing into the chasm between the shiny, white hotels. Somewhere within that maze of glistening towers we would soon find our battleship and ourselves…and the yet unknown Mr. Brockett.

A change in the motor told us we were beginning to descend for our landing. It was like being in a rocking chair. As we slid back down toward the waiting crew, we hoped we had captured this enchanting experience on film. Our documentary for schoolchildren had begun.

One special visit was to the Miami Shores Elementary School. The 5th and 6th graders put on a production called "Tom Jefferson." It was an amazing extravaganza complete with speeches, singing and dancing. As an elementary teacher I felt that the teachers and students had way exceeded their ability level. The polished, mature performance was so special. To our surprise we were suddenly introduced as the "the people you've read about in the paper who brought the USS BICENTENNIAL battleship to Miami." Thrust into my hands was the mike and we were "on." We have had to learn to speak in unexpected places and at a moment's notice. I spoke briefly about our journey and introduced my admiral. What a warm welcome we had from this student body.

That night we talked with Bill Leary, who wanted some of our film footage taken of us from the Miami Beach Boat Show. A tax override election was coming up in April, and Bill thought our publicity might be useful.

A phone call to Bill Brockett, still back on the west coast, gave us some dismaying news. The new Land 'n Sea houseboat would not be ready for our use, but we were told that a couple, Florida residents and owners of an older Land 'n Sea, would be willing to sell their boat to the company. And the stipulation was that they wished to accompany us. We drove to Melbourne, 100 miles north, to meet these people and found Mary and Don and two poodles. (Five adults and two dogs on board! We wondered how this arrangement would work out!) The plan was for Bill Brockett to go immediately to Melbourne and check out the boat and do any repair work necessary. We would put her and the battleship in the water at the Miami Yacht Club on March 16 and sail the next day. We kept in touch with Mary and found that Bill had landed and was already working on the boat. We waited impatiently for the 15th to arrive so we might meet our skipper.

We well remember the night he came to see us. He walked into our apartment, our lives and our hearts. Tall and slender, boyish and friendly, and we were to find out a sometimes wild ex-Marine (vintage Korean War). But at this time we did not know these things. We didn't know the three of us would become welded into an unbeatable, smooth functioning, happy team. We were to find that we needed each other, that each of us had his/her place and there was no obstacle that we could not overcome with the "can-do" spirit that infected our whole trip. For now we were happy that we had such a competent, fun friend with whom to begin our voyage. Our only concern was crowding on a 28-foot ship. Privately, we decided we would be good sports and be grateful for the boat transporting us. There was much transferring of clothing, food and gear to be stored. We stepped on each other, but all seemed determined that the crowding in tight quarters would not be a problem.

The day before our big launch, Bill and Cec had a practice session. We had been sitting around trying to figure out what name we should give the mother ship. It was decided that she would be CELEBRATION II in honor of our nation's 200th birthday. Signs were made and Bill and Cec put them on the bridge of Land 'n Sea. The signs mounted on both sides of the fly bridge read "LAND & SEA ESCORT BOAT FOR THE MINIATURE BATTLESHIP USS BICENTENNIAL." Then the men took the two boats out into the bay. They practiced going tandem and they practiced tying up the BI to the stern platform of CELEBRATION II. They practiced a proper speed. Bill felt that anywhere from eight to twelve knots would be about right. Twelve knots was likely best. A tide change threw the boats together slightly and tore off the starboard rub rail, so in they came at 5P.M. for repair and dinner at the Miami Beach Yacht Club.

The warm, humid 17th of March arrived, and so did the photographers. Our friend from the boat show, Bruce, came to the docks. Joe Schaeffer brought me flowers! One photographer had a beautiful, leggy blond model stretch out casually on our battleship. She was very poised and lovely until one of the gun turrets poked her in an unwelcome spot. She erupted off the ship, spoiling some pictures. There were shouts of encouragement from our new Miami friends who had gathered to send us off. Photographers took numerous pictures, pleasure boats circled curiously to see what strange caravan was taking off from the yacht club. Newsmen from NBC and ABC were present. I posed for one last picture by the battleship with Cec, then pushed his bow out with a hard shove. Then Mary, Don and I ran for the cruiser. Bill had the 250 HP Chrysler motor going, and with one shove we were off. The space widened between the boat and the shore which was lined with our waving friends. My silent thanks reached out to every one of them. How much they had done to ease our way and to help us with this undertaking. And we were OFF! Ahead, we knew was Ft. Lauderdale.

We were to find that this was typical of the spirit with which we were helped along this whole odyssey. People were supportive of what we were attempting to do when it was discovered we were trying to instill a feeling of appreciation and love of country in children. They helped us in so many venues to bring our American history and heritage to life. The fact that we were two school teachers carrying pen pal letters, mayor's letters and filming history as seen from the waterways touched some kind of button with the public.

SKIPPER BILL BROCKETT

We tried to analyze what it was. We decided it was a combination of many factors—a patriotic battleship theme, a 1500-mile adventure, a documentary to be shared...the American public was eager to latch onto something which would celebrate our Bicentennial year. So many towns, large and small, were readying celebration plans and programs. They eagerly welcomed us with our particular interpretation of this Bicentennial festivity and did all they could to promote us in any way possible. We also decided "the good guys outnumber the bad guys" in this great polyglot country of ours, and we felt a resurgence of American pride in their heritage and freedoms. This intangible feeling of support surfaced over and over on this long trip, and we shall ever be grateful to the chance acquaintances who did so much for us. Though we knew we might never see them again, we tried to thank them all for the help they tendered us and the friendship so generously given.

SHAKEdown CRUISE

As we left the luxury of the Miami Yacht Club and our waving friends, we five were excited. The two dogs were, too. We were out with the big kids on the block. We passed the gleaming expensive vessels so native to Florida's coast. We passed some Navy ships. The crews lined up along the railings and yelled and waved at us. We went under our first bridge. Things seemed to be going along smoothly. Our communication on the VHF from CELEBRATION II back to the BI was good.

It was not too long before Cec began to complain about losing power. He and Bill could tell that the plugs were fouling. They decided that the ambient air was the cause and said that upon arrival at Ft. Lauderdale that afternoon, they would install a blower. Poor Cec—he constantly stopped to change plugs.

The ICW narrowed and we felt we were getting closer to Ft. Lauderdale. Here's where the boater's bible is so invaluable. Our Waterway Guide was labeled the Southern Edition and covered the ICW from Texas to the border of Florida and Georgia. We had purchased all the editions which would take us to NY. Each section or "leg" begins with a large chart, an appraisal of the overall cruising characteristics, and tabulated data on bridges (and opening restrictions), distances, chart numbers, buoy numbers. The book describes mile by mile the harbors, ports, hazards, points of interest. At the end of each small section is a table of marine facilities in each harbor and spotting charts showing their exact locations. The list includes detail such as length of boat accommodated, depth for keel, fuel available, repair and in-the-sling service. There are other charts which are very useful. General headings include charts, distance, VHF/FM, tides, fishing conditions, temperatures, restaurant and grocery supply availability. We could not have made mile one without this valuable book. We referred to it constantly. Bill and I had a morning routine. We would get Cec launched, being careful not to drop his 16mm Canon Scoopic or Belle & Howell cameras with which he was filming this trip. He would be piloting the BICENTENNIAL. I would bring coffee to the skipper and read the portion of the day's trip aloud to him. Bill faithfully kept his own logbook

We left Biscayne Bay and entered the narrow confines of this first part of the ICW. They had determined that 12 knots was the proper speed. The traffic in boats was something else. Even though it was not a weekend, the boaters were thick. We kept our eye on Cec as he threaded his way through the large craft. Bill was on the fly bridge, where I was to learn he would usually spend the whole cruising time unless weather was a problem. Now we came through a chasm—a jungle of white concrete hotels. We had seen these from the blimp, but how different it was to be right down in them. The buildings towered above us. This whole area was a sun seeker's paradise. Hotel dining rooms faced the waterway and outdoor patios held tables. As we cruised up the canal, people shouted and waved at us. Our sign "Escort ship for USS BICENTENNIAL" linked us to Cecil plunging along behind us. When people saw the battleship they applauded, cheered, vigorously waved to attract our attention. One dignified older lady yelled at us from her table, "Best thing to ever come up the waterway!"

We were impressed with the beautiful homes whose lawns swept right down to the shoreline. Yachts were tied up to the docks in front of these mansions. Homeowners came running out, all with cameras, dragging their children, gardeners, anyone they could find. We found a nice marina located directly in front of a beautiful restaurant. I watched with great interest as our skilled skipper brought in our house cruiser so easily. I watched with envy as Mary and Don tied up the ship so beautifully. My lack of experience was obvious, and Mary kindly showed me the simplest of knots and tie up skills. I wondered what Bill thought of my "crewing." I found out later. "You were GREEN! dearie." Bill and Cecil worked on the BI, and we had the usual onlookers with their many questions and some newspaper reporters. We were on display in a very crowded area and surrounded by extravagantly expensive yachts. We planned to stay two nights as logistics would force us to begin leap-frogging truck, trailer and two cars.

Our first night was a nightmare, but funny. Mary and I stepped all over one another getting dinner in the small but well-equipped galley. Outside the three men were fussing over the battleship, tying her to the mother ship. There was much shouting and discussing of line management and much tying and untying. All this time the two poodles were yapping and running about. With dinner over, I had my first initiation in to the bedding down process. With five of us on board it was impossible to take showers, and the shower was full of life jackets, anyhow. Thus it was I was initiated into one of the most discussed items on the waterway. "How are the heads and showers?" Boating people always volunteer important information to other boaters. Eagerly one asks about the facilities! "Are they good?" Qualifications for good means clean, no cracked plaster, screen over open windows to keep out critters, good lighting, outlets for hair dryers, no lurking snakes or spiders. I became convinced that the electricians who did the wiring on this 1500-mile trip were all bachelors. Where were the outlets?

The next most important things were the laundromats and grocery shopping. Boat people are hounded and driven by needing showers, clean washer/driers and markets. Water-borne, they are free as the gulls who escort them, but once tied up to the dock, they again become land people, flippers clipped and needing amenities. Certain marinas have wonderful reputations— "Remember the one that had the great showers and a grocery store within walking distance?" Also acceptable and sought after were the small towns where it was possible to tie up and walk into town using a cart that the marina would put out on loan. When these useful conveniences were found, we could always recognize the boaters. They were bronzed, wearing deck tennies and had that drip-dry look about their clothes. A local post office was definitely a bonus.

The five of us headed for the showers. Showers are usually back-to-back for the men and women, and the conversations were fascinating. This night there were five women in different states of disrepair. I soon learned that one does not care—or rather learns how not to care—how one looks, especially when bedding down. The night attire of people going to and from the showers is more like Halloween night. I have had many an interesting conversation with women adorned in curlers, mumus, shower caps, shorts and halters, and men draped in towels and very short bathrobes. The bond of sailing people goes far beyond appearance, and the exchange of stories and information is the important subject of the day. Appearance takes on a secondary position as safety, navigation and care of the boat come first. I complained to Mary about the distance from the boat to the showers. I grumbled I would need another shower after I made the long walk back in the humidity. "You'll get used to it," was her truthful reply.

We all rummaged about like so many nesting sparrows each making up his or her own bunk. We may not have known one another very well, but we giggled as we "pardon me'd" our way to bed. As I lay in my top bunk I looked at the interior of the boat. It was a mess and there were only three of us inside. Cec and Bill were topside on the fly bridge cushions. There was clothing all over, cushions stacked here/there, belongings tied to poles or hooks, dogs snoring. The creaking noises and soft scree of stretching lines were strange to me, but I fell into an exhausted sleep. I'm sure everyone else did, too.

The next A.M., Bill and Cec arose from having slept up on the bridge in fold out chairs and sleeping bags to find that they were dressing under the view of people having breakfast in the marina restaurant above us. They decided to be nonchalant and waved. What else could they do?

We had left our rig at the Miami Yacht Club. Bill needed his VHF license for installation of part of the Intech unit in the big boat. Cec, Bill and I rented a car and drove back to Miami to pick up everything. We felt like sneaking in the back way after our auspicious sendoff. Back to the boat we drove. When all communication instruments were in place, we were able to use our call letters. They remain indelibly ingrained in my memory: WYU 5904 for the BICENTENNIAL and WYU 5985 for CELEBRATION II. I learned the radioman's sea alphabet. We were Whiskey-Yankee-Uniform. I promptly forgot the names and was to regret this mistake later on. I will never forget it and Bill will not let me forget.

Mary and Don had brought their car and trailer forward, and that afternoon we decided to jump the two vehicles forward to the small town of Lantana. I would come with the rental car to bring us all back to the boats in Ft. Lauderdale. We became hopelessly lost trying to find a previously designated spot and did not get back to the ships until late that night. This hop, skip, jump routine was to prove tedious with all the moving required.

In addition to having a fouling plug problem, Cec also discovered that his well containing the engine was being swamped by wakes from the large boats passing us. This had a tendency to short out the batteries! So the two mechanical geniuses cut up a rubber inner tube and made a very high gasket which they wrapped around the opening. This seemed to solve the problem.

March 18 and Mary and Don drove to Melbourne, their home, and would wait for us. Nice as they were, it was a relief to have just three bodies on the 28-ft. ship. That morning I stood on the swim platform and helped Cec put the port and starboard harness on the BI so we could do a bit of towing and he could join us on the CELEBRATION II. We were gradually leaving the busy ports behind us and had entered a lovely canal. We were now out of the big cities and the pastoral scenes of meadows, coco palms, and an occasional home was all we saw. White egrets began to show up in abundance. We could see groups of them in the thick greenery along the shore. Their snowy bodies on toothpick legs we likened to two straws standing in a pistachio soda with a head of foam on top. This wild, uninhabited area was a reprieve from the bustle of the large cities. Ten years later we would come by the same area and it would all be built up with condos, the birds gone.

OFF AND RUNNING—
OR SO WE THOUGHT

The peace and quiet that descended on the three of us was wonderful. We were headed for the small town of Lantana. Mary and Don were off moving trucks/trailers. We went through areas of primitive looking trees; we came around bends which opened up on turquoise colored waters; we passed quiet stretches of wild coco palms displaying their bounty which was hanging out over the bays; we laughed at the awkward pelicans who plunged, then clung to the markers that guided us north up the channel. We spent most of the day on the bridge, sharing the beauty and the joy of the day together. The only break came was when I went below to prepare sandwiches for us. I soon came topside, for none of us wanted to leave the beauty that surrounded us. That day the three of us truly became friends. We bonded!

As CELEBRATION II continued to tow the BI and we came closer to Lantana, the wind increased. We found that late afternoon winds usually did come up and it was better to leave early and tie up before we had to battle winds as we came into port. Our *modus operandi* was not yet worked out for docking, and we learned to put Cec into his boat, then Bill and I would go into port with CELEBRATION, tie up, then bring in the battleship. This was one of our unintentionally late days, however, and as Bill tried to bring in CELEBRATION to a long pier, the tail wind shoved us headlong toward a potential ramming. He threw the engine into reverse and at the same time I fended off our large boat—all except Cec who was desperately trying to keep the BI from climbing into our back pocket. She was already nosing up toward us and we managed to come to a safe, if not very graceful stop before the expected crash. Locals watching were nice enough to tell us of a boatyard nearby which was more protected from the wind. We made our way to this spot and spent the night amid cranes and boats in various stages of disrepair. The two men discovered their towing distance had not been correct, for the BI was full of water and her batteries were shorted out. They spent a large part of the evening wringing her out and discussing a better positioning of her behind CELEBRATION II. The police chief and mayor came to visit us and were a great help in driving the men to buy parts and equipment.

With some boating problems fixed (we thought) and behind us, the three of us awoke to a beautiful day. Mary and Don had the vehicles and were waiting for us to pull into their hometown of Melbourne. We were to proceed north and join up with them at the Patrick Air Force Yacht Club. We launched Cec and his ship and proceeded up the ICW. We drew many stares as Cec shot broadsides at boats and people along the waterway. We journeyed a long ways through populated areas and when we came to a remote part, we put the BI under tow and got Cec on board. What a day we had. Up on the bridge together, sharing the beauty, munching on sandwiches, wondering at the fun of having this adventure and being so compatible…it was euphoric.

I left Cec and Bill on the bridge and went below to clean up the debris left over from lunch. Without warning, there was silence. The engine had quit and the silence was not golden. It is true panic time when a boat is underway and the power is suddenly gone. I reconstructed later what had happened topside. Bill had just passed a large dredging operation and was approaching a drawbridge. A large ship was coming south toward us and we were waiting for the bridge to open. As it swung up there were many cars stopped, waiting for both boats to proceed. Then the engine stopped, the excitement began. Cecil told me later Bill's understatement of the day was, "Don't look now, but I think we're in big trouble." We surely were. We were heading into the wind and there was a chop on the water. Right behind us was a long series of barges and a Corps of Engineer's dredge which was clearing out the canal. It had large rotary blades which, though half submerged, looked ready and waiting to gobble up a helpless cruiser and battleship.

I barely had time to assess all this when I heard Cec almost falling down the ladder from the bridge. He hit the stern deck and seconds later he came bursting into and through the narrow aisle to the bow. I was forcefully shoved aside by this 200-pound catapulting maniac. As I lay in a heap draped over the galley table, I stared at my supposedly better half as he clawed his way to the bow. He threw open the hatch and began to wildly throw things aside. At last he located the anchor and threw it overboard. It was none too soon. The dredging operators stopped everything and the men stood ready to fend us off. I unraveled myself from the pile into which I had been so rudely thrust and looked aft. The anchor had grabbed just in time. The battleship was almost in the maw of the giant teeth, the huge ship approaching us was sliding by, people had leaped out of their cars and were watching us from the side of the bridge. Chaos—but two big lessons learned. Bill found that one gas tank was empty and as soon as he switched over to a full one the engine started and we were able to wave at everyone and get underway. We also learned that the anchor and chain must ALWAYS be at the top of the hatch and ready for any emergency. Another boating lesson learned…piloting a boat is like piloting a plane. There are hours and hours of beauty and boredom punctuated by moments of stark terror.

We proceeded on our way and figured we could make Ft. Pierce before nightfall. I joined the boys on the bridge and we finally had time to laugh at our almost misadventure. I did manage to wrangle a semi-apology from my spouse for shoving me into an incongruous lump. Another lesson—male and female titles mean nothing on a boat. "Save Our Ship" is the cry—gender be damned.

MARKER 221—WATERLOO!!

As the afternoon wore on, the three of us continued to enjoy one another and ourselves. What an adventure. Although we realized there was a lot of work ahead of us, we felt we were settling in. Our troika was becoming welded, and we found we appreciated having more space to ourselves. It was a crowded situation with two more adults and the two dogs. We would not think about that until we arrived in Melbourne.

All our talk and musing together was brought to an abrupt halt when a most unwelcome noise came from the engine compartment. Cec took the wheel and Bill plunged down the ladder and looked under the engine compartment hatch. Then the boat slowed down of its own accord and began to heat up. Bill's assessment was that we had blown a head gasket. With each compression stroke, gases were being blown out and were hissing in the engine compartment. This dismaying circumstance made a change in plans imperative, for it was obvious we were in trouble. We would not make our intended port, and I was sent to the *Waterway Guide* to find the nearest marina landfall. Soon signs along the shore and in the water alerted us that the Outrigger Club was just ahead. The write-up in our book made it sound great. We turned in just before Marker 221 and were grateful to do this under our own power, even though very slowly.

What a spot we had stumbled into! Most full-time boaters are aware of the beauty and facilities of Jensen Beach where the Outrigger Club is located. We were unaware of the south sea island effect of this gorgeous place. Frances Langford, former singer with Bob Hope's WW II shows, owned this spot. She was married to Ralph Evinrude, whose name is on his sturdy boat engines. We could not have chosen a more appealing place had we tried. The whole marina had the exotic look of the South Seas with coco palms and thatched roofs. The restaurant overlooked the marina, and we were Bill's guests for dinner. How welcoming our hosts were. We were told where we could take CELEBRATION II to a nearby ramp and the BICENTENNIAL would be a guest of the marina.

The next day Bill and Cec scurried around for a gasket set, torque wrench and miscellaneous things needed for repairs. Cec had broken the gantry crane on the BICENTENNIAL, smashed a gun tub and salt water was beginning to makes parts of the boat rust. I held "open house" for all those curious about the battleship tied up dockside. The local paper sent down a reporter for an interview. Ralph Evinrude came by to see our boat and invited us on his 120-foot yacht. The boys continued to work on CELEBRATION II. In between repair work and the press, we did visit Mr. Evinrude's ship, CHANTICLEER. We were impressed with the luxurious living and how beautifully appointed all the rooms were. We enjoyed pictures hung on the bulkheads of the famous life Miss Langford had led—so many celebrities and politicians had been in her life. The boys were most impressed with the engine room. It was painted a spotless white with specks of gold glitter. Small pieces of white carpeting on the engine room floor confounded us all, and it was this that Bill and Cec talked about more than anything. Mr. Evinrude was most gracious and asked us to have drinks with him. What a setting in their ship's living room!

By this time Mary and Don had heard of our plight and drove down to Jensen Beach to see if they could assist in any way. Bill hoped he had done enough of a repair job that we might be able to drive the boat to a nearby ramp, then to a boat repair. The BICENTENNIAL was also in need of work, as the seawater was taking her apart. We planned to trailer up both boats and take them to Mary's home. There the boats could be worked on and repaired. We left the next morning. There was a strong wind blowing as we took off from the Outrigger. Bill and I watched Cecil head out into the waves and the battleship cut right through the foamy white caps. Onlookers helped us shove off, but as we headed out we nicked a guardrail when the wind gusted particularly hard and pushed us back into a piling. We followed Cec out and the others drove to the ramp to meet us.

Bill was unusually silent as we headed out to Marker 221. I could see him checking the gauges. Abruptly he jumped up. "Pat, you steer. That engine is heating up. I'll go check it." He disappeared below and I was alone and in command of this cumbersome vessel. At least I knew enough to head into the wind. I didn't like the sounds I heard and I knew Bill was having trouble. He came up the ladder. "It's no use. The engine is full of water and will not turn over." We were drifting away from the causeway rapidly, and Bill told me to throw out the anchor. After he helped me secure, I rushed up to check the fathometer. We had six feet under us. The ICW is channeled out and constantly worked on by dredge and shallow on the sides. We were in a wide spot, but we could see the shoreline on both sides.

Cecil, way ahead of us, saw us hanging on our anchor and came back. We talked via the VHF and told him of our problem. He circled for a while but there was nothing to do but wait until we could be towed in. Cec went in to join Mary and Don at the ramp and wait for us. Bill was still trying to repair the engine although it seemed fruitless. Then he said, "Get on the radio and call the Coast Guard. Tell them it's not life threatening, but we need a tow." My heart sank. Color me green with inexperience. How I wished I had listened, learned and memorized our call letters. How one called the Coast Guard left me clueless. Bill patiently yelled instructions to me. We were still in trouble for strong winds were jerking at our anchor and we were slowly being dragged. I managed to find the C.G. frequency and immediately made the blunder which stays with me to this day. "This is Whiskey-Yankee-Union," I began.

"Whiskey-Yankee-UNIFORM" Bill bellowed. Becoming more unglued, I struggled to explain our problem to the patient Coast Guard radioman. All the time I could hear Bill muttering, "Whiskey-Yankee-Unionsuit." Embarrassed, I asked him what further information I should give the Coast Guard. "Nothing," he said. "Leave the frequency open. We'll monitor it and see what they can do for us. Come back here and give me a hand."

The U.S.C.G. kept in touch with us and determined that we were in no immediate danger and they had a more urgent problem—that of removing a burned man from a ship offshore. They radioed the C.G. Auxiliary of our location and our problem, and those good volunteers said they would try to rescue us in the next few hours. Those on shore were listening to our communications and monitoring our problems. Bill's engine diagnosis—gaskets had blown, crank case full of water. We had to get ashore for repairs.

Defeated, we decided to get the ice chest out and see what beverages it might hold. I sat on the stern, cross-legged on the deck, with Bill on the foam chest. We watched the land slowly slide by us as we dragged anchor. We had found only one anchor on board and Bill swore to buy another. He talked about the problems of buying or using someone else's boat with no history as to its care or lack thereof. The sun was setting and there was no BICENTENNIAL in sight. We had not been able to raise him although he said he heard all our calls to the C.G. All were aware of our situation. Every now and then Bill would say, "Whiskey-Yankee-Unionsuit" and we would burst into peals of laughter. The third time he said this he fell through the lid of the foam ice chest. We were tired after two hours of this, so inconsequential things brought us to near hysteria.

Bill pointed. "Look at that. I'll bet it's our rescue ship." And SOUTHERN COMFORT came to assist us. We made fast the towline between our two boats. I watched in awe as the owner of SOUTHERN COMFORT expertly towed us toward land. What a help our Intech radio was. We were connected with our Coast Guard Auxiliary rescuers. Gracefully and without hurry, SOUTHERN COMFORT came into the Outrigger Club Marina. Just at the right time he swung us toward our docking area and we let go the line. Waiting on shore was a crowd of people—many had just seen us off. How awkward to return to the same place where we had had such a gala send-off that morning!

There were Cec, Mary and Don waiting for us. The dock master drove up in his golf cart. "Thought we'd seen the last of you," was his greeting. "Have you cleared our harbor of all the enemy? What can I do for you, Skipper?"

We accepted a lot of good-natured teasing but it had been a long, long day. "Would you like a ride up to the restaurant?" we were asked.

"No, but we'd love a ride to the head." Bill bowed me on board the golf cart and away we went. Was this afternoon occurrence lesson number five or six for me? I was too tired to care.

After a good night's sleep, we thought things looked a bit better. Bill and Don began to tear down the engine. They found the head gasket had blown on all four cylinders and the crankcase was full of oil and water. They scraped and cleaned all parts and the engine was reassembled by 7:30 P.M. They tested the engine for half an hour and announced they were back in business. Again—another dinner at Outrigger. They were like family by now. That night it was hot, humid and I heard a restless Bill go topside for a while. With not too much sleep, we were up at dawn for our trip to Melbourne and Patrick AFB. We gassed up at 8 A.M. and Don dropped his trifocals overboard at the dock to start our day. We said what we hoped were our final goodbyes to the Outrigger and headed out through the channel to the ICW and then northward. At Marker 221 (our nemesis) we began to lose RPMs and within 30 seconds the engine stopped, showing a temperature of 160. Oil pressure was 40 pounds. Opening the engine compartment, we saw steam and hot oil cooking. We waited one hour to let everything cool off in order to check out the engine and Bill took a compression test. All cylinders read zero. We were about ready to call the Coast Guard again when some very pleasant boaters saw our problem and offered to tow us to Bailey's Boat Works half a mile away (embarrassing—hoped they didn't spot us from the Outrigger Club). We made a few phone calls, Mary came down to pick us up, Cec trailered his battleship up and we dejectedly made our way to Melbourne—by car rather than boat. Bill's logbook states (after a full page of engine problems): "Arrived in Melbourne at 6 P.M. for dinner and another tragic day was done!" Mary and Don kindly let us use their home as headquarters. Our heads were full of logistics in moving truck, car trailers and boats. What an incongruous bunch we were—strangers a week before, but all caught up in the drama of making this dream become a reality.

Cec set up home in the driveway patching, repairing, bailing out and rewiring the battleship. Corrosion from seawater was to prove a severe problem. The men were up at dawn, drove to Bailey Boat Works and began the work of lifting CELEBRATION out onto the trailer. With a bilge full of water, full gas tanks plus drinking water on board, the owner was doubtful of lifting the boat. After nearly losing the boat twice, it was on the trailer by 11 A.M. Phone calls were placed trying to locate a new engine to no avail. We then trailered the boat to a nearby boat yard where Bill was joined to CELEBRATION perched high and dry. For days the hatch would be up and Bill would be inside, covered with grease. It was regrouping and decision-making time. Moving in to the hospitable Mary's home, we began to scout for an engine and a place to pull out the old one. Bill finally found one in West Palm Beach, one hundred miles behind us. Many phone calls later to Chrysler motors in Michigan, and in San Francisco, Bill finally made a deal. The three of us left immediately for the south and picked up a 225 HP Chrysler. The trip back was fun, as we stopped at Sebastian Inlet Marina and went out to dinner with the owners we had met at the Miami Boat Show. Bill had one dozen oysters on the half shell! The rest of us were more moderate. Back to Melbourne by midnight. Another full day!

By this time we were looking forward to having Bill install the new engine. To everyone's dismay the men found that the SBII engine we had picked up yesterday was a right-hand rotation engine. So, back Cec and I went to Palm Beach to exchange it. Bill and Don tore down the out drive and engine from the big boat. They replaced the bilge pump and cleaned out the engine compartment. All was in readiness for the big conversion tomorrow. Bill slept on CELEBRATION that night as two engines were sitting side by side in the open boat yard that had been hit by thieves for several nights.

We were hung up in Melbourne for a week. Cec had much repair work to do on his boat—fiber glassing, paintwork, engine well repair. Bill was strung out trying to put in the new engine. After six hours of work he ordered the forklift to set the new engine in. That took two hours, then there were all the parts to hook together. There was a one-inch difference in the fittings, but adjustments were made and it was possible to correct this problem; there were numerous trips made to buy parts. An electrician was called to connect the ignition. After six hours that did not work. Cecil did guard duty at the boat yard that night. The electrician came back, worked another five hours— to no avail. By mid-afternoon Bill had figured it out and had all wires functioning. Since there was nothing Cec or I could do, we took off for Cape Kennedy to do some filming. The magnitude of the space program struck us as we filmed exhibits and rode the moon rover. We got some good footage and headed back to Melbourne.

We went to see Bill immediately and he told us the water pressure was so low he could only run the engine for five minutes; however, he announced all systems were functioning and we towed CELEBRATION back to the house for a good scrubbing in order to have it ready for a sea test the next day.

Next day was Easter Sunday and we again packed the boat with our belongings preparatory to launching it at Patrick Air Force Yacht Club. Don, a retired AF Colonel, had a slip there. The test was successful except there was a bad vibration at certain speeds and Bill could not get the boat up on plane. A change of props would probably fix all. The radio equipment also had poor reception after the new engine was installed. We left CELEBRATION in the slip and prepared to mount up!

That night we made plans to go off in two directions. Cec and I would take the truck and battleship to St. Augustine and leave them there. Big plans were underfoot about using our ship and us in their Bicentennial celebration. We would meet with city officials, catch a Greyhound back to Daytona Beach and take a taxi to the Daytona Marina. Bill would meet us there in CELEBRATION II. We all looked forward to getting underway again.

It had been determined that the two dogs were just a bit much with five adults on board, and arrangements were made to leave them in Melbourne. Off we all went, Don and Bill on CELEBRATION, Mary driving a car to Daytona (we thought) and Cec and I to St. Augustine. We had a great day with the Bicentennial committee people planning our part in the festivities. We were taken to the Greyhound bus and made our way to Daytona where we grabbed a cab to the waterfront. We hurried along the docks looking for CELEBRATION. All the boats were white and we could not pick her out. The taxi driver waited patiently for us and we had him drive us to the other side of the marina. We were confounded. Where was our boat? Had they had another breakdown? We were sure Bill would be there if he possibly could. Our patient taxi driver became a little less patient. "Shall I leave you here to wait for your boat or do you want to go some other place?" We looked at the darkening sky.

Still unwilling to accept the fact that we had been stood up by our boat, we reluctantly got into the cab. We asked for a motel near the water. The driver drove us to the deluxe Howard Johnson motel. It occurred to us we did not have luggage. I trailed Cec into the desk. The clerk asked him to fill in the license number of our car. "We didn't come in a car. We came via taxi," Cec answered. The clerk looked at both of us. It was obvious we had no luggage. "I see," he said with a slight smile. "What do you see?" I thought. He handed us a key and we went to our room. Feeling a bit wicked, we waited until we got into our room, then had a big laugh. My eye fell on a calendar. Tomorrow was April 1—we had had our April Fool's Day one day ahead.

We collapsed in chairs. Where was our crew? The only link we had was a last-minute instruction from Don that in case we did not find one another at any port we should try to make contact through the police. We called the local station to see if there was a message—nothing. Later we were to find that Don had left a message at the station, but the police were too involved with college students on Easter break. Daytona was jammed with young people on vacation. Some were destroying property and most were going through the mating season. The police had their hands full. Lost mariners were not in their jurisdiction that night and our low priority problem became lost in the maze of all the extra calls from hapless landlords calling for help.

Knowing what a great skipper Bill was, we hesitated to make any calls to the Coast Guard. We waited until 9:30 P.M., hoping some miracle would bring communication. Our dilemma was obvious—we had no idea where we were to find our boat the next day and our transportation was back in St. Augustine.

We called the Coast Guard. Skilled, dedicated men, they are patient with people less experienced than they. I explained our problem and the man on duty said he would try to trace our boat, but we would have to file a missing boat report. Thanking him, I hung up. Should we file this and possibly embarrass Bill? Should we trouble the C.G. with this when we were sure no mishap had occurred? We mulled this over and at 10:30 P.M. filed our report. The C.G. was thorough in their questioning of us. They wanted every detail right down to how many life jackets were on board. We felt better about notifying the C.G. and at 11:30 the phone rang. They had located CELEBRATION. The bridge operator identified the last bridge the boat had gone under. The C.G had also called the marinas between that bridge and the next one and had located our missing home. With effusive thanks we heaved a sigh of relief and called the New Smyrna Sea Harvest marina. We were sure we would find all three on board. The dock master reported the boat was locked and all were gone. The mystery deepened and we had the dock master leave a message on the boat telling Bill where we were and left our phone number. Surely, somehow we would unravel this whole cops and robbers merry-go-round and would find one another. At midnight the phone rang. Relieved and happy to hear Bill's voice, I shouted accusingly into the phone, "WHERE were you??"

A tired voice explained that they had heavy winds which slowed them down. Bill finally got in a trough behind a 50 ft. Hatteras which smoothed things out, but it was dusk and they were nowhere near Daytona Beach. Mary had been in contact with them via VHF and felt that they should meet at New Smyrna Beach as she had the truck and trailer with her. Bill wanted to continue on, but the other two wished to pull into a marina. He had little input. When we called they had gone out for a late dinner. We made plans to meet the next morning. Thankful that we had linked up we fell into bed. My last thought was, "What's a nice girl like me doing in this bizarre situation?"

TORPEDOED BY A NAVY DOCK

Before we left the motel we had to place several calls up the Florida coast. The Navy was expecting us in Mayport (their port near Jacksonville, FL), and the Bicentennial committee was expecting us in that city. Our trip was beginning to have a domino effect. People ahead of us heard about us and called all along the way to find us, hoping to welcome us into their harbor.

We were at the dock at 10 A.M. and we found CELELBRATION II and our skipper waiting for us. We were glad to see one another. I threw my arms around Bill and hugged him. Cec pumped his hand an extra long time. We were finding we needed one another on this bizarre voyage.

We took off full bore for St. Augustine and I went below for a welcome change into boating clothes. It was a sparkling day and the sunlight danced on the water and beckoned us northward. We continued up the channel. The wind grew stronger and the channel more narrow. Bill had to allow for much drift at a higher speed. Just 5 miles south of St. Augustine, the temperature took a sudden drop of 15 degrees and we were into a fierce storm with water breaking over us. The Waterway Guide warned, "Pay careful attention to ICW markings when crossing the inlet. For the best water, follow the chart's magenta line closely. Favor the inlet side and give the inner shoal and its buoys a good berth until finally across on the Conch Island side. Here the channel turns sharply to starboard, sweeps around the peninsula of land then turns up the Matanzas River." We watched carefully. It continued on, "Currents flow swiftly through St. Augustine and surges from the inlet can be strong. When coming into the marina dock against the current. Keep its direction in mind when undocking, also." OH! Even though the storm was fierce, we could see the fort's turrets and towers in the distance. By the time we arrived at the municipal yacht marina in the center of the city it was 4:30 P.M. It took all five of us, the dock master and his assistant to tie us down to the heaving gas dock. We fueled up and they moved us to a better slip because of the rock and roll. The Bicentennial committee greeted us and we secured for the night.

Revolutionary War history tell us that St. Augustine is the oldest inhabited city along the east coast and had been under four flags since 1672—Spain, England, France and the U.S. This historic city's officials planned a yearlong series of celebrations for the Bicentennial. That night we were taken to dinner, then to a band concert near the marina. The rain had stopped in time and a local high school group put on a production for the townspeople. The support for the show and music was at a high level. We all stood or sat on benches out under the stars. The air was cool, the air of informality was warm. To our surprise, our "fame" had spread before us and when we were spotted in the audience we were asked to come up on stage for an introduction. The three of us were wearing our Johnson Outboard look-alike jackets which were bright yellow with red and black trim. We were introduced and each of us spoke briefly about our trip and what was ahead of us. We told the audience of our planned battleship visit to the old fort in the morning and our boat would be ready for all to see. We were to slip out of the harbor, then enter it again to meet the press and TV. A Bicentennial committee would be waiting for us and at that time the reporters would be able to get their pictures and interviews. They would then go to the famous fortification and Cecil would attack St. Augustine's fort!

Cec was up early as he had a ride to retrieve his battleship and help to launch. It was a very foggy morning. As soon as he was out in the harbor he became hopelessly lost in the fog and ended up "attacking" a surprised dredge operator before he could find the marina. He had to cut his engine and listen for the traffic on shore so he knew which direction to go. We sighted him hovering out in the bay and went to rendezvous with him by the fort. The fog was lifting and the fort looked impervious to attack. We put a few of the committee on board and rendezvoused with Cec. The press was on boats and on shore. When they saw the USS BICENTENNIAL they grabbed their cameras and began shooting with a vengeance. The little boat was clipping along. She dipped through the swells as she headed for all of the fortress and us. Pictures were shot of the ship silhouetted against the fort, cannons blazing forth with jets of water. It brought a big laugh when the cannon from the citadel let go with a big bang in retaliation. We ended the picture taking session back at the marina and had long interviews for the paper, TV and radio. St. Augustine gave us a two page picture of our Bicentennial in their local paper. She looked as long as a city block.

We had a wonderful time in this city. The metropolis is restoring much of the pre-Revolutionary history and preserving their long and unusual heritage.

Our hosts toured us through the old part of the city and the vice president of the committee entertained us at a cocktail party.

One highlight was taking CELEBRATION II and the BICENTENNIAL out into the harbor for a special visit in front of a retired Brigadier General's water front home. The general had been ill and we heard he was in a wheelchair. He had been unable to attend any of the festivities and we were asked to cruise in front of his home. We could see a figure in the wheelchair waving at us. We dipped the colors for him and he saluted us. My vision blurred momentarily as this gallant figure waved across the water. We were glad we had made a special trip for him. This visit had been a most rewarding one and we were most grateful for the hospitality from the St. Augustine people.

Ticonderoga

Philadelphia, PA   New York City

Baltimore, MD

Wash. DC

Newport News, VA

Wilmington, NC

Charleston, NC

Savannah, GA

Jacksonville

Daytona

Cape Canaveral

W. Palm Beach

Miami, FL.

USS BICENTENNIAL
went from Miami to
New York in 1975

USS BICENTENNIAL
went from New York
to Montreal in 1976

USS ARIZONA
went from Miami
to New York in 1985

1500 water miles on
the Intracoastal
Waterway from
Miami to New York.

That night Bill, Cec and I sat out on the stern for a long time, talking and assessing our trip so far. It was proving to be a logistical nightmare, but also high points of great reward. We were beginning to see that our journey represented something special to others. In applauding us and urging us on they were applauding their own heritage and expressing pride in their own country's birthday. We were happy to be a part of this.

Bill studied the charts carefully that night in preparation for leaving St. Augustine in the morning. The ICW crosses an inlet within a short distance of open ocean and this adds to the strong tidal currents that come sweeping in. Consequently, the inlet frequently shoals and the buoys are changed to match the changes brought on by wind and tide.

In the morning we sent Cec out first and he reported strong winds in the harbor. As CELEBRATION II took off, I could tell there were strong currents working against us. Water was surging toward us as Bill fought his way out.

We reluctantly left this lovely city, but were looking forward with excitement to our next stop—docking that afternoon at our first Navy port of call, Mayport. We would go in, tie up and film some of the Navy ships berthed there.

The winds were fierce at 20 knots as we started to clear the harbor. We approached the outlet to the Atlantic into a port turn northward and under the massive Bridge of Lions. The wind was so strong that sailboats would not attempt going under the bridge with the current coming in off the ocean. The battleship did it after much time taken maneuvering and with water breaking over her. There was no way we could leave the dock with the battleship under tow. We did not have as much control as Cecil had at this point. He was having an easier time than we were. We watched with apprehension as his boat disappeared from our sight as he paralleled our course 1400 feet away and on our port side. With relief we could see the red funnel suddenly thrust skyward as the tossing waves momentarily let go their grasp. Bill was having his own problems with our larger ship, fighting current and wind. We knew hooking up the battleship with the mother ship would not be easy. Gradually we narrowed the distance between us and made three attempts to get a line on the battleship although the wind would drift us far from one side of the ICW over to the other in a matter of seconds. We finally hooked up and had to run at 4000 RPM to control the crafts. Going up the waterway that day, we bucked 45 knot winds. It was rough and hard. Some wind gusts registered 50 knots and it was cold. We found a channel marker out of place. With the wind blowing so hard and the fathometer registering a three ft.

depth under us, Bill had to search for the channel. After a few minutes he found it again and we proceeded on course.

We knew we were approaching the channel for our turn into Mayport. After some calculations from the chart, Bill found the pivot point. Coming into the St. John's River and the mouth of the Atlantic was a shock. We had to make a starboard turn into a wild current and the heavy, continuous winds were making control difficult. We were unprepared for another "first." A wild wake and the current caught the USS BICENTENNIAL and she proceeded to try to portside CELELBRATION II. Bill throttled back and in a panic Cec and I raced for the stern, tumbling over each other as we struggled to get down the ladder. And the now familiar battle cry rang out, "Fend her off! Fend her off!" We barely managed to shove the battleship back where she belonged. She plunged wildly about behind us, tossing her bow and shaking water off much like a wild mustang tosses its mane.

The struggle was on to get into the Navy Base. Although the wind had not calmed down, we released Cec and the battleship from the towing position. This was not an easy job. Both men wanted to make a grand entrance in for the Navy and we knew the BICENTENNIAL had since proven her seaworthiness and she would plow through the waves. She started in under her own power. We began our run into the Navy port. We could see the gray Navy ships in the distance tied up at their docks in orderly precision. They reminded me of so many dignified elephants, trunk linked to tail, ready for the march into the ring. Bill had to fight to keep our mother ship headed into the wind.

By this time the Navy was very much aware of all the commotion a civilian ship and miniature battleship were causing in their harbor. As we cautiously approached the dock, we could see a captain motioning us into a slot which looked to be two feet wide. We were to tie up beside the captain's gig. The piers and tall pilings looked ominous. This was definitely not a pleasure boat marina. Everything looked to be made of steel and there were no cushioning tires or bumpers for us to bounce onto. I went up on the bridge and spoke with Bill. He looked tense and tired from wrestling with the elements all day. "I've got a side wind and this thing is behaving like a kite. I WISH I had twin engines." How many times I was to hear this as he cursed and cajoled CELEBRATION II up the 1500 miles of the east coast. "There's nothing to do but head in. I'll give her the gun, then reverse and hope for the best. Go get your lines ready."

Obediently, I clambered down the ladder. Don, Mary and I all headed for our stations. I could see two sailors with lines ready to throw. There was a crowd gathered on the dock waiting for us and watching Cecil, who was tossing about in the harbor, attacking destroyers and causing all sorts of excitement.

I held my breath. Even with my lack of experience I could tell this would be a hairy docking. We headed in and I felt the wind buffeting us on the starboard beam. Bill fought to guide the ship in on a straight line. Just as he had it made a strong gust of wind slammed into the starboard stern side of the boat. By now our bow was 10 ft. from the dock. Then it was as if a mighty hand had plucked us up and out of the water and flung us against a steel corner of the dock. I heard the sickening crunch as CELEBRATION's side opened and she bled foam. The wind picked up the pieces and hurled the foam far beyond the reach of anyone. We had a two-foot-square hole dug out of the hull, but it did not go through the inner lining. I watched in disbelief as pieces of our boat spilled out.

The Navy came to the rescue. They had a line on us immediately and Bill came back to assess the damage. We were fortunate. A hole was obvious, but in this double-hulled boat only the foam had ripped out. Our wiring was intact. It was incredible that such a blow had not done more damage. The only real damage was to our skipper's pride. No one ever wants to pile up his boat, particularly with the Navy watching; but they were most sympathetic and understanding and joined Bill in cursing the winds of Mayport. They even offered their help and tools for a repair job.

We couldn't believe the welcome we were about to receive. A Public Affairs Officer (PAO) took us in tow and laid out our evening and our visit in precise, military fashion. We were to have a Navy car take us up to the BOQ where we could shower and change for dinner. We were to go to the Officers' Club and enjoy the facilities of their lounge and use their club for dinner and the evening. A car would take us back to CELEBRATION at 10 P.M. What a welcome offer this was after the day we had had! How grateful we were to friend Admiral Tidd in Washington who had made this visit possible.

The evening was a memorable one, not only for the Navy hospitality, but for the remainder of the night on board the ship. After we had gone through our usual "pardon me, sorry to have stepped on you" routine, the five of us heaved a grateful sigh to have engineered another bedding-down process. Then it began. "Squeak, groan, squawk, scree-ee-ee!" Metal against metal. The I-beams on the dock were riding up and down on their pilings. It sounded like an orchestra tuning up—all trying to find "A" and never quite making it.

"Moan, groan, growl, squeal." It was akin to fingers running down a blackboard. We slept fitfully through this banging until 2 A.M. The wind was still very much with us, although not as strong. We could hear our own lines heaving and straining that were lashed to the steel piers. The hammer-hitting, screeching sounds became ear-splitting. We were all awake by 3 A.M. and Cecil went outside to tape the sounds. We still laugh when we replay it, but at the time we were irritated and sleepy. To add to a sleepless night, the battleship tried to break loose, so Cec and Bill had to go out and make her fast to the side of CELEBRATION II.

The night finally ended, and in the morning we had coffee with the Navy personnel. They brought us phone messages from the Bicentennial committee in Jacksonville. They were expecting us later in the morning. Before we left, Cec, Bill and Don were invited aboard an ocean going tug tied up next to us. The three loved this tour and told me in great detail that the tug had 3000 HP engines run by diesels which run generators which, in turn, run props. This permits the tug to have quick stops and starts. When the diesel is not connected to the props by the transmission, this permits the tug to turn a 12-foot wheel at full speed. I tried to sound properly respectful and fascinated with this technical talk.

The Navy's last good will gesture for us was to take Bill to the pilot's headquarters to check the tides and currents. We knew it was 23 miles up the St. John's River, and we needed to go in on the flood tide. The Navy predicted a rough trip. Actually the terminology should be down the St. John's, for it is one of two rivers that actually flow south to north. At 10 A.M. the Navy gave us a final sendoff with toots, waves and admonitions not to sink their destroyers. Cec took off ahead of us and ran down the line of gray ships one more time. We took off in our escort boat and met him about one mile from the port. Once again we snubbed the bow to the boat and hauled Cecil on board, then we streamed the BICENTENNIAL out about 13 feet from the stern where she danced gaily along behind us. The only thing marring our appearance was the hole in the port side of CELEBRATION. This bothered Bill who took pride in having his boat ship-shape.

About 10 miles "up" the river, we found a Coast Guard auxiliary boat hailing us and we knew this must be our escort craft for the trip into Jacksonville's downtown harbor. We were pleased to have a guide. By this time the ebb tide had turned to a flood tide, which made for much easier going. We made good time for the river runs at four to five knots. Soon we saw the tall buildings of Jacksonville looming ahead of us. We were not quite sure where our meeting with the few people with whom we had spoken was to take place. Fortunately our escort boat knew. Then Jacksonville's twin railway-bridge was ahead of us. As we were admiring this giant span of steel, the largest, reddest fireboat I had ever seen came bearing down on us. We watched in admiration as it came closer. When it came to a complete stop in line with us we were incredulous.

"You don't suppose they have come out to meet us?" we wondered. I was sent down to the radio and contacted the fireboat. Instructions came that Cec was to attack the fireboat. A boatload of photographers was coming to film the whole affair for the evening papers. We quickly cut Cec and the BICENTENNIAL loose from us and he was off chasing the fireboat. What a sight. The tiny battleship came cautiously toward the shiny, new fireboat. We could hear the captain on his hailer, talking to Cec. He warned him that the fireboat would turn loose with all her streams of water and the battleship should watch out as she might be inundated. Not wishing to be the target of a deluge, the battleship and her driver motored off to a safer distance. The fireboat let go. What a glorious sight it was. Four gigantic jets of water surged into the sky. The big boat came about and paraded by us. Then, Cecil ducked in for his attack.

The picture the camera captured for the evening papers showed the tiny streams of water the battleship hurled at the fireboat. The contrast was obvious. It provided the newsmen with some excellent pictures which were on the front page that night. In our hurry to get Cec off, we had forgotten to give him his walkie-talkie. We always seemed to be shoving him off in great haste and regularly chastised ourselves about our carelessness. Communication was impossible because of the noise from his engine, and we had to resort to wild hand wavings and gestures which proved to be about 50% correct in our batting average ratings. After quite an undignified display of hand and body signals, we were able to indicate to Cecil that we were to come into the municipal dock.

We proceeded in and met the head of the Bicentennial committee, who gave me a long list of important names to memorize and instructions as to what we were to do. We were to leave the dock, go back out into the harbor and at a signal on our VHF we would re-enter, tie up and meet the dignitaries. We managed to convey all this Cec when he came close to our ship. Soon a message crackled out to us that all was in readiness and we were to proceed to dock. As we came around a bend, we saw a huge crowd on the docks. Bill and I suddenly grasped the enormity of our welcome. This was no small informal gathering such as we experienced in St. Augustine. This was on a big scale. We looked at the pier. What a crowd awaited us. I looked at my blue jeans and thought about the way we were all dressed. It was too late for any last-minute changes. Anyone who has been on the water knows it is not a fashion show, but hard work.

Against a strong current CELEBRATION II came in first so we would be able to catch Cecil as he came in. With the powerful current there was no way he could drive, lift the battleship lid and dock himself. He always needed help. Someone had to get a line on the battleship's cleats. Willing hands reached for our lines and some experienced boaters came to our rescue. It took four people to tie us up. We were finding the tide on the east coast to be a bear. The 7-8 foot change in tide level was astonishing. If we came in at low tide we could be looking underneath the dock at eye level with the barnacles. Someone was always getting cut from these critters and the first aid kit was forever out. If an unsuspecting boater was not careful about the tide change the tied up boat could snap lines and capsize. We seemed to manage to come in at low tide on most occasions and many a time I chinned myself before clambering up and out. It was always nice to come in at high tide and step right out on the dock.

Even with the swift current and the low tide, we managed to make a smart tie-up, which is always nice to do when you have an audience. We hurried to get our lines secured because Bill could hear Cec having trouble with his engine. We turned to watch him, hoping he would not lose his engine and begin to drift downstream. We knew his gas mixture was not right and the plugs were fouling. He careened about in the water and we could hear his engine missing.

Closer in he came, Bill leaned down and just managed to catch him and get a line on him when the engine gave a final cough and conked out completely. Immediately the crowd of well-wishers was upon us. We barely had time to tie up the BICENTENNIAL before we were welcomed up on the dock which must have been ten ft. above us. What a reception! What a welcome! Greeting us was the mayor, the superintendant of schools, a rear admiral and captain from the Naval Air Station, the captain of the port, the president of the Coast Guard Auxiliary, the chairman of the Bicentennial committee, members of that committee and a retired C.G. captain who was in charge of the fireboat. There were several secretaries who were curious to see who and what we were, plus a good-sized crowd. It was a red carpet greeting. We were given a letter to the Los Angeles school superintendent, some Bicentennial license plates, some beautiful signs and a heavy brass key to the city which was hung around Cec's neck. We were surprised and touched at this presentation. The last time a key to the city had been given, it was presented to a full admiral who was in charge of the fleet. Along with these gifts, these nice people gave us their warm Southern hospitality. They even gave us the use of a motel overnight. The motel was within walking distance of our tie-up. We were to be guests of the city, then guests of the Florida Yacht Club, which was just outside the city. I delivered our L.A. mayor's letter to Jacksonville's mayor and gave my pen pal letters to the superintendent.

We tried to thank these fine city representatives as graciously as possible. Cecil did his thank-you up in his own inimitable way. In the rush to tie up his boat, climb out and scramble up onto the dock, he had hit his hand (again) on the piling's barnacles that had lain in wait for him. He had gashed a fairly sizeable hole in his hand. Unbeknownst to any of us, he was trying to stem the flow of blood with his handkerchief and still appear gracious and smiling as the crowd, TV crews and newspaper reporters surrounded him. Later on we were to see the finale of this accident. That night the three of us were in a bar, watching our TV coverage from earlier in the day. We watched as Cec shook hands with the mayor while thanking him for the key to the city. He also bled all over the mayor, who was dressed to the teeth. In dismay we watched the mayor surreptitiously grab for his handkerchief and carefully wipe the blood off his hand. Bill and I were horrified at this breach of etiquette. We told Cecil his performance was tacky. One just does NOT bleed on a mayor.

The Bicentennial committee had made arrangements for us to have a better tie up nearby, out of the current and close to the downtown area. But the logistical problems surfaced that afternoon because Cec and I had to go back to St. Augustine and pick up the truck and trailer and jump it forward to Jacksonville. Two navy lieutenants kindly offered to drive us to St. Augustine and took us back to our former stopover. The yard that had been loaned to us for parking our rig was locked. It took a long time to find the right person with the key to let us in. The logistical problems connected with this constant moving of land and sea crafts sometimes seemed overwhelming. We got back to our boat and Bill by 5 P.M. We had given our motel room to Mary and Don to thank them for letting us use their Melbourne home. Bill was sitting alone and his face lit up when he saw us. "Thought you'd never make it back," was the remark. We sat down and told him our troubles with the delay. We decided it was time to celebrate the day's finale, and Bill suggested we go out and find out what the key to the city might do for us that night.

On this trip we all walked—walk, walk, walk. Many times our transportation was in another city and we learned to become independently mobile. This night we took off across the grassy park area to the brilliant night-lights of Jacksonville. We barhopped to three different places, watching carefully for the evening news as we knew we would be on it. Wearing our Johnson jackets, we would order a drink, then ask the bartender what the key would open. Most people had seen us on TV in earlier shows and we seemed to be welcomed. We found the best answer at the Casablanca Restaurant where a lovely lady bartender told us her best Southern accent, "It opens the hearts of the people of Jacksonville, ya'll." This enchanted Cecil and Bill and we prolonged our stay. Eventually we made our way over to a Hilton Hotel and had a late dinner.

We were hungry, tired and on a high with our key to the city. We felt the hospitality and the outreach and as we walked back to the boat we discussed the fullness of the day. It had been a long one. It was heady stuff but we had a great sense of appreciation along with all the adulation. People were so nice and kept reaffirming our feeling that good guys do outnumber bad guys. We walked across the grass and out onto the long dock toward CELEBRATION. Cecil stopped to talk with some men who had been viewing our battleship tied up near us. "Are you really the builder? Why did you do that? Where are you going?" It was the usual barrage of questions, and Bill and I knew Cec would be there a long time talking and explaining. We padded silently back to the boat and went on board. With just three of us the boat seemed commodious. The water was quiet, the moon was up. Bill and I sat on the stern and looked at the city. It had been a beautiful day.

SHANGHAIED!

We spent April 5 in Jacksonville, shopped and made preparations for moving to the Florida Yacht Club where we were to be guests. We would be grateful to leave this rough tie-up, for although the winds had subsided somewhat, we were still rocking and tossing on our lines. Don and I spent the morning moving truck and trailers to this yacht club which was 14 miles from Jacksonville. Just before we left, I watched from the dock while Cec proceeded down the St. Johns River. Bill and Mary took off shortly thereafter. When the two boats were about five miles from their destination they were met by a C.G. Auxiliary boat, who told them they were in the middle of a race, but to follow them. By VHF they told Cec and Bill to follow them and according to the boys they were "shanghaied" to the Rudder Yacht Club. Everyone wanted to see the battleship. When Don and I arrived at the Florida Yacht Club, we were met with much courtesy at this 100- year-old club. It was an old, elegant established club where memberships were passed down through families. Everything was done to make us comfortable and after we toured this posh club we reclined on chairs by the pool awaiting the two boats arrival. A message was delivered to us that CELEBRATION II and the USS BICENTENNIAL had been "captured" by the Rudder Yacht Club. We were to drive over and join them.

The blue-jeaned crowd was loud in their welcome to us. CELEBRATION and BI were the objects of much interest, and Bill and Cec were surrounded by admirers and were answering questions. We enjoyed the company of these nice people. The men called it a "working people's marina." As the sun began to set, we knew we had to get the boats back in their slip for the night. Mary and Don drove back while Cec, Bill and I had a C.G. Auxiliary escort to the Florida Yacht Club. After three miles of travel I hooked Cec up to our stern, but he declined to ride with us saying he would stay in his boat. Bill decided to have some fun with Cecil and revved up CELEBRATION's engines. We soon had the battleship and Cec up on plane and made a few circles in the bay. When we came in to dock at the club, Cec was all wet, and the air turned blue with his description of his ride. As we doubled up in laughter at his appearance, he swore to get even with Bill.

We cleaned up for dinner and enjoyed the facilities of this beautiful club. The dining room and bar were overlooking the pool, a large expanse of grass and the masts of the tied-up boats. We dwindled over dinner and then stayed to listen to the piano of one of the most talented men we have ever met. Into our lives came another gem, Robin Springer. His piano playing in the bar was superb, and as the crowd thinned he began to play more of his own compositions. We were all enchanted with this gentleman. He seemed enamored with our boats and our trip, and there was much talk back and forth with the small crowd left. We planned to be at the club one more day and knew we would again be in the dining room/bar to hear this talented pianist at the keyboard. His personality was warm, his gift was multi-faceted and we wondered what his real occupation might be. We speculated he must be a Broadway star in disguise. I was sitting on the piano bench with him when he told me his true occupation. "School principal?" I was stunned. Immediately I could see how the faculty and children must love him, but all this talent—so hidden.

How we enjoyed the huge showers in this club. We took our time and made our way back to CELEBRATION. Cecil, Bill and I stayed up on the bridge for quite some time speculating about the creative man we had just met.

The next day a reporter from the *National Enquirer* came out to the dock to take some pictures of us. "Some" pictures turned out to be 350 shots, and Cec performed for the reporter for three hours. The water turned out to be choppy and the shots were good. We were to find out later that out of 350 pictures only two were used in the Enquirer; however, with all the filming we were doing, we were learning that when cameramen have what they consider to be a good subject, they never conserve film. By this time we had done magazine stories with *Houseboating*, *Rudder* and *Southern Boating*. We were scheduled for some TV shows later on—*To Tell The Truth* was one. The publicity about this trip was snowballing. Bill took some club members out for a demo in CELEBRATION, and when he docked I got dinner on board. We were anticipating another evening of music with Robin. We were not disappointed and stayed until very, very late that evening. Robin invited us to visit his school in Yulee, FL. We made plans to trailer up our battleship and bring a short film clip with us for his 500 students. How else could we thank this man for the music he was giving to all of us? We said our goodnights cheered by the idea we would see him again. We could not have guessed the circumstances.

Mary and Don were waiting for us at the boat when we made our late return. They thought they would leave the boat as soon as they spoke to Bill. We wondered why. All of us had smelled gas for several days and we did comment about this to one another. Don said it seemed particularly strong when we opened the closet and our clothes were getting permeated with the gas smell. Bill tried to locate it, but the odor would be swept away by the strong winds we had been experiencing. He could not pin down the source. Mary and Don were uneasy and left for a motel, and Cecil went to bed up on the fly bridge since it was a balmy, though windy, night. I had just crawled into my lower bunk when Bill came back to the boat after seeing Don off to his car. Without saying anything he jerked back the carpeting and opened the hatch to the bilge. He put his head down and gave it the Brockett sniff test. Getting up, he said, "You'd better get dressed. I think we likely should leave the ship. The smell of gasoline is worse. I'm going up on the bridge to talk to Cec." Up he went and I could hear a sleepy Cec. Still in dreamland, he heard Bill say it was quite possible we could be sitting on a potential bomb. I could also hear Cec saying (several times), "Now wait a damn minute." I climbed up the ladder and under the stars we evaluated our situation. It was obvious Bill felt a great deal of responsibility for our safety. We decided we should do as he suggested. In the small hours of the morning we abandoned ship in the dark as we did not dare turn on any lights in case there might be a spark. I grabbed a suitcase and packed some things for all of us. We were all struggling in the dark with mixed feelings and various assorted bags and equipment. And things had been going so well!

Bill directed Cec and me to walk some distance away from the boat as he pulled the power cord to the dock plug. He feared a spark could send us all flying. "Thank goodness tomorrow is Monday!" Bill said. "We won't have the visitors we've had over the weekend. I don't want to leave this bomb in their harbor. We've got to drain out that gas and find the leak. We've got another big problem tomorrow, Cec." Wearily Cec agreed and we all went to a motel, Bill bunking in with us. It was 2 A.M. by this time, and Bill's log book reads, "Another full day was through."

The next day the three of us drove all over Jacksonville looking for 50-gallon drums to siphon out the gas since the men had no way of knowing which 50-gallon tank might be leaking. Bill decided he would drive the boat to a ramp for trailering. Cec would also have to trailer up the BICENTENNIAL in our trailer. I held my breath while Bill started the engine. It took awhile with Don (who had come back) maneuvering CELEBRATION's trailer on the ramp, but both boats were put in their respective trailers and the boys siphoned the gas and water into the drums which we put in Cec's truck. Now the search began for a place to dump our load. We finally found a dump station, then came back to our motel. We had dinner at a crummy restaurant and fell into bed. What a comedown from our previous enchanting nights.

Breakfast at a Holiday Inn revived our spirits, and we started for the small town of Fernandina, passing through Robin's equally small town of Yulee. We stopped to see the school. Robin told us of a motel where we could stay in Fernandina. After checking in, the three of us located a boat yard where the boys could work on CELELBRATION II and rip apart the gas tanks.

This is where we had our introduction to sand fleas. These tiny insects are known up and down the waterway and appear in the spring. Various names for these annoying creatures are "widgims," "no-see-ums," and other unprintable names. We decided they were all mouth and no body. We were plagued with these pests and when working inside the big boat had to put mosquito netting on the bow and stern hatch.

As long as we were stuck in this town in this situation, Cec decided to go off and film the city and the dock area. Mary and Don went to visit friends for several days. I stayed in the boat and typed and paid bills. Bill savagely tore away at the foam encompassing the gas tank. It looked like a hopeless job. He used a butcher knife and chopped and whacked all afternoon. Still he did not get the tank out. Cec returned and the two of them could not get the tank out. We were about to leave for the motel when a car drove up. There was Robin and his wife, Shirley. They had been looking all over Fernandina for us and had about given up when they saw the silhouette of CELEBRATION awkwardly perched high and dry in the boat yard. These good people insisted we accompany them for a fish dinner. We headed back to the motel for a shower and quick change. What a gala evening. We were taken down dirt roads and into a back woods area, which we could never have found. We found a restaurant in the back bayous and all ordered our favorite seafood— Bill outdid himself with 24 oysters on the half shell. Joining us was Robin's vice-principal and her husband. We were a compatible sixsome.

The next day we left Bill to his struggles and went to Yulee elementary school and put on two shows for Robin's students. We stayed and had lunch with the faculty. As a primary teacher I was surprised to find the children had

20 minutes for lunch—then it was back to work. *Probably cuts down on accidents*, I thought, remembering *long* one-hour lunch times at most schools and the visits to the nurse after this lengthy time. It was obvious how everyone loved this kind man. We were received with much warmth and filmed the pleasant Southern children for our film. When one boy asked Cecil if he had brought his boat all the way from California and he responded in the affirmative, the expletive to this was, "I'll be a blue-nosed goat!"

When we arrived back at the boat yard, Bill had jerked the gas tank out and showed us the rust spot where the tank was leaking. Seawater had been trapped under the tank and had slowly rusted a seam. Corrosion had set in and made the tanks paper-thin. With the pounding the hull had taken it had been enough to break the thin membrane. Bill and Cecil commiserated with one another, denouncing the lack of care the mother ship had had. Now we would have to travel on 50 gallons of gas instead of the safety factor of 100 gallons; but why worry about this now? We had another invitation from the same two couples to join them for another night. How hospitable could these great people be! This time they picked us up and took us to one home for cocktails, then it was out to dinner to a 1752 vintage home turned into a steak house. What atmosphere, completely different from the night before. We were surely being shown the special restaurants in their town. How we enjoyed their company.

After steak and champagne, Robin insisted we go with him to a famous old saloon in town. There, he ended up playing the piano for the crowd, and the three of us watched the listeners place themselves in the palm of Robin's talented hands. Many had been his former students and it was obvious all cared deeply for him. Robin's favorite expression was "Merry Christmas," regardless of the season. It seemed to be an all- encompassing greeting similar to "aloha." What a way to end our stay in Fernandina, and it was with some reluctance we made plans to leave this beach city the next morning.

COMING IN ON FUMES AND A PRAYER

Before leaving, Bill ordered another gas tank which would be flown into Charleston, S.C. That was the best we could do. Meanwhile we would limp along on one tank. We pulled the boats from the Fernandina boat yard to the downtown area where the boats would be launched. Off went Cec in the BICENTENNIAL, then CELEBRATION with Bill and Don. Mary and I were to jump vehicles and trailers up to Lanier Island. Many people were there to see them off. So were the gnats. Bill's logbook reports fighting the current for two hours with little wind, then the rain started and poured the whole trip. The battleship was hooked up for cruising, and Cec came aboard CELEBRATION. After all three were properly soaked, they decided to leave the bridge and pilot from the cabin. They switched the depth finder to the lower station and it refused to function. The markers were hard to see from inside as the rain was so intense. Bill went back up on the bridge despite the rain, but the depth finder did not work there either. All they could do was carefully follow the charts while Cec tried to find markers through his binoculars. Another worry was the fuel gauge said they were running on empty. They finally spotted a gas dock. They tied up and filled the one tank and it took 38.9 gallons. They were getting less than one mile per gallon. They had eight more miles before they were to meet Mary and me at Lanier Island. This took ten gallons of fuel. Bill reported the tides were rough especially with a six- to eight-foot tide which runs fast like a moving river.

Apparently the rain, the sand fleas and the worry about running out of gas did them in. We were all tired; but we had made it over the border of Florida into Georgia! Mary and Don decided to stay on the boat and bed down early. Our trio went out to a pizza place and sat for hours by a fire, drinking beer and eating pizza. We stayed an unusually long time. The restaurant was comfy and the company was good! Cec said we should have stayed longer. It poured all night, and at 4 A.M. Cec and Bill had to get up and retie the battleship and adjust lines. This is when Cec discovered his lower bunk was soaked and I was the culprit. I had left my upper bunk sliding window open just a crack but it had been enough for the water to slide down the side wall, soak his foam cushion and sleeping bag. There was much gnashing of teeth and grumbling as we did our best to dry Cecil and his bedding out. It was a miserable night. My guilt drove me out of my bunk early and to the marina drier. Wet towels, blankets, carpeting—it took hours to dry out. The men went out looking for five-gallon jerry cans that would carry extra gas. It was a worry about not having enough gasoline on board. We also had a wonderful mail stop, General Delivery in Brunswick, GA. Mail stops were always fun. We did take time out to tour Fort Frederica late in the afternoon. The fort is reportedly the largest and most costly built by the British in North America. General Oglethorpe selected this site as a strategic one to guard against the Spanish invasion. The Spanish fleet from St. Augustine tried to wipe them out, but a small group of Scottish Highlanders managed to hold them off. This turned the tide for the future of America.

Bill tried to get the fathometer repaired but there was no one in the area to help. Another skipper looked at it and said one component was out in the unit. We knew Bill was anxious about the next day's run. We were headed for some swampy, remote areas where there would be little help. Surely we had run out of jinxes by now.

As we came back to the boat from our fort visit, I was fascinated to watch a black 50-foot Chinese junk coming into the marina. We soon met the crew, which consisted of a retired professor, his story-writing wife, and Edward— a female gibbon. Edward delighted in flying up and down the rigging, hanging upside down and peeking into portholes. She had been living aboard for seven years with this boat-oriented couple, and the only way they could entice female Edward to go to bed was by giving her a jelly bean. We watched this bedding-down procedure with amusement. Edward went obediently to her quarters promptly at 5 P.M., hand in hand with the lady of the boat—and her jellybean. We needed no jellybeans to bribe us to turn in. Tomorrow would be a long day.

Because of the lack of gas and extra demand on CELEBRATION, Cec decided to trailer the battleship to Savannah. Ditto Don and Mary with their rig. It was a cold and windy morning after the storm, and Bill insisted that we pilot from topside. We were beginning to wend our way through narrow rivers and channels which made up this part of the Georgia ICW. He was quite concerned about depth and no fathometer. Coming into Dobay Sound, we found it was wide open to the Atlantic and the wind hit us at 40 knots. After getting across this area, we proceeded through marshy land with no signs of habitation. As I navigated for us, I learned! The skipper was quite patient with his still-green crew member, and I spent hours on the bridge absorbing as much as I could. We had heard that there was a gas stop somewhere "up a creek" but it was off our charts. It was imperative we find gas for we had used all four five-gallon cans of extra fuel.

We hung a starboard and began to navigate our way up the unmarked Newport River. It was five miles up a treacherously shoaled river as we kept looking for a gas dock. We had no chart and the only guide Bill had was the crab and lobster pots, which he followed up the narrow channel. He knew the pots are planted on the shelf between the narrow and deeper part of the channel and he carefully followed these, trying to avoid any entanglement. Coming around a bend we saw a tiny settlement, a fishing village AND a welcome gas dock in sight. We nosed into the dock, which was located on a bend in the river, and made a wild landing in a 10-knot current which was hitting from the port side. I made a great leap and snubbed up CELEBRATION. After gassing up, we went to the small restaurant where the owner told us that NO ONE can come up the river without knowing it and without going aground. It is very shallow. Bill worried out loud as he told him we had to go back. The owner had some charts which he had made into place mats and with his red pencil drew a line that we should follow for the six miles back down to the ICW.

Our takeoff from the dock was more spectacular than coming in. Bill tried to swing the stern into the main stream with no success. He then pulled forward to a gap where small boats were berthed, and the current caught our boat and spun the bow into the opening. He threw the engine into reverse and poured the power to CELEBRATION, finally clearing and getting out almost to mid-stream. He barely had time to put the throttle forward and we almost ended up against the dock again. We felt our way back out and what a relief it was to see the well-marked ICW ahead. What a lesson it was for me in navigation that day. We used up 2 ½ charts on this little jaunt.

As we continued on, we went through more narrows in a bewildering labyrinth of swamp area—across St. Catherine's Sound into the Bear River; Ogeechee River, Vernon River, Burnside River and through Skidway Narrows. There we caught the Wilmington River and a 40-knot wind. Rain was pouring down on us. As the afternoon wore on and there was still no sign pointing us toward Savannah or civilization, Bill began to again worry about gas. We knew we were nearing Savannah, but there was no mile marker. I went below to call Cec on the VHF as he had taken his unit with him. To my surprise he picked us up, and after comparing notes he affirmed that we were very close to the Thunderbolt marina. I went topside to report this welcome news. It had been a harrowing day, and Bill and I were both on edge. His remark was, "We'd better sight Cecil soon. We've been going on empty for 15 minutes, and if we don't find him in the next few seconds we're going to have trouble." Just as he said this, we rounded the last bend in the river and there was Thunderbolt Marina and Cec, both a welcome sight. Just at that moment I heard CELEBRATION II "shlurp" her last gulp of gas, cough and quit. We must have been 40 ft. from the dock. I ran to the port bow and grabbed the 100-ft nylon line. I threw the rolled-up line and watched it uncoil and slither its way right into Cec's waiting hands. He grabbed the end and we were home free. Bill cheered and I felt partially redeemed from the bad things I had inadvertently done previously.

Even though the Georgia rains had begun again, nothing dampened our spirits at this moment. Well, only one thing, maybe. A black man in the uniform of a self-appointed admiral made it his duty to greet every boat that tied up. A flashing smile and a wonderful personality greeted us. Helping us tie up, his one remark remains etched in my memory. "Y'all don't want to fall in this river!"

"Why not?" Cec asked.

"Becuz ya'lls gonna die!"

It was then we found out the Savannah River runs at eight knots and one could easily be swept away. We went to our assigned slip after gassing up and decided to celebrate our successful arrival by dining at the nearby Greek restaurant. Mary and Don joined us. All vehicles were parked in Savannah and we would have to launch the BICENTENNIAL tomorrow. We went through our usual bedding-down process—five of us in the 28-foot boat, more or less conditioned to the chaos and stepping over and around everything and everybody.

Thunderbolt Marina in Savannah is well known among the boating nomads. It is no wonder everyone told us, "That marina will spoil you. It's the best one on the waterway." It didn't take long to find out why. We awoke the next A.M. to gray leaden skies dumping buckets of rain on us. But what was that on our deck? A newspaper securely wrapped in plastic was on the stern and ONE DOZEN donuts in a secured plastic bag! Every boat in a slip had this delivered to them. We were in shock to find service like this. This latter was not only a surprise, but we had a lengthy discussion about the welcome cleanliness and first class heads (important to boaters). I found a hair dryer attached to a comfortable chair. Twenty-five cents dried my hair after a wash job in the super clean-tiled baths. No chipped paint, bare bulbs or cracks in the plaster. No critters. The gigantic laundry room offered plenty of washers/driers for wet boaters. It was here in this cozy room that many of us would meet in the morning. Who wanted to leave? The rain was steady, heavy and enduring. We were all semi-comfortable on our boats but we found we enjoyed bringing our donuts and coffee to the laundry room. We dwindled over coffee with our fellow boaters, exchanging stories, questioning what lay ahead. This marina completely spoiled us. We found nothing to equal it in the next 1000 miles. The hospitality was easily matched, but not the appointments. We were pampered and loving it! A small grocery was within walking distance, and in between cloudbursts Mary and I would go to the store. We stayed in Savannah 3 ½ days waiting for the rain to stop and procrastinating about leaving. Cec enjoyed filming for the children in this city, and Bill and I entertained many visitors. The newspaper articles on us brought numerous visitors to our door.

How does one telescope into one package all the wonderful people we had met and were meeting? All the Bicentennial participants we had met, the visitors who brought their children to see our ships, boating people anxious to give us a hand, marina operators who gave us free berthing. When in port in a slip, there was hardly a moment that someone wasn't out looking at the battleship, looking at CELEBRATION—hoping that one of us would come out and talk. We took turns, for "our public" was so supportive, so enthusiastic, so amazed about the trip we were doing that we felt their interest and were always glad to talk. They seemed particularly to want to talk to Cec regarding the building of his battleships. The usual questions were answered over and over (just as at a boat show), but we never tired of answering these nice people.

We did some filming in Savannah at a fort called Fort Pulaski. Because it dates from Civil War times, we decided to film the young man in a Civil War uniform. He loaded his musket and gave our camera a good dose of history for West Coast children. We visited the beautiful old homes and the boat museums. We enjoyed sumptuous seafood meals night after night. In between we shopped for food to put in our small refrigerator, did laundry and tried to keep dry. A steady procession of reporters, TV camera people and visitors besieged us hourly. Press coverage from Savannah and surrounding towns was great. The men visited a nearby factory which built tugboats that carried 20 men for crew. The men were making it a point to extend my boating knowledge, and I found I was more and more interested in the details of engines, power and handling of boats. Was this a "if you can't lick 'em, join 'em" thing? Whatever it was, I began to appreciate my ongoing water education.

The night before we were to leave, we were walking the docks and saw a transom that said "NAWILIWILI" (Kauai) on it. Cec couldn't believe what he saw. His father had built the breakwater in that same harbor when he and the Gates family were living in Lihue, Kauai. We knocked on the bridge. Three cheery voices welcomed us aboard and asked us to come below. We were soon seated in the cozy interior of this comfortable sailing boat. My schoolteacher heart was excited when I found that we had stumbled into the hideaway of Marion Rumsey, famous authoress of children's books—many I had read to my class! *Lion On The Run, Seal of Frog Island, High Country Adventure*—most written on the boat. Conversation flowed about Kauai and books. We learned that these interesting people had two sons and all had lived aboard for 26 years. The oldest boy could hardly wait to leave the boat and complete his education and had settled down in the Mainland. The youngest boy was 18 and was still on board. When I asked him if he had missed the contact of other young people in not attending a regular school, his answer showed a great maturity. "I can't miss what I've never had and I love the sea. I'm going to get my skipper's license and spend my life on the water." This mature young man obviously enjoyed his nomadic life, and we learned that each one had his own station on the boat. The finale to our visit was an autographed copy of *Lion On The Run* from Marion. We were beginning to gather some treasured mementos.

The boating fraternity is a close one, and barriers rarely exist. Friendships can be instant and the glow of stories, warmth and hospitality shared is special. Although paths probably never cross again, I learned to savor these special times and always felt richer for having done another "ships that pass in the night" relationship.

THE BATTLE OF BEAUFORT

We awoke to our last morning of home-delivered newspaper and donuts. Time to begin A.M. logistics: who drives what vehicles, who rides on what boat. The Coast Guard weather report promised a sunny, mild day. We were glad to see the sun. "A Rainy Night In Georgia" proved to be true—there had been 24 inches of rain in three plus days. Cec wanted some good film of CELEBRATION towing the battleship, so he took off with truck and trailer and positioned himself on a bridge that we would go under. Don would stay on the boat with Bill and me, Mary would drive to our rendezvous which was to be Beaufort, South Carolina. We realized that compared to the time it took us to get out of Florida, Georgia did not have a very long Atlantic seaboard coastline. We would be going just over the border into Beaufort, S.C., an inlet city. We discovered we were to be in two Beauforts. The South Carolina Beaufort is pronounced "Bewfort." The North Carolina is "Bowfort." We were off and running by 9 A.M. Cec was upstream one mile, and as we approached the bridge he was on our starboard side.

A brisk, cold breeze was coming at us, and there was Cec with camera and tripod at the ready. His waves indicated he wanted plenty of film, so we made five passes before he waved us on. We proceeded up the Wilmington River. Then it was into the Savannah River, New River, Ramshorn Creek, Cooper River to Calibogue Sound. With only one 50-gallon tank and a little extra, it was imperative to make a gas stop at Hilton Head Island. We were anticipating a new gas tank being flown into Charleston. Meanwhile this refueling left us with mixed feelings, as this part of the ICW went through many sounds and the water was rough off our bow. This made fuel consumption very high.

On this day our forced stop proved to be a beautiful one. Going into the marina, we saw where many boats were wrecked and their hulls still protruding out of the water. This beautiful island was rapidly becoming a tourist attraction and many people are retiring on Hilton Head's island paradise. This morning was a lazy, hazy day and we loved the calm of the small marina we entered.

With Don catching the battleship, I was able to help tie up CELEBRATION easily.

Out we went into the ICW and rounded Pigeon Point, which gives way to Beaufort River. The route gradually widens and becomes easier to follow. We carefully checked the time for the opening of Beaufort's bridge. Many bridges have restricted hours, and the *Waterway Guide* gives the vertical clearance to a close tolerance. One had to check the tides due to the tremendous fluctuation on the east coast. Beaufort sounded like a small town but with plenty of supplies within walking distance of the marinas. We were to find that this was a large seafood center with a crabmeat factory. Happily we found that our scheduled rendezvous with Cecil and Mary had worked. After greetings, Mary and Don drove the rigs on into Charleston and Bill, Cec and I stayed on the boats.

Messages were delivered to us from the Navy's PAO (Public Affairs Officer) about our entering Charleston. Apparently this was to be another gala meeting near the battery of this history-laden town. After dinner the three of us went for a walk and discussed an early morning take-off for Charleston. We would be up by 6 A.M., and cast-off time would be no later than 7 A.M. The plan was for a C.G. boat to meet us in Charleston Harbor by 1 P.M.

We were heading back to the boat when Bill spotted some Marines who were stationed at nearby Parris Island. He decided to follow them into a bar and talk with the newer generation Marines. He said he would have one beer and join us soon. We headed back and were soon sound asleep. I wakened at 3 A.M. and listened to the usual night sounds of the boat. The uneven "squeak-squeak" of the lines, the gentle splash of a wake and the even breathing of only one crewmember startled me. An uneasy feeling crept over me. Cec was peacefully sawing wood; Bill's bunk was empty. I rechecked my watch. Three A.M. and no skipper. I got up and walked out on the dock. There was no sound of returning footsteps to break the stillness.

My getting off and on the boat had wakened Cec. "What's wrong?" he called.

Funny, I thought. *Whenever one gets up at night on a boat everyone else wonders what new crisis lies in wait.* "Bill's not back yet and it's after 3 A.M. What do you think could have happened to him?"

We speculated about this for a while and came to no conclusion. He knew of our early morning commitment and we had learned we could depend on him. He was always there for us no matter what the problem. Daylight was beginning to show and sleep was out of the question. By now it was 4 A.M. We debated walking in the direction he had taken to see if we could find where he was going to have a beer. After wondering about what we should do, we heard footsteps way down the dock. I peered out my bunk window into the misty morning. There was a familiar figure, head down, hands in jacket pockets, making his way back to the boat. Relief swept over us. We waited. In came Bill as quietly as he could. I watched him sitting on the edge of his bunk. I could resist no longer.

"Bill, WHERE have you been? We've been so worried about you."

"Well, Dearie," said a rather blurry voice. "It's a long story and I shall now tell you the whole sad thing." Thus began the narrative that we have since named "The Battle Of Beaufort City."

When Bill followed the Marines into the pool hall the night before, he found that they were stationed at Parris Island, which was a huge Marine training base. Bill found some new recruits who were with their sergeant. All were in civvies. Bill began to listen to the tall tales spun by what he called the Marine's "heroic leader."

"He was a bull shipper," stated our skipper. "You know what a bull shipper is—he's a guy who ships bulls from Texas. Well, this great Marine leader was a bull shipper." We laughed. This whole thing was beginning to be funny. Our relief at finding Bill in one piece was replaced by low-key hysteria at his description of his long night. It seemed that the sergeant had begun to describe in vivid detail a 500-mile march he had taken while serving in Korea. His valor and fearlessness was obviously attracting the young Marine squad. Bill was an ex-Marine, vintage Korean War, and had been in some of the toughest combat there was. When he began to question the sergeant about places he had been on the 500-mile march, the sergeant began to back down. Soon he disappeared, and Bill was left with six young Marines.

The evening wore on and more beer was consumed. He obviously was upset at what he felt was a lack of toughness in training the newer Marine Corps. His pride in his own training and his unit led him to give a long and detailed description of his own boot camp nightmares. He bemoaned the fact to us that the Marines had had to draft men during the Vietnam War instead of counting on enlistments. His sad tale of the evening with the Marines went on for some time. As he rambled on, Cec decided to tape the narrative, and to this day we occasionally play it when he visits us.

Finally, at 4:30, we got him to bed. He moaned pitifully a few times about the old-time Marines. "The new ones are sissies," he groaned, and then fell asleep. At 6:15 when I got up I saw the supine figure of our skipper. Cec suggested I brew some strong coffee, ready for the moment we would awaken Bill with the fact that it was daylight and he WAS going to drive a boat. Poor Bill. I am sure he was in shock when we tried to wake him up. The smell of coffee didn't seem to do much but a cold washrag was introduced. This did not help his usual sunny disposition, but there was no other way. He kept moaning about "cruelty to skippers" but I persisted. After two cups of coffee and more cold water, he made it to a vertical position and decided he was up to piloting us to Charleston.

50 GALLONS OF RELIEF

We were off by 7:15 A.M., and the cold air on the bridge made everyone shiver. From the looks of the two men, I decided they could use a hearty breakfast. I went below and cooked up a good one consisting of fried eggs on toast. This may sound easy, but it's difficult when the boat is up on plane and everything keeps sliding back and forth on the gas stove. In triumph I carried this repast up to the bridge. It was worth all the trouble. I was greeted as if I was the chef from *Maxim's de Paris*. The gentlemen's obvious enjoyment of their breakfast made the mess below seem immaterial. I looked out over the stern at the BICENTENNIAL. She was jumping and cavorting around as if reflecting my own mental feeling. I was glad I had fed them well. Bill seemed to improve with time.

We had a long run of 65 miles to Charleston, and we fought a current the whole way. Twisting and turning, in and out of rivers, creeks and sounds we went. Our compass pointed in all four directions as the ICW zigged and zagged. We had to chase fuel six miles up the South Edisto River by Bay Point Marina on Edisto Island. Even though we carried three five-gallon spares and one six-gallon can, we were just barely making it from one fuel stop to the next. Many a weird inlet was penetrated by our strange-looking crafts. These lovely upstream stops were off the usual channel, and we wished we could spend more time. The people were always friendly and the usual curiosity had many marinas calling their friends to come down. We passed out thousands of PR sheets on our Bicentennial story. How glad we were to have them as they saved us a lot of talking. If only we could have tarried in these lovely locales.

Our 1 P.M. date made us hurry on, and soon it was lunchtime and we were still far from Charleston. At 12:45 I was sent below to try to raise the Coast Guard. This I did and was glad to hear them say they were waiting for us. They asked for our position and I told them of the red marker we had just passed. They located us on their chart and we anticipated a meeting in 15 minutes. As we approached Charleston, the huge Ashley River widened and we were there! We could see a large C.G. boat and a press boat. Mary and Don were on the cutter all waiting for our arrival. What a greeting and a grand escort right into the harbor. We tied up at the city dock. Another remarkable job of maneuvering was done by Bill. He managed to squeeze CELEBRATION's 28 feet into a 30-foot slot. A superb job and we congratulated him on his performance. We privately told him it was almost as good a performance as the night before in Beaufort. He grinned—no comment.

Here we experienced one of the biggest tide drops of our entire trip. When it was low tide we had to board the ship from the fly bridge. I remember the surprise I had the next morning when I looked out the galley window. The night before our lower deck had been even with the dock. This morning I looked out on pilings under the pier, which were covered with oysters and barnacles. The drop was eight feet. Spring lines were needed!

The Navy PAO came down to tell us we were the Navy's guests that night at the Charleston Navy base. We were to have dinner with them. With Don's service background, he and Mary could stay over several nights at the BOQ. Then the mayor came! Resplendent in a colorful patterned jacket, he gave us a letter for our mayor and his business card. He "allowed as how this card will keep you out of the pokey for 10 days." (Oh, Good. We'll give it to Bill.) Then the press and TV came down and swarmed all over the dock. We answered the usual questions, posed for pictures, talked to the TV people. We gave out our mayor's letter and the letters for the pen pal schoolchildren. Four more deliveries to go! The press had been wonderful to us in small and large cities, and they spent a long time interviewing us. We became crass about counting our time on TV—sometimes we had 45 seconds, sometimes almost three minutes (see TV log).

After everyone had left except for the usual visitors who hang around docks, we showered and left for the base. We joined Mary and Don and surely enjoyed Navy hospitality. We could not get over the fact that the steak dinner cost us $2. We decided if young people knew about the great deal waiting for them in the services they would join more quickly. The three of us said our goodnights and went back to our bunks and a much-needed rest. The winds were beginning to pick up, the tide was smashing in under the concrete marina walls. and the boys tied up both boats with extra lines.

We awakened to a 40-knot wind whipping across the marina. We were glad to be inside the concrete buttress surrounding the harbor. The men were busy tying, retying, hauling down our flags and battening down anything that moved. This wind lasted for three days and we could hear the waves splashing against the outside walls of the breakwater. That afternoon we headed out for Old Charles Town, the first US settlement, and did some filming. Then we went eleven miles up the Cooper River in our truck looking for a quieter marina. We found a good one, but the boys decided that the currents were too wild along with a 30- knot wind, so Bill elected to stay where we were. We had another fish dinner on the way back to the boat. By now we were "fishaholics."

Cec kept calling the airport to find out if our gas tank had been flown in yet. We were impatient to get it installed for felt we had a long ways to go and should get underway. The enforced three-day rest, however, was a good one, and we took advantage of our tie up to explore historic Charleston, do laundry, see a movie and film for our documentary. Cec took the ferry out to film Ft. Sumter while Bill and I stayed in port to do laundry and to begin to sand the hole in CELEBRATION's side. We were always entertaining visitors who were intrigued with both ships. Our days were filled with people, shopping, picking up the gas tank (hooray!) and fittings. Cec went out twice in his BICENTENNIAL to "terrorize the natives" and clear the port of all the pirates. The onlookers and Coast Guard loved it.

The gas tank had been flown in from Utah, and as soon as we got it back to the boat, the boys began to tear up the floorboards to put in the new tank. Such chaos. Then Bill discovered the fittings were wrong, so it was off and all over town for the right parts. It took the two of us all day to find proper fittings and there was much gnashing of teeth at this point. I retreated to the bow dining area with my typewriter, bills and correspondence. It was a welcome chance to get caught up. When we were underway there always seemed to be an emergency of some kind to cover. When Bill and I were alone on the bridge he needed someone to navigate for him, and I spent hours pouring over charts.

A day of tearing the floor up, then putting things back together, finally ended. The fittings were tested and not a leak was to be found. Soon it would be back to 100 gallons of gas and a more relaxed time between stops. Mary and Don came down to check out Bill's sanding on the mother ship's battle wounds. I went shopping one more time before tomorrow's scheduled take off for Georgetown, N.C. I found some California poppies and brought them back to the two California men. I was thoroughly teased for spending $1 for a dozen poppies, but they did comment that the flowers looked good on that night's dinner table. We took CELEBRATION over to the gas dock and filled her up, preparatory for the morning's departure. We awakened to a quiet day with no wind, but the no-see-ums came to bid us *adieu*. We decided they had a two-foot mouth, no body, and they left unsightly red welts. Vicious little things. The Southerners curse them and told us the secret weapon was to spray oneself with Avon's "Skin-So-Soft." But where was the Avon Lady? We departed with this recommendation.

BOTTOMS UP!

Away everyone went in different directions—Cec was to drive truck/trailer to Georgetown and get mail, Don and Mary left to visit friends, Bill and I were to take CELEBRATION and BICENTENNIAL to Georgetown, a distance of 50 miles. There was to be a mail stop ahead in Georgetown and we all anticipated this. What a day after the winds of Charleston. Heading out of the harbor, we entered a beautiful area of the ICW. Up rivers, through creeks and swamps we churned. White egrets and awkward pelicans accompanied us all along the way. We speculated about alligators lurking in the marshy areas as we had been warned. At one place on the chart we came to the intersection of two rivers. Having left my chart-reading momentarily, I became disoriented. When I pointed to Bill where I thought we were, he corrected me. "We are at the mouth of the Pee Dee River."

"We are not, Bill, you're making that up!"

Previously I marked our triple look-alike jackets with our initials—C, P, and B. For some reason Bill tied this in with the Pee Dee River and my nickname became Pee Dee. This is mentioned as an in-joke only because of what we learned. If one of the boys would call me Pee Dee in front of others, the visitors would ask how I got the name. Thus, we found an interesting fact. When Stephen Foster wrote "Swanee River" he was really writing about the Pee Dee River, but he obviously could not use that name and he chose something different. To hear people sing "Way down upon the Pee Dee River" would be a bit bizarre—thus, Swanee River. I was to be badgered by this name throughout the rest of the trip, sometimes to my embarrassment. The name still sticks.

Late that afternoon we sighted the old Georgetown Lighthouse which has been in use since 1901. We went in the big ship entrance, and the main channel led straight to a paper mill dock. Pleasure boats turn right at the inside light for the deep channel serving the city waterfront. Here we found the marinas with their conveniently-located business section just behind them. Passing some fences anchored out in the bay for fishing, we came into the

Belle Isle Marina. It was a beauty. Marinas, all different—some "first cabin," some badly run down. Eventually I shall write a book entitled *Heads and Showers I have Known On The ICW*.

Cecil was there ready to tie us up and we could see we would have another tremendous tide fluctuation. There were ladders nailed to the pilings so one could climb up to the dock from the boat. This was a new facility, still under construction. Our only complaint was that the showers were so far away. Don still insisted the life jackets be kept in the shower. We decided that since we had a truck, we would drive to the showers then go to dinner. We elected to have a flounder and she-crab dinner and got into a great discussion about "she-crabs vs. he-crabs." We had mail call at the dinner table, played ping-pong and pool after dinner and had such a wonderful time we stayed an extra day.

By this time the press had been alerted and would be dockside the next morning. Cecil took a photographer for a ride in the battleship and we entertained the press people on board. After they left we explored the newly built condominiums in the area and checked out the lake. Cec went out again to continue filming. He was doing a wonderful job. We found out that Battery White was nearby and was used during the Civil War. Lafayette had landed nearby. Ahh-h-h, history for the children at home. Our documentary was going to teach them a lot about the East Coast.

We were getting ready to leave the next morning and watched a Boy Scout troop approach us. They were coming for a visit after reading about us in the local paper. They were twenty feet away from us and suddenly, pandemonium broke out and the boys dispersed in all directions. I heard a splash and saw the scouts leaning out over the docks. We went over to where they were watching the water and they explained that a water moccasin had entwined itself around one of the ladders leading up to the dock.

It had been frightened by the boys and had dropped into the murky waters. The three of us looked at each other. We were glad the snake had not wrapped itself around our ladder. Cec had learned to always look inside his battleship before he climbed into it. After a brief visitation from the boys, we were about to take off when we heard another shout. Three scouts came running toward us carrying something long and slender. Proudly, they displayed a very dead water moccasin to us. Whether it was the same one we had heard drop into the water or not we would never know. The snake had been swimming close to the shore when one of the boys shot it with a .22 rifle and brought a very dead reptile for Cec to film. The boys were so proud that Cec got out all his camera equipment and filmed a bunch of happy, laughing boys all holding a portion of the battered snake. The snake looked lethal up close and we were not sorry to leave. We all decided, "No one falls overboard today!"

A Pennsylvania marina with all the wonderful boating amenities

A peaceful backwater bayou in South Carolina

Cecil decided we could tow the battleship today and he would jump the rig ahead to Little River, S.C. The only other incident we had before leaving Belle Isle marina was when the gas pipeline from the dock to our boat fell into the water and pumped gas all over the harbor. A cautious skipper had us pole our way out of the dock area and out into cleaner waters before starting up the engine.

What a day this was to be. Bill and I sailed past many wooded areas full of chattering birds. Flowers, vines and unusual greenery marked this part of the channel. We loved the isolation we felt and the joy of exploring such seemingly untouched territory. The Waccamaw River may be the most scenic part of the southern route. Side streams wind back through moss-draped cypress. We had to refuel once on this long run. In the midst of this beautiful trip we were suddenly aware of one bad odor. Good grief! The holding tank. I had forgotten my job. We called it "Doing a Code 4." I hurried down the ladder to take care of this delightful duty. After getting gas at Wachesaw Landing, we went under many drawbridges. The charts indicated we were paralleling the Atlantic Ocean with less than a half-mile between the sea and us. After checking our Waterway Guide, we headed for Palmetto Marina. It had a very shallow inlet and was only three feet deep at low tide.

That night's tie-up was another one of those gems that come along frequently in the southern part of the ICW. We came into Palmetto Marina late on a Saturday afternoon. We had been in touch via VHF, and the owner recommended this spot. A young couple had taken over the marina and were making a beautiful place out of it. Paula, who turned out to be a lovely lady, promised us a musical evening at their "Salty Dog Tavern." We had dinner on board and after this we went into the bar/dining area for the Saturday Night Stomp. We had another never-to-be-forgotten evening. Paula was an accomplished guitarist and singer and her music held everyone spell bound. Locals drifted in and out all evening.

A tired Cecil left for CELEBRATION II, then along about 2 A.M. I began to think about my bunk. By then, there were only a few of us left. It was then I watched the most fabulous Southern "back woods" dance I have ever seen. Paula's music enchanted everyone, and as she launched into a lively folk dance a plumpish woman and her husband got up to dance. Soon, they were doing one of the most complicated, foot-stomping bits of Kentucky clog dancing that I had ever witnessed. The woman was shy, but enjoying herself. They rapidly got into the spirit of the music and we watched a whirling dervish type of stomp and spin which is impossible to describe. Her Kentucky drawl gave us a clue as to her background. When it was over the couple fell exhausted in their chairs and the few remaining onlookers applauded wildly. Deciding that this was the crowning glory to another full day, I managed to find my way back to the boat. Bill came in later. What a night.

The next day was Sunday and we slept in. We had many visitors, and Cec took out the battleship and began his forays up and down the river where many fish restaurants overlooked the water. He began attacking boats and diners at the restaurants, so Bill and I decided to take out CELEBRATION and join him. We also asked some newly-made friends to come on board with us. We sat on the bridge in the warm, spring-like weather and watched the many speedboats hurtle by. It was Sunday and the waterway was crowded. We estimated some were running at 60 mph when the water was calm. We passed so many restaurants advertising fish dinners that we decided we must have one, too. We could see that there were 30-40 waiting in line for the well-known fish places.

After bringing both boats back to their berths, we climbed into the truck to look for a dining place overlooking the water. We never really wanted to stray far from the water, for we were happy when we were near it and our boats. Cec and I had another flounder dinner and Bill did his oyster thing again. When we arrived back at our slip, we found the local sheriff ready for a visit and a tour. He was a huge fellow, with a slow Southern drawl. As we stood by the boats and talked, we swatted away at the sand fleas. The sheriff said, "The weedjums out maghty bad tonight. Thay'll carry y'all away if yo don't tie yo'self down." We concurred.

Mary and Don joined us, as they had been visiting friends for several days. Mary and Cecil elected to pull the vehicles ahead, and Don, Bill and I would pilot and tow the boat. It was to be Don's last run with us, as he and Mary missed their dogs and would head back to Melbourne. We would part with a gala dinner at Myrtle Beach.

After a fond farewell from Salty Dog Tavern friends, we were cruising through a very isolated, swampy area. The channel was narrow and we were doing 2900 RPM. I was navigating for Bill on the bridge and Don was below— doing what we knew not. We only knew it was a gorgeous morning and all was well with our world. We saw a huge boat approaching us. Bill identified it as one of the boats on his hate list. It was a gigantic sports fishing boat hurtling toward us at full speed. People who own them love them, but boaters who have to meet them on the waterway shrink from the tremendous wake they create. Their hull design is such that the wake has far more size and force than the usual powerboat. We were about to enter a turn, and Bill sped up, hoping to get past the turn before meeting the wake from the Striker. I was kneeling down on the bridge deck beside Bill between the seats. It was a cold, brittle morning and I was keeping out of the wind reading my charts on my knees. Bill had only time enough to warn me, "Watch out! Here it comes!" Absorbed in my chart reading I looked up just in time to see a huge wave coming right at our bow. We headed directly into it. The boat left the water and I left the boat. Down on my knees and legs I came with a crack. I looked back at the speeding boat, heard Bill cursing and also anxiously checking the battleship. He shook his fist at the disappearing missile and added to the blue of the sky. "You'd better go down and check on Don," he said, recovering from the onslaught. "If we got a jolt like that up here he must have gotten it twice as much below."

Obediently I obeyed and staggered off as quickly as I could with my bruised knees. Seconds later I came shrieking up the ladder to Bill. "Don's gone!" I shouted.

Bill's hand cut the throttle immediately and he looked back along the waterway for a floating body. "Go back down and check the head," he ordered.

Plunging down the ladder, I raced through the companionway. Banging on the door, I shouted, "Don, are you in there?"

"Yes," said a muffled voice, "and you wouldn't believe what happened."

Immensely relieved, I trotted topside and reported that Don was still with us. Relaxing, we sank back into our seats and tried to recoup. Bill was laughing at how panicked I was when I thought Don had been bounced off into the swamp.

Our side of the story was minimal compared to what was reported by Don. According to him he was having his morning moment of meditation. To quote him, "Some moments are sacred. Everybody has one of these moments every day." Suddenly the bottom dropped out from under the boat for Don. He reported it was like being on an elevator that had hit the bottom of the shaft. Right after that he was hurled up and hit the top of the holding tank. Then he was thrown into the shower. He was just hauling himself out of the shower and settling back when he heard my hammering on the door. With my shouting at him and his feeling the throttle pulled back by Bill and the wake hitting us, Don thought something was terribly wrong with either Bill or the boats. Poor Don! He hobbled out, his trousers down around his knees. Lurching out and up the ladder he peered at us on the fly bridge flaked out on our seats. The air became blue again only this time it was Don's turn...His description of what had just happened to him pushed us into the arena of near hysteria. "I'd come up on the bridge but my trousers are down around my ankles," he reported. "You all regard this with a great deal of levity and I'm all bound up." We doubled over, too weak to laugh anymore. Reportedly, Dave was so shaken by the whole incident that it took him two days to get back on schedule.

SPLASH!! OH, NO!

After this morning crisis had passed, we headed out to mid-channel as much as possible, for we knew there was a great deal of shoaling at bends. There was also a lot of flotsam and jetsam and the *Guide* warned us about submerged objects. The fixed bridges we went under were no problem, but the swing bridges (closed vertical clearance seven feet) are usually regulated. Some open only on the hour. Having a boat under tow, we did not want to have to circle and wait for a bridge to open. Planning ahead was critical. We only had 30 miles to go and enjoyed cruising through the heavily wooded land and the wild isolation that gives no hint of any nearby population. However, we had heard that a multimillion-dollar complex is definitely set for the Briarcliff sector near Myrtle Beach. Although Pine Island Cut looked tranquil, we were warned to watch for more shoaling as the banks had slid down and formed a hard slate bottom. This needs more dredging by the Corps of Engineers.

When I brought sandwiches topside for the three of us, Bill remarked that the boat seemed to be dragging, pulling hard. We all just looked at each other. There surely could not/would not be another problem. Let us ignore whatever it is! As we found our way into Myrtle Beach, there was everyone waiting for us on the dock at a beautiful marina. Another tie up done—with five hands it was a breeze. Now to gussy it up for a gala farewell dinner! Don and Mary deserved a huge 'thank you' for all their efforts to assist us. With a gourmet meal and a fond farewell, the evening was done and we went back to our two boats. Tomorrow, another day. We still had the leap-frogging logistics to handle with our truck/trailer. Well, ho-hum. Worry about that later "Night, night, boys." Za-a-a-Zoop from every bunk.

First order of the day, April 28, was to rearrange the interior of CELEBRATION. Out came the life preservers from the shower. We would celebrate by having showers on board tonight. We secured the BICENTENNIAL into her halter and took off for Wilmington, N.C., Cec in his truck, Bill and I with our two boats. We began to come out of the sparse, wild areas of the South and into the more industrial area of North Carolina. About half an hour before coming into Wilmington, we made a 90-degree turn into the Cape Fear Inlet. This stretch of water lived up to its name and the wild ride began.

Waterway Guide says: "Respect it. While the channel is deep, wide and well marked, the very number of lights, buoys and big ship ranges tends to confuse even the seasoned waterway traveler. There are side channel passages and we advise a compass course. Currents run strong and swift, winds get a good sweep up along the river's long, straight length. When tide and wind are in conflict, batten down for a wet uncomfortable ride."

Oh dear. We were coming in on an outgoing tide. As we approached Wilmington we could see the outline of the Hilton Hotel, which we had read was located right on the waterfront. *The Guide* had made the tie up in front of the hotel sound good, particularly since it was right across the river from where the battleship USS NORTH CAROLINA was enshrined. We anticipated a comfortable marina but such was not the case. By this time Bill was not feeling well and it was all he could do to bring in the two boats to the dock where Cec was waiting for us. Again, we were faced with a huge tide rise and fall. This six-foot difference made the tie- up extremely difficult and we had to bring the battleship alongside CELEBRATION's port. We had to secure our lines on the tar-covered pilings on our starboard side. Riding these lines up and down with the tide soon covered our boat and our fenders with a messy black tar which we never did get off completely. Bill prided himself on the care and feeding of his ship, and he fussed for days trying to erase the remnants of our Wilmington visit. To be fair, the Hilton Hotel was not really prepared for pleasure boat tie-ups. We were fortunate to have shore power, but that was all they provided. The boys did the best they could and we watched CELEBRATION as the gooey black pitch rubbed against her gleaming white sides.

We decided we should take rooms at the Hilton, since by this time Cecil was not feeling well either. We took two adjoining rooms on the corner of the hotel so we could view our boats and the USS NORTH CAROLINA. This also enabled me to play nurse with only a door in between.

The gentlemen with me were in no mood to admire any views. Bill disappeared into his room, obviously not very good company for anyone. While Cec went down to check the spring lines, I walked to the downtown area in search of a hot water bottle and some juice. Upon my return I found Cecil flaked out and in the same condition as Bill. It was obvious the two of them had been a bit greedy the day before when they sampled some salt-dried fish which a local fisherman gave them. Since I had two sick men to care for, I moved Cec into the twin bed near Bill and kept one room for myself. I spent the night running the hot water bottle back and forth between them as they alternated getting up and racing for the bathroom. Thank goodness we were not on the boat. Between bouts of stomach upheavals I made several trips down to the restaurant. Since it was between hours, the waitresses were not busy and were most accommodating about supplying me with soup; but when the chef found out that it was our ships tied up outside the hotel, he was most helpful and he had several trays of toast and tea delivered to upstairs headquarters.

Sometimes I was a successful nurse and was thanked; sometimes they eyed me belligerently. I felt alone without my two security blankets and realized what a big job the two had with the boats. Around 2 A.M. they woke up feeling better and decided they would live, but they became restless. After draping a blanket around both of them, I put them in front of the TV. They gazed morosely at it. Neither would speak but sat there like two lumps of clay. They were feeling better, but both looked so unhappy and grumpy that I decided to take a few camera shots of them. They faintly objected, and then dejectedly resigned themselves to being filmed. They glared at me, but I still have the pictures today. (I have been threatened with mayhem if I ever show or publish those pictures.) As if by a hidden signal they both went back to bed next door and I grabbed an hour of sleep. The next thing I knew Bill was up and had decided to go for a walk. Cecil slept on. Bill came back in at 4:30 A.M. and went back to bed. Lights out—it had been a long, long night.

By 8:30 the next morning, life began to look a bit more appealing to my two sallow-faced friends. They perked up when they saw the fruit, juice and coffee I had ordered from downstairs. Apparently they decided that they could once again face the world, although I noticed they were not consumed with energy. We had a TV date with two channels at 10 A.M. and made our way down to the boats. We helped Cec get his BICENTENNIAL ready for the camera debut. The goo on CELEBRATION was awful. She was not camera ready. The sun was out after a refreshing night shower, and the world looked bright once again. What a day this would be. We knew nothing could go wrong.

By 10 A.M. our TV people were with us and ready for picture taking. A representative off the NORTH CAROLINA had come over and wanted pictures of us up against his ship. We made a date to tour her later. We cast

Cec off and out into the harbor he went. How tiny he looked up against the "mommy" ship, the USS CAROLINA. The TV men laughed at the comparison and seemed to enjoy their filming. One beautifully attired anchorman had come for an interview and wanted to ride in the battleship. He was a gorgeous creature with his wavy hair and canary yellow slacks. We hesitated about having him climb into the battleship. We had had a lot of anchormen riders but none so nattily attired. Unfortunately, the last thing riding in the rear bucket seat had been a gas can, and when the anchorman stepped out we were horrified to see some large grease spots on his yellow slacks. I tried to wipe the spots off for him, but he hurried away. We felt badly about this. Was he off to the dry cleaners? He proved to be more than forgiving for that night on the news he gave us the longest TV interview we had experienced to this date (and he had changed his pants!).

When the next TV station was through filming the BICENTENNIAL on the water, they asked Cecil to come in to the dock and tie up for a personal interview. This he did, and Bill and I thought we should have some footage of the TV people filming Cec. It would be good stuff for our documentary. We hurried back to CELEBRATION. The tide was low and Bill had to climb way down to get into the boat. He picked up the camera case and started to hand it up to me. As I stretched way down to reach for the case, it suddenly flopped open and Cec's 16 mm Belle and Howell hopped out and sank in 14 feet of water. We looked at each other in horror. Bill swore. I whispered, "Don't tell him. Don't tell him." We agreed not to say word of this until Cec was off the air.

I slunk over to where his interview was being conducted. Bill stayed to tell the cameraman about our blunder. When the interview was over, Cec sensed that something was wrong. Our guilt must have stood out in plain view. I couldn't bring myself to tell him alone. Bill came over and faced up to Cec. Poor Cecil. Speechless again! But he took the whole thing with great composure. His Belle and Howell was his working camera. His Canon Scoopic 16 mm was his more expensive indulgence. He used them interchangeably, but he relied on his B&H in tight spots when he had no time for adjustments. He was so nice to us after he had overcome his first shock that Bill and I felt worse than ever.

As we were sitting on the dock discussing this awful happening, the Wilmington fire truck drove up and out climbed three scuba divers in wet suits. We couldn't believe our eyes. The TV cameraman had asked the fire chief if his scuba team would try to rescue our camera. The scuba divers readied their equipment masks in place. Someone made a comment about watching out for "Charlie." I looked around. Who was Charlie? We found out Charlie was the local alligator who frequents the dock area. Three loud splashes and 30 seconds later, one diver surfaced. Up came his arm triumphantly holding the camera. Poor wet, soaking camera. It was covered with silt and water. Wonderful, brave firemen. I almost hugged them suit and all when they climbed out. How grateful we were to these fine people, and I wrote a letter to their newspaper telling of the help we had been given. This was just another example of how supportive and wonderful people were to us as we journeyed along the waterway with our boats. So many reached out to help is in any way they could.

We sat on the dock and the men took the camera apart and sprayed it with what they called "Mother's Milk"—WD-40. I learned early on that this miraculous chemical was good for wiping down teakwood, spraying stubborn engines, cleaning off spots and cleansing white fenders. The camera had been in the water approximately half an hour. Cec called a camera headquarters in Norfolk and explained what had happened. They didn't sound too encouraging about repair, but told him to send the camera in and they would try. Off it went on a Greyhound.

That evening we stretched out in our room and watched the local news. Our coverage was excellent and we were given almost three minutes. We became a bit crass about this as we made comparisons between different cities. After the news we went down to the boat and I cooked a light dinner for the three of us. We locked her up for the night and went back to our rooms. One more night living like real people in beds should help us. It had been a long, emotional day for all. Tomorrow we would leave for Wrightsville Beach.

Leaving our rig back in Wilmington, the three of us had a most pleasant day as we ran northward. Before settling in to read charts, I checked the BICENTENNIAL to make sure she was tracking as she should. It had become my job to fend her off when we docked and to make sure she swung around properly when Bill guided us out. Most of the time it was not too difficult, but when the tides and currents roiled I was usually down on my stomach, grabbing the bow of the battleship as she tried to climb aboard with us. I felt a little more professional now. At least I rarely embarrassed the skipper. He was a good teacher and I was making progress in chart reading and visual navigating.

We read the usual warnings from the *Guide*—crosscurrents were strong in some areas and it is easy to be carried out of the channel. Since shoals tend to build up inside these small inlets, we were instructed to favor the ocean side of the main channel on flood tide, the landside on ebb. Back down the Cape Fear River we went looking for the secondary route that joins Myrtle Grove Sound. We also found out that in 1861 President Lincoln ordered all ports south of Hampton Roads blockaded. Profiteers rushed to the sea in ships to create a lifeline that brought supplies from abroad to the Confederacy. More than 2000 boats made for Carolina ports and 84% got through the blockade. One of the busiest and most prosperous of blockaded ports was Wilmington. The proximity of Fort Fisher kept the port open until the last months of the War Between the States. Then the fort fell in the largest land/ sea battle fought up until that time.

Bill still complained about the way the boat was handling. There was much discussion about this. And it was agreed that it didn't work to avail yourself of a boat that had had a previous owner—one who had not taken care of it. The narrow channels brought us closer to Wrightsville. Glory be! Floating docks and a nice tie-up—except the outside tie made us subject to outsized wakes from large craft plying the narrow channel. We had been published in the Wilmington paper that morning even before our arrival, and people streamed down to the docks to welcome us. More press and TV, then we spent the afternoon up on the bridge watching the weekend boaters come by. Occasionally one would come careening along much too fast for the narrow area. Courtesy has it that boats slow down so as to create no wakes for tied-up craft. Most obey this rule of the water, but there are always some that don't know or don't care.

We watched many barges tied end to end with 50,000 tons of logs aboard. They would come by with only a single tugboat towing them. It was almost frightening to see the gigantic powerhouses on the move. One mistake and a whole marina could be wiped out. It did happen once. A barge got out of control and went under the restaurant across the river where we were tied up. The whole restaurant building with all their guests ended up on top of the barge. They still talk about this. What a way to have a fish dinner!

We stayed in this marina for two days. That night a distant rainstorm lured us to the beach and an ice cream cone. We walked out onto the pier and watched the lightning criss-cross the sky. When we returned to CELEBRATION, the storm had moved in closer and we sat up on the bridge debating whether or not the storm would reach us. It was an eerie spectacle. The squall was so violent looking, the air so balmy and warm. Lightning crackled and thunder boomed—yet not a drop of rain. We were reluctant to leave Mother Nature's show, but one by one we went below.

Bill's logbook says, "It was a good, full day."

Cec's tape says, "What a fantastic trip."

My diary says, "I like living in this boy's locker room."

NO OUT DRIVE—NO DRIVE

May 3, 1975—up and at 'em! 7:30 A.M. and we left port. Cec elected to jump truck and trailer forward to Swansboro. We passed Sloop Point, Snead's Ferry. We loved these eastern names because they represented so much colonial and Civil War history to us westerners. Many of the commercial fishermen from Snead's Ferry were great-great-great grandchildren of men who had been fishing for generations. Here the Waterway cuts for five miles through government property where signs prohibit landing. Camp Lejeune uses this area for firing practice but mariners are not generally inconvenienced except for annual amphibious landings. Mile 234 found us south of Swansboro where there was a big new plant belonging to a major Pacific coast yacht builder.

We were moseying along at 2900 RPM meandering with the curves of the waterway. We didn't have a care in the world and life was good. I made just one trip below to make sandwiches. The egrets were our only company in this grassy, swampy area and all seemed idyllic. We laughed about our past problems and Bill's comment was, "The only other thing that could go wrong for us would be the out drive. I've replaced everything else." Was he a prophet? A seer? One hour after this remark we heard some strange noises coming from the stern of the boat. "What in $%#X@ is that?" Bill left me to throttle back and pilot as he leaped down the ladder, up to the bow and threw out the anchor. Then he dove into the engine compartment. "I don't like it one bit," he said as he came topside again. "It's either the out drive or the damper plate."

My boating vocabulary had improved somewhat so that I no longer asked, "Is that bad?" That could always antagonize my roommates with female-type questions. Instead, I made intelligent sounding noises which seemed to satisfy Bill that I had some idea as to the seriousness of the nature of the unwelcome noise. He started up the engine again and we must have gone a few more miles when CELEBRATION gave a final WHOOP and would not budge another inch. Bill hit the ladder for the anchor while I rushed off behind him to fend off the battleship. As the anchor bit into the bottom, we drifted off to the side of the channel—thank goodness, out of the boating traffic. There we swung. "Maybe you shouldn't have spoken about the out drive out loud," I ventured. "It heard you talking."

Bill's blond head lifted briefly above the edge of the engine compartment. "Any other theories, Dearie?" he growled. I retreated. Should have kept my mouth shut. Better I should fetch him a beer from the refrigerator. As he climbed out of the engine compartment he said, "I hope it's not the out drive, but I'll bet it is. We hit something yesterday which really bumped against the hull. I heard it smack. But I thought everything was OK until this happened." We sat there and debated about calling the Coast Guard for a tow in. We knew we were not too far from Swansboro where we anticipated meeting Cecil. We figured we were only a few miles out. As we were sitting there, discussing this unfortunate turn of events an 18-foot motorboat with a man and a boy in it came by.

He hailed us with, "Hi, are you in trouble? May I help you?" We must have looked like the now extinct do-do bird, dangling from our anchor with the red/white and blue battleship waggling her tail behind us. Bill jumped up and shouted our problem out across the water. "Throw me a line," the man instructed, "and I'll tow you to Swansboro. It's not very far. You can get into a sling there and they can take a look at your out drive."

I gazed with some apprehension at the small boat. It looked no bigger than a good size rowboat with an engine mounted on it. "Can he really pull us in?" I asked Bill.

"We'll give it a try, Dearie. At least it's better than sitting out here." Bill coiled a line and it landed in the bottom of the boat, which was now positioned in front of us. The man made it fast and slowly eased the throttle forward as he took the slack out of the line. Bill took in the anchor and we watched as CELEBRATION and the BICENTENNIAL began to move out into the main channel. Our rescuer eased the throttle forward a bit more and we began to pick up speed. Then our special do-si-do began. Or call it the grand right and left. We sashayed back and forth across that channel as if we were square dancing. It must have been quite a sight, the three boats all harnessed together, whipping back and forth across the water like a bouncing football. Our friend obviously knew what he was doing. We took four glides across the water from side to side for his one thrust forward, but we were making headway.

I hoped we were within calling distance of Cec, who must be expecting us to check in with him. Bill directed me to try the radio. "This is WYU

5985, CELEBRATION II calling WYU 5904." No answer. I repeated the call letters and still no answer.

"Try him again in a few minutes," the skipper said.

Minutes passed and we continued our crazy dance up the channel. Again, I sent out my message and this time came the welcome answer: "This is WYU 5904 calling. Where are you? I'm waiting in Swansboro for you."

Bill was busy taking care of the line to see that it did not become fouled. I poured out our latest problem over the airwaves. Cecil had already made a reservation for us at a marina, but we would have to change plans now. Our friend in the boat was taking us to a marina that had a sling so we could be pulled out. I relayed this to Cecil, who said he would drive to the new spot which was not too far from where he was calling us. I went out to watch as we began our approach into the small harbor. The man in the boat certainly was skilled. Unhesitatingly he made his turn in toward the marina, which we could see off in the distance. The winds were not bad even though it was late afternoon. At this moment we didn't need a chop.

Bill stayed in the bow, I was on the stern to catch the battleship when she would try to cozy up with us. Closer in we came. We could see high pilings coming up out of the water. "Must be another huge tide drop here," I thought. There was no further time to speculate. This tie-up would have to be a good one. With no power we would have to do the first pass right. Bill and the man were shouting to one another as he stood on the bow. Bill would untie the line and let it drag for the motorboat to pull in. He would have another line ready to throw to Cec, who looked ready and apprehensive. I was on the stern with a line ready and knew I would need my hands and feet to fend off the pilings and help save CELEBRATION and the battleship. If I didn't do this right I might as well buy a plane ticket home if I messed this up.

"NOW!" yelled our rescuer to Bill. Off came the line and the motorboat veered quickly off to port out of our way. CELEBRATION II was on collision course with the dock. In we came as the last small surge of power shoved us, but with inertia slowing us down. Sixty feet of water separated us from the dock and Cecil's outstretched hands. Breathless, I watched our awkward approach. From the stern I saw Bill's forward line shoot out to Cecil. It was a perfect throw and a perfect catch. I turned to my charge trundling along behind us. Sizing up the remaining slice of water between the boat and the dock, I sat down and stuck out both legs. I managed to fend CELEBRATION off and away from the dock. Then I made a dive to my right and caught BICENTENNIAL's nose with one hand. As CELEBRATION slowed and stopped, I stretched out on my stomach and gave the battleship a hard shove on the bow. Heavily, reluctantly, she slowed as she pushed against my arms. As I continued to shove her back she began to respond. Soon there was five feet between her nose and CELEBRATION's out drive.

People on the dock, anxious to help us, jumped on board and tied up our stern. Boating people! They were marvelous. Always tuned in to another's problem, always quick to respond to anyone in distress! We were grateful to them.

Cecil jumped on board and helped me tie up the BICENTENNIAL to the starboard side of the mother ship. To say we were relieved was the understatement to the whole affair. What a reprieve to be all in one piece with nothing damaged. At least I wouldn't have to buy a plane ticket west this time.

The following was written by author unknown, (undoubtedly female), but I could easily have penned this:

MY JOB

It's not my job to run the yacht—the horn I cannot blow.
It's not my job to say how far the yacht's allowed to go.
It's not my job to throttle down—or even clang the bell.
But let the damn thing hit the dock—and see who catches hell.

(Ah, yes.)

SLEEPING IN A SLING

If we had to have a problem, it couldn't have happened in a nicer place. Swansboro was small, quaint, friendly and hidden away. We looked at the small working marina and appreciated the compactness and the efficiency of it. We had an outside tie-up but we were far enough from the main channel that any passing wake should not affect us. We would be gently rocked, but not rudely jolted from side to side.

The usual questions came from the local fisherman nearby. Cec had told us that this was a very small town and we likely would be a curiosity. That we proved to be! After we had explained our mishap and told our battleship story, the locals drifted away and went on with their fishing. We thanked our rescuer profusely and complimented him on his skillful handling of us. He turned out to be a former tug boat captain and was anxious to leave so he could bring his other son down to see us and our battleship.

We had arrived in Swansboro in time for the weekend. After dinner on board, the men went off with the dock master, who drove them all around the small town and vicinity. Cecil and Bill were impressed with the casualness of the whole area and more specifically with the bicycle which was laid carelessly in front of a house on the main street. It was lying on its side six feet from the street on a dirt sidewalk. "That bike would be ripped off in five minutes in any large city," they said.

The next day was Sunday and the men who operated the marina would be back to lift us out of the water early Monday morning. We had a lazy day ahead of us. French toast was served on board around 11 A.M. Early afternoon a very large young man came loping down the incline to see us. He was waving a magazine. It was one in which we had appeared. Mike had enshrined it, always hoping to contact us one day, but never dreamed we would end up in a marina near him. He so wanted to shake Cecil's hand and told him how he admired his battleships. Shyly he asked us if we would like him to take us on his special tour of the waterway. He owned an 18-foot boat with a 150 HP engine. We agreed. That day Mike got his boat out and picked us up. How he did enjoy cutting the canal in half and how we enjoyed riding with him. He reported we were doing 48 mph. I was duly impressed.

Dredging machines when they were cutting out the ICW channel had formed many man-made islands. The islands were partially covered with growth, but they seemed like typically mysterious desert islands, and we loved exploring in and around these spots. Mike took us around one island to the mouth of the Atlantic Ocean. We could feel the surge of water as we faced the elements from the sea. It was good to be protected from that body of water by the narrow strip of sand and islands that lay between the Atlantic and us. Mike told us he wanted us for a fish dinner some night. We accepted and made plans for this in the next few days. I would bring fresh fish and the dessert. Mike would prepare the rest and would fry the fish. We had no idea what lay in store for us.

After all this exploring Cecil decided he wanted a sequence in his film which would involve exploring with our yellow inflatable life raft. Back to the boat we went to pick up all this equipment. Before we had left L.A., a salesman friend for a sporting goods company had given us one of the dinghies his company carried. This yellow, deflated package had often been the object of speculation by Cec and Bill as to how they could film a scene around it. We had had many a laugh at the dinner table imagining a pirate flag on the dinghy, a sinking of it—or the battleship ramming the dinghy. They were not quite sure what type of sequence they would film, but seeing the sand duned islands throughout this area it seemed like a good time to begin picture production. Cec put his tripod and remaining camera into Mike's boat, Bill got the life raft and the California flag, Cec started up the battleship and we were off to film our extravaganza. We hurtled back to our desert island. Shoes were tossed aside, jeans were rolled up and we waded ashore. There were quite a few remarks from Cec to Bill and me about "DON'T drop the camera!" We chose to ignore these remarks, but I noticed Cec was filling Mike in on all the details about our hurling his other camera overboard in Wilmington.

We were enjoying a hazy, lazy, slightly humid South Carolina day. The sun was filtered through the clouds. Cec set up his tripod at the water's edge preparatory for the Keystone Kop routine.

There was much shouting of orders from Cec. Mike and Bill were holding both boats, knee-deep in water. Cec was giving directions about what he wanted to film. Bill was to get into the battleship, go out into the channel, circle and come to shore. As he came close, he was to lift the superstructure, hook it so it would not fall, then pull out the deflated life raft. Next, fill it with air, climb in and with the one paddle, aim for shore. After doing this, he was to put the California flag into the raft. When he hit the shoreline he was to pull the raft ashore, grab the flag, run up the steep 18-foot sandy slope to the top, plant the flag and fall to the ground. The scenario sounded good. I giggled—three grown men, splashing about, getting ready for their production. It all looked so funny and I sat down to watch. Everyone was in readiness for their Cecil B. DeMille production.

Bill had discovered the only way to blow up the raft was with a plastic bag which came with it. One corner of the bottom of the bag had a valve which screwed into the raft. Bill was to hold the bag up like a pillowcase and when it had filled with air he would close the top, thus forcing the air into the raft. It all looked quite simple. "Ready!" yelled Cecil. Bill put out to sea, coming smartly about, heading the battleship for the camera. Coming in close to shore, he pushed up the superstructure but it did not latch properly. Cec began to laugh. Bill swore. Mike looked quizzical; I said nothing.

They decided to try it again. Out went Bill. This time he came in successfully. Up with the superstructure, out with the life raft which was now a curled up, smashed looking piece of rubber. The wind was blowing (of course) and the pillowcase full of air was forced into the raft by the hard-working Bill. We now dubbed this our "Yellow Submarine" film. Bill continued working. Up would go the bag and fill with air. Bill grabbed the top forcing air into the raft which began to look like a dinghy. Cec stopped filming because, as he told Bill, "I'm not going to waste all that film watching you fill up that raft."

Bill looked harried and we began to laugh again at his dilemma in trying to pump so much air into the raft. "Ready, here I go," shouted our pirate. Then Bill climbed awkwardly out of the battleship and into the raft. He reached into the boat to grab the flag and the paddle and discovered he was sitting backward. He got up to change position and almost fell out. Paddling on both sides of the raft, he finally made it to shore and dragged the raft up on the beach. Then he unfurled the California flag and clawed his way up the steep sand dune. Reaching the top, he planted the flag and flung himself to the ground, arms outstretched. By this time we were laughing so hard we were weak. Cec sunk to his knees and announced he knew he had shaken the camera so badly that the film would be jerky. Bill must do the whole thing again. Poor Bill.

Out he went and again ran through the whole scene. Collapsing in a heap on top of the sandy hill, he could not believe Cec wanted him to run through the scenario one more time. Ex-Marine Bill told Cec in no uncertain terms exactly what he could do with the flag; but he gave it one more try and landed exhausted and triumphant at the top. He was covered from head to foot with sand. We piled everything back into Mike's boat and made our way back to CELEBRATION for a much-needed rest. The galley person served refreshments and hors d'oeuvres and we speculated as to how our great burlesque would turn out. Much later we were pleased that it was one of the funniest things we captured on film. And I had had a brief moment to escape over the sand dunes and collect seashells to mail to my class—way across the U.S. I would never forget this day!

Next morning we were hauled out. It's a traumatic experience to see one's water home lifted out of the water. Somehow she's out of her element, loses her dignity and looks clumsy. Poor CELEBRATION. Bill and the dock master did their best to place the boat in an exact upright position so that we might not have to live at full tilt for the next few days. It was bad enough trying to get up that first step onto the boat. It was a good three-foot stretch for me but every time I did it I figured it was good for the waistline so ceased to think about it. The two tall men with their long legs had no trouble. (I received no assistance or sympathy. Is this called being "one of the crew"?) Bill tore off the out drive for a checkout. He pulled the shaft housing plate off and found that the teeth were torn up at the upper housing with possibly a lower broken shaft. The oil was full of metallic grindings. It was very much as he expected although he had hoped up to the last minute that a miracle might occur. Next he got on the phone and tried to locate an out drive. He found one in Norfolk, VA and after several calls they arranged to sell us a 280 out drive from a warehouse in Norfolk. Since the boat was still in a sling, we decided to start for Norfolk immediately, as this would make the trip shorter the next day. We had 200 miles to drive, so I quickly packed some clothes for all of us and we managed to get as far as a motel in Ahoskie, North Carolina, 50 miles south of Norfolk. After a late dinner we got to bed just before midnight. We seemed to be having many late nights, but there always seemed to be something going on or people visiting us.

On the way to Norfolk we had our first encounter with a Southern sheriff, the kind you always read about but didn't think existed. Cecil was driving and slowed down for a roadblock. As we approached, an officer stopped us. The sheriff with him noticed our California license plate and said in his drawl, "Ah see y'all fum Californy. Y'all got yoself a good driver's license?"

Cecil allowed that he had, and as he pulled out his wallet the sheriff pushed his Stetson back on his head. "Well, that's mighty fine and ah's glad tuh heah that. Sho would hate to put a Westerner in our lil ol' jail" He smiled benignly at us but we had the distinct impression that we'd jolly well better be legal all the way or we'd end up in a Southern pokey with corn pone and hush puppies for breakfast, lunch and dinner.

We had a good breakfast the next morning and headed for the Volvo plant in Norfolk. We located the warehouse in the waterfront area. Bill's sense of direction was uncanny and we found the factory with no trouble. He signed for the out drive (thank you, dear Preston—our supportive benefactor) and we were on our way to Elizabeth City for mail call. We drove much of the time beside the Dismal Swamp where we were slated to come by boat if we could ever pull ourselves together again. It was a beautiful drive and we arrived at Elizabeth City where we went to three city post offices before we found our general delivery mail. We stopped for hamburgers and shared mail. We knew a lot about each other's family and friends by now. Coming back into Swansboro, we drove by the bike which still lay in the street. We found our boat had been set back in the water so the lift could be used to haul out another boat. Shortly it was up and out again and I cooked dinner that night on a boat which was high and dry—very high. We were fortunate in having electricity, for the dock master saw to it that we had shore power. While I was getting dinner, the boys pulled off the out drive again so they could get an early start on repair in the morning. That night the boat under us seemed unusually quiet. We missed the slap-slap of the water, the gentle wakes and the murmurings of the water.

In the morning I readied some French toast to fortify two mechanics. Bill wasted no time in assembling all the parts, and the afternoon found him partially finished with the repair job. We took time off for a local news reporter and a TV interview from a larger city. Then it was time to get ready to go to Mike's for our anticipated fish dinner. Not only were we invited for dinner, but also for showers. Since we were in a sling it was not possible to have water, and the showers at the marina needed help. Off we went to Mike's home with fresh fish, dessert, soap and towels in hand. It was a lovely place, located right on the water. The house was built over the garage and the view was beautiful. We took turns showering and enjoying the parade of boats going up and down the ICW. As yet we were in no hurry to join those who were churning along through the water. We were enjoying our enforced stay in the quaint environs of this town. The people made us feel like one of them—and the bike was still lying near the street. We wondered if these good people knew how fortunate they were to live in such a peaceful manner.

We couldn't keep away from the windows. As the twilight crept in we stood, fascinated by the changing light on the water. The sun was doing its best to put on a show for us visitors, sharing a kaleidoscope of colors with four earthlings. Our reverie was interrupted by the sound of pots, pans and dishes being banged about in the kitchen. Our bachelor host, Mike, was beginning dinner preparations and I turned to go help him. My curiosity in watching him haul out a five-gallon bucket turned to amazement when I found it contained five gallons of pure white pig lard. I called the boys over to view this. We listened while Mike told us how his family gathers for the killing and rendering of a hog on his uncle's tobacco farm. Each family would go home with a five-gallon container of hog fat. This one was one-third empty and Mike dipped into the grease with his hand and scooped out cup after cup of fat. He went on to fry the French fries in the fat, then the hush puppies—finally my blue fish. Soon we were sitting around a circular table enjoying a repast that could not be matched for cholesterol. Mike's cole slaw and my dessert filled out the dinner. We were all considerably filled out, too. It took us two days to get over our gorging.

The next day the men completed the out drive job and tightened the belts and nuts. We were dropped back into the water early in the afternoon and gave some demo rides to different locals who had been so nice to us. Everything checked out to our skipper's satisfaction, so we tied up by the dock glad to be back in our element again. Three classes of kindergarten and primary children came down to see the battleship and us. I strolled over to explain more about the Bicentennial and our journey to the teachers and youngsters. It was a pleasure to talk with those in my profession who were so far removed from big city problems. Mike wanted to take Cecil out in his boat one more time so Cecil could film Bill doing maneuvers in the battleship for the children. This time I was in the audience sitting on the shore and enjoyed watching the delight of the children and the comments from the adults.

Over the battleship's speaker I heard Bill's voice say, "Now hear this. This is the captain speaking. I am sorry to report this battleship has run aground." Bill and the BICENTENNIAL were stuck on an oyster bed. The children clapped with glee and we all laughed at the incongruity of the situation. I could well imagine Bill's dismay to founder in full view of his audience. Up went the superstructure and he waved at Mike. I could see Cec getting a line ready to throw to Bill. He caught it and held on as Mike gradually tightened the rope between the two boats. With a roar of the engine, Mike lurched forward and the BICENTENNIAL came off the oyster bed. Our forgiving audience applauded. Down came the superstructure, Bill zoomed around the small harbor in circles for a few minutes more, then sped off and back to a tie up with CELEBRATION. I hurried over to meet him.

As he came in slowly and threw me a line, I hauled him toward me. "Show off," I accused. "Time for you to walk the plank. How would you like your bottom scraped on an oyster bed?"

Laughing, he told me what a strange feeling it had been. "I wasn't going very fast. All of a sudden the damn boat just wouldn't go. I put it in reverse and she wouldn't budge. I couldn't rock her loose, either. She was stuck. I could see oysters and the water was pretty shallow. I came onto them so slow I know the bottom wasn't damaged, but probably there's no paint left in spots. I'm sure she's OK." We finished tying her up beside the escort boat and I went in to prepare dinner. A call came from Southern California to the marina for Cecil and he came back to report we would be on the cover of *Family Houseboating* magazine in August of 1975. Janet Groene, a fine writer whom we had met at the Miami Boat Show, had done a lengthy article on us. It would be coming out in a few months. We had a toast before dinner to this news.

As I continued with dinner preparations, I kept glancing toward the bow and out to sea where some advancing clouds and evening were rapidly settling in. I kept telling my companions, "Do you see where we're eating dinner tonight? Can you ask for a more beautiful setting?" Each time we found some special spot, I always served meal up forward at the big table so we could enjoy the view. Despite our numerous problems, we were milking every second of this trip for its beauty and fun, and we didn't pass up a thing. This was one of those special nights, so forward to the bow we went. "Sure beats looking at those oysters glued to the pilings at some of the places we've seen," said Cecil.

We watched the clouds lowering and assume a more threatening pose. We turned on the C.G. weather report. A storm cell was moving toward us and we could expect rain soon. The wind picked up, but it was not cold. On the fly bridge, the sky looked black and there were no stars. Occasionally lightning split the sky in half, revealing boiling, bubbling clouds intent on catching those of us who venture forth to watch nature's show close up. We were transfixed. The air vibrated with unspent electricity. The smell of the ocean over the barrier island blew in. Each of us, I am sure, felt small and rather insignificant with the magnitude of the spectacle being presented by Mother Nature. She seemed unable to make up her mind whether to unleash a deluge on us or to merely leave us in awe of her pent-up power. Was she angry with us as uninvited guests viewing her temper tantrum? Like an undecided woman, the threatening squall danced and feinted. We decided to take advantage of her indecision and scurried below. Bedding down in our bunks, we were subdued by what we had just witnessed. We said our goodnights.

The storm must have changed its mind once we stopped watching. The rain hit the bridge above with a cloudburst effect. We were bombarded with a moisture-laden machine gun. Nature was going to have the last word tonight. Almost asleep, I suddenly had an uneasy feeling. I sat up and closed the partially open sliding glass window. Remembering Georgetown's drowning of poor Cecil, I thought, *Good night for leaks*. Not wanting a repeat of that catastrophe, I sank back as the storm raged without. *I must be the luckiest woman in the world*, was my last waking thought.

LOST IN OUR OWN WORLD

A bright and shiny day greeted us. What were today's logistics? With only 25 miles planned to get to Morehead City, we were feeling confident. Cec decided to let us tow the battleship, and he would jump the rig forward. He checked the battleship for towing and made sure the self-bailing pump was functioning so it would take care of any unwelcome rough water. We pored over the charts for what should be a four-hour run to Morehead City and we would meet Cecil at the marina. It was a short trip, but it turned out to be a rough one, taking us longer than we thought. The channel was shoaling and the winds were blowing hard from the north onto our port side. Sitting on the bridge we could see over the barrier islands and we kept the Atlantic in view most of the trip. We drifted badly, continually fighting our way through the channels. It was particularly bad when we came to Boque Sound. The area we cruised by was never monotonous. The landside was so close you could almost touch it and is high and well wooded. The opposite side was a direct contrast. The long, slim island had a dense growth of pine, myrtle and scrub oak. We read that the explorer Verrazano sighted this island in 1524 and left what is believed to be the first written description of any land in America.

Our musings were brought to a startled end when Bill heard a bad noise. Out went the anchor and by the time it caught we were in three feet of water. The steering belt had come loose. He repaired it and we were on our way. We were glad to round the bend and find the entrance to Morehead City. The shelter from the wind was welcome, and I soon had Cec on the VHF who continued talking us into our place at the dock. We made fast our lines and two boats and none too soon.

Again word had gone ahead of us about our pen pal letters and battleship. Here came Tony from the famous Tony's Sanitary Fish Restaurant. Well known up and down the whole Waterway for his great fish dinners, he hurried down to greet us. We had come in on the low tide, so getting down onto CELEBRATION was not easy. The three of us were used to being half person/

half monkey by now, but Tony was amazed at the difficulty in getting down and onto the ship. He greeted us warmly and said the newspaper and TV people were following him down.

Tony stayed with us while we spent the next three hours with reporters and newsmen and did quite a bit of performing for them. This necessitated Cec getting into the battleship and we turned him loose in the harbor. We watched the reaction of different workmen on a large dredge across the bay. We couldn't hear what they were saying, but the gesturing and pointing made it clear that they were intrigued with the strange vision in their harbor. The news people were quite thorough in their interviewing and questioned us about the whole trip. Tony listened with great interest. As soon as the news people had left he got up and announced, "We have a mayor, too. I know he has a key. You *must* have a key to Morehead City."

Off he went climbing out a little more easily than he got in—the flow tide had lifted us three feet during our interviewing. Within 15 minutes, Tony and the mayor were back. The elderly little mayor came tottering in and made a most touching presentation to Cec. The key was not accompanied with all the hoopla and finesse that had gone with the key to Jacksonville, but the warmth and hospitality were certainly there. We were moved by the generosity and spirit behind the act.

After several hours of interviews, we ended in the late afternoon with a final radio interview. This was played over the local station for two days. Consequently we had many visitors who heard about us. How pleasant the small cities were turning out to be. We were to appreciate them so much when later we began to come into the large cities lining Chesapeake Bay. The visitors came flowing in and we barely had time to run up to the marina lounge and watch ourselves on the 6 P.M. news. Ah—2 ½ minutes we clocked. It made us feel great although we knew it was not us that were important. It was what we represented. I was ready for another fish dinner and made mention of this fact. But dinner was already planned. The gentlemen said they would consider taking me to lunch at Tony's Sanitary Fish Restaurant the next day.

Cecil got up early the next morning and left for Ft. Macon to do some filming of that Civil War fort. Upon his return he regaled us with its history and told us the fort had fallen to the Union forces. We were fascinated as history was coming alive for us Westerners. That morning I found a marina laundry not to be passed up. I kept making noises to the gentlemen about lunch and we decided to take in Tony's restaurant. Cec wanted to go over in style and took off in his battleship. Bill and I walked over to the restaurant, several blocks away, and waited for Cec so we could tie him up. We could always tell when he was coming. Boats would slow down, they would begin to circle, people would come running down to the docks and much yelling and pointing would be in evidence.

There he came, bouncing gaily over somewhat choppy waters. We waved and he came in for a tie-up but not before he squirted us with his cannon. He and Bill seemed to have a oneupmanship game where one would hose down the other. I asked them once what happens in the men's restroom. No answer—just a glare.

After the usual flurry we went into Tony's, where we asked if he had a vacant table by the window. We were so happy by the sea, so married to the water we never strayed too far. We enjoyed watching the boats come in and tie up—the home port name on the stern told of coming from as far as New York and Miami. We found out why Tony was famous up and down the east coast. The fish, the oysters, the hush puppies—superb food. This long, leisurely lunch was another never-to-be-forgotten meal and we promised each other we would someday return. How fortunate to have stumbled on to this place.

We lazed around for a change, shopped to lay in supplies for our next run. Turning in early that night—10 P.M.—we enjoyed a great night.

The next morning a radio station announcer came on board at 6:30 A.M. to share his broadcast with us. Bill and I slept through the whole thing. Cec reported the announcer had brought coffee and donuts on board and that we were two zombies to have missed it all. This turned out to be a gray day, and the C.G. weather report made us feel that we should stay an extra day. This would give us a chance to get caught up on correspondence, do logbooks and tapes. The three of us spent almost the whole day on board doing our various chores, but had many interruptions from visitors. We always enjoyed them. That afternoon some recent University of North Carolina graduates, three delightful girls stopped by to talk. They were on their parent's boats for the weekend and had heard about us on the radio. We invited them on board and they told us about all their friends who were located on boats throughout the marina. They decided their friends must see the battleship and meet us, so off they went. When they returned the boat was full, forward, aft and on the bridge. Late afternoon turned into evening and conversation and liquid refreshments flowed freely. The students brought their own and we chattered, philosophized about their job opportunities. They pumped us about California and our way of life. We in turn asked these friendly southern young people about their education and ambitions.

The three of us thought we would go to Tony's for dinner but he closed at 9 P.M. We were not sure where to go, so the students showed us the way to another great fish restaurant and they joined us for another flounder feed. We found our radio friends there, too, so it was a great fish-feeding frenzy. We sat and talked until midnight. Then we were told of a party that one of the recent North Carolina graduates was having at their summer beach home. We were flattered to be included, for we were at least one generation apart. They drove us to a beach home, which was one of many lined up along the shore. We learned that these homes had been handed down through several generations of families and that coming to the beach for the summer was a ritual. We enjoyed our peek into the lives of these newly-minted graduates. We floated from group to group and listened to the talk. Lingering into the wee small hours, we were interested to hear about their hopes and dreams for the future. We were eventually driven back to CELEBRATION, which was a small island of peace and happiness that the three of us had created. Morehead City had been a super-great stop!

Before we left for the big crossing of Pamlico Sound, we reevaluated what lay ahead and what was behind. We had traveled 265 miles since leaving Charleston. We were not yet halfway to NY from Miami. Our usual logistical problem was with us—what to do with truck and trailer. The unanimous vote said to leave it in Morehead City and we three would head for Belhaven. Just how does one get to Belhaven? As we left we pointed out to Bill that Beaufort, N.C. was just across the bridge from Morehead. We reminded him about "Bewfort" as opposed to this "Bowfort."

As we came out of the marina we found that the route doglegs through marshes and shoals to the 65-foot fixed bridge. The adjacent railway bridge is usually raised. We began a compass course (034) to (058) into the Neuse River. Many yachtsmen equate this river with the upcoming Albemarle Sound and say that the two are equally matched as strong contenders for the title "meanest water on the Intracoastal."

Cec took over navigational chores and I spent time below cleaning up from our parties and visitors and thinking ahead to the dinner we would have that night. I had found that I could even make a Jell-O salad by putting a lid on the top of Tupperware. Even if we hit rough waters, my dinners could usually be ready ahead of time so that when we came into port and were besieged with interviews, I didn't have to worry about feeding two hungry men. I kept climbing up to the bridge that morning to check our progress on the charts. We were accumulating quite a stack of charts by now and we always felt we had one more notch in our belt when Bill folded up another one and tucked it away.

We had been forewarned about Pamlico (and Albemarle) Sound and had read how tricky and rough they could be. Thus, we were prepared for a bout with the ocean in this huge sound where land is not visible on either side. It looked to be a huge body of water on the chart and as we approached the river widened and before we knew it we were actually in the Sound. As Cecil later described it to the other boaters, Pamlico Sound was "a piece of cake." It was windy and we experienced some chop, but it was not near as severe as we were told it could be when highly agitated by the openness to the Atlantic. We were LUCKY!

We found Oriental, N.C., on our charts and the earlier article in *Trailer Boats* magazine provided us with more friends. In the small town of Oriental, a couple named Doug and Wade had read about us and our proposed journey from Miami to NY. They wrote us before we started and said that they hoped to make contact with us along the way. We had written to them from Miami and had just received an answer from them in Elizabeth City. On the appointed day at approximately 11 A.M. they would try to be in radio contact with us on the VHF. This was the day and it was closing in on 11 A.M. I had the VHF on, monitoring channel 26. After checking the charts Cec and Bill decided that our course must be quite close to the spot where Doug said he would try to contact us. I was sent below to call his unit. To my surprise he picked me up on my first call. Great luck! I called the gentlemen to come below where we took turns talking with this unknown voice. When Doug found out we anticipated tying up at Belhaven at the Riverfront Plantation, he told us he would like to drive his family to meet us that night. We agreed and signed off, anticipating meeting another new friend.

Back to the bridge we went again because the markers were scarce and we were now on a compass reading. The atmosphere was hazy and the wind picked up to 20 knots causing a heavy chop. Visibility was reduced to one to two miles. There was no land to be seen and we checked our chart and kept searching with binoculars to see if we couldn't find a distinguishable checkpoint. We had read that the wind sometimes moved the markers or storms ruined them so we were not surprised that some markers just were not there.

Finally a marker appeared on the horizon and Bill plowed for it. Upon arrival it had no number on our chart and Bill doubted if it was the 90-degree pivot marker we needed. We milled around a few times discussing this, then spotted a large power cruiser coming up behind us. This was the first ship we had sighted all morning. We decided that if that ship turned 90 degrees on the marker, it must be the one that we were searching for. The boat closed in and made the turn! "That's it!" shouted Cec and off we went in hot pursuit heading toward what we hoped was Bay River. The boat soon outdistanced us, for we had to throttle down with the battleship in tow.

The BICENTENNIAL's nose bobbed about and turned from side to side as if she was an unruly horse trying to throw her reins. We passed two interesting sights. One was a sailboat aground, but as they seemed to be in no other trouble and we could not spot a distress signal, we continued on. We did see one gigantic apparition blot out the horizon. A huge barge came by with a whole restaurant on top of it. Bill contacted the captain and we learned that this restaurant was making its way from Lake Okeebogee, FL on up to the north end of North Carolina. The barge size was 95 feet by 32 feet. They had had some hairy times when bad weather hit them. We realized they had many more problems than we would ever have.

Our elation at finding our way gave way to sudden apprehension. We all heard the noise coming from the engine compartment. Bill dived in and soon located the trouble. The water-pump pulley had lost its key and the pulley was coming off the engine. Fortunately we were in sight of a Coast Guard station. Pleasure boats were instructed NOT to tie up there, but if we didn't our engine would overheat and we did not want to perpetuate another problem. Bill said he would need another pulley before we could go on. We were without transportation and it looked as though we were in a very unpopulated area. With some trepidation we pulled in and the men went up to talk to the two Coast Guard men on duty. They came down to assess our situation and to exclaim over the battleship tied up at their dock. We were intruders, but they could not have been more helpful. One drove Cecil into town and to several stores and he managed to find a pulley. In the meantime I made sandwiches, and when the shoppers returned I invited the C.G. men to join us.

Bill tried out the new pulley and because Cec had not been able to get the correct size it was necessary to change the V belt. Then, it worked! "Any port in a storm," seemed to apply to us. Being a boater is not all smooth sailing but constant vigilance and maintenance. We enjoyed the protected area we were in. It was out of the wind and the sun shone and if we had to

144

break down this was a great place. But we still had more of the Sound to cross and we knew we must get going for Belhaven. We were anxious to tie up long before dark as the Sound was shallow and any kind of afternoon wind could create a problem for us. Any strong wind brings up five to six ft. waves, reportedly ten feet apart, and this could hinder our towing.

With much picture taking and shaking of hands and thank yous, we departed up the Pamlico River to the Belhaven Marina. What a pleasant sight, and we saw that the marina was jettied out to block the wind and tides. Later we were told that this sound can have all the water blown out of it and everything is aground. This marina was the only one half way between Morehead City and Elizabeth City, but its popularity was not only due to that fact. What a charming, sleepy beautiful Southern town. It had all the services a boater could want, and this tree-shaded town had an old plantation home. We tied up with ease alongside the dock. The large grassy area surrounding the plantation looked restful to us. No wonder this is one of the ICW's favored stops. The full-service marina had emergency service even at night. The tree-shaded streets have a good selection of stores within walking distance of the harbor. Belhaven has three shellfish factories and one of them, as a favor to traveling boaters, will sell fresh crabs. In season boatmen can tell whether the crabs are running by listening for the 5 P.M. "crab whistle." When the whistle blows its blast signal then there is enough crab to make it to work the next day. No whistle—no crabs—no work.

As we walked up to the entrance of this gracious plantation home and inside, we were transported back to another era. The place was crowded with antique furniture and dishes. We could envision the leisurely pace of the Southern people and the opulent way of life they must have enjoyed. We climbed the stairway admiring the hand-carved balustrade. When we peeked into the rooms upstairs, it was to find them seemingly left exactly as they would have been when the original owners lived there. It must be fun to stay overnight here, we said, but we belonged on our boat and decided we would come back after dinner to join Wade and to share an after-dinner drink and some get acquainted conversation.

Back at the boat I prepared dinner while the gentlemen enjoyed the cocktail hour up forward. "Do you two see what our dining room window is looking out on tonight? Look at that sunset."

I joined them and we sat in silence, digesting the show Mother Nature chose to share with us this time. We felt suspended in time. We all agreed we did not want this idyllic life to end. We were soaking it all up to be stored away for memory examination later. Right now our cup of contentment was full. We had the first of the two roughest sounds behind us. Our mechanical troubles all seemed to be small ones. We had many miles yet to go. The companionship was the best. We were content in a world of our own making. Our only challenges were from the water instead of the abrasiveness and complexities of the crowded cities from which we came. Days went by without a newspaper. The only TV we watched was when we were on it and could find a nearby set. Our biggest radio listening was to the Coast Guard weather report. Isolationists? Yes, but thoroughly enjoying every second of our withdrawal into this remote, insulated life on the water. We had created this insular idyll ourselves. Through problems solved and everything shared, we had become welded into a cohesive force. We enjoyed our port stops, loved meeting the people, jousted with the press and shared experiences with other boaters. We were also sufficient unto each other. We were alike in our purpose, there was total trust in one another and we functioned smoothly as a team. We knew that together we could meet any challenge. I might add also that there are no secrets on a boat! Two hungry men demanding dinner interrupted my reverie.

The first thing we saw on our way from the boat to the colonial mansion were the lightning bugs. Being Westerners, we had not seen these small insects. We were entranced with the darting creatures. They looked like miniature flashlights held by invisible elves who pranced around on the lawn intent on sending out their own fairy lit Morse code.

Entering the hotel, we could see the evening was in full swing. The dining room was filled and the table was laden with smorgasbord delicacies. The whole ambient scene had an air of elegant times from the past. We found a table and soon spotted a couple with a young boy coming in.

That's got to be the Carters, we decided, and waved at the man whose voice could now be attached to a person. We spent the next three hours talking with these nice new friends, hearing about their C.G. Auxiliary activities and learning about the small North Carolina town in which they lived. It was an interesting night. The Carters left and we stayed on. Mayor Smith, owner of the hotel, invited us upstairs, and we spent the rest of the evening in his secret hideaway. A few other fortunate guests were there, and we spent the time talking and dancing. Another late night and we threw ourselves into our bunks in the small hours.

Cec and I were up early the next A.M. and enjoyed a walk in the fog along the quaint streets of Belhaven. What a peaceful way of life these people enjoyed. Their lovely two-story homes, the flowers, the graceful, arching weeping willow trees all presented such a feeling of peace and uninterrupted harmony. Mayor Smith was up early too, and we joined him for coffee. Then it was time to waken Bill, get some breakfast and study our charts for today's run. It was on to Elizabeth City, where we planned to spend time repairing both boats. They were showing signs of wear and tear from their immersion in salt water and from the banging they were getting from unavoidable bumps.

We headed out of the jettied protected area and to challenge Albemarle Sound. The chop was very heavy, the compass was set to the chart, but the wind was causing plenty of drift. We searched for Alligator River, which was deep but has frequent snags outside the channel. Any departure from the main channel carries the risk of wheel damage In other words, don't take shortcuts.

I left the two boaters up on the bridge and went below to do chores and prepare for lunch. They were taking a beating from the wind, but didn't want to drive from the lower station because markers were not visible due to high waves. They needed to stay topside, but I could see they were tired. They came down one at a time for lunch. When it came time to find the marker for the two passages to keep on our course, the boys were unable to determine that the marker located was the current one on the chart. It had no number. Bill, stating he was going to use the "Brockett method," headed 330 degrees north, hoping to spot the correct entrance to the Pasquatank River. After several hours we did see a marker a mile or so ahead. Fortunately, it was a marker in the river which by now was three miles wide. From this marker going up the river was a snap. We arrived in Elizabeth City Marina by 4 P.M. and tied up. The marina was quiet, and since this was a weekday there were few visitors. We heard from several boaters that local fishermen get lost and go aground in the Sound. The C.G. stays busy trying to locate them. We had been successful and were proud and pleased that we had the two difficult sounds behind us. I prepared a good dinner for the mariners who had taken a beating on the bridge. Our late hours from the night before caught up with us. We fell into bed early and slept soundly.

Elizabeth City is a good stopover for the beginning of the Dismal Swamp Canal route. The marina/boatyard is located right on the town waterfront, and it was a place where they allowed us to pull out the battleship for some necessary face-lift repairs. We were in good company. The shrimpers hauled out here, too and did their clean up operations. Cec and I were up early for he had a 7 A.M. Greyhound bus to catch for Morehead City to jump the rig forward. I walked him up the dock and bid a fond farewell. He would be gone all day.

Back to CELEBRATION and I found an unrecognizable lump in a bunk; however, the aroma of coffee soon filled the interior of the boat and Bill finally decided to join the land of the living. We had decided that the morning would be given over to cleaning up the interior of CELEBRATION II. That afternoon we would take her out and explore the outer bay and look for the childhood haunts of our friend and benefactor, Preston. After breakfast I pulled all the carpets and lined them up along the dock where they received a much-needed sweep down. Bill scrubbed the decks and sides of CELEBRATION, and by the time we were finished we were quite proud of our handiwork.

After checking with the dock master about our course, we were off to find Old Wharf Bay. Everything looks different from the water, and the only description of the property was as if found from a land base. We had fun poking in and out of inlets. The water was very shallow, only 2 ½ feet in spots and we did not linger long in those areas. The river at this point is very wide since it is the beginning of Albemarle Sound. By late afternoon it was beginning to cloud over, and the threatening scud which enveloped the sky looked as if it had a potential for liquid downpour. The suddenness with which weather could suddenly erupt never failed to surprise me. The forces of nature treated us kindly this afternoon. We slowly made our way back to port, enjoying the beauty surrounding us. The silver streaks of rain sliced down and across the wind ruffled waters. The gray/silver of the streaming tinsel-like showers had an eerie, unreal look. An occasional fragmentary appearance of the sun gave the water a shimmery, tremulous light. It cast a spell and we said little, but watched the unfolding of this special show.

We docked in late afternoon and it was necessary for me to go shopping as we had been several days without replenishing the ship's larder. Wishing to give Cec a sumptuous welcome back dinner, I told Bill I was going to walk to the store. He wouldn't hear of this mundane way to go. Borrowing a loaner bike he had noticed by the marina store, he ordered me to ride on the back of it with him. With misgivings I climbed on. Prudence bade me close my eyes. We took off down hill, over the bridge, gathering great momentum. The out-of-control was terrifying. "Slow down, slow down," I shrieked at him. I might as well have been talking to the wind as the bike had no brakes. Thank goodness he didn't drive the boat as he did that bicycle. We came careening into the local supermarket and made an abrupt stop against a post.

I slid off onto the pavement, actually glad to have terra firma under me. With a few well-chosen words about Bill's background, I picked myself up trying to salvage a bit of dignity. At least it would be uphill all the way back.

I was enchanted with Southern shopping. There were so many new mysterious things for me to learn about Southern cooking. One table in the produce section was devoted to a table piled high with "greens." I watched with curiosity as ladies filled their brown bags full of mustard greens, okra and strange looking weeds. We loaded up with groceries and proceeded back to the boat in a more dignified manner.

We watched for Cec and soon spotted the truck and trailer pulling into the repair yard. After hearing about his long bus ride and the trip back, we sat down for dinner. I was glad I had prepared a gourmet-type feast: gray fish, fruit salad, vegetable, homemade biscuits, cake. My crew seemed to appreciate my culinary offerings. We talked a bit longer, took a walk and hit the bunks around 10 P.M. It had been another long day for everyone.

After breakfast Cec and Bill worked on setting up the battleship in the marina repair yard. They hauled her out of the water on the trailer, then cranked her onto sawhorses. She was battle wounded and needed repainting. Some interior equipment needed repair or replacement. They worked all morning on her. That afternoon we took the truck and went looking for a proper pulley for CELEBRATION's Chrysler engine. This was to no avail.

Not being very successful there, we decided to amuse ourselves by trying to find Preston's property by land, since we had not found it by sea. We drove down some fascinating dirt roads which were always protected by hordes of dogs that all barked and chased us with a fierce demeanor. Eventually we found the acreage by Old Trap. It faced the Pasquatank River and we could see the ICW markers way off in the distance. It was a lovely, quiet spot, but we noticed that the land was being eroded at the water's edge when the waves washed on to the land. We would report this to Preston. We spent an hour, not only checking out the land, but Bill had heard there were water moccasins about, so he passed the time beating the bushes for snakes. We speculated what he would do if he actually hooked one. He found nothing. It was a lazy afternoon, and by the time we were ready to leave, the thunderstorms were trying to do their thing again. The clouds seemed to create their own moisture, and it showered for a while on the way back to the dock. The humidity seemed high that night and the temperature was 60 degrees.

We decided that Bill needed to have time to do more work on the boat and make contact with people who were interested in purchasing a Land n' Sea craft. Cec and I took the truck and headed out for Kitty Hawk to film the spot where the Wright brothers had left their mark on history. We enjoyed our trip out to the N.C. coast. We were fascinated with the site of the first airplane flight. The lonely, windswept sand dunes were an ideal spot for what the two brothers were attempting. We were transported back in time and imagined how exciting it must have been for the two bicycle repairmen to have accomplished what was said to be impossible. The site is well preserved and the first plane is housed inside a building where it is protected from the weather. As we walked slowly around the tiny plane, we were impressed with its fragility. It looked to be put together with wire, cloth and glue. We filmed the bicycle chain and sprocket which turned the propeller. We wanted our future audiences to be as impressed and admiring as we were at the wonderful accomplishment.

We arrived back at Elizabeth City to find that Bill had done a lot of paperwork and had picked up a new 'ah-oo-ga' horn for the USS BICENTENNIAL. He had also taken some would-be customers out for a demo on the river. It had become rough and they had to head back. With part of the late afternoon left, Cec and Bill put the battleship back in the water. Bill would give her a test run and try out the new horn. He disappeared down the waterway and later reported he had attacked the canoe team from Albemarle College. The schoolchildren then saw him and came back to the marina, following him along the shoreline. We soon had the usual gathering of fascinated youngsters. The local press came down for a lengthy interview and many pictures. Again we were impressed with the friendliness and hospitality of the Southern people. As the day drew to a close, we found we were somewhat unwilling to leave this lovely spot. We sensed the big city crowding of larger ports which lay ahead and we were not anxious to leave this golden part of our expedition

Checking the chart, we realized that we had two choices to head for Chesapeake Bay. One route is for large, commercial traffic. The other is the narrow, quiet Dismal Swamp, most appropriately named. We chose the latter course. This route is one of the country's oldest canals. It was first surveyed by George Washington and still has vestiges of some of the original bulkheads lining the banks. Abundant wildlife and unusual plants line the canal. We read that there was a nine-foot projected depth and two locks, one at each end. We had never done a lock before. We anticipated cruising slowly through this area, for we had heard much of its history. There are numerous tales of lost hunters, renegade Indians, runaway slaves and bootleggers. It is also full of deer, otter, rattlesnakes, water moccasins and birds.

We headed out of the marina and began searching for Turner's Cut, which is a man-made cut leading to the first lock on the Dismal Swamp. The lock was to raise us nine feet. The skipper gave us our instructions for trying our first lock. Ordinarily a lock is a fairly simple procedure, particularly a small one such as we were approaching. If the lock is open, one is free to enter in. Sometimes the lockmaster shouts instructions as to which side he wishes the boats to tie on. As we peered ahead we could see that there was already one sailboat in the lock tied up to the port side. We were to proceed in slowly; Cec would be at the bow for that tie-up, I would be on the stern, doing my usual "fend off the battleship" routine. It looked simple. We were going slowly. Nervously, I looked forward. By now we were a competent, smooth-functioning team. Why did I feel this sense of apprehension? Perhaps because by this time I knew that even the best laid plans of an experienced boater can suddenly go sadly awry, and peaceful moments of boating bliss can instantly be turned into excruciating minutes of panic. Although Bill had slowed down it was not enough and in we charged. *Quel horror*!! Both craft came hurtling into the middle of the lock. The dock master and everyone on the sailboat were watching. We were not exactly inconspicuous with our battleship tailing us. They were fascinated as we suddenly did a 180 and ended up facing the wrong way. We were quite embarrassed with this amazing gyration, but decided to brazen it out—as though everyone entered a lock and ended up backward. Of course, when the lock filled with water we had to execute the same maneuver to get back out. We did another 180! *Oh well*, we thought. *We'll never see these people again.*

We soon forgot about our acrobatic circus performance and became lost in the beauty of the swamp waters. The waters are stained a clear, dark amber color coming from the trees' roots. The water is sweet, pure, long-lasting and was widely used for drinking and storing in barrels during the 19th century when sailboats used this canal. It is said the tannic acid is what keeps it sweet so long.

We could not have petitioned for a more beautiful spring day. The sun was out, the no-see-ums were taking the day off, the clouds floated by in lazy clumps of cotton. The water was so quiet that we could see the sky silhouetted in it with a sharp staccato outline. We talked about casks of this "juniper water" being carried aboard sailing vessels on long ocean voyages. It was the Dismal Swamp water that sustained much of the blockading Union fleet in the War Between the States. The uniqueness of the strange shaped swamp trees fascinated us: drooping moss with their gentle, grasping tentacles, wound in loving embrace around grotesque, gnarled tree trunks. White egrets and birds belying description ornamented the woods as cherished ornaments decorate a Christmas tree. We were so surrounded by beauty that we could not go below for fear of losing precious minutes of just looking.

Boats using this canal must slow down to at least eight knots and the Corps of Engineers suggests six knots so that wakes will not damage the shoreline. "No Wake" signs are posted for the boater, but we needed no reminder to cruise slowly through this magnificent scenery. That day remains indelibly etched in my memory. Bill and I were on the bridge, lost in silence and awed by what we were seeing unfold on all sides of us. Cec had gone completely wild with his camera and was hanging over the bow, shooting cloud reflections in the water. He tried to tape some of the birdcalls we could hear from deep within the swamp. I did manage to go below once to make sandwiches for all of us but was back topside as soon as I could scramble up.

The three of us were sitting quietly munching sandwiches when Bill let out a yell. He was pointing down, and as we looked we realized we had an escort. A water moccasin was swimming lazily through the water on our starboard side, keeping perfect time with us. It undulated languidly as it glided through the tobacco- colored waters. The enchantment of the swamp embraced us. The snags alongside the banks looked like sentinels guarding the secret lairs of long-gone pirates. The channel gave off an eerie, otherworld aura. We wished we could anchor, take a canoe and explore some of the hidden side passages which beckoned us into the heart of swampland.

As all things must, our suspension in time had to come to an end. We saw ahead of us the lock which would lower us to Chesapeake Bay's level. This time, we swore, we would execute our entrance into the lock with cunning and skill. This we did and were soon tied up in the lock along with a few other boats. The lockmaster had apparently heard of us for he came hustling along the wall of the lock hastening to check out "a battleship." Evidently, the lockmaster at the other end had telephoned ahead and alerted this one that "a battleship is coming through." The lockmaster at this end was obviously relieved that he did not have to deal with the real thing. As the water drained out, we were gently lowered and could see that the canal was broadening out into the Chesapeake Bay and the busy Norfolk shipyards. We were in no hurry to end this less populated southern portion of our trip, but on we must go if we were to be the Paul Reveres of the waterway and deliver our schoolchildren's letters before school was out for the summer. We were very content in our semi-isolated world and our connection with the water. Both men said, "Coming ashore is a bummer!"

HOW TO PLAY ADMIRAL

A few miles of twists and turns and—WHAM—there we were, right in the midst of the busy Norfolk shipping area. What a shock—big industrial buildings, cement walls, brick factories, steel mills, gigantic drawbridges. Huge barges and tugs were all around us, oil was on the water and we found we were alternately repelled and attracted by this sudden shift in scenery. This was an assault on our senses and it was difficult to adjust to the abrupt change from our love affair with nature. We had felt like welcome guests in the labyrinth of the prehistoric phenomena we had just left. Now we were bombarded from all sides by man's inventions—awesome but overpowering in their gluttonizing of the land and bay waters.

We were accustomed to our slower speed and found that boats were scurrying about the enormous harbor, very busy in their workaday world. We felt no kinship with this rapid pace of life; however, we found the industrious activity of the bay very interesting and we began reading names of vessels from faraway ports. There were freighters, merchantmen, and Coast Guard vessels. Destroyers and small naval craft represented the Navy. Tugs were puffing determinedly at large cargo ships, busying them into position at nearby docks. It was a scene of great activity. We felt small and insignificant amongst the tonnage of steel surrounding us; but then we discovered again that even though we were tiny amidst the behemoths, we were unique. Horns began tooting at us, friendly waves came from passing ships, cheers from a passing Navy cruisers—it made us realize that we were a welcome break in the working world in these waters.

A Navy ship passing reminded us that we had better begin to look for our docking area. What a privilege to have permission to come into the huge Norfolk Navy shipping area. This proved to be no easy job. Although the Mayport and Charleston naval personnel had previously briefed us as to how to approach the docking area, it all looked so big and spread out that we were not quite sure where to turn in. It would never have been a problem if we had been just a cruising ship alone, but we always had our appendage tied on behind us and never relished getting ourselves into a position where we had to back out. We approached with caution and tried to identify buildings and harbor openings.

Bill, with his uncanny sense of direction, decided upon one channel which looked like a quiet area and in we went. Rounding a point, we were startled as we gazed at the huge Navy ships docked all around us. We felt like intruders when we saw the aircraft carriers USS Nimitz, USS Kennedy and various destroyers. Our small battleship in her red, white and blue colors and fluttering flags looked like an overdressed midget cavorting about amidst a group of dignified, solemn-faced, gray judges. We were uneasy. Would the Navy welcome us? Had they even heard of us or were we the intruders we felt we might be?

Our fears proved to be unfounded as we unerringly came right into the proper dock (thank you, Bill) and were met by several friendly sailors who helped us tie up. The PAO (Public Affairs Officer), Lt. Scott, came rushing down in his car to greet us after a message was radioed to him. We could not have been welcomed in a more hospitable way. We were finding that the Navy loved our boat as much as we did and had a great appreciation of the patriotism and filming of history that we were trying to accomplish. In a short time we had been cordially received and were escorted over to the yacht basin which was the admiral's dock. We had a *safe* three-day tie-up ahead.

Thus began another chapter of our trip, which we called, "How To Feel Like An Admiral In One Easy Lesson." Lt. Scott escorted us onto the Norfolk base and showed us different places we could visit. We were to have PX privileges, coffee shop availability, the Dog mess (?) and the Officer's Club. The *coup de gras* was when the PAO drove us on to Admiral's Row and we pulled up in front of one of a series of old gingerbread three-story mansions. This particular one was built during WW II to house the many brass who were based here.

We were escorted into this spacious, columned colonial home and found that we were three of only five occupants. Two officers were housed temporarily in the visitor quarters. Downstairs we found a steward who was always ready to serve breakfast...or do anything! He brought out coffee every time we appeared. We wandered about this beautiful place looking at all the pictures of former Navy officers who had ruled over this grand residence. We imaged receptions and parties which must have taken place in the many great rooms downstairs.

We located a TV and vowed to watch ourselves here after we did "our thing" for the Navy and Norfolk media. My first job was always to call all the media contacts we had been given or to answer phone calls from ports ahead anxious to know when we would arrive. I learned to carry change for pay phones, a credit card, pen and paper to write down information for future meetings. The boys expected me to disappear and set up the press dates. Today was no different. It was late in the afternoon when we were finally squared away. A lieutenant was kind enough to take Cecil to the Greyhound bus depot, where he caught a bus back to Elizabeth City. This was one of our "movement of equipment" problems, but Cecil never seemed to mind going back for our transportation. Many times he would take his camera and film things that we had missed along the way. Later on when viewing our film, we were glad he had filled in so well.

Bill and I decided to eat at the closed Officers' Mess that night and did so. Considering the very low price of our steak dinners, we had a discussion as to whether he and Cec should have stayed in the Marines and Army. After dinner we went over to the Officer's Club where we danced and waited for Cec's return. Several parties were in full swing and there was a good band playing. The Naval base seemed like an island unto itself in the midst of all the industry we had just seen. Cec came in around 10 P.M., and after hearing the tale of his journey we all danced to the great music, then turned in at midnight. We made our way up three flights of stairs where we had the whole floor to ourselves. We felt very special…and honored.

We awakened to the sound of rain, and it proved to be an off and on day of clouds and showers. We were due at Lt. Scott's office at headquarters, where we met several ranking officers. All seemed interested in our battleship's story and were eager to help us. We felt that any publicity we could give back to them was the least we could do to help out their Navy recruiting. That afternoon they sent two TV stations and four newspaper reporters to cover us. We had lunch at the Navy exchange with the base photographer who wanted a story for his Navy news. We had many visitors on board that afternoon and welcomed quite a few sailors. Bill struck up a friendship with one particular CPO who said he could procure some Coors beer for him. This, being more of a West Coast product, delighted Bill. When we left he had several six paks of Coors in our ice chest. That night we had dinner at the Officers Club and watched our two TV appearances. They gave us several minutes, and we were pleased the way Cec and the battleship had come across. The weather report said that tomorrow, Armed Forces Day, would be another repeat of today's weather—cloudy, showery, with intermittent peeks at the sun.

Armed Forces Day! The base was open to the public. May 17 and the day was colored gray. The steward noiselessly appeared and we had a healthy breakfast. We walked over to the boat where Bill checked CELEBRATION for fuel and pumped the bilge. Cec readied his ship as he was to go out and "attack" the *Nimitz* and *Kennedy* carriers. This was a request on the part of the PAO that we participate in Armed Forces Day We launched Cec then took CELEBRATION II out to watch him perform. It grew rainy and chilly on the bridge and the water was rough, not a perfect day for boating. We watched with binoculars while the tiny BICENTENNIAL skittered along the gray sides of the aircraft carrier. Cec said he had never felt quite so small as he looked up, up at the floating giants. Rain was driving in on him and for a while he sought refuge under the deck of the immense vessel. We watched the sailors and visitors gaze down at the miniature ship and wave. His attack with the water squirting turrets must have brought about some laughs for everyone as we saw them gesturing and pointing down at him.

After a final cruise we escorted Cec back to the yacht basin and our dock. Both men were soaked. We tied the ships up and the men went for dry clothing. What would our game plan be for the rest of the afternoon and our last night on base? We knew we could not pass up a meal in the O Club. The food was delicious and the "price was right." We sat around on CELEBRATION a bit too long and barely made it to dinner on time. One learns that the stewards set the protocol for Navy meals. One arrives for dinner at the correct time and one does not dilly-dally overly long. The waiters really lit a fire under us. Fast-moving white-jacketed mess boys whisked our meals out. As soon as we laid down our forks, our plate was whipped out from under our nose. We managed to get down the main meal and dessert was upon us, lights were going out and we were the last in the mess. Feeling properly chastised and repentant, we left for a base movie. We consoled ourselves on licorice and candy bars and saw a very funny movie.

We were up early and were greeted with clouds and fog. We said goodbye and offered profuse thanks to our Navy friends for all their hospitality. We checked our charts; Cec checked his road map, for he had elected to take our rig across the bay to the next stop, Wormley Creek in Yorktown. He would pick up our mail and we would meet at the marina. We needed the truck because we wanted to drive to Jamestown and Williamsburg for filming at the next port.

With a final wave to all, we cast off and stopped within a few miles to top off our gas tanks and buy a ship chart we didn't have. I got out the charts and joined Bill topside to help him wend his way across the very crowded channel. Norfolk is an exciting harbor. The piers are enormous and filled with every kind of craft. We watched the tugs maneuvering great ships into cargo piers. The wake created by big ships, even when going dead slow, was scary. Our *Guide* advised us to keep well to our side of the main channel, ready to dodge outside if need be. Depths alongside would permit this. We had to set a compass course because of visibility. Markers were far apart and after some hours we were pleased to find the entrance directly into the mouth of the York River. We rode great swells that were four to five feet high, but they never broke. The markers were closer and we proceeded inland to Wormley Creek which had a very narrow channel and was quite shallow in spots.

Since this was a Sunday, there were many visitors and yacht club members to help us tie up our two craft. Cecil was nowhere in sight and we found out 30 minutes later that he had become lost. Going by water and going by land to the same place are two entirely different processes. Cec reported many unmarked roads, street signs hard to find, no shoulder on the road and everything was so green and overgrown that he was frequently lost. It always seemed simple when we compared charts and road maps, but trying to find a marina alongside the water often proved to be a difficult task. When he did arrive, he promptly climbed into the battleship and put on a fine show for the visitors. Our press and TV had gone ahead of us, and our reception could not have been nicer. We ate dinner on board and since we had an outside berth with a beautiful view I insisted we use the forward dining salon. We might not be as posh as the Navy's O. Club, but we were happy to be back in our own quarters. As I lay in my bunk that night listening to the slap-slap of the waves on our boat, I was glad to be back in a quiet marina, but I also wondered what it would be like to go into New York Harbor. What a challenge must be ahead for all of us. Navigating and reading charts was old stuff, but having experienced the heavy traffic in the lower part of the Chesapeake, I wondered about future busy, city ports.

We were up by 7:30 A.M. and I gave the crew ham and eggs, which put them in an excellent mood. Today, we decided would be "pick-up-mail day, cut-hair day, deliver-schoolchildren's-letters day and meet- the-mayor day." Into Williamsburg we would go and hopefully get our mail in General Delivery at the first post office. So far mail stops had been successful, although in larger cities we sometimes had to go to two post offices before we found the right one.

Williamsburg was enchanting, and the drive from Yorktown to get there was beautiful. There is no place more colorful than the South in the spring with the green trees, the winding, unmarked roads and the profusion of flowers. We found Williamsburg well preserved. We were unprepared for the extensive renovation and adherence to detail that we found. Cars are not allowed to drive the streets in the old section of town. We found that parking was a problem and we finally went into a "no-parking-don't-do-it" lot. We debated the wisdom of doing this, but decided that as we were Californians, the city fathers would be lenient with out-of-state-visitors. (Hah on that! Three months later a letter found us, and we PAID.)

We started out on foot and thoroughly explored the famous old city. What fun wandering the wide streets and grassy areas of colonial times. It was easy to be transported back 200 years. The clip-clop of the horses pulling the carriages through the streets matched the era of the homes and buildings we filmed. We were captivated by the gracious old homes and the craft shops with their European-type signs hanging out in front of the stores. Children played in the stockades where Black Beard's pirates had once been held. We were impressed with the history of our country's heritage. Since the three of us were Californians, we knew intimately only of the missions and Gold Rush days to visit; but here were our early beginnings, our roots, and we were reliving the history of our forefathers. Two hundred years suddenly didn't seem so long ago. The courageous people of colonial time seemed close to us, and we sympathized with their fierce desire to be independent and to forge this new land into a viable, workable nation of freedom for all.

After this remarkable visit, we wandered back to the newer section of Williamsburg where we had lunch at a lovely restaurant. After some shopping it was back to the truck. Alas! The city fathers had not been compassionate with out-of-state visitors and we found a king-size parking ticket tucked in our windshield. We were ordered to pay a $2 fine. Casually, we filed the ticket away in the glove compartment, "intending" to pay it. Suffice to say we completely forgot about it, but the police force is efficient. Three months later and our fine had increased in "value"!

Our next stop was city school headquarters. We found the superintendent's office in an old home that was covered with ivy. After being ushered into this lovely place, we climbed three flights of stairs. There we found the superintendent and one of his assistants, who personally accepted the L.A. schoolchildren's letters. This small town lack of bureaucracy was in such contrast to our own L.A. city system with its monolithic officialdom set up that we simply could not take in the modesty and informality of it. We were warmly welcomed and assured that the children would have our special letters and that teachers would be urged to have their classes respond to the pen pal mail.

Our next stop on the way back to the boat was to the Yorktown Naval Weapons Station. Lt. Scott from Norfolk had notified this Naval station that we were on our way, and the PAO was expecting us. The commander of the station invited us in and we told him our story. He was typical of the courteous, friendly Navy people we were meeting. At the conclusion of our visit we were given cigarette lighters with the emblem of the depot and coffee mugs inscribed with the insignia of the C.O. Commander Young also had his PAO notify Washington D.C. of our anticipated arrival date. The local papers were notified and tomorrow we would have interviews on board boat at our marina.

On our way back we also made one phone call to someone Cec and I kept referring to as the "balloon lady." We set up an interview with her for the next morning in Newport News, VA. Since it was late we settled for dinner at a small steak house. Hair cutting would have to wait until the light of another day.

We were early birds the next day, for it promised to be a full one. We had a press interview for the local paper, then it was off to meet Mrs. Valerie Horner in Newport News. At last we were to meet our balloon lady. We had no trouble finding Valerie Horner, and soon Cecil, Bill and I were seated in her comfortable home. We taped her story of how she had noticed a bright-colored balloon in her backyard. It had shrunk considerably in size. She picked it up and was about to toss it in the trash. When she noticed the card tied on to it, she read it and her surprise and shock surfaced when she realized the distance it had traveled. Even a year later as we talked with Valerie, her amazement was evident. We filmed her in her yard and she pointed to the spot where she had recovered it. Her description also explained that a few more feet and she would not have found the balloon, for there were dense woods directly behind her home. We all surmised that many of the balloons sent up from San Fernando Valley schools must have been carried out into the Atlantic Ocean, although no boats ever reported finding any. It was enough to know that quite a few balloons had made their way 3000 miles across the USA.

Valerie gave us a newspaper clipping of the story which was printed at the time of the discovery. Later, it was our privilege to deliver the newspaper article directly to the 5th grade California girl who had sent the message. We decided this day should be called "coming full circle."

After this fun morning, we went back to the boat for haircutting time. Bill sat quietly under a tree while I performed hair surgery to the best of my ability. Cecil escaped my razor this time, for he did not trust my cutting talents. He always seemed to be able to be absent at this particular time, and it was not until he became desperate with hair in his eyes that he would finally consent to a trim.

That afternoon many parents brought their children down to the docks to see us after school hours. Cecil and Bill took turns taking the battleship out. They engaged in a mock war with many teenagers who were charging about in small rafts and canoes. The afternoon was fun! I watched all these antics from the bow windows where I was ensconced with my typewriter. The shrieks from the youngsters corresponded with the water being shot from the turrets. Cecil filmed much of this and we laugh today over boys clutching at their hearts, then toppling over into the water. I thought, *Men never seem to tire of playing war.*

A FREE DINNER AT A GREAT PRICE

That night we had been invited to dinner at a famous restaurant called Nick's Seafood. Mr. and Mrs. Matthews' restaurant was well known in the area and the Greek owners were beloved by the surrounding community. These successful immigrants to America had prospered and grown from small beginnings and were so grateful to live in our land of opportunity that they had just given some large acreage to the US government for a historical site. This generous one-million-dollar gift would further enhance the area, for Yorktown was very close to this place. These kind people had heard of our Bicentennial efforts and invited us to be their guests for dinner.

What a welcome we later had at the restaurant, but first we had to get there. Mrs. Matthew wanted us to come by boat(s) and this we did; but the usual afternoon breeze had turned into a strong, stiff wind. With some trepidation we launched the battleship and CELEBRATION separately, then put the BICENTENNIAL under tow out in the bay and headed into the wind for a journey of a few miles. The wind increased in velocity, and although it was not a cold wind, it certainly was a strong one. There was considerable chop, and when we came in sight of the restaurant which overlooked the water, we released Cecil, who had climbed into his ship. By this time we knew how seaworthy the little craft was, and I did not feel any apprehension about his going alone. In fact, he was having an easier time of it than Bill and I were. Our tie-up was going to be a bad one, we could tell. There was no dock for us, and we would have to tie up to a rusty old water scow which was using the only docking space available.

Bill ordered me to put out fenders on the starboard side. It was hard to judge what our approach should be for the *Gungha Din* (as the inhospitable looking rusty scow was named) was tossing and throwing her bow and stern like a wild horse. Bill made several passes at the hulk and each time pulled away. Welded pieces of metal protruded from the *Gungha Din*, and I tried to anticipate where the bumpers should go. Cecil was patrolling off our port, helplessly watching us attempt some kind of a tie-up where the sides of

162

CELEBRATION II would not be ripped apart and damaged.

Then Bill yelled, "This is it. Get ready!" He cut the engine just as we came within reach of the tossing vessel. Simultaneously, we both jumped for the *Gungha Din*, Bill from the bow, I from the stern. By this time we had a large restaurant audience. One seasoned boater took pity on us and came to help. CELEBRATION pitched and tossed like a wild thing. It was almost impossible to control her. It was all we could do to jump from her onto the *Gungha Din* and keep our balance. While our boat plunged up and down, we kept pushing her away from the lethal spikes protruding from the old water tanker. Bill managed to tie his end fast with a couple of bumpers to cushion the distance between the two boats. Our rescuer had been helping me hold off the stern while Bill wrestled with his part. Between the three of us we did do a tie up which was secure, but wild. "Only took us 40 minutes for that one," announced a tired skipper.

Now it was time to turn our attention to Cecil, who was patiently patrolling the waters and watching our dockside antics. We could see it would be next to impossible to tie the BICENTENNIAL up to CELEBRATION, so Bill decided we must string her out between the stern of CELEBRATION and a gigantic piling along the shoreline. This was no easy feat. First we had to get Cec out of his tossing boat onto our tossing boat. As he slowly edged his way toward CELEBRATION, I wondered how we would ever catch him. Up went the superstructure, and Cec threw us a line. Bill caught it on the third try. At least we had a line on him, but how to get Cec out without dumping him into the river and without damaging the boat was another challenge. Both boats alternately rocked and rolled, never simultaneously coming to the same level at any one time. Bill and I sat on the port side of the mother ship and used our feet to catch the battleship. By this time we were already tired battling the elements and were anxious to get this production over and done—ON with our social life!

Our kindly benefactor hopped onto our boat and stretched out a hand to Cecil. While Bill and I held the boat, Cec awkwardly climbed out, long legs stretching across the wildly churning waters. One size-12 shoe was at last on the deck and he managed to pull the rest of his 6'2" frame under the railing and onto the stern. "Wow! She's a bitch out there!" was Cec's only remark. (*Why*, I wondered, *is everything always a "she"?*) It didn't seem to matter if it was a truck, car, boat, refrigerator or anything balky, men always referred to the item as "she." (I made a mental note to challenge this derogatory inference at a later date.)

More shouting interrupted my reverie. "Pat, grab the stern line!" Obediently I grabbed, then handed it up to our rescuer, who climbed back across the *Gungha Din* and onto a high dock. Cec and Bill eased the BI out diagonally across CELEBRATION II's stern. Now she was controllable. They made her fast between the boat and the piling, and even though everything was pitching and rolling, we felt everything was safely secured against the elements. With one final check of lines, we decided it was time to abandon our unruly charges. We were all dressed for dinner, yet here we were with our usual boating problems. By this time we knew we could usually lick any obstacles that crossed our path, but I had not planned to do this in my gussy-it-up outfit. Spending the better part of an hour on docking and tie-up was decidedly not in our plans.

With relief we clambered over the rusty frame of *Gungha Din*, up onto the high dock and made our way up to the restaurant. The restaurant guests applauded all of us. We were made to feel so welcome by Mrs. Nick Matthews, who complimented us extravagantly on our Bicentennial efforts. Then she told us to order anything we wanted on the menu. She made us feel very special. We dwindled over a delicious seafood dinner in elegant splendor. Again that feeling crept over us as the three of us sat there. How lucky could we be? We dilly-dallied over dinner for a long time and thanked Mrs. Matthew when we reluctantly felt we must leave. We had the feeling that she and her husband did generous things for others whenever they could.

We were relieved to find that the wind had died down considerably and our two boats were still tied securely to the rusty wreck at the dock. At least we could cast off in the moonlight and make our way back to our marina with no problem. As usual, when we came near enough our boats to be identified with them, a crowd would gather. This time it was people sitting out on the terrace of a next-door bar. They had been wondering about the battleship and CELELBRATION II. When they found they had the owners within their grasp, they insisted we stop at their tables and have drinks with them. We spent the rest of the evening sitting outside, conversing with interesting people while the red hurricane lamps flickered in the breeze and cast their dancing shadows on us.

Around 11 P.M. we all decided it was time to call it a day, and several of our new-found friends offered to help us cast off. Climbing back over the dirty barge, I laughed to myself. Here I was, all decked out in pink pants and top, yet groveling my way through rust and tossing seas. How many women "get" to go through what I did for a lovely dinner? Miraculously, I had stayed clean with no grease or rust marks on my party pants.

Stepping over greasy lines and equipment, I made it onto CELEBRATION II. It was good to feel her under my feet. Cecil climbed into the USS BICLENTENNIAL and we shoved him away from our stern. He circled a few times, his port and starboard lights doing dances, low to the water. Bill turned on our riding lights, started the engine, and I readied our lines as our friends gave us a shove. We were off. What a gorgeous night. Bill took the bridge controls and I sat beside him watching the shadowy shape of the battleship as she led the way back to our marina home.

We discussed the generosity of the people we were meeting and the reception we were receiving. It still surprised us. How anxious people were to hear good things about their country and how eager they were to help those they felt were trying to spread the word. After a half hour of travel we found our starboard turn into Wormley Creek. Slowly we made our way in and tied up quietly. Cecil waited for us to finish securing, then came on in and as the BICENTENNIAL's bow gently bumped the stern of CELEBRATION. It almost seemed as if a tired puppy was nosing up against the safety and security of its mother. The two boats had been through a lot together. An invisible yoke seemed to connect them in some mysterious way. Maybe it was our shared adventures which produced this invisible phenomena. Whatever it was, we knew we were sharing an unusual and special experience, probably never to be repeated. The now-quiet water, the moonlight shimmering through the trees, and the wail of an unidentified bird—all these things wove a spell around us. Quietly, we made everything secure for the night. No words needed to be spoken. We all "just knew."

JAMESTOWN AND THE 'JIMMY' RIVER

In keeping with trying to film "East Coast history for West Coast children" (we used this expression A LOT with the news people), Cec and I headed out early the next day A.M. for historic Jamestown. We went by truck rather than by ship, as there are no facilities for transient boats in the Jamestown area. This interesting spot is famous for being the first English settlement along the East Coast. At Jamestown there is a small reconstruction of life, as the first settlers knew it, including mud and thatch houses and the old fort. Moored near the dock are replicas of the original colonizing boats. It was a memorable experience to board and walk the decks of the sturdy *Susan Constant*, *Godspeed*, and *Discovery*. Part of the narrative in our film was to include our remarks, "Imagine living on these tiny boats in crowded conditions. They are so small." My admiration for the sturdy pioneers who crossed the Atlantic continued to grow. Having been in rough weather on some large cruise ships, we could not visualize how the tiny boats survived the rough seas they must have encountered.

That afternoon we picked up Bill and headed for Newport News, VA. Cec and Bill were to visit the Mariner's Museum while I borrowed the truck. My afternoon mission was twofold. One errand was to try to find a trophy shop where I could buy a plaque which could be engraved to present to Bill at the completion of our trip. Although we didn't want to think about it, we could begin to see that our trip might be over in about a month and we wanted something special for him. We had decided upon an engraved plaque which Bill could hang on his wall.

The other part of my afternoon turned out to be an emotional one. Some 50 years before, my parents had suddenly married in a small church somewhere in Newport News, VA. I had heard the story from my parents many times. My father had been slated to go overseas during WW I and had sent for my mother to come from Iowa and bid him goodbye. My grandfather's last words to her as he put her and my grandmother on the train were, "Don't you marry that man under any circumstances." My father, being an excellent salesman his whole life, had sat my mother on the banks of the St. James River one night (they called it the Jimmy River) and talked her into marrying him the next day. With only her own mother and my dad's Army buddy for witnesses, my parents were quietly married in the small St. Paul's Episcopal church, Newport News, VA. I had heard the story about how loud the men's Army boats had sounded as they clomped down the aisle for the ceremony— and my mother's feelings of fright that she had disobeyed her father. There had been five participants in the ceremony. Nevertheless, I couldn't help but feel that she had done a remarkably courageous thing, for the two enjoyed almost 50 years of a happy, fruitful married life.

Although my mother had passed on, I knew that my father would enjoy hearing that I had finally seen the little church where it had all started. I eagerly sought out the address of the church and found it in a quiet area, near the water. A delightful caretaker showed me into the church, and when she heard my story she insisted on leaving me alone with my own thoughts. It was a half hour which alternately delighted and pained me. I walked down the aisle my mother had walked as a young, probably timid young girl. I was able to transport myself back into her position and imagine what the small wedding must have been like. The details were vivid in my thoughts as I relived her experience. In the vestibule I even found a picture of the minister who had married them. I made a mental note to call my father in California that night.

With my wooden and copper plaque in hand and my memories stored away, I headed back to pick up my crew. I found them—still wandering around the mariner's museum, still fascinated with the leftovers from ancient sailing days. Both were expressing great respect for the ingenuity and accomplishments of the early mariners. I listened with interest as they described to me the courage of the early seamen coming to this vast, unexplored land. Then it was their turn to listen to me while I described my emotionally-charged time.

All three of us were breathlessly chattering about our different experiences and discovered we were hungry. We ducked into a restaurant and had a hamburger while we continued to fill one another in on all the details of our experiences since we had been separated. We all decided it had been time well spent and drove contentedly back to our boats.

A crowd of locals were inspecting our two vessels and waiting for our return. Bill immediately took the BICENTENNIAL out and gave quite a show of squirting the children with the turrets. When several shows were over, Bill and Cecil took off to film the Yorktown Battlefield and capture this memorable spot on film. I enjoyed pulling together a dinner of Southern pork chops, salad and a veggie casserole. The crowning achievement was a fluffy chocolate dessert. Their "oohs and aahs" of delight were more than enough to satisfy any cook who wanted to please her crew. Another good day was almost finished.

That night we got out the charts and studied our next stop. We would head down the York River and into the Chesapeake Bay, then turn north toward Smith Point. Chesapeake Bay! A scary thought. We had been cautioned all the way from Miami about watching out for weather, commercial vessels, buoys, and crab pots. We decided we were ready for "The Chesapeake Challenge." Taking out our "bible" we read about this mighty inland sea—it was almost 200 nautical miles long and up to 20 miles wide, with 1500 miles of navigable waters. It has 40 rivers, hundreds of creeks, inlets and coves. The great bulk of yachtsmen like to linger in the Chesapeake, gunkholing, crabbing, fishing, exploring. The "through-travelers" hurrying south in fall and north in spring consider the 200 miles a necessary evil to be traversed as quickly as possible. Autumn and spring are considered to be Chesapeake's finest time to cruise although the weather can turn unexpectedly, seas can mount, and afternoon thunder squalls are the rule rather than the exception in summer.

And the *Waterway Guide* further cautioned: "Boatmen cruising the Chesapeake will do well to check their charts to be sure they have the latest. Buoyage has been changed, new markers added, old ones removed, numbers changed, buoys repositioned." WELL! Great!

Chesapeake has five distinct sections, all great cruising grounds. The five parts are the Upper Eastern Shore, Upper Western Shore, Potomac River, Lower Eastern Shore and Lower Western Shore. As we tried to plot our course, we searched through sixty-two pages related to the five sections in this huge bay. Intimidating? A bit! Our friends docked near us at Wormley Creek reminded us to "watch out for freighters and tankers in the middle of the bay." We were properly cautioned and uptight!

We felt we had done our homework and put away our charts and Guide. Now we planned our logistics for the next day. Cecil would take the truck and meet us at a pre-determined marina. We admonished him not to get lost. He laughed. This seemed to be part of the journey. Finding a marina was a difficult task on small, two-lane back roads. It was usually a red-letter day when he said he "drove right to the marina!"

OUT OF GAS AND FACE

We were up early, bade Cec a fond *adieu*, fueled up and were off down the quiet York River. We had to work off a ship's chart, which was all compass settings from one marker to the next. The visibility was one mile. There was considerable haze and fog with some sunlight filtering through. The water seemed placid. So far, so good. The river continued to widen until we found the Chesapeake. Again, I learned some new lessons in navigating from our astute skipper. Because of the fishing area and crab pots, we had to follow the ship's channel which is in the center of the Chesapeake. We were fortunate this A.M. We found the waves were deep, but far apart and we began to have the feeling we were riding a roller coaster. The crab pots were out by the hundreds, and we were forced out where we could not see land. One fascinating marker was the Wolftrap floating lighthouse, which was now abandoned. Living quarters were actually in the lighthouse, but now it was automated and no one lived there. We wondered what it must have been like during a storm. We slowed down to explore this interesting old landmark and speculated about what must have been a lonely vigil for the lighthouse keeper. We tied up on the floating lighthouse for almost an hour waiting for the fog to lift.

Our boats slid up and down on giant roller swells. Liquid mountains rolled under us. We were not alarmed, but I remarked to Bill about the unleashed power I felt beneath us. He agreed he was glad it was the end of May and not stormy weather. We knew we were traversing unpredictable waters. We glided and swooped along in an eerie, fogbound silence. The rolling waves did not break but kept trying to shove us off course. We kept checking our charts and our compass for a very important pivot marker which would be the location for our 90 degree turn. As I was preparing lunch in the galley there was a shout from the bridge. "There she is!" (another she). "I found it. The buoy number is the right one!" I went racing up the ladder to the bridge and checked the charts. Right on! How comforting it was to know we were not lost in this huge body of water.

We knew we were heading for Smith Point and our *Waterway Guide* always proved to be an invaluable aid when attempting to find an unfamiliar marina. Although charts tell us where we are, the *Guide* always had a blow-up of the area approaching the marina. We were careful to check out the approach, for there is nothing worse than coming into a marina the wrong way. It's tacky navigating and is much frowned upon and discussed by those on shore. Rules of the road are necessary and important for boaters, and there usually is a good reason why one cannot choose his own shortcut. The dock masters can make or break a visit by their welcome or their disapproval of a captain and his crew. Better to come in carefully than to be what the two men titled the weekend skippers—"one big smart-ass."

We were not so lucky this time. There were absolutely no markers to guide us into the channel leading to Smith Point Marina. This was a small marina, a narrow channel. It was a weekday so there was no boating traffic, and the only markers we could see had bird nests on top of them which measured three feet across. Numbers were obliterated (due to bird droppings—one big white-out!). Bill nervously read that he had only five feet under him and suddenly we ran aground! Fortunately it was all sand beneath us. Bill threw an engine into reverse and plowed out. I ran for our following battleship and caught her just in time before she crashed her nose into our stern. Warily we looked again for the channel in to the quiet marina. We could see Cecil's truck parked on shore and knew he was on the VHF to us, but we were too busy to answer. We searched for the channel, which turned out to be the opposite of any calculated guess we could make. Later on we found that Cecil had been watching us and reported that we made a "weird entrance." He called it "how to run aground in one easy lesson." He also said we had spun around and dug a channel of our own. Sarcastically, he also wanted to know if we were going to become part of the dredging crew for the Corps of Engineers. Bill glumly took this kidding and immediately asked if Cecil had gotten lost. "Certainly I got lost," answered Cec. "Those unmarked roads all look the same and I ended up having to cross a river on a one-car ferry."

We soon tied up and went up on the bridge under the canopy and discussed our morning. There Bill was happy to see some locals run aground, and he didn't feel so badly. Cec felt we should all see his one-horse ferry, as he described it, so we were off for a short afternoon tour through beautiful Virginia countryside. We did indeed ride across on the one-car ferry. What an operation. It slid back and forth on a cable and brought us to a delightful, small town where we watched the local fishermen come in from the bay. We visited the small mercantile/general store. We enjoyed these visits, as the storekeepers were as unusual and quaint as the products they carried. We always found the Southerners to be friendly, curious and refreshing. How we enjoyed the South! I busied myself picking some wildflowers for the dinner table that night. The boys laughed at me, but I noticed they, too, were beginning to be flower collectors and occasionally I would be handed an unsolicited bouquet for our table.

Back at the boat I readied dinner while Bill and Cecil entertained the usual number of visitors on board. We loved these times. The lazy weekends brought a different type person to our hearth. It was a time when we felt suspended in limbo. The hurrying workaday world was somewhere "out there," but it didn't touch us. We didn't miss it and rejected the thought that eventually we would have to rejoin them.

What interesting people visited us. This time it was an out-of-the-ordinary college professor and his lady friend. We spent some time talking with them and others who drifted by, curious to find out what the red/ white/blue apparition might be. Everyone was always so pleased when we handed out our press release, complete with picture and short story. They would hurry away with the sheet of paper clutched in their hand. It was obvious they were happy to have proof when they left that "there was a battleship tied up at the marina today."

The evening was a humid one and the clouds became more threatening. On our way to the showers, we felt the first few drops of rain. At the same time we watched a mother duck and her fifteen (yes, fifteen) babies swimming madly for shelter under a bridge. What a picture they made. By the time we made it back to the boat, the rain had begun in earnest and we went to sleep with the *rat-a-tat-tat* of the downpour drumming down on our bridge above us.

Next day the weather had not improved. The sky was lowering and looked as if it held promise of bad weather later on. Our usual morning question— "to go or not to go?" Having some dates set up in concrete in the days ahead with mayors etc., we felt we should forge ahead. Cecil would drive ahead to the Ft. Washington Marina, which was on the Potomac River. Bill and I would have a long run this day for the charts showed the Potomac River going a long, long way up toward Washington, D.C. from the Chesapeake. We were all up early for the day ahead. We compared our charts with Cecil's road maps and ascertained a time we would hope to meet later in the afternoon.

With a bit more courage this morning, we forged out into Chesapeake Bay, found our course and held closely to it. There were too many opportunities for us to go completely off course and wind up going up other rivers which branched off the bay. We loved names new to us and stumbled over their pronunciation—Chickahominy, Appomattox, Piankatank, Tappahannock, Rappahannock…so much history along their banks.

We slowly churned our way north, checking every marker carefully. Ultimately we were looking for our pivot marker to turn into the eleven-mile-wide Potomac River. We had to rely on compass settings from the chart, and the way ahead was confusing. To confound our problem, the water began to be very rough, and a storm was obviously brewing.

Eureka! We sighted the pivot marker and turned northwestward. We hoped the river would narrow enough so we could see land. We knew we were to meet Cecil on the starboard side of the Potomac. He had planned to stop at Mt. Vernon and Stratford Hall (the home of Robert E. Lee) and do some historical filming. Then he was to go on up the opposite side of the river from the marina and find a bridge where he could cross over to our meeting at Ft. Washington Marina. We knew we had 40 miles left to go and Bill began to talk about the fuel being used up so rapidly due to heading into rough waters and an ever-increasing wind. We had looked for fuel stops along the west side of the Chesapeake but could find nothing. As we proceeded up the river, water began to break over the bridge. The river was full of planks, trees and other debris. We could tell the storm was coming toward us and had already filled the rivers above. The junk had floated into the Potomac and was being washed down. Bill was kept busy dodging all sorts of obstacles and I was equally engaged seeing that the battleship was protected.

Proceeding cautiously in the turbulent water, we began to hope we would soon sight the marina. Eight miles from the marina it began to rain, and we ran out of gas. Waves and a strong current had made us consume far more fuel than anticipated and we knew it would be close—but not this close! We immediately began to drift backward and shoreward. I ran to fend off the BICENTENNIAL. Bill threw out the anchor with all the line and secured us so that we were only 30 feet from shore. As we edged toward the shoreline, we were able to get out of the rough water. We tried and tried to raise Cecil on the walkie-talkie but to no avail. Then we found that the Ft. Washington marina had a channel they monitored. We were able to contact them and told them that we were out of gas and where we were. The marina people would notify Cec of our trouble and would try to get someone out to help us after

172

the cloudburst was over.

We found that most people in that area used CB units and after we called the Coast Guard and apprised them of our situation, people intercepted our call and put us in touch with a huge houseboat. The houseboat people were put on our frequency and they soon found us. They tied on to us and began to tow us back to Sweden Point, which was up river eight miles. The downpour caught up with us and it became very rough. They were unable to pull us all the way in to the marina so turned us over to a Maryland police boat who tethered us to their side and took us directly to the gas dock of a private yacht club. While Bill fueled up I was astonished to have to fill out a police report and explain why we had run out of gas. We were grateful for their help, but were sure to insert that we had a battleship under tow and that did not help our fuel consumption. Skilled boaters do not really like or appreciate those that run out of gas. We giggled over the sergeant, who might read our report about a battleship. The fueling process took an unduly long time as the pump was faulty and it would repeatedly go off and on. We did stroll up to the yacht club where there was a big celebration ongoing. We were invited to have a drink and did so. I called Cecil, who was drying out at the Ft. Washington Marina. We were very glad to finally be in touch with one another. He had driven through heavy rain and was anxious for us to be on our way.

It was late afternoon by the time we could depart. We had thirteen miles to go to find our safe port. Cecil had made arrangements for us so we knew we would have a slip. The weather alternately spit at us and stopped. It was not a good afternoon for boating and we were tired. Almost two hours later we found the shallow inlet going into Ft. Washington and were surprised to come into a huge covered shed which housed hundreds of boats. After the deluge we had been caught in, we realized the need for this type of large shelter. Inside everything was wet or damp. High ceilings made the whole area sound like an echo chamber. The flotsam and jetsam in the water made coming in to tie up a chore. Carefully we edged in, and Cec caught our line. Our crew was together again, and the usual curious visitors streamed onto the narrow dock to see us. Cec was a good sport and took the BICENTENNIAL out for a spin, and there was much whistling, clapping and approval shouts as he came back in. We passed out our press releases and had a welcome and warm reception. These boaters were all victims of the bad weather and many had sought shelter from the storm.

We then noticed that in his haste to take off, Cec had broken off one of the port cannons and a vent. He and Bill always had to repair and improvise. So many accoutrements were attached to the battleship that they protruded and caught on the docks or onto the mother ship.

This time they fixed the vent and the port gun with a painted beer can. Bill announced he would be happy to supply us with as many cans as we needed for necessary repairs. He promptly went off for two six packs, confident he was doing his bit to "save the ship."

We were lured into the marina restaurant that night by the seafood menu we found posted on a piling. As we ate by candlelight we described the adventures of our afternoon to Cecil, who made several unkind remarks about "people who run out of gas." Bill retaliated about "people who were always getting lost and could hardly locate marinas." Our waitress discovered we were the owners of the strange craft docked outside and told everyone in the restaurant about us. We had many visitors again and equally as many questions.

We walked back on the squishy, floating docks way out to our tie-up. The air was damp and the bedding felt wet as we crawled into our bunks. It dripped rain all night. One bonus was the great showers at this marina. We all stayed in a long time. This was pleasant, but we would not be sorry to leave this unusual spot. We felt constricted and closed in with the shed wrapped around us. Undoubtedly the boat owners appreciated the protection for their boats, but we had long been used to the freedom of the open waters of "The Ditch." We would leave early for the rest of our trip up the Potomac into the heart of Washington D.C.

A CAPITAL TIME IN THE CAPITOL CITY

In the morning the water was full of floating debris. Logs, planks, junk surrounded us. We saw several water moccasins swimming lazily about, and we watched Cec as he carefully opened up the superstructure of the BICENTENNIAL and looked inside. "Hello, down there. Anyone living in here?" Finding no slithery creature had taken up quarters, he folded his long frame into the battleship. He would check out the motor, see how she (she!) was running, then tie her to CELEBRATION's stern. Again, Bill and I would take the two boats up the river and Cecil would go ahead to D.C. and meet us at the dock of the Washington Municipal Marina. Gingerly, Bill edged out of the crowded marina, constantly looking back to see if I was fending off the battleship. Cec, too, was watching from shore. So far I had managed to keep the BICENTENNIAL from getting terribly banged up and felt my crewmember rating on the boat depended on my continuing good performance. I refrained from ever saying anything when either man gouged a dent or knocked off something. I found it much more tactful and expedient to cluck in sympathy and offer snacks or liquid refreshments while they were making repairs.

Very carefully we proceeded out the narrow shallow channel in a drizzling rain. We plowed mud all the way out to the Potomac River and into the main stream. We dodged debris constantly. The morning was cold and damp, and we shivered on the bridge deck as the chill wind blew off the Tidal Basin. We passed tour boats headed for Mt. Vernon, which was located on our port side. We followed tradition by ringing our ship's bell as we passed George's plantation. This custom is said to have begun the night of Washington's death and the bell ringing is to honor him.

On we went, ticking off mile after mile through floating logs and junk. Would there be a lot of Washington D.C. boat traffic? Would we find Cecil in the huge city? Coming into strange ports was easy when the cities and ports were small, but the large northern cities were a challenge. We saw several marinas along the way on either side of the river, but had planned to meet Cecil at the public marina in downtown Washington D.C. The long, leisurely trip was beautiful and the weather began to improve, as did our spirits. To our dismay, when we arrived at the municipal marina we found it to be closed to all boat traffic for repair. Thank goodness for our VHF. As we put out our call hoping to contact Cecil, we were grateful he picked us up immediately. He told us that we had been invited to be guests at the Capitol Yacht Club. He had met the commodore of the private yacht club next to the one we had hoped to be in, and Commodore Dooley made room for us! What a welcome this was and we quickly checked our *Waterway Guide* to locate this spot. We wasted no time coming in and found Cec and his new friend there to help us tie up the two boats. There were no floating docks, so tie-up was not easy; but what a privilege to be guests of these delightful new friends and to enjoy the elegance of their club, their showers, their facilities. We spent four wonderful, relaxing days at this marina over the Memorial Day weekend. We had learned it was better not to be out on the water with the weekend warriors when they were at the wheel of their boats.

We met many of the club members over the three-day holiday weekend and welcomed many aboard. We found that business people live aboard their boats in the marina and avoid the high cost of buying or renting a capital city home. We were parked in front of the famous Flagship Restaurant and the main walkway was above us. We were the focus of a lot of attention and had numerous visitors. There was an open-air fish mall next to us with fishing boats of all kinds. Many ships were selling fish from their boats. We were in the hub of Grand Central Station. On one busy day Cec went out and "attacked" all the fishing boats to everyone's delight. After dinner our nights were spent playing blackjack in the yacht club. I learned quickly that the men were all ex-servicemen and were merciless. Due to sheer luck I won all the silver in sight, and everyone was astonished. Hah! Retribution for past indignities.

Cec and I enjoyed visiting all the monuments and filmed them for the Los Angeles schoolchildren. We did them all: Washington Monument, the Lincoln Memorial, the White House and the Capitol. Later on we would use all this as background film for our interview with Barry Goldwater, Jr. We did have one restful night including dinner on board with several visitors coming to the dock. The next day the deputy mayor of Washington D.C. came down and we gave him the letter from Mayor Bradley and the schoolchildren's letters. He was most gracious, and Bill filmed this bit of protocol for us so we could show the youngsters later on.

That day it took a bit of maneuvering to avoid Bill. We had purchased our trophy plaque for him in Newport News, VA, but had not been able to stay anywhere long enough to get the engraving done. I made a secret call to an engraver who said he would meet me at the entrance to the Capitol Yacht Club, pick up the trophy, engrave our message on it, then bring it back the next day. We were all so glued to each other by this time that I found it difficult to evade Bill. He kept turning up when I most wished to be unobtrusive. I finally met the engraver, gave him our message along with the plaque and fervently hoped I would see the trophy returned.

That afternoon we had a most pleasant surprise. Barry Goldwater, Jr., our California congressman, was in the midst of painting his home, but when he heard that the USS BICENTENNIAL for California was in town, he hurried down to the marina and spent three wonderful hours with us. We took him into the yacht club and treated everyone to beer and hors d'oeuvres. Barry was a most interesting and gracious visitor. He gave us a marvelous interview, which we taped for the children at home. He generously gave us his whole afternoon. His casualness (he came down in paint clothes) was much appreciated by his constituents, and we counted ourselves fortunate to have had so much of this busy representative's time. He gave a very serious and direct charge to the children as he urged them to become involved in politics and give some service to their country.

We were up late the next morning and had many visitors. We were amazed at the huge pleasure crafts, some with a 15-foot beam. We passed out a lot of our literature and found that a "Spirit of '76" ceremony was going on out in the basin. Cec climbed into the BICENTENNIAL and joined in on the boating parade. The TV cameras turned to him and caused much excitement. The people in charge of the ceremony asked him to leave since the press and TV were focused on the battleship and they wanted a floating restaurant to be featured. We watched TV that night and were a bit chagrined to find that Cecil and his boat had a great deal of coverage.

We all journeyed out to Arlington Cemetery to film and met Rear Admiral Robert McClinton, who was in charge of recruiting for the whole United States. By this time RAdm. McClinton had replaced VAdm. Tidd. His official letters now were COMNAVCRUITCOM. The admiral has been a part of our boating life, and we have had some visits over the years with him. We have appreciated him, treasured his friendship and were so grateful for his support when we took the USS ARIZONA to Honolulu for the 50th anniversary of Pearl Harbor. We were delighted to hear that the Navy was 100% behind our up-with-America travels and supported our pen pal letters and boating with enthusiasm.

That night we three decided it was time to push ahead so we readied the two boats for another long trip. It was decided that Bill and I would take both boats down the Potomac, Cecil would drive truck and trailer and we would meet at the next marina at the mouth of the Potomac—Clayton Marina. It was May 29, 1975 and we had a marvelous run down the river. We even circled in front of Quantico Marine Center perched high on the bluffs overlooking the river. We saw quite a few commercial vessels and sight-seeing ships. We looked for the presidential yacht but did not spot it. The day was sparkly, but as we plowed on toward the Chesapeake, the weather suddenly changed. We were 40 miles out from Washington and the river became choppy, then turned wild. The rain descended and five-foot waves began to slap at us. Bill throttled CELEBRATION down to 3000 RPM and we crept down the sullen, turbulent Potomac. The spray drenched us on the fly bridge. Visibility was so bad that we could not use the lower, protected station because we could not see the markers or tugboats due to the waves and white caps. We found that every fifth wave would be a deep hole, then we would plow over some small waves, then BANG! We would end up behind another large hole. Bill explained that the tide was running one way and the wind was blowing the opposite direction. We were reminded that this river had a mind of her own (her?). Had it always been this way? We wondered about this river during George and Martha's time. How many sailors before us had fought their way up and down this tempestuous river?

It was a long 85-mile trip back. It meant constant checking on the USS BICENTENNIAL to make she wasn't climbing onto the aft deck of CELEBRATION II. She seemed to sense the capriciousness of the day's journey and our tension. She tossed her bridled nose back and forth and dared me to control her. We "limped" into the Clayton Marina around 6 P.M. Shooting for Smith River was quite treacherous, as it was a crooked channel and shallow on both sides. Markers were few. The marina was off the chart so we navigated from the *Waterway Guide*. Cecil was waiting for us and as we came into VHF talking distance his was a welcome voice. The marina did not look like much from the river but we could see it was a safe port.

After a most welcome tie-up we went in for dinner at a cozy restaurant connected with the marina. The fish dinner was superb. Cec had picked up our mail, and along with dinner I read the most welcome letters from my little class left far behind. I found a bundle of "I miss you, Mrs. Gates" letters. The printing had improved since I left those precious cherubs, and I was delighted. As I read each love note I could picture each little face. A momentary pang set in. How could I have left them? I knew they were in the capable hands of a dear substitute friend and were making the progress they should. My two "boys" listened courteously to the letters. They likely were bored, but they were polite. Both made a few unnecessary comments, but they seemed pleased that the little ones would send such nice messages across the miles.

We found two huge shower rooms available, and since there were few boaters at the marina, we had them to ourselves. There was much shouting back and forth over the partitions, and we were happy to have this difficult day behind us. Tomorrow would be a switch. Cec would ride with Bill and go out and around the difficult Pt. Lookout passage where the Potomac emptied out into the Chesapeake. I would drive the truck and trailer as we headed for a marina close to Annapolis. I hoped I would be able to find the marina by land. I knew by now that was the hard part. Having the huge white trailer behind made me a bit apprehensive, as I had heard Cecil talking about the narrow back roads in the countryside. Oh well. I planned to have my hair done, the first time in months. This gave impetus to my plan to visit a beauty shop and a supermarket *if* I could find them. With this upbeat female thought, I fell asleep.

POINT LOOK OU-OU-OUT

It was with mixed feelings I watched the two take off the next morning. We had been warned about coming out at the mouth of the Potomac and rounding the point as we headed for Annapolis. The winds were capricious and difficult to predict. The point had been described to us as "wicked, 40-knot winds, some shallowing."

As I watched CELEBRATION II head out, I sent out a prayer for their safe journey. I found I was lonely as I began my truck/trailer trip for Annapolis. Strange country, new highways and back roads, but then came the thought that somewhere, someplace I would get my hair done. Now THAT would be a treat. As I drove mile after mile through the small Maryland towns, I looked for a beauty salon where parking with a trailer would be easy. I found just what I wanted, parked, went inside and found that I could be made presentable in a very short time. Lucky me! The luxury of having a shampoo and set after so many, many marinas and CELEBRATION II showers was a treat. Soon I was on my way, and in the outskirts of Annapolis I found my supermarket. With the continued luxury of being able to drive my groceries to the boat rather than having to carry them, I loaded up. The boat refrigerator was a small apartment size, but I had learned to compact everything. There were frequent complaints from the crew about my stacking yummies inside and on top of one another, but I found that this prevented snacking on my dinner essentials. They complained, "We can't find anything!" I never told them my scheming on this, but always told them "I just don't have any space."

The traffic grew heavier, and I pulled over to check my city map. Everything looked so different coming to a marina by land. New respect for Cec's navigating surfaced. Before I was even aware, I found myself in the parking lot of the Oak Grove Marina. It was delightful to have found our rendezvous spot with so little difficulty. Stopping at the marina office to inquire if a battleship and escort had arrived, I was surprised to find they had beaten me in. The boats were berthed and the men were on board. I raced down the docks to CELEBRATION II and jumped on board anticipating and expecting a huge welcome from both gentlemen. It was noon and I had not seen them for six hours. Relief and joy swept over me as I jumped on board and poked my head into the cabin. "Hi, you guys." No answer. Both were flaked out on the bunks, sound asleep and obviously totally exhausted. What a welcome! But the satisfaction of seeing everyone and everything safely around Cape Lookout drowned out other feelings. Cecil finally awakened and gave me a drowsy hug. Ditto Bill. Happy to be back in charge of the galley, I prepared lunch. The smell of food brought life back, and soon we were sitting together, ready to trade descriptions of our two trips.

Bill's logbook says, "We bucked steady, strong winds as we headed out into the Chesapeake, but after Cec and I rounded the point, we had our most favorable day yet. Heavy wind blew us from the stern and the tide moving with us helped us breeze along. We pulled in for fuel at Plum Point, the best-known point when storms hit the bay. This is the only shelter in the area. We approached the inlet, which looked to be only five feet wide and had a wicked current and rapids. I hit the narrow inlet at 3500 RPM, and after clearing the mouth throttled down to 1000 RPM with good control. After we fueled up I hit the exit fast, and off to Annapolis we went. Our run was 6 ½ hours, and we tied up at the harbor with crowds and crowds of people coming in for June week and the Navy Academy's graduation." With all these people visiting this week, we were inundated with visitors and passed out much literature and had many visitors on board.

We very much wanted to be in the Annapolis Municipal Marina, which was a keyhole/gopher hole narrow inlet with boats tied up alongside. This narrow inlet ran right into the heart of town and was located under the Annapolis Hilton Hotel. We did not have too many miles to go, so Cec drove the truck and trailer into the city dock mid-town. Bill and I had a nice ride in, but an arduous time getting into our berth. It was difficult maneuvering the 28-ft. CELELBRATION and fending off the 18-ft. BICENTENNIAL. Once again, we had many helping hands and finally tied up in time to greet hordes of newspaper people and the TV crews. Our welcome could not have been nicer.

Annapolis as the capital city for Maryland is the seat of government and once—briefly in 1784—it served as our nation's capital. For yachtsmen, however, it is called "Queen of the Bay." It is the principal yachting center of the Chesapeake. Annapolis is homeport to more sailing craft than any other port on the Atlantic Coast. For yachts going north or south, it is a logical break in the long passage. It is a prime source for boating service and has many sightseeing attractions. Not too many years ago the activity in the City Basin centered around the commercial watermen. Buyboats came in to sell their wares off the deck—fish from Virginia, watermelon from North Carolina. Black ladies hawked peppery crab cakes from baskets; tonging (handling oysters) and dredging gear, repaired and ready for pick up, was piled high on Dock Street. The city was replete with history, from the gray and white State House dome to the original red brick sidewalks.

The British-accented street names—Duke of Gloucester, King George and Hanover—held shops that offered art and craftwork, elegant or offbeat clothing, exotic needlepoint, and restaurants of all kinds serving foreign and familiar foods. We visited the crab boats and the campus of St. Johns College, founded in 1695. There we saw a 600-year-old poplar where colonials and Indians made their treaties and where patriots plotted Annapolis' own version of the Boston Tea Party.

We had a wonderful four days in this city. There was great press coverage and from this numerous invitations to visit new friends. Both Cec and Bill took the BICENTENNIAL out to do a "show" several times each day. On one occasion Cec came floating directly in front of the Hilton Hotel and on his loudspeaker announced, "Surrender! Or I shall be forced to fire upon you!!" We were all shocked when many windows and balconies opened and white sheets, towels and pillowcases were frantically waved at him! One night we were invited to go up Spa Creek and visit new friends who said we could tie up at their dock. This meant going under the Spa Creek Bridge, whose closed vertical clearance was 15 feet. Like so many bridges we had gone through, this one had morning and evening closed hours and does not open to boat traffic. We heard it had the dubious distinction of holding up almost 2,500 cars daily in summer.

Up we went to wine and dine at the lovely home of the new Spa Creek friends. That night we came back down to CELEBRATION and noted that we bedded down at 2:15 A.M. Being tired the next day, we did not leave to return to the city dock until noon. We tied both boats up carefully and took off for a walk. About two hours later we were across the channel from our tie-up and Bill suddenly shouted and sprinted around to the opposite side of the gopher hole. "My gosh, look at that!" We turned and saw BICENTENNIAL hanging by her nose. Her bow must have been elevated five to six feet in the air off the water and the line was taut. We had forgotten the tremendous tide lifts and drops. Bill remedied this before any damage was done. Later that afternoon Bill took the BICENTENNIAL out to please the crowds, and as he was coming in to CELEBRATION, I reached out to get a line on him and pull him in. Losing my balance, I began to slowly fall in the river. I yelled at Cec, who came running through the cabin and grabbed me just in time. Another close one!

We felt the crowning Annapolis jewel was the Naval Academy. What a coincidence and a privilege to be there during June Week. Cec went out and "attacked" the midshipmen's boats on a side creek near the academy. They loved it! Despite the contacts, fun and sightseeing, we had the usual boating problems to contend with. One day a line broke on the battleship and she began to drift off into a piling and had to be rescued. These were always what we called "Hail Mary" times. The great highlight was going to the Naval Academy to enjoy some of the graduation events. What a thrill to see 2000 midshipmen marching in perfect order. A flyover by the Blue Angels completed a great filming day. The super-trained pilots put on an incredible show for us as they zipped, dipped, flipped all over the sky and in all directions. We also learned that the Navy museum housed such curiosities as George Washington's comb and a real three-dollar bill (Maryland currency, circa 1780).

Our final night in Annapolis was very special. A retired general who had read about us invited us to be his guests at the elegant Annapolis Yacht Club. The three of us were generously wined and dined along the way. We shall always be grateful to these wonderful people who treated us so kindly. We realized we were ships that pass in the night, we would glow briefly together for a short time and then pass from one another's sight. The spirit of the Bicentennial and the love of country was what bound us all together in one common purpose. It was not us, but what we represented that appealed to these good American citizens. It was tempting to stay another day, but we had some dates ahead in Baltimore, a greeting due from the mayor of Philadelphia and by now we knew we had to allow for the boating problems which were sure to arise. We held our usual pow-wow regarding logistics and decided that we would leave our trailer at the private yacht club and our truck would stay with our new friends up Spa Creek. The three of us would forge ahead together. Out came the charts and we checked out the Patapsco River which led to Baltimore and, we read, had a wide, wide mouth. The *Waterway Guide* said this is a commercial river and does not appeal to the cruising yachtsman as it is big, crowded and has an active marine industry. The docking facilities would leave a lot to be desired, but we had a date with schoolchildren and some Baltimore city officials. What lay ahead? We decided there was nothing the three of us could not overcome, so with confidence we retired. Our abilities were about to be tested in a way that we could not have imagined!

THE CAMERA IS JINXED

We were up early, and within half an hour we found ourselves under the massive Chesapeake Bay Bridge, which connected Washington D.C. and Baltimore's west Maryland side with the eastern side. We felt very, very small as we forged north on a compass course in the middle of the bay. We ticked off our markers and looked for our pivot point to enter the Patapsco River. We knew we had found it for the commercialization of the river was obvious. Warehouses, some abandoned, factories, and marine industries abounded. We could see the river was not cruiser friendly, but we had no choice.

Suddenly on our port a prominent landmark showed up! Fort McHenry stood out in the haze! This is where the original Star Spangled Banner flew. Here Francis Scott Key was held prisoner by the British and took inspiration for his immortal anthem in September, 1814. We wanted to stop but there is no wharf at the fort for visiting boats. The water is shallow, a bar reaches out from the seawall and we could see rocks close in. We contented ourselves with filming the flag waving over the fort. The banner Key watched as he wrote was the largest battle flag ever flown. It is 30 by 42 feet and can be seen at the Smithsonian in Washington D.C. It was made oversize so the British would see it miles off.

As we continued up the river, a fireboat appeared on our starboard, water jets shooting high into the sky. Over the VHF we were told they were going to escort us into the harbor. As we approached the harbor I was instructed to get the binoculars and find out what the crowd was doing on top of the seawall. We drew closer and I could tell there was a huge band and a crowd of people all waving American flags at us. What a surprise. There were no docks, no cleats available. We had a terrible time securing the two boats. The brick bulkhead was 8 ft. high and sloped down to a small cement curb. There were a few posts to which we could tie a line. We had to get the swim ladder out and lean it up against the seawall so we could even climb up to the huge, flat acreage above.

We struggled up and were surprised to be met by the mayor and made honorary citizens of Baltimore. The more than one hundred children presented us with a book, gifts, and flags. The press and TV were there and we gave a long story to the Baltimore Sun. Four classrooms of children sang to us! We passed out literature, pictures and the story of our trip and enjoyed a lovely visit from these young people and their teachers. At the teacher's request Cecil went out in the BICENTENNIAL and "attacked" the old USS CONSTELLATION. This magnificent old frigate was built in Baltimore in 1797 and now is moored at a specially-built pier and open for visits. As the battleship's turrets squirted water on the USS CONSTELLATION, a white handkerchief waved a surrender signal from one of the frigate's small windows. What a laugh this brought for the visiting youngsters.

After an hour's ceremony and talking, everyone left and we looked around the area. It was desolate. There were no shops, no fuel, no water or electrical hookups, there were obsolete loft buildings and crumbling warehouses. We knew there was to be a renovation of this waterfront, but we were obviously way ahead of that time. (We would visit this harbor again in 10 years and the transformation would be hard to believe.) But right now, WHAT to do? We needed fuel for the 67-mile run from Baltimore up to Chesapeake City, MD. Looking off almost a mile, we could see buildings, some skyscrapers and some cars. We felt abandoned and misplaced. We really did not want to stay, but where could we go? There was no yacht club and we needed gas before we could venture very far.

A policeman unexpectedly showed up to see our boats and to meet us. He asked us if he could help. We told him we had heard of the famous Obrysky's (steamed crab) Restaurant and would like to go over for dinner. He answered, "You mean you're going to leave your boat tied up here alone?" We looked around again and could see no reason why we should not. Both boats were locked and there was no one in sight. When the policeman saw that we could not be dissuaded he called a taxi for us and left making *tut-tut* noises. We wondered, thanked him, then shrugged this off. The taxi picked us up and delivered us to the well-known restaurant, which was jammed, and what a meal we had. Large sheets of butcher paper were ripped off the roll and placed on our table. A pitcher of beer was brought in, then we were astonished to have a bucket of steamed crabs dumped on the paper in the middle of the table. What a feast! We gorged and drank and gorged some more.

Totally satiated, we made our way outside into the dark evening. Being Westerners, we were interested to see the brownstone buildings we had heard about and seen in movies. Since it was a warm evening, the neighbors were all sitting on the brownstone steps and enjoying talking together. Just like in the movies! We went into a local bar, as we knew our TV coverage would be coming on the news. We always seemed to find ourselves in a bar asking a cooperative bartender if he could check the channels for our appearance. But bars were the only places where we could drop in and see the reporting.

After viewing our television interviews, we found a cab that took us back to the seawall which was in darkness. We slid and stumbled carefully down the ladder and onto the deck of CELEBRATION. Unlocking the boat, we felt our way inside and turned on a dim, battery-operated light. Bill discovered it first! "Look at the screen over the galley window," he shouted. We looked! The screen had been kicked in and the window forced open. We all began to check lockers, closets, cabinets and the USS BICENTENNIAL tethered to us and quietly riding up and down. Our search showed nothing missing. We were immensely relieved and said the officer was correct with his warning to us. But we were also a bit paranoid about the intrusion, and the men decided that we would not spend the night tied up to shore, but should go out into the middle of the harbor and anchor out for the night. "Good decision," we all felt, so Cec and I cast off lines and we slowly moved out in the darkness. The BICENTENNIAL obediently sloshed along, tied on our port side bow to stern.

We went out about 400 yards and dropped anchor. With a scope of 100 feet out, we secured everything, Bill shut down the engine and we went up on the bridge. It was beautiful at night as the distant lights of the city twinkled, and a half moon played hide and seek with the clouds. Tired, full of seafood, resigned to staying in this dreary harbor, worried about fuel, we were at least semi-content that we were safe from intruders.

We sat silently, each with our own thoughts, and someone mentioned it was time to hit the bunks. Just as we were about to head below, we heard the splashing of something in the water. It came closer and closer. We peered into the blackness of the water. A small boat emerged from the shadows and a man's voice said, "Is there a Mr. Gates on board?"

Surprised, we answered in the affirmative. Who could possibly know where we were?

"See that tiny light back on shore?" the man questioned. "There's a man there who has something for you."

"Something for Cecil?" What kind of a setup was this? We had more questions, and the man sounded so sincere Cec decided to go find out what the mystery was, but he also took his walkie-talkie VHF with him so we could communicate. We all went below and helped Cec climb into the small rowboat. Off they went, disappearing slowly into the blackness.

Bill and I went back on top and discussed this. The more Bill evaluated, the more nervous we both became. Abruptly Bill said, "We're going back to shore. I hope that guy doesn't have a 38 gun for him. We've got to go see that he hasn't gotten into some kind of a trap!"

Up anchor, engine started, VHF on, throttle forward and we began to creep back toward the tiny light. As we were wending our way back the speaker crackled. Cec's voice said, "Would you check under my bunk and see if my Belle and Howell camera is there?" Back I went. No camera. It had been stolen during the break-in and the man by the light had Cec's camera!

The honest man returning the camera unraveled the bizarre series of events that led to its return. He was a construction foreman on a crew that was working on a downtown project during the night hours. A ten- or eleven-year-old boy came up to the foreman and wanted to sell the camera for an apple. The surprised foreman made the trade and the boy ran off. The foreman looked inside the camera and found Cecil's full name, and went home for dinner. While there he read an article in the evening newspaper about our battleship coming to Baltimore and connected the name inside the camera with the newspaper story. At the same time he wondered if we still might be somewhere in the harbor. He got his friend to find a rowboat, and after they saw our faintly outlined silhouette in the half-moonlight, his friend rowed out to us. What an honest man!

Once again, we climbed wearily up and out onto the deserted bulkhead. We all shook the man's hand, tried several times to give him a reward, but he staunchly refused. His only comment was, "You'll do the same for someone else at another time." What a NICE person. I did take his name (David Nicely) and address and mailed him our press clippings from New York Harbor. That was the one thing he wanted to see—the finale of our trip under the Statue of Liberty.

Tired, we slowly let ourselves down onto the narrow cement curb at the bottom of the slanted bulkhead. Bill went up to the fly bridge and started the engine. Cec took the bowline and carefully balanced himself on the narrow curbing. I stood on the stern of CELEBRATION untying my line. The usual "Ready to cast off?" from Bill. We confirmed all was ready.

Abruptly and with no warning, all hell broke loose. As Bill put the boat in gear, the lower controls jammed. CELEBRATION leaped out into the water at 30 mph. Cec was thrown back against the brick bulkhead and almost fell in. I was thrown onto my knees to the deck on the stern. To compound our problem, the bow and stern lines were dragging in the water as we went roaring off into the black. As I picked myself up off the deck, I looked over at the BICENTENNIAL. To my horror she had been dragged stern to bow under the water and only her red stack was showing. She had tunneled under during our brief wild ride. Bill cut the ignition and we heard Cecil shouting, "How's the battleship? How's the battleship?"

We hated to tell him. "She's half sunk, but won't go down any farther," Bill answered back. I grabbed and coiled up the bow and stern lines so they wouldn't be caught in the prop and we limped for shore. Sadly, the men surveyed the damage.

"Pat, go get the buckets and we'll start to bail." What a disheartening occurrence. We had a date with the Mayor of Philadelphia in two days and now we had a drowned battleship. I was devastated for all of us.

As the two boys began to bail, there was an exclamation. "I'll be damned," said one. "The self-bailer is working." Sure enough, it had gone to work despite its immersion. The men bailed and bailed and I brought coffee, solace, sympathy and support. After getting the boat as dry as possible the men sprayed our "mother's milk" (WD-40) on the engine. Shock! The engine turned over and with a few more starts it purred as usual. Jubilation overcame weariness. It was 2:30 A.M. and we stayed right on the seawall and fell into bed at 3 A.M.

We were up at 7 A.M., as Cecil had to walk to catch a taxi to the Greyhound to go back to Annapolis and pull the truck and trailer forward. Bill and I would have to find gas. We would meet Cec in Chesapeake City IF fuel was to be found. After being in this harbor for some time, it seemed an impossibility to find gas anywhere.

After a quick breakfast Bill said, "Follow me."

"Where are we going?" I asked.

"To a bar."

"WHAT?? At 9 A.M.? You've got to be out of your mind. Only drunks go to a bar that early!"

Bill's only response was, "Never mind, come on, I may need you!"

Being the obedient crew slave, I followed him up the ladder and onto the brick pavement. "Why are we going to a bar?"

Exasperated, tired, but patient, he answered, "You'll find out. Now COME ON!"

Walk, walk, walk, walk. Tired from the night before, I could hardly keep up with him. Then he found what he had been looking for and into a dark, smelly bar we went. Getting accustomed to the dim light, I looked around and saw three men sitting at the bar. It was almost 10 A.M. I sat down beside Bill, who immediately ordered a beer, turned his back on me and began to talk to the man sitting on his right. Feeling rejected, thrust outside the male parameters and miserably tired, I sat on my stool and sulked. Barely able to overhear the animated exchange going on between the two men, I wondered what all the conversation was about. Then Bill turned to me and said, "This man is going to help us get gas."

"Really? But, HOW?"

This time I received an answer. "He's a salesman and has connections with farmers and engine companies. He knows where he can get two 50-gallon drums and he'll fill them with gas. Then he'll put them in his pick-up and drive down to the dock. I'll have to take the gas out by the bucket and pour it into our tank, but we'll have fuel this afternoon." Hooray! Another NICE man.

Bill went back to the boat, and I went out walking to find some food for the refrigerator and to buy some *Baltimore Sun* papers. We had had a nice spread with them. Hoofing it back to the boat, I was ready to make lunch for both of us; but there was a crowd of children with two adult supervisors. Getting closer, I could see that Bill's friend had delivered the gasoline drums and Bill was busy transferring gas into CELEBRATION's tanks.

What caught my teacher-attention was the fact that these children were all seriously retarded...mentally and physically deformed. Very sad! But Bill, not being accustomed to this, hissed at me that he was supposed to tell these children about our boats and what we were doing and he didn't know what to say. Tossing our groceries on board, I made a simple, direct talk to the children and did my best to help them understand. Bill kept doing his bucket thing as I talked and was muttering, "Let's get out of here. Let's GO!" The children seemed happy with my simple explanation and straggled away.

Bill was almost finished when one of the adults carelessly (thoughtlessly) lit up a cigarette. That was the last straw for poor, tired, frustrated Bill. "My Gawd, we'll be blown up! Get on this boat and we're GOING!" I was barely able to get on board; Bill had cast off both lines before scrambling to the bridge and I just managed to leap onto the stern. We were off and getting away from this nice city, but lackluster/no facilities port. I looked back as we left. All I could see were the two lonely fuel cans left on top of the bulkhead for our friend who would later retrieve them. *Goodbye, Baltimore*, I thought. *It's been a long thirty-six hours*. The BICENTENNIAL, under tow and bobbing quietly behind me, seemed to nod her head up and down as if to agree.

CANAL PILOTS, POLICE DOCKS
AND PLAYING VIPs

We exited Patapsco River as quickly as we could and made our pivot point at the mouth of the Chesapeake. How free we felt to be away from the industrialization and commercialism of the area we were rapidly putting behind us. Out into a friendly, quiet bay with sunshine, screeching seagulls, and few freighters with their wakes to confront us. We knew we had 56 miles to go, but felt confident we could be tied up in Chesapeake City at the mouth of the Delaware River before dark.

As we churned along we recapitulated the problems left behind, wondered about Cecil working his way northeastward and what was ahead. Coming into a wetland area that seemed quite isolated, we heard something in the engine compartment that alarmed us both. Throwing out the anchor, we stopped to investigate, but Bill could not discern anything wrong. We finally decided something dropped or misplaced itself and was the sound that startled us. BICENTENNIAL seemed quite happy now that she was dried out, and she cheerfully and obediently followed right behind us.

As we approached the C&D Canal, the southern end of the Delaware River, we sat up on the fly bridge and I read to Bill about the canal. It is a vital connection in the vast ICW system and is a timesaving link between Delaware and Chesapeake. The twelve-mile cut has no locks and no toll, but does have a great deal of big-ship commercial traffic. We were surprised to learn this canal was first proposed by a mapmaker in 1661, backed by Benjamin Franklin in 1788 and finally opened in 1829—complete with four locks and a six-mule team which towed boats through. The canal was straightened out in 1921, the mules abandoned and the canal was made wider and deeper. It is one of the world's busiest ditches and carries thousands of pleasure craft, big ships and barges.

We knew that dredging equipment would be inevitable, as the canal is always being deepened. Accustomed to staying away from large ships due to their tremendous wakes that would almost capsize us, we knew the only thing to watch out for was debris. A TV monitoring system controls traffic and the Corps of Engineers watches and tracks all vessels within the canal limits. Though there is no speed limit, captains know (or should know) that one does not speed, race or crowd alongside other vessels. We found that we would be going under five bridges in this short stretch, four fixed and one lift. The current was only two knots, and we were pleased to see that we would be riding the incoming tide, which traditionally gave us the right of way.

We knew this was the transfer point for Delaware and Chesapeake pilots and anticipated watching how they might transfer. We slowed way down as we approached the canal and began to watch for Schaefer's Canal House, which had a restaurant, market, fuel and dock facilities. That sounded "A Number One" to us after the desolation in Baltimore's harbor. Standing on the stern, I was checking on the BICENTENNIAL when I heard Bill give a shout. "I see Cec's blue truck parked up there so he's made it before us." Good news! I could always use help in tying two boats up at one time. As we drew closer we could see that the protected inside area of the marina was completely full of boats already in their slips. We slid alongside the long face dock that sat directly on the canal. After our greetings and tie-up chores, we all agreed it was great to be secured and together after our harrowing Baltimore experience. We still had some extra hours before we had the Philadelphia appearance and planned to spend two nights here. We all needed some sleep and R&R.

Since we were tied up right alongside the canal, we caught every wake of the huge, passing freighters and everything that went up and down the canal. We were shocked that small boats came roaring through and made enough wake to turn us on our beam's end. What had happened to the rules of the road? We heard many complain about this lack of manners, but no one seemed to do anything about it. We sat up on top of CELEBRATION II and watched the show the pilots put on for all. The tugboat pilots scramble down swinging rope ladders and hop into their pilot boats. Since the freighters cannot stop in the canal and must move at a fairly good clip to maintain steerage, the pilots are amazingly sure-footed and agile as they leap about. We watched all the activity with great interest and discussed our vantage point, problems and hazards.

As our talk continued, I began to experience the fraternity hazing about my Pee Dee nickname. "Pee Dee, Pee Dee," they both teased. "Immortal Pee

Dee." There were a few inside jokes along with all this. After giving me a bad time, they felt badly, so Cecil said he would treat for a fish dinner that night and Bill would host the next night. Nice to live with two men that had money. Off we went for lobster bisque and clams.

The next day was devoted to laundry, grocery shopping, numerous phone calls ahead to Philadelphia contacts and entertaining some Coast Guard Auxiliary (Philadelphia) guests who came to meet us. The auxiliaries always had willing helpers and they had been wonderful links for us up the ICW. These nice people were setting up our Philadelphia docking with all stops pulled out. We would have a marine police escort into Philly, a welcome by the mayor and a docking spot unknown to us, but certified by the Coast Guard Auxiliary. "Just follow your police escort," was all we knew.

That night it was Bill's turn to host at the famous Schaefer's, and we had another seafood dinner. I was politely told I was growing claws. Still tired from the traumatic sinking of our battleship, we turned in early. We just had lights out when a tremendous eastern thunder and lightning storm hit. What a show and how loud it was on our fly bridge! We listened to our radio and learned there was a tornado watch. We sloshed about, the boys worried about our tie-up and argued for a while about whose turn it was to get up and check on our numerous lines. Bill finally stumbled out with much grumbling and cheering from us "stay insiders." I was relieved that nighttime tie-up checks did not include me. I never volunteered. That's one job I escaped.

Up early, we breakfasted as we tossed about from passing wakes, but we were so used to our deck moving about under us that we really did not like the few nights we spent ashore. Leaving the rig at Chesapeake City, the three of us took off together on CELEBRATION II. As we emerged into the Delaware River, we realized that this was a big-ship oriented and commercial area. We could see chemical plants, shipyards and oil refineries lining the banks. Yacht facilities were not too numerous, and we read that one must take an estuary off the main river and wander upstream to find a marina.

We had not been in the Delaware River long when a marine police escort boat greeted us and we talked on the VHF. As we cruised along, the officer described the spots we were seeing. We fielded many questions about the red/white/blue lady trailing along behind us. As we came closer to Philadelphia, the officer explained that the waterfront was still undergoing restoration. The ugly brick warehouses that fronted the river had been torn down and there were plans to build a park and a 2,000-boat marina in their place. The project had come to a standstill for local political reasons, and this is when we found out where our dock was to be. We were directed right into the Philadelphia police docks. A formidable dock looked belligerently at us, we had a six-knot current running against us. Another hairy one! But we had been told this was the only safe place in the whole boating area to dock, and they were putting us right beside the police for our own protection.

Hastily we got Cec into the battleship and cast him off. Bill and I gingerly took CELEBRATION into a very tight spot, tied up and pulled Cecil in beside us. Since we were tied on our starboard side, we rafted the BI off our port side with large fenders as usual. Our Coast Guard friends had come out to welcome us in a boat and they, too, tied up near us. Then we saw a crowd coming toward us. The press, TV, mayor and schoolchildren had come to welcome us. During the ceremony we were awarded a beautiful replica of the Liberty Bell, and we exchanged our last Mayor Bradley letter with the Philly mayor plus schoolchildren letters.

By this time it was late afternoon and we could see there was no place to walk, no place to find supplies of any kind. Large police boats were tied up eight feet away from us, and there was much coming and going among the police. It was a bizarre but safe haven. Our Coast Guard friends came on board and we shared libations with them. They had a car parked nearby and told us they would drive us to the famous Bookbinder's Restaurant, which was to be a great experience. They had been so helpful to us and generous with their time and we asked them to be our guests at the restaurant. And so it proved to be—another gourmet seafood dinner! We had learned to appreciate and enjoy these quaint, famous spots and had become spoiled from east coast seafood. We decided it had to be THE best-prepared anyplace. We invited our benefactors on board for a nightcap and finally, after profuse thank yous, retired. We were tired from our last month's push to keep up with our schedule.

We had no sooner fallen asleep than the three of us were startled awake by someone stepping onto CELEBRATION. We quickly tilted to the starboard. The footsteps continued and we tilted to the port. No unusual noise, just footsteps. This was supposed to be a police-protected area. What was going on? As quickly as the footsteps intruded, they retreated and we were alone. We discussed this mystery. Cec's turn to get up, but he saw nothing. Back to bed, back to sleep and it happened again. And it happened again and again and again all night. The police had heard about us, and as they changed night shifts they all wanted to see the BICENTENNIAL. So, onto CELEBRATION with heavy boots—*clomp, clomp*, a quick look, then off. We have no idea how many visitors we had that night, but at least we felt very safe.

What a plethora of filming we did in Philadelphia. We knew the Los Angeles teachers would be pleased that we filmed the Liberty Bell, Philadelphia Hall, Carpenter's Hall, Constitution Hall, Ben Franklin's burial spot and the oldest church where Washington worshiped. After spending a great portion of the day doing this, we felt we wanted to get away from the busy docks and find another quiet retreat. We had only to go eight miles north of Philadelphia and found just what we wanted, Dredge Harbor. As we headed upriver the industrial character of the area faded, homes lined the riverbanks and yacht facilities became more frequent. We even found California floating docks—a peaceful spot. This was a working marina and it gave us time to polish up CELEBRATION, as Bill planned to sell her for his company in New York. Don and Mary did not want her back. We also had to work on the BICENTENNIAL, which was looking battle-scarred. In a few days we had a date with the Freedom Foundation people, who wanted us to trailer our battleship to their grounds.

This was a lazy, kickback time for us in the quiet marina. Time to go banking, pay bills, drive to find our mail in Trenton, NJ, do laundry, check charts for New York—and, most importantly, try to figure out how to get from north of Philadelphia up to Atlantic Highlands, NJ. There used to be a canal similar to the C&D Canal that would cut through, but it had been closed and we did not want to venture out into the Atlantic Ocean. Off Bill went in Cec's truck to find an owner of a Land 'n Sea craft in New Jersey. He had carried a list of owners with him as a back up and now he found an owner of a vessel like CELEBRATION close by. When Bill came back he was elated. The Land 'n Sea owner had agreed (at a nominal fee) to pick up our boat and trailer it on a Sunday to Atlantic Highlands, a distance of almost 100 miles.

With that detail and date taken care of, we prepared for an appearance at Valley Forge's Freedom Foundation. This meant taking the BICENTENNIAL out of the water and locking up CELEBRATION. We had no idea how they wanted us to display the battleship as she always rode enclosed in her trailer with her stern jutting out 18 inches. We soon found out! Heading through Philadelphia with our charge behind us, we found that we were the object of toots, hand-waving and salutes. Our publicity had been extensive by the police dock and Dredge Harbor and we received a wonderful reception on the city's freeways. When we found Freedom Foundation at Valley Forge, another warm reception was held for us. Immediately we cranked the BICENTENNIAL out of her trailer and onto two saw horses. She was now on display and had large crowds gathered around her all day.

The president of the foundation and his officers all greeted us and put us up in the executive quarters that night. We first met the general public, then were introduced to several hundred high school teachers who were gathered for a seminar. Our introduction included a greeting from an admiral who thanked us for our contribution to the nation's two hundredth birthday celebration. We were given a tour of the extensive grounds and were impressed. Banks of red, white and blue petunias covered the area. We were surprised to find a Medal of Honor building which held the names of every receiver from every service, and the list began back before WW I. Bill, being a Marine from the Korean War, went through the books and announced that the Medal of Honor recipients were 80% Marines! We pulled the California list, two books, and thumbed through them. The men had devoted their lives to our country. Most were privates, PFC's and a few high- ranking officers. Cecil and Bill were very touched by the pictures and what they read. We saw the statue of George Washington with his hands clasped in prayer as he prayed over his freezing troops. The history and memorabilia on these sacred grounds was most moving.

Our hosts were exceedingly hospitable toward us. We were swept into stranger's lives for a period of hours or a few days and warmly welcomed—because we represented something special to them…their country's 200th birthday of freedom.. They all loved our ship and took us in under their hospitable wing. The battleship proved to be a catalyst and we were so embraced. It happened over and over—people, like ships passing in the night, disappeared over the horizon, but the glow of the warmth and outreach stayed with us long after the names and faces faded.

The next morning we packed up our boat and all our displays and were touched to find that one of the Freedom Foundation docents had stayed up most of the night doing a watercolor of the USS BICENTENNIAL. We were very moved by this lovely gesture. Off we went for Dredge Harbor to get ready for our trek across New Jersey and on to Atlantic Highlands. The Sunday that our friend would trailer us to New Jersey was also Father's Day, so I gave both men cards. There was much silliness and some in-joke discussion. Again, I silently thought, *I live in a men's locker room.*

Our driver came with his empty trailer, and for the first time in months we drove CELEBRATION to a ramp and cranked her onto the boat trailer. She looked out of place and we felt out of place being back on the road with her rather than in the water. We made a strange procession with CELEBRATION's escort signs and flags announcing the battleship's coming behind her. The Sunday traffic was not too bad, and our driver took us directly to the municipal marina. Atlantic Highlands is near Sandy Hook and is protected by a long seawall. Behind this breakwater was the sheltered anchorage. It was an enormous marina, well-run, with an accommodating dock master, restaurant, marine store with charts, yacht club and capable of berthing anything from a day sailor to the largest yacht. We looked at the crowding, the restless harbor waters due to so much traffic, the hundreds of boats and were dismayed at the noise and over-activity. We realized it was another Sunday and boat traffic was at a peak.

As we were discussing the situation, two onlookers wandered over to check out our rigs. As we visited they could see our reluctance to launch two boats into the teeming harbor. With the warmth and hospitality that we had come to appreciate, they immediately invited us to be their guests at the private Channel Yacht Club. What a difference! We were accustomed to tranquility most of the time and had avoided the large marinas whenever possible. We trailered everything over to the Channel Club and happily welcomed all the Sunday visitors who greeted us. This was a beautiful, quiet spot and had all the amenities that boaters need—without the noise and over-crowding. It enabled us to lay our groundwork for the press in New York, telephone those expecting us and bring a finale to this ICW trip. We were grateful…again! This would be a great spot for our jump off into New York Harbor.

And there was a scary thought! What lay ahead and what would we find in that packed harbor? We told Bill we knew he could do it! Over we went to the chart store for the latest, updated Chart 369-C. On the highly commercial waters, some kind of dredging or adjusting buoys is always underway. Our homework for several nights was becoming highly acquainted with the NY Harbor chart.

HIGH WATER MARK—DOWNHILL RUN

We awoke to a foggy morning. We knew that in poor visibility pleasure craft can run the buoys just outside channel limits where commercial craft do not venture. If anything, the waters are too well-marked. The many lighthouses and buoyage tends to be confusing and compass courses are helpful even in clear weather. Our direct run would go via The Narrows— fourteen nautical miles to The Battery where the Hudson and East Rivers meet. This is one of the most heavily trafficked areas in the water world, and the bay carries a nonstop stream of craft, ranging from small fishing boats to glamorous liners and fast-moving supertankers. There is too much going on and we were warned the more you know about navigating that area, the better off you are. I read to Bill that our *Waterway Guide* cautioned, "This is no place for the skipper to doze at the wheel." The other problem is floating debris, much of it massive and a lot of it submerged. The Corps of Engineers tries to remove it but 3,000 acres of rotting piers and 2,000 abandoned, drifting boats and barges fill up the bay quickly. We read that 8,000 pleasure boats a year are damaged, and timber, tires and boxes sink some.

With all the above in mind, the three of us sat up on the fly bridge, poised for our last great adventure. The direct run from Sandy Hook to The Narrows is almost due north. We wove around fishing boats of all sizes. The current was running at two knots and we were going with it. We crept along, undoubtedly a strange site to observers with our red,white and blue lady behind us. Our first sighting of the Verrazano Narrows Bridge was exciting. It is the world's largest suspension bridge, named for Giovanni da Verrazano, who explored there 84 years before Henry Hudson. The bridge crosses the Narrows from Staten Island to Brooklyn. We found the Upper Bay waters roiled by traffic. Now the whole panorama of the harbor and city spread out before our eyes. This spectacular view is unseen by land visitors and residents. The high rises, the densely packed skyscrapers of Manhattan's lower district loomed ahead. To our port was Miss Liberty, serene, lovely and 300 feet high. She faces southeast to look yachtsmen squarely in the eye. Even though we could go fairly close to the coppery-green lady, there are no pleasure boat docking facilities. The island is surrounded by riprap made of gigantic boulders.

The weather had cleared up as we made our way north and the visibility was good; however, we noticed off to our west that the sky was beginning to blacken. We proceeded farther north than needed just to see the silhouettes of well-known skyscrapers. We had made a three-way decision that we wanted to anchor out under the Statue of Liberty, have dinner and sleep under her shadow. The next day we would head for the only marina on the west side of the Hudson River, the 79th Street Yacht Basin. Tonight we would be different; we would be independent, autonomous, self-governing, self-sustaining and… we were beginning to feel the pangs of "this is the end."

I had stocked the refrigerator and we had plenty of food and beverage. Now, to find a special spot in which to anchor. We checked our charts to make sure we were out of a channel. It was mid-afternoon and few boats were around us. We could see three anchored off in the distance. We checked the depth finder and were busy chattering about the proper spot. Then the rain hit. It shocked us as we had been busy jockeying into position. We pulled up anchor and headed around behind the statue where the ferries were. We thought we might be in the lee of the wind and rain. We were in eight feet of water and anchored temporarily, waiting for the summer storm to pass. We watched the ferries taking people to and from their Staten Island homes and watched people who were visiting the coppery lady.

The rain stopped, we upped anchor and made our way back to the other side. The tide turned out to be a nautical nightmare. Flood tide in, ebb tide out and 20 minutes of no movement. This looked like a 12- anchor job, but we only had two anchors. With much conversation and heave ho-ing, the lines and anchors were finally placed to Bill's satisfaction. But not before one more "evil" befell us. Cecil leaned over to tie up his ship. Effortlessly, his traveler's checks and glasses slid out of his shirt pocket and into the muddy water! We watched helplessly as they lazily floated down into the murk. There was much gnashing of teeth and blue-colored air, but life had to go on. We would worry about replacing the TC's later. And Cec had an extra pair of glasses.

Now, it was time to take care of the BICENTENNIAL and tether her to our port side for the night rather than leave her dangling out behind us. All three of us had a line on her as we pulled her in to CELEBRATION's stern. All three of us relied on the others to hang on to a line. And all three of us threw our line on the battleship's deck at the same time. Gasp! Another horror story! There went our lady, all alone, bobbing about on the water and drifting rapidly toward the boulders that rocked in the statue's foundation.

Pat and Bill on

CELEBRATION's

bridge

Approaching

Statue of Liberty

July 3, 1975

USS BICENTENNIAL

under tow

coming into

New York Harbor

(memories)

Getting into anchoring

position in order

to spend the night

under the Lady

Shock! Disbelief! Consternation! Dismay! Had we come 1500 miles for tomorrow's anticipated huge publicity barrage at a New York marina only to have our ship dashed against the rocks? God must watch over fools and boaters. A young man who was on one of the boats anchored away from us had just thrown his dinghy over into the water, climbed in and was going to take a closer look at the statue. He saw our problem and rowed madly for BICENTENNIAL. He caught her and grabbed a line! Then he rowed her back to us and we had to go through our whole story of the who, what, where, when and especially why. But we were happy to do so and leaned way over to give him our literature and pictures. This writer had another close one, but did not fall in the river. That would have been another horror story. There was the chance "they" might not pull me out!

It was not quite dark, and a telephone friend who we had not met came roaring out in his jet speedboat to meet us and see the BICENTENNIAL. We had looked forward to this, as he was editor of *MAD Magazine* (Dick de Bartolo) and this promised to be a fun meeting. Tying up beside us, he gave us a copy of *Family Houseboating* in which we had just come out, hopped into the battleship and Cec gave him a ride around the statue. Dick thought it was great if not incongruous as Cecil attacked the statue with his water squirting guns. When they came back and tied up the BICENTENNIAL, Dick offered the two men a ride in his jet boat. Never have I seen any boat go so fast, unless it was the powerboats at the Seattle show. Dick cut the river in half and they disappeared up river from my sight. My only thoughts were, *My gosh, they're going to crash and I'm going to be left to bring two boats, two trailers and a truck home by myself.*

They finally returned some 30 minutes later, and both men announced they thought they must have gone all the way to Lake Champlain. They talked about this ride all through dinner that night. I learned that Dick had been clocked at 52mph. They also saw about 20 boys swimming in the river despite the sewage. Both Bill and Cec thought maybe the bacteria in the water fight each other and it all comes out negative. Their advice and comment: "Don't fall in."

After drinks and dinner, we rechecked all lines for the night ahead. We had a dangling good time! The tide came in at six knots, then reversed at the same speed. At times we had only two inches under our prop. The coming and going of the tides impressed us. Water was going somewhere all the time. It flushes out rivers, stream inlets and carries rubbish back and forth. We decided New York Harbor needed a lot of flushing. In fact, the remark was made that the river was composed of millions of flushings. Enough.

That night we made many VHF calls and had numerous TV stations and newspapers contacting us to find out when we would arrive at the 79th Street Yacht Basin. Our channel call letters were picked up by news and TV stations and sent back and forth. We made a date with all of them for 9:30 A.M. to meet at the 79th Street Yacht Basin. Since the rain had passed, we climbed up to the fly bridge for a New York look-around. What an impressive sight. We were isolated on our own island, had food, drink, beds and were having a privilege few enjoy. We would long remember this magic moment. Cec even taped the sounds we heard—the horns, squeaks, toots, engines. The beautifully-lit copper green lady stood guard over us, and there were few boats anchored around us. This was a night never to be forgotten. With reluctance we left the night's magic and went below. I noted the boys got up several times to check our position and our lines and seemed satisfied that all was well. That night job was one I never seemed to have to assume. Besides, it was easy to pretend to be in a deep sleep.

June 17: Early next day I fed a good breakfast from my overloaded larder to the men. We would be having a long day with a run from the statue up to 79th Street, a tie-up of two boats in a small area and a date with the news media. We were amazed at the debris which had surrounded our boats during the night. It was a dirty river, and as we hauled up anchor and started north we saw floating tires, rims, logs (Hudson River torpedoes), boxes, inner tubes, two chairs (not matching) and a bird cage. Good Grief! What a mess. Some of the obstacles looked downright dangerous and we wove a zigzag course up river.

It was a brilliant, cool morning and the chart matched every marker. We were nearing the yacht basin when Cec said, "What's all that out on the dock?" I grabbed the binoculars and could see a long lineup of men and women sitting on the pier, dangling their legs over the edge. I could also see suitcases and packs strewn all around.

"My gosh, do you think that's the press?" It was. We were besieged by most of the TV channels and most of the NY newspapers. After docking and saying hello, we launched Cecil outside the marina and into the Hudson River. At this time it was the ebb tide, and every time he circled outside the marina the river tried to sweep him downstream. Bill and I tied CELEBRATION securely, then pulled in Cecil. We had found that the press or TV people rarely had any nautical knowledge and asked innocent but impossible things of poor Cec. He was glad when his demo was over! We gave interviews to all and even came out in the centerfold of the *Daily News*, which had a 5,000,000 circulation.

When the press left, some of the local businessmen who lived on boats in the marina invited us aboard. We made a date that night to watch ourselves on TV on one 55-foot yacht and enjoy cocktails with him. ABC, NBC and CBS all gave us ample coverage, and one station did one minute, twenty-five seconds on us. By this time we had become somewhat insensitive in checking out the time given to us. We felt NY had been good to us. One of the newspaperwomen had been particularly nice. She had brought three tickets for that night's show of the Rockettes at Rockefeller Center. What a thrill for us sea-goers.

We busied ourselves during the afternoon cleaning up the boats as best we could and checking out our environ. We were surprised to note a very, very tall, probably 20-foot, chain link fence that encircled the marina. It was explained that the marina was not in a good neighborhood and the fence was locked, so no one could come out on the docks and break into the boats. After school was out we realized why the fence was there. Young teenagers came out, tried to crawl to the top of the fence, were unsuccessful, threw garbage over at the boats, made rude comments and were most unpleasant. How were we going to get outside without a problem? It was pointed out to us that we could make a dash out the locked gate (with guard), run for a tunnel which went underground and catch a taxi out on the main street. After a quick dinner this we did….and were successful.

How we enjoyed the bright lights and magic of New York. For three months we had been in a sheltered, focused environment, and we found that the dancing Rockettes and the movie were a wonderful break. Catching a taxi outside the theater, we made our way back to the 79th Street Marina. As we emerged from the tunnel we were grateful to see that the poorly behaved young men were gone, and the night watchman let us in to our safe haven. It was midnight. We all three showered and remarked we were glad to be back on CELEBRATION.

June 18: After a lazy morning Cec took the BICENTENNIAL out into the Hudson, and Bill and I followed. The marine police came by, curious as to what we were. Cec "shot" them from the battleship, to their amusement! It was tricky tying him up in the rapidly-moving Hudson and getting him on board, but we managed. Cecil filmed the Statue of Liberty as we glided by her. This time we felt we knew our way back, and we headed for Nauvoo Marina in New Jersey. We got in around mid-afternoon and had a most pleasant tie-up. The dock master said he would have the news media out the next day. That was fine with us and we went to dinner at a well-known restaurant in the area and had—what else? A seafood dinner.

June 19: This day was devoted to beginning to pack equipment and load things into our pickup truck cab. We were overwhelmed with "stuff" we had acquired. The battleship had souvenirs given from friends along the way, CELEBRATION had her share of linens, towels, keepsakes, charts, nautical needs, etc. We had three more nights to go and tried to filter out what we needed to live on and what could be packed or shipped in boxes. Cec and I had our pickup truck, but Bill would be flying from New Jersey to his home in San Francisco. The taking apart of our boats and relationships and the undoing of our miraculous trip was taking its toll in our silence and seriousness as we went about our jobs. That night I got our "last supper" as I began to clean out our refrigerator. We all greeted the thunder and lightning storm with the usual comments—"There it goes again." We sat up late and talked in the coziness of our "island" before bedding down.

June 20: Cec off on another errand with his truck—this time to tell his sad story about his TC's and pick up replacements checks for our truck trip cross country. Bill and I continued to clean, sand, scrub and discuss our trip and our parting. Cec and I had a prearranged date with the Johnson/Evinrude factory in Waukegan, WI as their guests, but our need for traveler's checks was obvious. Cec returned after some hours with a long tale about being turned down at several banks. We listened with sympathy. Later that afternoon a good friend with whom I had taught in Los Angeles came with her husband to visit us. They had moved to New Jersey and had seen our publicity in the newspaper. They came to invite us to dinner that night. What fun that would be and we looked forward to being with them and in a home. It was a most enjoyable night and helped us forget that we would soon be parting and off the water.

June 21: Another day of cleaning, packing, mailing boxes at the post office and generally "mounting up" for our departure tomorrow. Bill would stay on a day or two to repair the dings and dents in CELEBRATION and make arrangements to sell her. We had one consolation that we kept referring to; despite our parting we kept saying, "at least we live in the same state."

That night we took Bill to dinner at a lovely restaurant where the food was gourmet and the dance music ideal. It was time to give him our plaque which had been hidden from him for so long. We dwindled over dinner and wine and finally presented it to him. Here is what we had engraved:

To Bill: forever our Skipper—Miami to New York up the ICW, March 17—June 14, 1975. "Filming East Coast history for West Coast children." With deep gratitude and always our love.

Pat and Cecil

One more dance each and we left for CELEBRATION, now high and dry on blocks. The truck and BICENTENNIAL in the trailer nestled next to her ready for us to leave in the morning.

June 22: My diary entry: "Left at noon. VERY difficult."

RECAPITULATION
or...WHAT MADE IT WORK?

We started our trip west on Highway 80 with mixed feelings. A variety of thoughts enveloped us. We were reluctant to leave our boats and the water; reluctant to leave the ICW challenges, the meeting of new people; reluctant to have another boating experience ahead of us at Johnson Outboard headquarters and not have our threesome together. CELEBRATION II had been our oasis and home for three months, and we were loathe to cut the cord with the water and become land creatures. Most of all we realized that being back on land meant assuming responsibilities of a different nature. Ahead of us lay resumption of teaching and a return to home responsibilities. Psychologists would likely interpret our feelings as "coming off a high." True.

We turned off Highway 80 and headed north to Waukegan and a grand reception by Bill Au Coin and the Johnson Outboard people. They treated us like VIPs. Despite phone calls to Bill Brockett still back in NJ, he was not able to fly and join us in Waukegan. He was having problems gussying up CELEBRATION and needed to finish up and fly home. A tour of the factory was fascinating and we saw how our faithful 9.9 hp motor was assembled. The Johnson people treated us royally. We were given a lovely suite in a local hotel and were speakers at a banquet. They even pulled out the stops with quite a bit of press/media coverage. We were grateful for the opportunity to thank all these generous people for their help over the three-month period. We will never forget the new engines, the spark plugs freely given, the repair service at Johnson outlets along the ICW. We could not have survived the rigors of 1500 miles without their help.

Back south to Highway 80 and we trundled our red, white and blue lady behind us. Across the flat prairie land and over the Rockies she went, with truck drivers riding our tail and demanding to know (via CB) "WHAT is she?" This was old stuff by now and we were happy to answer questions as to where she had been.

It was all a jumble of memories now—happenings, problems, challenges and FUN! Never could we have anticipated the experiences we would be having. We were pleased that our exchange of mayor letters and children's letters was received so well. Later reports of pen pal exchange letters were gratifying.

How does one explain the camaraderie, the chemistry, the comradeship that develops between three disparate people who come from different backgrounds? The joy, the solidarity, the adversities faced together, the pulling together as a team, the ying and yang of male/female, the treasured friendship and trust shared—it is difficult to encapsulate in words, but it bonded us forever.

Others have undoubtedly experienced the same. Richenbacher, the famous WWII pilot who floated in a life raft for days with two other men , described such feelings. POWs, sharing such terrible experiences, have expressed the same thought. People who have been trapped in dangerous situations together and have survived express similar feelings. The kinship, the bonding must come from the hardships and danger faced together. When people climb tall mountains and faces harsh conditions, they are welded into a closely-knit collection never-to-be penetrated intimacy that outsiders recognize but do not comprehend.

There was a period of time in the beginning where I had to evaluate. Do I go along with this crazy battleship idea? What about the dollar outlay? How do I overcome my fear of water? Do I want to put myself into uncomfortable situations? What do I know about boating?

Am I ever glad I joined the parade!! I know the three of us would not trade what we did for gold or creature comforts. Lucky lady to have had two such good men in her life plus the many, many wonderful people who assisted us along the way. What a rich treasury of instant friendships. What gratitude we feel toward the Navy and the Coast Guard, who so patiently rescued us along the different waterways. How kind the many Bicentennial officials were to us. How generous people were in taking us into their homes—three unknowns, but they took us to dinner, loaned us their cars and trucks, helped us repair our boats, did truck and trailer storage and drove us to our destination when needed. People are good. We saw the face of America and we met its potpourri of citizens. They come in all shapes and sizes; they run the gamut of educational background, their walks of life range from the Cajun fisherman to tugboat pilots to CEOs of famous corporations. They all had one thing in common. They reached out to a tiny microcosm—a symbol of "up with America." Spontaneously they gave us their dollars, their food, their time, their help—and their hearts. We remember them all and we thank them again.

1976

New York, Hudson River; Lake Champlain, Montreal, Canada

USS BICENTENNIAL

Dru and Paul Stewart
Walt, Cecil and Pat

New York, Hudson River; Lake Champlain, Montreal—1976

COMING ASHORE IS A BUMMER

Fortunately it was the beginning of summer and we had July and August to adjust to having our land legs. After dropping off the well-traveled USS BICENTENNIAL at Lake Almanor, we drove south to Woodland Hills. We picked up dear dog, gave our renter a hug and said we would be back in time for school's opening in early September. Off to our northern California cabin on Lake Almanor we went. This gave us time to polish off the log book, check out audio tapes Cec had made, view the 16mm film he had taken, put two boats out on the lake and "attack" all other boats much to everyone's amazement. There was a great deal of memorabilia to sort out—lovely, sentimental gifts given to all of us along the ICW. Bill came up to see us and we had a grand time out on the lake, reviving wonderful memories. We did one feature TV show on the lake that summer—the NBC *Kent Pierce Show* from Sacramento.

A few weeks before school started, we drove back to our home to find that our wonderful renter had found another place to rent (a mutual decision), had partially moved out, then had the offer rescinded and his boxes were piled high in our kitchen. He was distressed and without another rental. By this time he had become so special to us (and dear dog) that we invited him to continue to stay with us and rent his end of the long ranch house. After three years of living together we all jokingly called him "The Man Who Came To Dinner." He had a business which took him out of the house by 4 A.M. and he was long gone before we ever got up. Late afternoon he would return, we would have a brief hello at the refrigerator (he had his own shelves) and that was it. Weekends he was always out and the relationship turned out to be a treasured one. He continued to take care of dear dog as we went off on more boating trips!

After settling in in Woodland Hills, it was time to bring our summary of the pre-Bicentennial, 1975 trip to the Supervisor of our San Fernando Area school district. The school officials had been well aware of our mail delivery— not only of Mayor Tom Bradley's six letters, but the numerous Los Angeles

City School's letters to the six major cities on the East Coast. They were very interested to hear the outcome. We had a special interview with our wonderful valley supervisor, Tony Rivas, who enthusiastically listened to our narrative of the three-month tableau on the water. He felt the liaison established between the West and East Coast children with the pen pal letters was so important a contribution to the next year's 1976 Bicentennial that he took us to downtown Los Angeles school headquarters and introduced us to the superintendent of all Los Angeles City Schools.

Those of us who were still teaching in the classroom called it "being on the firing line where the rubber meets the road." We also called super-district headquarters in downtown L.A. "The Kremlin." This last is self-explanatory. Down we went into the plush headquarters of the then superintendent. He rocked back and forth in his chair and "our" local superintendent told him of our enthusiasm of the just finished project and how he felt we should be given release time from the classroom to further uphold the Bicentennial year. "Our" superintendent suggested we be given September, 1975-February, 1976, free from the classroom to trailer our red/white/blue lady around to different schools, show the children where the letters had gone and share the film of the history we had taken. Tony felt that our contribution was invaluable to continuing Los Angeles school's participation in the Bicentennial. The finale of this rather interesting meeting was that we would both be required to teach in our classroom three days per week, and would be given two days per week "free" to trailer our ship around to 76 schools.

We suspect that the budget could have given us the "free" semester, but the L.A. superintendent only gave us the "concession" of three days in the classroom and two days "on the road." We and our local superintendent were disappointed, but were grateful for something.

And thus began a semester of juggling three days of teaching, preparing for a substitute for two days of the week, trailering to three schools per visiting days and winding up totally exhausted at the end of the week. We felt badly for our classes. They deserved better. The juggling of "three on/two off" was not what we felt the children deserved from us. Fortunately, I had a substitute who was in my classroom on a consistent basis most of the time. Poor Cecil—his high school subs could not always be that reliable due to other commitments. It was very hard on the children (we felt) and equally hard on us. But we did it.

One of the hardest parts to this whole affair was Cec setting up shop in L.A. school's Channel 58 TV station where he had to learn how to edit his 16 mm film. His 30-minute film had to be ready within a few weeks. Many days he would drive downtown after school and on Saturdays to learn to edit, cut and splice. The managers were very nice about putting in the proper music for a background and gave us many helpful hints when both of us did our voiceovers. Then we were ready to roll on this difficult fall schedule.

Friday and Monday we trailered up and did two schools in the morning and one in the afternoon. The modus operandi was to trailer onto the playground in an accessible spot. Some large schools required two sittings which would bring in the primary youngsters, then the upper grade. After the 30-minute film the classes would be brought out to the playground to see the USS BICENTENNIAL. There we stood on the trailer and answered questions. It was a wonderful finale to be able to tell the children about the East Coast and the Waterway. Many told us they were already corresponding with youngsters in the Midwest and the East who had found their balloons in odd places.

One of the most fun times was going to Chatsworth Elementary School and surprising the 5th grader with Valerie Horner's nice note and her story and picture of the young girl's balloon. When we came to that part in our film, the whole auditorium full of children gasped and applauded. Our 5th grade friend was an instant celebrity for the day. The children were amazed how far the balloons had floated.

There were many appearances that winter and into early spring of 1976. The Bicentennial festivities were in full swing all over the country, and we had many calls for appearances with our ships all over Southern California. One gathering was at the celebrated old Ebell Club in mid-Los Angeles. Only Los Angeles's oldest families seemed to belong to this prestigious group. We were invited to bring our trailer and speak to approximately 700 members. We were on stage ready to go and the electrical power for sound went out. After much fussing about by the custodian and with the audience obviously restive, we were asked to "wing it" with our voice over the film. We used one mike, passed it back and forth and tried as best we could to reconstruct what was already on the film. It was a challenging time, and the applause at the end was appreciated.

With two battleships in our backyard and the possibility of another—or even an aircraft carrier(!)—we did research to find out what we should do with this fledgling fleet. Attorney advice indicated we should form a non-profit corporation and write a preamble, design a logo, have stationery designed. All this would reflect the thrust of this impossible dream. There were piles of paperwork to complete just to form a California non-profit corporation, but eventually it was done and we began to put boats and trailers into this shelter. We were now THE FRIENDSHIP FLEET, INC. Soliciting some close friends who already loved and had driven our boats, we found five enthusiastic, supportive people who would serve as our board of directors. Cecil and I would make a total of seven members. Cecil was president, a neighbor was vice president and this lucky lady was voted secretary-treasurer "because you're so good at it!" Sure!

In the meantime the Navy had viewed and used our boats and wanted to buy three of them for use in the Midwest waters. Not being near an ocean, they felt they wanted them for a high profile attraction to help with their recruiting. Here was another after school and night job for Cecil! We had three more battleship molds shot up and Cec put one together so the Navy could see how to fiberglass them collectively. A CPO visited us and pronounced them "just what we need." As soon as this was done we had to get all three boats up to a Naval Base 40 miles north of us. This necessitated two round trips, and on a Saturday we met a C-130 and watched our gray ladies being loaded on board in the plane's tail section. Off they went to the Midwest and eastern rivers and we still hear reports that they are floating around somewhere!

At this same time Cecil and I decided we would be wise to take a power squadron course put on at night at a local high school. This long and technical course covered a great deal of boating ground and I realized, as I took notes, how much I had learned the hard way. We covered everything: safety, knot tying, embarking, disembarking, charting courses, compass readings, boating courtesy, who is the burdened ship, shipping channels and lanes, learning the mathematical computations for ETAs—all the basic navigation the novice boater should know and use. We took the final our last night of the course and both of us were delighted to pass it 100%. I immediately called Bill and proudly told him of our accomplishment. He was not surprised that the Hawaiian born boat builder Cecil had done so well; but his dry comment to me was, "Sure would have helped, Dearie, if *you* had taken that course before we all left Miami." Recalling my inexperienced times where I was more hindrance than help, I couldn't help but silently agree with our skipper.

With the Los Angeles Schools hoping we could do a next summer 1976 boating trip with more pen pal letters, we made some trips to Bill's Land 'n Sea factory in San Jose. He called for us to come up one weekend when his firm was having a meeting of West Coast Land 'n Sea owners. There was no way Bill could take the time to go with us in the summer of 1976, nor were we eligible for another sabbatical leave yet; but there was great interest from the boat owners who considered loaning their boat and going with us.

After showing our 16mm film and describing some of our adventures, we found two couples ready to go! One couple was older, retired and anxious to be an accompanying boat for us on the next voyage. The other couple, they decided, would leave the wife at home with the children and her husband would house us on his boat and tow the Bicentennial when needed. The two couples were so intrigued with our trip, adventurers at heart, so they elected to join us. We figured time to drive across the country on Highway 80 to New Jersey's marina (Nauvoo) would take a week. Then, we would plan to be by the Statue of Liberty for the fireworks the night of July 4, 1976. From there we would go up the Hudson River, into Lake Champlain, through the Richlieu River, hang a left onto the St. Lawrence Seaway and end up in Montreal. Again, we would be carrying pen pal letters from West Coast children to East Coast children and on to Canada. There seemed to be great enthusiasm on the part of the volunteer boaters to be a part of this voyage. And we were very grateful for their help.

We had towed our USS BICENTENNIAL to San Jose and Preston put her on a forklift and placed her next to a major highway outside his factory! We were glad to leave her in the Bay area because we had had a call from Hank Ketchum's office that they wanted to do a story on the USS BICENTENNIAL's ICW trip. On a weekend we flew to Monterey, Bill trailered the battleship south some 100 miles, and we launched out in Monterey Bay! It was fun to see Dennis (the perfect size) and our ship on the front cover of the comic book. We distributed hundreds of the *Dennis the Menace* comic books later on other trips.

Over the winter we planned our trip, kept in touch with our newfound friends, bought more charts and were publicized throughout the San Fernando Valley Schools that we would once again carry pen pal letters. We continued teaching school and laying our plans—reluctantly without Bill, but looking forward to another waterway trip in unexplored territory. Our trip would end with letters to the Montreal Prime Minister's office for Canada's schoolchildren.

We left L.A. as soon as school was out, June 16, 1976, and headed for Las Vegas. It was hot (107), so we spent more time in the casinos than in our camper. The next day we headed north and made it through Utah into Evanston, WY. On we traveled with the red/white/blue lady behind us. Buffalo

Bend, NE was a memorable stop. College students put on a terrific show at this out-of-the-way restaurant and we were enthralled. Everywhere we went we were the usual curiosity. "I seen ya on TV last year." "WHAT is it?" Navy men would tell us their stories; children were ecstatic over a boat just their size.

We slogged onward to the east. Unfamiliar toll roads were driven. The acres and acres of Midwest corn reached for the sky. Taking some back roads, we met wonderful people in RV parks where we stayed with our camper. We drove through the Iowa city where my parents were born and raised. Nostalgia! As we neared the East Coast, the rain began and our battleship looked red, gray and blue. We continued to drive to the northeast as we wanted to do some filming for the Los Angeles children on Boston history.

We ended up in an RV park south of Boston where, at last, we could drop the trailer, clean her up, and head out with the truck to do some filming before we met our boating friends. What a plethora of history we filmed in the Boston area (again). We even visited the USS CONSTITUTION (Old Ironsides) and were daunted with the lack of facilities the people on board had. What courage the early settlers had!

We visited Fall River where the USS MASSACHUSETTS was now a museum. This time we had to trailer our battleship into that harbor for the museum people wanted their battleship as a backdrop for ours. Again, great news coverage, and Cec repeated doing "his thing." We only had one bad beginning to this trip—our renter had generously given us two walkie-talkies and we were going to use them for communication when we were launching the battleship. I was the watcher; Cec, the driver. Somehow one of us (not labeled here) launched not only a battleship, but also a walkie-talkie. Dismay! What an inauspicious beginning. On another day we drove to Mystic Bay and filmed the sailors and taped their sea chanteys for background music for our new film. We also toured the Coast Guard Academy and filmed the cadets in training. This gave us an opportunity tell the Coast Guard officials how very much we appreciated their services to mariners.

With all of this filming out of the way, we trailered back to Nauvoo Marina as it was near the end of June and we were to meet our new friends: Walt, with whom we would live on his boat; Dru and Paul on the other Land 'n Sea. How could we go back to Nauvoo Marina without Bill? But he had wished us well, spurred us on and told us it would work again.

We met our three friends and were grateful to have company and a boat to live on! We began our transfer of clothes, equipment, pen pal letters, food, etc. into Walt's boat. Dru's was already provisioned. We were introduced to a surprise member of the crew, Sunny. Sunny turned out to be a beautiful, sweet Sheltie dog that was used to living on a boat and became everyone's favorite. That night we took everybody to a spaghetti feed, a get-acquainted time, got out our charts and checked out our next day departure for the Statue of Liberty. Not unexpected was a tremendous thunder and lightning storm. Cecil and I wondered if it saw us coming again!

Reprinted with permission by Hank Ketcham Enterprises, Inc.

HAPPY BIRTHDAY, AMERICA!

Dru and Paul proceeded ahead of us, out of the marina and into the turbulent waters of Sandy Hook. Unlike the previous year, this day proved to be a tough one for boaters. The water was in turmoil, we were with a most pleasant but unskilled boat driver plus we had put the BICENTENNIAL under tow. The hours dragged as we anxiously fended off the battleship, watched the increasingly heavy boating traffic and worried about a tie-up by the Statue. It was July 2 and *everyone* who owned a boat or had a friend who owned a boat was out on the water to get a good view of the July 4 parade of Tall Ships and the fireworks. We saw the Tall Ships from a distance, watched in awe the splendiferous yachts that churned by us, waved at small cruisers such as ourselves and talked on the VHF with Dru and Paul. Sunny did a good balancing job on the stern (lashed with a leash) and barked happily at strange boats, noises and waves. We churned our way toward the coppery-green lady and were amazed to see the powerboat and sailboat congestion. Apparently everyone in the New York area wanted a right-by-the-channel anchorage to see the parade of the Tall Ships. Our two boats eyeballed the traffic and decided we had best back off away from the main channel. This, after Walt almost collided with a passing sailboat. We could also see six large gray Navy destroyers lined up along the channel, each one swinging on a gigantic anchor chain. We had toots, hoots and whistles from the Navy as we tried to "sashay" into place. By this time we had cut Cec and the BICENTENNIAL loose and he was out in the harbor busily engaged in water attacks on the Navy ships. I was left to anchor with Walt. He chose a location which proved to be a poor choice. Out to the deck I went to hoist up the anchor. YUK! What sludge, slime and unmentionable goo was on the chain. My first thought was, *Cut the anchor line.* My second thought was, *This is not my boat and at this early stage in the trip I didn't want to have to walk the plank.* Three times Walt tried to anchor and three times I had the privilege of pulling up that blasted chain. "Bill, where are you?"

Finally we were settled to everyone's satisfaction and had a chat on the

VHF with Dru and Paul who were anchored near us. Cec came back, we tied him up on our port and hauled him on board. We were about to settle in for the evening, have a drink while I prepared dinner when we heard shouts, whistles and the whine of engines starting. We looked out. It was the tide change. The inexperienced boaters by the main channel had not anticipated the ebb and flow of the tide and were anchored much too close to the Navy ships. Slowly, the ponderous destroyers started to swing around in the opposite direction. Pandemonium! The day cruisers were about to be wiped out. Frantically, everyone on board at least a dozen boats ran around, orders were shouted, anchors hoisted and all narrowly made their escape. It was quite a sight and we could envision the conversation on board. We had one other episode to watch. Right where we had originally started to anchor a small tornado hit and caused damage to some boats in its path. That night the boaters in our area all had VHF chit-chat as we discussed the weather, Tall Ships and the nuances of boating. Exhausted, we crawled into bed, thinking about spending another 24 hours on the water before the parade began.

The next morning was a bright one, and cheerfulness descended on the five of us. I took the dinghy and rowed over to Dru's boat where I played with Sunny. Dru, Paul, and I and got into a wild hearts game. Cecil went out to terrorize the local, anchored boats, and Walt busied himself on board his boat, the UNICORN. More boats came in and anchored and Tall Ships were positioning themselves for the July 4 parade. It was a spectacular sight and Cec took his cameras and did a lot of filming. (East Coast history for West Coast children?) We had numerous visits from TV and the press and many magazines. The media was out covering this 200th birthday with a vengeance. They were looking for anything unique or unusual and we were "IT." Word had spread in the harbor via the many VHFs to "go find that funny little battleship." That night we watched the fireflies that out-maneuvered everyone. As Westerners we never ceased to be fascinated by these flying flashlights.

Operation Sail '76 had ships coming from all parts of the world—Argentina, Italy, Spain, Norway, Poland, and Portugal. Some of the fleet raced across the Atlantic to participate. We anticipated seeing them close up. In the morning we put on the radio as the 200th birthday was to be broadcast to the whole world and we were there! It began with the Tall Ships parading north up the Hudson. What a sight to see glorious ladies of old, sailing magnificently, grandly up the parade route. Brigantines, frigates, schooners, square riggers, sailing ships of all descriptions from as many nations—all paraded by us. The U.S. Coast Guard's training ship EAGLE was there giving cadets a chance to "learn the ropes." Cec went out near the ships, giving them a wide berth, and was hailed, applauded and tooted. What a sight. We were on Walter Cronkite's *OP' SAIL '76* (ABC).

The five of us had dinner together under the Statue and awaited the evening's fireworks. What an event. Everyone was up on their fly bridge with a radio. Fireworks had been planted on numerous barges up and down the Hudson. The cacophony was astounding, the fireworks magnificent and the finale was mind-boggling. The fireworks were set off to the music of the "Star Spangled Banner." When the words, "...and the rockets red glare, the bombs bursting in air..." came over the ether waves, the brilliant red fireworks dazzled us all. We could hear shouts, yelling and applause up and down our section of the river. What a sight! There were many happy boating spectators that evening and I am sure we were all amazed at the choreography. Happy Birthday, wonderful country. Happy Birthday.

LET'S HEAR IT FOR THE WOMEN!!

July 5 and we left the harbor. We waited until many of the boats had gone their ways. Being under tow increased our boating problems, and we thought it wise to wait until our passage north up the Hudson was more clear. We left after reading in our *Waterway Guide* that the first 12 miles of our trip should be made on a flooding tide. Currents run as high as four knots and bucking it can be costly in time, fuel and comfort. In the lower river the usual debris was everywhere, the water is polluted and the only scenery are the tall skyscrapers. We carefully edged our way northward and nostalgically checked out last year's 79th Street Yacht Basin. As we came up to 123rd Street, we could see Grant's Tomb and ahead, the George Washington Bridge. This bridge connected New York with New Jersey and it was necessary to slow down to five knots within 200 feet of workboats, barges and other floating barges. I was delighted to see beneath the bridge the little red lighthouse made famous in the children's book of the same name. How many times I had read that to first graders!

What history we were viewing! Verrazano had discovered the Hudson River in 1524, but he named it for the Englishman Henry Hudson. The latter had thought it might be the "Northwest Passage," and it has been used for almost 500 years for exploration, trade and for war. During the American Revolution the Hudson and the next link north, Lake Champlain were the gateway from and to Canada and was used by Gentleman Johnny Burgoyne and his invading British troops. America had also used the Hudson when they tried to invade Canada. This busy river had seen a great deal of history over the many years of its use. The Hudson valley is dotted with forts and battlegrounds from West Point to Saratoga where Benedict Arnold "defected."

As we left Manhattan's towers we began to see our country's spectacular history and scenery—The Palisades, High Tor, Dunderburg, Storm King and Bear Mountains, the Catskills. High bridges gave way to estates or farms once the property of patroons. We were seeing gabled Dutch stone houses and medieval German castles, but we also saw power plants and cities, large and small. WHERE were we headed? This neophyte, relatively unacquainted boating camaraderie group—where were we headed, where would we tie up tonight? Hello, *Waterway Guide*! What do you suggest? Dear *Waterway Guide*! You said, "Tarrytown Marina." (Reading on.) "North of Tappan Zee Bridge, sheltered basin, over 200 berths (floats and docks) for boats to 65', water, electricity, showers, rest rooms, ice, near village center. Named thus because men 'tarried at the tavern' after delivering produce to the market." OK—we can do that! A marked channel leads into Tarrytown harbor, which is protected by barges from either the north or south and boats of six-foot draft use it without problem. Stores and shore accommodations are located within walking distance of waterfront facilities (which included the marina, restaurant—cruising boats are accommodated). Oh, did this sound good! Let's GO.

What a WELCOME! These good people were celebrating the Bicentennial, having a carnival that promised to go on forever, and invited us to participate. After spending some quality time with these patriotic citizens we thought we had best get back to our ships. What a nice night. To have water, power, showers—things were looking up. The next A.M. we told our newfound friends that we would be leaving; we must get going to West Point where we anticipated filming the first women to enter the Army Academy.

We wished we could have stayed there. Both our boats, UNICORN and PEANUT, were docked at the gas dock. After fueling, Walt forgot me, took off in UNICORN and I was left stranded on the docks as he left. Cecil was off filming! Dru and Paul were waiting to cast off. They saw that I was boatless, called Cecil, rescued both of us and took us out to Walt's boat which we privately named "I'm headed out" ship. There we were shoveled onboard out in the channel with apologies from Walt. "No problem we assured him. Forge on." Great to be onboard.

We trundled on up the Hudson River. What a different situation confronted us. We really had no idea where we were except for the (bible) the *Waterway Guide*, '76. We could see densely wooded Dunderberg Mountain, 1100 feet high. It was thought that Captain Kidd might have buried some of his treasure at the base of the mountain. The river narrowed sharply here to less than one third of a mile in width, and for the next nine miles it threaded around sharp turns between high rising mountains on both shores. Blind curves were scary. Thank goodness for The Waterway's guidance. It truly is/was a bible. Hopefully we were heading for West Point! We knew we were in military country. On the east side of the Hudson was New York's National Guard

Camp Smith, and farther along on the west bank was West Point. We were getting close!

At last, we saw an anchorage on our port side with a dozen moorings but it did not look easy. We cast Cec off in his battleship and our two escort ships gingerly made their way in. West Point! Excitement! We were thrilled to be there. We tied up both ships and BICENTENNIAL at the bottom of the steps. We encountered a surly 1st sergeant who was not overly welcoming and paid the tie-up fee. When we excitedly said we had come to film the first women to be admitted to an academy, his reply was, "We are training for war. We don't need NO women!" OK, so much for any more comments.

I could not resist retorting, "If I were 20 years younger, I'd be right up there with them." He glared at me, harrumphed and we exited. Despite his lack of enthusiasm, we were excited to be there, and we walked and walked and walked up, up, up to the top of the bluff. Huff/puff. We climbed. Huff/puff and we ascended up to the campus! Nothing could discourage us true blue Americans at this point—watching the FIRST women to apply for and be accepted into a military academy!

We had a wonderful afternoon walking the grounds and watching the young women cadets saying goodbye to their tearful parents. A few more hours and the women belonged to the academy. There were tears, a high level of excitement, hugs, kisses and some mean-looking upperclassmen who looked ready to pounce on the new cadets the minute the parents' visiting time was over. As the afternoon waned, we felt it was high time to find a resting spot for the night and we hurried down the path we had so laboriously climbed. Thank goodness, we had a good take-off. We were grateful. Out in the middle of the Hudson we pulled in BICENTENNIAL and helped Cec climb on board. The charts told us the river would soon turn almost 90 degrees to port through Worlds End. The latter is the Hudson's deepest with 140-175-foot-deep holes.

We passed Sing-Sing and had some interesting comments between our two boats. Dru entertained me with the wonderful tricks Sunny was doing in the cabin. Suddenly, over the VHF came a familiar, but unidentified voice. "Ahoy there, UNICORN. Is that the USS BICENTENNIAL you have behind you?" Surprised, Cec and I looked off to the starboard. It was CHANTICLEER, Mr. Evinrude's huge yacht we had been on last year at Jensen Beach. We reminded him of our pleasant visit aboard his boat, thanked him again and he wished us well. With some envy (color us green) we watched the luxurious yacht pull past us and disappear. We could see his wife, Frances

Langford, sitting with friends on the stern deck having cocktails. Sigh!

On into the Catskills, and we found our marina with the unlikely name of Hop-O-Nose. How good it read in the *Guide*...."water, power, heated pool, bar, restaurant, showers, ice, pump-out station, marine store, gift shop, rental cards"...hooray! We were impressed with the write-up. We were grateful to have an unimpressive tie-up for all three boats. The only problem was a very grumbly dock master. Usually they welcomed us so pleasantly, but this one seemed to have had a bad day or night. He was unimpressed with our battleship, which was a total one-eighty degree attitude for us and equally unimpressed with the two escort boats. He probably felt the same way about the five of us. We assured him we would be taking off early the next morning. Whether he cared or not we have no idea. We had dinner on board and walked into town. The rain began! We raced back to the ships and battened everything down for the night. Into the bunk. Another day.

Early the next morning the local newspaper came down to cover us, and off Cec went for a show of battleship power in the river. After this interview we set off for our next commitment which was to be Albany, NY. There we would have the men go back for trucks, trailers and Dru and I would do big-time laundry. What interesting, beautiful country we went through. We went under the bridge which joined Newburgh and Beacon. We read that General Washington headquartered at Newburgh and it was here he angrily rejected a letter promising support of his officers if he would accept the crown of an American monarchy. At Beacon hilltop signal fires told the Continental Army of the movements of the British. It was fascinating history for all of us! Mansion after mansion we passed, reminders of earlier times when land and labor were cheap. As we neared Kingston, the channel swung around the broad shoal area called Esopus Meadows and extended well out into the west shore of the river. We zigged and zagged as we gave mud flats that dot the river a wide berth. North of the Saugerties were more mud flats, and buoys were carefully watched. Onward, under bridges, uninhabited areas except for wading birds, some marinas, a few breakwaters and some interesting looking homes. We took this all in. We were so close to the city of New York yet, but in such a lovely area. We were nearing Albany, which was 144 miles above The Battery and the capital of the state. Here we would deliver our first set of pen pal letters. The commercial traffic began to grow heavier as this was the principal port above New York City. The banks slowly filled with industry. We began to look for a likely marina.

Some unidentified mariners who were members of the Albany Yacht Club came out to greet us and invited us to stay at their private yacht club. With no chart, Walt and I argued about which way to go. Walt went left when he should have gone right, but we made it in to a lovely marina. This yacht club is a favorite layover for many having 1,000 feet of floats for boats going on through the Troy locks. What a nice outreach to tired boaters. Weary, we walked to the nearby restaurant. We left a saddened Sheltie who howled when she saw us leave. After dinner we walked uptown. Where was everyone in this capital city? We found out that Albany emptied on weekends. They must be in the Catskills! What history we were finding. We were told that it was here a British soldier wrote "Yankee Doodle." To the soldier's dismay, the Yankees adopted it for a rallying and marching song that we still sing on July 4.

Sister ships!

Lake Almanor

Marina

It gets lonesome

out there all alone

on the Intracoastal

Waterway

We did not have a chance to visit the state capitol or the Schuyler Mansion where Alexander Hamilton was married, but we knew there was a lot of history in this area. One of the obstacles ahead was the Troy locks, and we were advised to buy inexpensive hay bags to protect our sides from dirt and slime in the locks. Oh, goody. We were told that the lift bridge ahead had been removed and a 60-foot-high fixed bridge had replaced it. Good—one less worry. With all the advice and looking forward with some trepidation about getting through the locks, we all turned in for the night.

WE ATTACK THE DUTCH

Rising early we discovered that a Dutch lugger (lug rigged on two or three masts) had come in at night and was very curious as to what we were. Adding to the fun was the fact that the four people were Dutch. They came over to visit us and were very interested in our battleship and the Bicentennial celebration. They were quite well-informed about our nation's 200th birthday and seemed to think we were unusual, quaint and pure American. They were so nice and wanted to get pictures, so Cecil, who was going to drive the USS BICENTENNIAL anyhow, went out into the large harbor. When he came in close to their lugger, he surprised them by squirting them with his 16-inch cannons. They were delighted to be "attacked" and Cecil said over the PA system, "Welcome to America!" We knew their pictures were going to be shown everywhere in Holland where the four might have friends!

Our usual nightmare of leap-frogging trucks and trailers was always with us. This time the men had left all the equipment north of Albany. Without leaving anything behind, the five of us took off, anticipating our first lock. As we cruised along we were so aware of the numerous mansions along the high bluffs of the Hudson. They were living museums and we wished we had the time and car to visit some of them. We were amused to read that the town of Watervliet had been instrumental in giving us the caricature of "Uncle Sam." A man by the name of Samuel Wilson supplied the army with meat, and soldiers in the area decided that the "U.S. Beef" stamp stood for Uncle Sam Wilson's beef. By extension anything stamped "U.S." became "Uncle Sam's." We discovered another bit of trivia. The town of Troy ahead was made semi-famous by a housewife. She tired of laundering her husband's shirts when only the collars were dirty, so she detached the collars and they could be washed separately, thus creating a new industry. My, there were some amazing details to history in the Northeast…all news to us Westerners.

We knew that the Troy Lock and Dam were the largest and first of many that boats headed north to Lake Champlain must pass. Also, if one was heading west via the Erie Canal, one must lock through. Troy Lock was designed for commercial traffic—it is 500 feet long, 44 feet wide with a low water depth of 13 feet over the sill and a lift of 17 feet. This was the biggest we had done yet. We were early-morning arrivals as traffic can be heavy, debris around the entrance is a problem and the current approach is tricky. We knew that maneuvering around would be difficult with our boat under tow, and boats cannot tie up to the walls but must wait 100 yards downstream. We found that lockmasters are VERY particular about boaters following the rules of the road, approaching them slowly with care and following their directions. Lockmasters can make or break your entrance and exit to and from the locks. One exercises the utmost caution and courtesy and listens carefully to the VHF. We knew that pleasure craft are locked through on the hour and that sometimes they can go through with commercial boats if there is room. The latter always enter first, with others following in the order of waiting. Red, green and amber signal lights tell you what to do. Many times the lockmaster will yell over the PA system or contact you politely on the VHF (or sometimes not so politely).

Ready, set, go! We had our four plastic, hay-filled bags hung over the starboard side, strategically set. Ditto Dru and Paul. The BICENTENNIAL was tethered to our port side. We should be OK for the 17-foot lift and be lifted in 20 minutes. It was our friend's first locking experience and our second. (Pros? Hardly!) Cautiously we proceeded into the lock and found our space behind another cruiser. We found two bollards and threw lines around the bow and stern. Walt was in at the VHF, Cec and I on the bow and stern lines. We would ride 17 feet up on the bollards. We looked at the slimy, ooky-book walls. Yuk. No wonder those handling lines going through locks wore gloves. We were surprised to have a crowd awaiting our arrival at the top of the lock. Word had spread that a red/white/blue battleship was locking through and many townspeople came out to wave to us. We were also delighted to have the father of a lady reporter who had done a big story on as at the Miami Boat Show suddenly appear on his bike. He wondered if he could hitchhike with us up to Schuylerville. We were delighted to have him on board, lifted his bike on and enjoyed his company for several hours.

Safely detached from the slimy bollard and a bit smug that we were all so good about locking through so professionally, we enjoyed an afternoon of chitchat with our visitor. His daughter, an excellent writer, was obviously the pride of his life and we were reluctant to see him leave us. We let him off approximately 20 miles south of his destination, but that's what he wished— he wanted plenty of miles to ride his bike. Quite a gentleman.

We saw so many complexes on either side of the river: automobile plants, marina/country clubs, protected anchorages where one could tie up alongside a canal and walk to town. Then we came to Watertown. Here a signboard marks the junction of the Erie and Champlain Canals. As we saw the huge commercial vessels coming out of the Erie, we were glad we were staying to the starboard. Few cruising grounds can match the canals and waterways that lead to Lake Champlain. Ahead of us lay 270 miles to Sorel, Quebec on the St. Lawrence River. But before reaching the St. Lawrence, we had eleven locks to negotiate. Off we went for Lock 1, which had a lift of 14 feet. We timed our arrival perfectly, as northbound traffic is allowed through on the hour. After locking through, we cut to the western shore to avoid rocks and shoals on the east bank. We had a pleasant run for quite some time. Just before Mechanicsville, Lock 2 appeared. Again we were fortunate and did our 18-foot lift successfully. Beyond Mechanicsville, Lock 3 proved to be the highest lift in the Champlain system and took us up 19 feet. We felt we were beginning to be quite skilled. Word of our battleship's arrival was sent ahead by the lockmasters, and we had many townspeople lining the sides of the locks with the usual questions and cheering. Newspaper reporters from the small towns jumped on board with us to do their interview, then got off after we left the lock. A few more miles and there was Lock 4, a lift of 16 feet. With little delay, we wound our way through. Sometimes we had to retie the BICENTENNIAL to the opposite side as the lockmasters directed us to a port or starboard bollard.

Our route wound toward Schuylerville. The hay bags were doing their job in protecting Walt's UNICORN. We did hear a horror story about a boat that had preceded us by a few days in Lock 4. Two ladies and their teenage sons were taking a cabin cruiser down the Champlain locks. They tied their lines—bow and stern—to the two stationary bollards at the top of the lock. As the water went down in this 18-foot drop, their boat did not go, as they were hanging by their two lines which were tied to their cleats on their deck. The crew had not let the lines slide around the bollards to release them in a downward path. There was much shouting by the lockmaster and townspeople. Panic by the crew of women and teenagers was evident. Everyone was frightened. There they were—the water going down, their boat hanging by two frail lines, suspended in mid-air. With the water quickly draining out below them, the teenage boys did the best they could. They grabbed an axe and chopped the two lines. CRASH!! The boat fell five feet down the side of the lock and into the water. Most of the windows were broken and there was glass all over. The engine jumped out of its mount. We heard that someone towed them to a repair marina and that's the last we heard of their sad tale. Live and learn, we all decided. We would be careful.

We realized we were in a "colonial scorched earth" policy territory. We were traveling in Revolutionary War country. Surprised to read this, we found that General Schuyler's wife had burned the wheat fields to keep them from the British. Good for her! We decided that four locks in one day were enough; we needed some supplies and Cecil and I wanted to take off and film some Revolutionary War history for our next film for the schoolchildren.

Tying up at a lovely Schuylerville marina, Dru and I did laundry, prepared dinner where all five of us would eat together, and planned tomorrow's journey. Walt, Dru and Paul would work on their boats, Cecil and I would take the truck and drive to Saratoga to film the history there. What a thunder and lightning storm we had that night. We played hearts through most of the onslaught. Although our boats were tied side by side in the slips, we were drenched when we ran from Paul's boat to UNICORN. Good to be inside. We'll think about Lock 5 day after tomorrow.

Waking to a brilliant, crystal clear day, Cec and I took off for Saratoga and some Revolutionary War history. This was of particular interest to Cec, as he was named Cecil Horatio Gates, Jr. after a general who was in both the British and Colonial Army. General Horatio Gates had been a British general, had retired and moved to the "new country." He had bought a plantation in Virginia and was considered a country gentleman. He was a friend of General George Washington. The latter had faith in General Gates and asked him to come out of retirement and be a general in the Revolutionary War. Gates agreed and led the battle of Saratoga. The Battle of Saratoga was the most decisive of the Revolution. The Continentals under General Horatio Gates's command frustrated a British plan to split the colonies by taking New York. We drove to the spot where the battle took place and tried to envision Cecil's ancestor as a leading contender in this fray. The marker was there and we tried to imagine what war had been like in the days when men stood in line and marched toward one another, muskets at the ready. It was primitive warfare and many lives were lost. This battle ended October 17, 1777 and the colonies persuaded France to give us help with her fleet. This eventually led up to Cornwallis's surrender to Washington at Yorktown four years later. The crowning finale to the story about Cecil's relative was that we had been told and had read that when Burgoyne was forced to surrender to Gates, his remark was, "Do I have to surrender my sword to an old granny of a man like that?"

So much for ancestors.

Back to the boat, a dinner out, more hearts; Sunny for some reason wanted to visit our boat, but soon went back to PEANUT. Another day/another night. It was July 12, 1976. Tomorrow we were determined to get as close to Lake Champlain as possible.

DRU'S TOE COUNT

Logistics! After three newspaper interviews it was decided that I would drive the truck and trailer forward to Lock 7 and the men would do 5 and 6 on UNICORN. Dru would do ditto for their PEANUT Land 'n Sea trailer. We left together and the trip took us through small towns, beautifully located along the Hudson River. Dru and I, always looking for a laundromat, found one and felt very virtuous. We were glad the men would have some time without us! Perhaps there would be great appreciation to see the two cooks later that day!

We met them a few hours later, did a BBQ steak dinner on the stern of PEANUT, played another wild game of hearts and planned ahead for a Whitehall stop. The men told us of going through two locks and we found they missed the extra deck hands. Beyond Lock 6 they went through two miles of land cut to bypass a long river curve. The canal rejoined the Hudson near Billings Island and they ran past farms and countryside. It sounded like the same area we had driven through. There was another channel with no boat facilities and they shared it with oil barges. Anyhow, nice to know we were missed.

We were up early, and the men and Dru were off for Whitehall, the northern end of the Champlain Canal and midpoint between New York City and Montreal. Hooray! Half our goal accomplished. I would pick up the empty trailer. Dru and Paul elected to pick up their rig at a later date. I drove through more beautiful country with the trailer behind me. The others were going through Locks 7, 8 and 9. Lock 8 would be the last one to lift as 9 would drop the boats 16 feet into Lake Champlain.

What a lovely small city we found at Whitehall. This town is where the first U.S. Navy ships were built. These were four galleys and eight gundelos or gondolas. They were built of green lumber. With a sloop and three small schooners, all but one had been taken earlier from the British. The little fleet commanded by Benedict Arnold, gave the British a hard battle at Valcour Island on Lake Champlain in the summer of 1776.

We all met at a lovely marina right in Whitehall that had a restaurant with dockage. It was perfect for a truck and trailer and five hungry people with one small dog. What a surprise to find that this marina was run by two women—our first "dock mistresses." They were very knowledgeable and very efficient. They told us a wild tale that had happened just a few days previous to our arrival. A man and his teenage son had come in for the night and were leaving early in the A.M. The dock mistress watched them tie up and felt they were careless and rather cavalier in their attitude about boating. The next day when they left the father put the throttle forward full thrust and went roaring off into the lake. The son had not yet untied the lines that held them to the dock. The dock mistress saw them careen off into the lake dragging 200 feet of floating dock behind them. There was no attempt by the man to turn back and return the dock! The marine police were called and found the two farther up the lake, arrested them, made them tow the dock back and ticketed them with a large fine. So much for unethical boaters!

What a wonderful tie-up we had at this lovely spot. The following morning was Sunday. We had heard that a very elegant hotel nearby served an equally elegant brunch on Sunday mornings. We looked pretty grundgy, but Dru and I searched around in the dark recesses of our "extensive" wardrobes and found something "Sunday brunchish" and semi-passable....ditto the three men. We climbed off the ship as the water was so high that it was sloshing over the top of our dock tie-ups. We started to ascend. Up, up a steep grassy slope we all went. As we approached the top of this hill, we could see a beautiful white hotel with many equally beautiful white outbuildings in this luxurious setting. As we came closer we could hear the cacophony of many voices, the clatter of silver and a distinct sound of many at brunch. We looked for the entrance, not having come in our Rolls Royce or our chauffeur driven limo. A-HAH! We found the entrance. Dru and I checked our attire and looked at the seafaring men. Oh well—OK. Best we could do! We were graciously ushered into one of the most beautiful hotels we had ever seen. The graciousness, the ambience, the whole setting was so eastern, so high class—we loved it. We were seated, given menus, but were also invited to partake of the most heavily-laden Sunday brunch table we had ever seen—cruise ships excluded. What a feast for five weary travelers who were used to doing hard physical labor and juggling logistics. We had a wonderful time. A few curiosity seekers wondered where we had strayed in from, but were really trying to be friendly. When we told them about the USS BICENTENNIAL being docked below them, they took off their shoes, marched down the steep grassy slope and demanded our story. A few had read about us in the local newspapers. What a bizarre happening—to intrude in on a weekly Sunday ritual, but find such wonderful new acquaintances. Again we were impressed with all the good Americans we had met and were meeting. Whatever the bill was, it was well worthwhile the expenditure for all of us. We tromped back down to our lower "servant's quarters" and settled in for a heart game, an analysis of what we were doing and a long sleep. Tomorrow—Chipman Marina or bust! What a goal.

Leaving Whitehall, the channel turns to port. One more lock to go, and #12 ahead looked formidable. We got in with little trouble and watched and listened as the locks clanged shut. The water began to boil as we were lowered. The lockmaster was not overly friendly as he apparently didn't like the TV coverage we were receiving as the boat was lowered. For the next 15 miles it was well buoyed and the channel winds through marshes in the southern narrows of Lake Champlain. There was a river-like stretch with wildlife on either shore in the foothills of the Adirondack and the Green Mountains. We followed the markers closely past strange sounding names—Maple Bend, Narrows of Dresden, Pulpit Point. We proceeded slowly. We found Stony Point on our chart, and the channel began to broaden, the marshes ended, the buoyage thinned out and our navigation became easier. Open water was still almost 17 miles away, and land points projecting out from both shores had to be given a wide berth. We knew that at Chipman Point, Vermont, the first boating facilities on the lake would show up. We read that from here on there would be many, generally well equipped to serve cruising boats. We began to read our "bible," check our charts, visit on the VHF and try to figure out where the next landfall would show.

Chipman Point Marina proved to be exactly what we wanted. It had all facilities, fuel, laundromats, showers, and marina supplies. New acquaintances tied up next to us and invited us on board to view our TV coverage from the early-morning lock. The Bicentennial celebration was going full swing in this town. We went to a fair where all the old-fashioned foods and games brought everyone into town. Children were bobbing for apples, many were dressed in the 1776 clothing style complete with bonnets for the women; we filmed the boys climbing a bacon-greased pole. The incentive was a $20 bill pinned to the top. We watched a girl beat out the boys in catching a greased pig. It was all very simple and refreshing to watch. We invited many to visit us at the marina to view our battleship. Our publicity had preceded us, and we were delighted to have visitors. All five of us sat down for a pow-wow as to the next jump, and I was voted to drive our truck and trailer to Ft. Ticonderoga.

Twenty three miles north, Fort Ticonderoga stands on a broad spit of land, high on a hill on the New York shore. It was built in 1755 by the French, captured in 1756 by the English, taken in 1775 by Ethan Allen and his Green Mountain Boys, then retaken in 1777 by the British. Our *Waterway Guide* advised us not to approach the fort by water, as landing facilities are poor. They did direct us to a state launching ramp just to the north of the fort, and there the crew elected to meet me.

The Vermont and New York countrysides were beautiful. Coming into Ticonderoga, I stopped for our general delivery mail, picked up bus schedules for possible backtracking which lay ahead and drove to the marina where my crew was waiting for me. We had lunch and all piled into our truck for the trip back to visit the fort.

What a hike to reach the top—up the hill, across an open field. Sunny did better than all of us. We were intrigued to find that when the British controlled the portage from Lake Champlain to Lake George that it fell without a shot. However, the Americans were unable to keep it armed because the artillery had to be shipped to Boston, where it was badly needed. We enjoyed the lessons in early colonial history we were learning. Our early education in history was greatly enhanced by visiting the various areas. We were surprised that there were so many forts along the whole eastern coast. After a fascinating visit we went back to the boats and decided that we would have to anchor out that night. It was late in the afternoon and the next marinas were far ahead. Anchoring was always a dilemma. We wanted to be near one another, yet we had to account for wind, scope and swing. After much maneuvering and gnashing of teeth, we found an acceptable compromise. We brought the BICENTENNIAL to our starboard side and tethered her bow to stern. Content that we had done an excellent job in anchoring, Dru and I each cooked a good dinner for our men. It had been a busy day and we all turned in early.

Five hours later we were awakened by a severe wind. It was howling through the boat, the mosquito netting had been ripped and we heard Paul shouting at us from his boat which was much too near. All three of us rushed topside and saw that our boats were dangerously close to one another. The rain came down in buckets. Even though two anchors each had been put on the boats, they both were dragging their anchors. Closer and closer PEANUT came to us. Then we saw that while we slept, the anchors had become entangled with one another. What a dilemma. It looked impossible to untangle the whole snarled up mess. Closer PEANUT came to our UNICORN. The men were on their stomachs trying to untie and disentangle the anchor lines. Sunny was barking hysterically at the commotion. As Dru's boat came close to us, she put one bare foot on her boat and one bare foot on our stern to fend us off. The wind was howling and Paul started his engine so he could pull away from us when we were untangled. I was helping Dru keep our two boats from smashing into one another when I heard Cecil shout.

"Hey, Dru," he yelled through the sound of the wind and breaking waves, "you've only got four toes!"

Dru, being the good sport she always was, shouted back her story of "I had it cut off because it bothered me, Cecil. Now untangle the darn rope!"

My goodness. We would have to hear the rest of this story later! After thirty minutes of thrashing about, we finally were able to part without too much damage and resettle our anchorages far apart. The rest of the night was spent fitfully, as one of us was always getting up to check on our drift and position. Dawn came none too soon, and with it, calm.

We were all happy to weigh anchor and leave this supposedly sheltered cove. We rowed Cecil ashore in the dinghy as he was going to hop the truck and trailer forward to Basin Harbor and we would meet him later. Onward! The river began to widen and was very turgid after last night's rains. We had been under numerous bridges on the Hudson—a count of 33 thus far. As we read about the midsection of Lake Champlain, we found we had a choice of marinas. There were facilities on the New York side to the east with pump-out stations, fuel docks, etc. On the Vermont side there were equally fine amenities. We passed Port Henry, Westport and Split Rock. The latter was a 30-foot-tall half acre outcropping and was a sacred Indian site that once marked the border between Algonquin and Mohawk tribal lands. Next we passed the small hamlet of Essex. From here the lake began to widen and we knew we were approaching one of the largest expanses of open water on Lake Champlain. By now we had covered 100 miles in a little less than two weeks. Our mileage was not great, but with twelve time-consuming locks behind us, we felt we were on schedule.

Swinging more over to the Vermont shore, we began to hunt for Basin Harbor. We knew this was a private yacht club, but we knew they extended courtesies to cruising yachtsmen. With the binoculars we could see the blue of Cec's truck from quite a distance. He must have found a space for us. Dru and Paul went in first and tied up, then all three helped us come in alongside. It was a beautiful spot. A decision was immediately made by the two cooks who threatened to go on strike unless we went to dinner at this enchanting place. The restaurant was very elegant and we had a delicious smorgasbord. This was obviously a popular local spot. Again, we had visitors who came down to our dock to see our battleship. We could expect TV and the press in the morning as calls were made to come cover us.

Next A.M. after answering the usual press questions, we untied and were on our way together. We would later catch a bus back here and pick up our rig. It was a beautiful July 19 day, and we had only eleven miles to go. We looked for Shelburne Point, rounded that and entered Vermont's Shelburne Bay. Inside, we knew, was a full marina and repair facility. We also knew that the Shelburne Museum was five miles away and one of the area's special attractions. We would plan to visit this and film it. We were pleased that we were now half way between Whitehall and the International Boundary. Our curiosity was piqued as we wondered how we would cross the border into Canada by water. Would there be a border patrol in a boat?

As soon as we docked, a lovely couple with two small children came down to see the USS BICENTENNIAL. They saw we were without transportation so asked us if we would like to be picked up and go to a restaurant with them for dinner. We readily accepted. Our larders were low and we would have to replenish soon. We were picked up and driven to a very nice Shelburne restaurant. The couple was absolutely charming and invited Dru and me to do laundry at their home the next day. Just before leaving, Kathy dropped her contact lens and could not find it. We all got a bit hysterical as we crawled around under the table of the lovely restaurant on our hands and knees. We never did find it and they took us back to our boats. The next day when Kathy picked us up to do laundry she told us that the night before as she prepared for bed she suddenly found her contact high in her eye and took it out. She also informed us she and her husband were hardly speaking. Our many minutes scrounging around on the floor were not to his liking. We noticed later they had patched everything together.

That afternoon we went out to the Shelburne Museum. What a display of 35 restored old New England buildings, an old side-wheeler, antique buggies and a locomotive! It was all late 1700s memorabilia. We did a lot of walking and it was good to get exercise. Everyone slept soundly that night, and only two of us heard the deluge of rain.

A BLUNDER RECEIVES
THE NAME OF "FORT"

Saying goodbye to our supportive and patriotic new friends, we waved goodbye as long as we could see them. The water was relatively calm, and it was easy to bring Cecil and the battleship in to the stern and put her under tow. For some reason this always excited Sunny, and she barked from across the water whenever this procedure was underway. We enjoyed the peace and quiet of the day and threw out anchors while we had lunch on board.

We began to look for a marina for the afternoon tie-up and headed for Burlington, VT, on the east side. Burlington is Vermont's largest city, and our charts showed manufacturing and a resort center near the downtown area. As the afternoon wind was picking up, we took the first marina on our list. We encountered another grumbly dock master! Fortunately there are not too many. We had a bad tie-up on the outside where we caught the wakes from passing boats. We had to put the BICENTENNIAL in a different location. This made it difficult for pictures when the local TV people came down. We were always uneasy when she was out of our sight and care. We went off for a walk to a close by MacDonald's and feasted on hamburgers. Dru and I grabbed the opportunity to abandon cooking duties whenever possible.

Our next pit stop would be across the lake to Plattsburgh, NY. We were hoping for a smooth crossing. Just north of Burlington is open water from shore to shore, and the crossing covers ten miles. Just before the boats left, a friendly boater offered to take me to the bus depot for the trip back to Whitehall to get our truck and trailer. I bid *adieu* to PEANUT and UNICORN, and I was wished a safe trip with the hope that I would not get lost. After an hour's bus trip and a two-hour drive, I located Plattsburgh. Driving across the long bridge, I hoped our boats were having a smooth crossing. We were to meet at Dock & Coal Marina. The address sounded good (1 Dock Street). That should not be hard for anyone coming by boat or truck.

Hallelujah! I found the street and all the boats just tying up. Plattsburgh proved to be the largest city in NY on Lake Champlain. Our US map told us Plattsburgh was "only" a one-hour drive to Montreal; but our charts said otherwise. We would continue up Lake Champlain and head for the US/Canada border, a distance of 19 miles to Rouses Point, the last US community. Then we would be on the Richelieu River, Chambly Canal and knew we had more locks ahead. With approximately 65 miles of this travel, we would be headed into the St. Lawrence Seaway. The Dock & Coal Marina proved to be a great stop. Cec and I were headed off for the Holiday Inn where we would celebrate our 30th wedding anniversary…and, of course, a dinner out! Our loyal friends would have a modern marina, laundry, ice, car rental, showers and a five-minute walk to the heart of the city. They were happy campers. Dru was always happy to be able to walk the Sheltie Sunny.

Plattsburgh was the site of a large air force base and scene of a War of 1812 naval battle. As Cecil and I drove toward our motel, we laughed about our wedding anniversary. It was July 23, and who would have dreamed 30 years ago that we would have ended up in Plattsburgh with our own battleship and people we hardly knew? Life has its bizarre twists and turns. The "big spender" treated us to a steak dinner and we marveled at the luxury of a Jacuzzi and a bed slightly better than our bunks on the UNICORN! Refreshed and ready to tackle the next obstacle, crossing the border, we returned the next morning to our shipmates, who were all fueled and ready to leave.

We decided we had done enough leapfrogging with the truck and trailer, and after checking the US map realized it would be much closer to come back by bus to pick up our rig and drive it to Montreal. It's a good feeling when all crewmembers can be aboard and all accounted for! We rounded Cumberland Head, cleared the marked rocks and shoals, and rejoiced that today's waters were relatively calm. Our chart indicated we were approaching Rouse's Point. Our bible said it was a full service marina and had a restaurant. Dru and I speculated about hitting up the male crewmembers for another night out. It worked, and after a complicated tie-up where Walt kept trying to get into the dock stern first, we were settled. But not without embarrassment, as we saw quite an audience of boaters watching UNICORN'S attempts. We never did figure out why he tried to go in backward, but it was his boat.

We could hardly wait to find Fort Blunder, just a mile ahead. Taking a taxi, the five of us (and Sunny) barely crossed the Canadian Border (with no problem—just proof that we were American citizens) and there was the fort. Why was it named Fort Blunder? It was built by the Americans to defend the lake from the north, then was found to be on what was at that time still

Canadian soil. It was promptly abandoned. Fort Montgomery was built 600 yards farther away in 1842 when the present boundary was established. Nobody was angry at anybody at that time, so the fort was never garrisoned. We had a great tour through the abandoned fort and speculated about the men who must have been quite sheepish when the US Government discovered their expensive mistake. We would put the early bungling behind us and head across the International Boundary into Canada's Province of Quebec...this time by water.

Back to our boats, more newspaper interviews and we tried to find a chart for the Canadian waters we would be entering tomorrow. We had no luck. The chart shop was all out. We felt very vulnerable. The *Waterway Guide* was our only pilot into unknown waters.

We knew we had a long day's trip ahead. Leaving Rouse's Point, we headed north and checked in at the first Canadian port of entry. Fortunately we had purchased a Canadian ensign and hoisted it as a courtesy to our hosts. We checked in at the Canadian Customs dock a mile north of the border on the west side. It took only a few moments to clear our boats for entry. We were given a permit for the Chambly locks, were told all locks lower boats northbound and lines are usually fastened to the shore, then passed to boats by lock men. Crew was to tend all lines. OK, we could do that. The water was quite high and we were told to place fenders just above the water line to give the best protection for the boat. To our surprise, the Canadians did not require us to don life jackets as we had to do in US locks.

Once on our way after answering many questions about our BICENTENNIAL and dropping our literature off with the custom agents, we headed north onto the Richelieu River. There were ten locks ahead of us with a total lift of 85 feet. The country looked green, tranquil. The people waved at us and seemed so friendly and so very French.

We cruised along, loving the scenery. The clear river was wide and slow, summer cottages lined the banks. Farmland was visible behind the buildings. We were coming close to St. Jean and read that if we needed to shop we could tie up at a concrete wall between the marina and a bridge. The men were a bit reluctant to attempt this maneuver, but when Dru and I told them about our supplies being low, they agreed to the stop. It was not easy. Dru and I apologized, scrambled up the ladder and walked into town. Laden with groceries, we were finally welcomed upon return, a decided improvement over the complaining when we made our speedy exit.

We should have over-nighted in a St. Jean marina, but elected to push on.

With no chart, we were not skilled at estimating our ability to make it to the next stop. We soon saw our first Chambly lock ahead with a lift of five feet. With some delay due to southbound traffic, we navigated out of this lock and found another lock nine miles ahead. After going through this one, we suddenly encountered eight locks bunched together in a distance of two miles. What a job that was and how very long it took to get though these locks. Northward we progressed from Chambly Basin and for 42 more miles along the Richelieu River. The latter was no longer so clean and clear. We debated going under the Beloeil Station railroad bridge because it only cleared 14 feet. We blew our horn and waited for it to open. The current was swift. Very soon we slithered into the last lock and were lifted five feet. By this time everyone was tired and we were ready to hang it up.

As the afternoon waned, we realized we could not make the marinas ahead before dark. At St. Ours we decided we would tie up to a cement wall. At least we would be more secure than trying to anchor out in the channel. It was an uncomfortable but secure night, and we were all glad to retire early.

When we rose the next morning, there was much breakfast discussion and anticipation about getting to the St. Lawrence Seaway. We all tried to recall our high school history, and between the five adults we found that we knew the river was wide, there were a lot of huge, commercial boats on it, there were ocean liners plying its waters, and we thought there were waterfalls somewhere near. We were pretty hazy about past history classes, and someone voiced the opinion that our teachers would not have been proud of our lack of retention.

We wished we had St. Lawrence Seaway charts. As we headed out the river looked to be about 150 yards wide and led us through more farmland for about 15 miles to Sorel. Here we thought we could buy charts. Sorel is a shipbuilding city and we were sure we would find something. We found a marina. Dru and Paul had the easiest time of docking and tying up, so we circled outside in the river. While they were inside trying to buy charts, the owner saw our apparition out on the water, and Dru explained who and what we were. The man immediately telephoned the local TV station, who sent a crew, and within 20 minutes Cecil was in the BICENTENNIAL, unhooked and doing maneuvers for the news. Back came Dru and Paul—no charts. We would have to feel our way to Montreal for the next 52 miles. We were now almost 400 nautical miles from New York City and felt we could see the end in sight. One more set of pen pal letters to deliver and we could head west! We would make a long run up the St. Lawrence that day and treat ourselves to several nights in a Montreal marina. This sounded great to everyone.

We kept in close touch with Paul on the VHF. Sorel on the east bank of the Richelieu and Tracy, on the west bank where the river joins the St. Lawrence are overhung with smoke from titanium and oil refineries. We timidly felt our way into the St. Lawrence, although when two large bodies of water meet there often is no definition of north/south or east/west. It all looks like one huge expanse of water. Thank goodness for compass settings. We hung a port to the west. We began to see the buoys, which proved to be very, very far apart. Commercial vessels are so big and travel so fast that it was no wonder. There were no pleasure craft that we could see. We began to get into a fairly bleak stretch, and the seaway was heavy with commercial traffic. Here the river is two miles wide, deep and dirty. The shores were flatlands with pastures and forests and a few small towns. We felt we were getting along fairly well, although alarmed at all the huge vessels off to our port side. Their wakes washed over us, and we thought we likely should let out the BICENTENNIAL a bit farther on her tow. As we were about to do this, the VHF crackled and Paul's voice came over. "Look ahead to the northwest and watch that huge black cloud. I think it's coming toward us. That's a bad squall line if I ever saw one. Batten down everything." Paul was an experienced mariner and we paid close attention.

We watched the oncoming, menacing cloud with apprehension. Cec rushed out to check the line towing the battleship. I grabbed everything moveable and stored it all in locked cupboards or down on the carpeting. Walt stood at the helm, lips pursed tightly and clutched the wheel. As he throttled way down, the storm hit. Within seconds we were engulfed in swirling, white, foaming waters. The clouds enveloped us in a garish mixture of purple, green and black. Our UNICORN surged up and down, port to starboard as we thrashed about in the snarling waters. Over the VHF Paul said, "Walt, let's circle that buoy that I can barely see out there. Keep away from the main channel. Those freighters don't give a damn about a storm like this and they do not cut their speed. Hang on. I'll try to keep off your tail and you do the same."

We were lost and had no clue as to where we were. The buoy appeared and disappeared as we tried to circle. The battleship stood up on her nose, then crashed down into the seething sea. We knew Dru and Paul and the tankers were out there somewhere—but where? Our mother ship leaned way over to starboard and we felt we were being pushed toward shore—or was it out into the main channel? We had no idea. We never did see PEANUT and only occasionally spotted our red buoy. Thank goodness that was still on our port side. Twenty long, hairy-scary minutes went by in the hellish thrashing we took from St. Lawrence Seaway's wicked ways with small cruisers. Just as suddenly as the storm hit, it passed, and the sun shone, the waves calmed and we spotted Dru and Paul not too far away. The airwaves crackled with what we both had been through. Relief swept over us as we counted two boats and a battleship still together. We must have discussed this escapade for the next 30 minutes on the radio as we put ourselves and our boats back together.

We still had some 40 plus miles to go to Montreal and felt we had had a hard enough day and would find a good spot in which to anchor. Then we would proceed into Montreal on the morrow. It was almost impossible to find a sheltered spot. We anchored several places, but the wakes from passing freighters caught us and we almost smashed together. We finally crept over to a swampy looking inlet, an abandoned canal. It was replete with mosquitoes, but by this time it looked good to us. The cooks passed out soup and crackers, and then we all passed out.

A MAPLE LEAF RECEPTION

In the morning, both boatloads of tired crew people shouted across the water at one another. We had quite a ride ahead of us, but knew we could make it to a marina in Montreal and the EXPO '67 that was still ongoing. We could see from our small, sheltered cove that the enormous freighters and tankers were out there, just waiting for us. We scanned the weather channel anxiously and heard no report or warning regarding any severe weather pattern. After yesterday's experience, we were not about to emerge from our hole unless all was safe. We rechecked the *Waterway Guide* and decided we would take the closest marina when entering the city.

With some hesitation and a lot of yak-yak on the VHF, we pulled up anchor and ventured out into the Seaway. We had a bit over 40 miles to cover and figured we could be in by noon or mid-afternoon. We kept way over to the starboard side just clearing the red buoys. Even so, the wash and wake from passing behemoths rocked us. The trip was pleasant, through flatland country. We could tell that we were beginning to get into the east end of Montreal because of the industry that was showing up on both shorelines.

There ahead of us we saw the Montreal skyline! It rose over the river from the north shore. With no chart we relied on our *Guide* and sighted St. Helene's Island and the entrance to the harbor. Elation spread throughout both boats. The end was in sight and all boats and people were accounted for. We let Cecil off and into the BICENTENNIAL and entered the harbor with him at the stern of our parade.

To Walt's and my shock a young man in a fast moving aluminum boat came out to our UNICORN. I went out on the bow to greet him. Were they going to tell us our battleship was not welcome? *Au contraire!* A pleasant voice said, "You going to tie up with us?"

I answered in the affirmative.

"Great. Follow me and I'll take you to your slips. How many boats?" He quickly went over to inspect Cec and said the BICENTENNIAL would have a free berth. How many times we had heard that from generous people in so many marinas. Happily we made our way in to a well-run beautiful marina. The dock master's assistant put us side by side, then helped to bring in the battleship. We thanked him for a very friendly Canadian/Maple Leaf reception.

We were delighted to find that we were in a marina near where the major portion of EXPO '67 was still on display. We remembered this world's fair and the theme "Man And His World." It was almost as intact as it was nine years before, except the Russians had taken their exhibits home. Buckminster Fuller's geodesic dome which housed the American exhibits stood out.

We basked in the tranquility of a well-run marina, the safety of being off the St. Lawrence and reflected on our almost 500-mile trip. We had one more set of pen pal letters to deliver to the Prime Minister, and then we must all go back and pick up our rigs. Tomorrow would be a good day for all of us to set out for the various places where we had left our transportation! We celebrated our survival by going out to dinner and welcomed many news people to the dock. One of the most outstanding TV stories we had ever had done on us was by a Canadian channel. Two of them covered us, and we wish today we had a copy of the anchorman's interview.

Off we went in different directions the next day. We would meet on UNICORN and PEANUT upon our return and visit some well-known spots in Montreal. Cecil and I would find out where to deliver our pen pal letters. It was great to have wheels and visit so many interesting sights in this Canadian city. We found the education department of the Prime Minister and delivered our letters. The education secretary felt this would be a good stimulus to the elementary grade teachers to teach some U.S. history to the Canadian children. We were pleased and grateful for our reception.

The five of us trotted all over the city with Cecil always filming. The EXPO '67 exhibit was outstanding, and we enjoyed the entertainment that the Montreal people continually put on there. We spent three days on the boats, packing up, exchanging pictures and discussing our scary and fun times. By this time we had all named Paul "The Crocodile" due to his tenacity, sense of adventure and sudden charge while playing hearts. Dear Dru—her silly inane comments and sense of humor had caused Cec to change her name. For some reason she had become "Dur." It was always said with affection. Walt, not the most skilled boat driver, but with a good heart and a desire to help us with our Bicentennial project, was toasted graciously. We were so grateful for his help. Some reflections along the way were from "Dur," who said she felt she had seen France and Germany as we went along the Hudson and the Richelieu Rivers. Walt said his memories would always be of me shouting, "Fend off! Fend off! Slow down, Walt!" (This latter is true). Cecil's memories included the problems climbing in and out of the Bicentennial, dealing with the demands of TV crews, strong winds, bad tides and unexpected boating problems.

We all agreed that one of the greatest parts of the trip were the wonderful, friendly people we met who took us into their homes, gave us rides, took us to dinner, enthusiastically supported Bicentennial activities and loved our USS BICENTENNIAL.

It was a short, one-month trip full of the usual boating problems, but the results were wonderful.

There was only one problem left.

The last night on our boats, Dru came over and announced, "Sunny is in heat!"

1977

Nashville, TN to Paducah, KY
Cumberland River

*USS ALABAMA, USS MASSACHUSETTS
USS BICENTENNIAL, USS BUNKER HILL*

Dru and Paul Stewart
Cecil and Pat

Nashville, TN to Paducah, KY—1977

THE USS BUNKER HILL IS BORN

Bidding our helpful friends a fond *adieu*, we trailered our well-traveled lady behind us. How do we get out of Montreal? A friendly Canadian who was going out of town offered to guide us up and over a huge bridge and out of the city. We appreciated the guidance and were soon on our way through the southern part of Canada. We followed the St. Lawrence all the way and felt a bit more comfortable from this vantage point than from being right on the Seaway. We decided this was our chance to visit Niagara Falls on the way down to busy Highway 80. Parking a big truck and trailer is always a problem, but we found a parking spot and were overawed at the power of the water.

It was the end of July and we had a bit of summer left before school started in September. We went back to Southern California to pick up dear dog and say hello to the man who came to dinner two years before. Then it was north to our cabin for the rest of our summer and another building project. On the way across the country I kept hearing that the corporation needed two more additions. We needed one more gray battleship and an aircraft carrier! A carrier? How do you do that? It was carefully explained that you use the mold for the battleship and give it a "rhinoplasty job" on the bow. Then you deck over the hull with a barn door overhang and build a special superstructure island. Oh! Sounded simple.

All summer work continued on two boats. Cec worked from early A.M. into late evening. Our logistical problems continued as we made two trips to Southern California to take our new boats home. School started, and we loaned our film out to quite a few schools to view as we were not eligible for any more release time. The end of 1976 was on its way, and many of the Bicentennial celebrations were shutting down.

In early 1977 we had a call from Disney to bring our USS BICENTENNIAL to a southern California beach and be a part of the newly launched Mickey Mouse Club. We had learned that a few people understand boating problems such as launch, retrieval, and parking for the truck/trailer—

but most had no conception of the space needed and the problems connected with finding boat ramps, parking for truck and trailer, etc. Sure enough, we arrived to find a mammoth camera crew, the Mousketeers and no ramp for a launch. There was much head scratching and a few bizarre suggestions made until one man said he would put the battleship in a sling and lower it over a railing and into the water. There was a large crane on the set for filming and the gentleman guaranteed his bowline knots. He was obviously a knowledgeable boater, but we watched with anxiety as he tied a bowline knot on the stern and bow of the BICENTENNIAL. Carefully the crane picked up the rope that was tied to the two lines and gently lifted it up and over the railing and down into the water. Heaving a sigh of relief, we now wondered how Cec was going to get into the boat for filming. Fortunately an onlooker who was out in the water offered to put Cec on board his boat and deliver him to the BICENTENNIAL. We always seemed to be getting into inappropriate positions with our burgeoning fleet.

The filming went well and we went nationwide that month for the opening of the Mousketeer TV program. About this time I was also beginning to hear noises about another river trip, but this time taking the four ships in our fleet. The new USS ALABAMA was finished and the USS BUNKER HILL was complete except for some of the superstructure and finding some folding wing Corsairs to place on the deck. They had to be screwed down tightly from underneath the deck, but could be taken off for travel. Hmm-m-m. Sounded complicated to me. And how do you take four ships anywhere, and who would go with us?

It seemed to me that such a river trip would be much too complicated, but my enthusiastic partner began to do research on the Cumberland River. Where was that? One would begin in Nashville, TN, journey down the Cumberland, take all four ships and entitle ourselves The Nashville Navy. We would stop the trip at Paducah, which is at the confluence of the Cumberland, Tennessee and Mississippi Rivers. By this time we thought our fleet of ships might be used for publicity or the logo for some company and Cec felt the exposure would be good. I suspect it was more the fun of driving his boats and the attendant excitement they brought to all.

The euphoria of our two Bicentennial trips was still upon us, but the concept of the celebration was slowly fading from the nation's perspective. We decided to take another summer trip, possibly find a Confederate Flag sponsor and see what 1977 would bring. It sounded like a huge undertaking and it was.

Supportive good friends, Dru and Paul said they would go with us and they would handle two of our boats. If we could get all four boats back to Nashville, they would trailer PEANUT back and tow one boat and tether one to PEANUT's side. For any water appearances for TV, Dru and Paul would drive two gray battleships and I would drive the BICENTENNIAL. Cecil would drive the new aircraft carrier. Logistics again! How were we going to do this? We would rent a houseboat in Nashville and tether two boats to one side of the houseboat. It surely sounded complicated and very much like hard work to me!

CRUISIN' DOWN THE CUMBERLAND

School was out, and two days later the long trip across the country began. We had our rig with the BICENTENNIAL safely in her trailer, and I was to drive this outfit. Cec and our great renter brought a Ryder van home and loaded two battleships inside the truck. A hitch behind the Ryder van took care of the carrier. With everything safely loaded the night before, I looked out the kitchen window at the circular driveway with the long, long convoy and silently questioned my ability to head this motorcade from Los Angeles to Nashville, over 2000 miles away! Were we gluttons for punishment using two boats (we would rent a houseboat) to live on plus four boats under tow, going through locks, jumping truck and trailer equipment ahead? It looked like a tremendous undertaking.

Off we went again. Through Las Vegas, Flagstaff, Albuquerque, Oklahoma City, Memphis and finally Nashville. It took us six days to accomplish this run and it is indelibly inscribed in my memory. Motel stops took many minutes for parking, critiquing and finally coming to a rest to everyone's satisfaction (this was always a challenging task). Whenever I looked back at the slow Ryder van behind me, the letters were always backward in my mirror— REDYR. I could write RYDER backward by the time Nashville city limits were in our sights.

We were into the Nashville city limits and began to look for a marina where we could unload, stay a few days, wait for Dru and Paul, then launch all four ships. We would live in our camper while we readied the ships. We were tired, dusty, dirty and near the end of the day. We found what we thought was a nice marina, and it was. The only problem was that the owner did not want us there. We were too big, had too much equipment and were rather rudely turned away. What were we to do? A young man on a bike saw our plight, loved our boats and said, "Follow me. I know a place just down the road where they'll appreciate having you." We followed the young man another half mile and found a warm welcome for us and our boats. We set up camp on a grassy spot amongst the cow pies. This was not an elegant marina, but a friendly/working one. We unloaded boats, turned in the Ryder truck and found that to take showers we must drive five miles. It appeared to be the usual difficult logistics, but Dru and Paul would join us in two to three days and we would be on our way.

That night there was a wild thunder/lightning storm and we heard there was damage from violent winds down the road. The next day we drove along the river and found the marina that had turned us down had been ripped apart, boats were tossed all over and damage was extensive. We were grateful to have escaped such violence!

USS

BUNKER HILL

Maiden

Voyage

Battleship hull

With a "nose job"

Decked over—
Superstructure
added
Corsairs-ready
for take-off

USS BUNKER HILL, USS BI-
CENTENNIAL, USS MASS-
ACHUSETTS, USS ALA-
BAMA

Sailing on Cumberland River
from Nashville, TN to Paducah,
KY

Hooray! Dru and Paul showed up with their UNICORN and we all went to look at the houseboat Cec and I would rent. It looked spacious and comfortable but again, the logistics of tethering two boats on the side was a problem. We found that the 32-foot houseboat's overhang prevented a good tie-up, and I went out to buy plywood to hang over the sides so the boats would not slip under the overhang. On July 4 we had great coverage from CBS and NBC for our fleet of four's launch. Our well-laid plans about our boat-driving configuration for TV looked wonderful on paper. Cecil diagrammed a great maneuver. We would circle, follow Cec, use our CBs to keep our fleet pattern, and we would be impressive. It all began as planned, but rapidly deteriorated into a free-wheeling free-for-all where we had no idea what the others were doing or where they were going. Watch out for your own boat! It was awful. The TV crew thought it was wonderful, and we must have looked impressive as we had one narrow miss after another, dodging each other's show biz antics and trying to maintain radio communication and avoid disaster. It was probably the most scary maneuver ever done in close quarters by us, and that night we watched our TV in horror. It may have looked spectacular to the public, but we wondered how we had survived without ramming one another. We resolved to always have more space between us and not do tight turns ever again.

We had one more day to move onto the houseboat and ready our four ships for tethering and towing. That was the day I fell in! I did too much leaning over the side tying on a line—and splash! There was much gnashing of my teeth and guffaws from the onlookers. Next day, hot and humid, and we left Nashville to go through lock one.

New friends were kind enough to drive our truck and trailer to the first marina ahead. We glided along for several days, in and out of locks, through very small towns, no newspaper or TV in sight and wondering if we had been crazy to do this trip. Were we gluttons for punishment and what led us to pursue this isolated river trip? The excitement of the Bicentennial events was behind everyone, our boats were still a source of amazement and amusement, but we began to feel we were lacking in purpose. Nevertheless Dru and Paul were a wonderful support. We finally made it to the Clarksville Yacht Club in a heavy rainstorm. This was our first major city in four days. All fleet boats were untied, and the four of us put on a show in front of the Clarksville Marina. It was rough water, made worse by the barges and their huge wakes. The next A.M. a nice neighbor delivered *The Tennessean* paper to us, where we read of our exploits in Nashville. On we plowed, anchoring out some nights because it was too difficult to bring six ships in to a marina. One night we anchored out in a quiet pond, but it was near a noisy steam plant. Bumpus Mills turned out to be a lovely, rural tie-up where some soldiers told us via the VHF that they were coming to see us. The soldiers came with their families and friends and offered to drive Cecil back to where we had left our rig.

July 11—Lake Barkley! We managed an accident-free tie-up and took the small boats out. The local papered covered us, and we just had time to tether the boats when a typical Southern thunderstorm enveloped us. We all seemed to have our own special logistical problems. Dru and Paul were such good sports and were so cooperative and supportive. We could not have done this trip without them, but Cec and I privately thought we had tackled too much. That night we took them to a smorgasbord feed to show our appreciation.

A local radio station interviewed us, and that brought people to view us from as far as 100 miles away. We pulled into the Grand River boat dock, a small marina, and found admiring fans. The towns were getting smaller and smaller as we approached the Ohio, Cumberland and Tennessee Rivers. We were really out in the boonies.

July 14 and we tied up in a large lock with two huge diesel-powered tugboats. When we had been lowered, Paul went smartly out, but we were suddenly held back. Cec shouted, "The boat won't go!" I rechecked my lines and discovered to my horror my carelessness had left a line dragging in the water. Lines have an immediate affinity for whirling props. They have an ongoing love affair and are always attracted to one another. They seek one another out and bond instantly. Cec shouted at me. I could not loosen the taut line.

The tug boat operator took out a bull horn and yelled, "Get that #$%&$ boat out of here and MOVE!" Frightened, embarrassed, bewildered with our inability to move, Cec's language matched that of the tugboat pilot. He came roaring back to the starboard stern. Seeing the tight-as-a-bull-fiddle-line did not improve his state of mind. He grabbed his trusty Swiss knife, climbed down the swim platform, which was under water by 12 inches, and began to saw through the unyielding knots. I stood by, wringing my hands, and tried to ignore the deep-throated rumbles of the nearby tug as he kept revving his gigantic diesel engines at us.

With half of Cec's tall body soaking wet, he climbed back up the stern ladder and ran for the pilothouse. As we pulled away and out of the lock, I retrieved what was left of our newly-purchased 100-foot line and swore never again to let a line fall in the water. We made our escape in great humiliation and the tug went roaring by us in all her haughty power, leaving us to rock in her large wake.

Contacting Dru and Paul, we told them via VHF that we needed to regroup, so we found a sandy beach where we could tie up side by side, have lunch and describe our most recent escapade. They expressed much sympathy as they had no idea we were in trouble. With our feathers partially smoothed, we went on to the moldy Clarks River Marina. Some marinas are made for pretty boats, pretty people and cruising visitors in white pants. Others are hard-working marinas full of ditto men, machinery, oil, machine parts lying around on greasy floors, and tug boats with engines in various stages of disrepair—definitely not for the jet set mariner. Clark River was the latter. Glad to find a marina listed in our *Waterway Guide* in this lonely spot along the Cumberland River, we gingerly made our way in to a very, very narrow opening. The only spot we could find was a tie-up next to a rusty old barge. Getting into position was most difficult as we maneuvered battleships, a carrier and our two large boats into an overnight spot. How welcoming the hard-working men were, and they didn't seem to mind that we needed to climb up and over their equipment to get up to the office at the top.

After a long climb up to the top of the cliff above the marina, we found our truck/trailer awaiting us. The good soldiers had delivered it for us. Out we went for groceries, laundromat and newspapers. We never did get over the surprise of coming into a city by water, then trying to find the nearby city by car. Locals were always happy to help, and we made this our headquarters before going to Paducah. We KNEW for sure we were never going to tie up in Clark's River again (famous last words!). Never say "never!" Eleven years later we were there again.

A few days and we edged out of Clark's River and headed for our last stop, Paducah, KY. Our publicity had gone ahead and the mayor met us and gave us a tour of his city. He showed us the high water mark from a flood when the Ohio River ran way over the banks and into the city. Here we had to part with dear Dru and Paul, our wonderfully, supportive shipmates. We also contacted people we had never met but had been directed by mutual friends to find them in Murray, KY. What an amazing couple! He had built a paddlewheel excursion boat which held almost 100 people. They decided to move from Michigan to Kentucky, and the whole family packed their furniture, dogs and cat, children, themselves and sailed down the Mississippi River, churned up a tributary and arrived at the dock of their new home in Kentucky! What boaters they were, and they welcomed us with open arms! These adventuresome people related with us and our logistical problems! Dick helped us find storage for two boats in a local garage, an acquaintance from Southern California offered to trailer the carrier home, and Cec and I trailered the BICENTENNIAL. We made arrangements to leave our rented houseboat on the Cumberland, where it would eventually be picked up. We would figure out later what to do with the two battleships we would leave in Kentucky.

We decided to go home, lick our wounds, do some boat shows and await whatever was around the bend. I had no clue yet that Cecil was going to give birth again. We were too busy discussing retiring from teaching and moving to northern California and Lake Almanor. We did not feel the Nashville Navy was a roaring success as the two previous trips had been, but the people were wonderful and their Southern hospitality was appreciated.

1985

Houston, TX to Panama City, FL

USS ARIZONA

Ernie and Peg, Cecil and Pat

Houston, TX to Panama City, FL—1985

WE RETIRE
...and GIVE BIRTH TWO MORE TIMES

It was now 1979 and the Bicentennial years are a misty memory for the nation. Since coming off the 1977 trip with dear Dru and Paul, we've done numerous boat shows—Sacramento, Los Angeles Convention Center (twice, using different facets of our fleet), San Diego...and have appeared on *You Asked For It* and *P.M. Magazine*, and did alot of pre-publicity for boat shows. We have five ships in our non-profit corporation now: four 18-foot battleships and one aircraft carrier. Surely, this is enough! We think retirement from 30 years of teaching. Cec had 30 years of high school architectural drafting leadership, I had 30 years in first and second grades. They were wonderful years, but enough already! We saw a lot of Bill, Dru and Paul and reminisced about our escapades over the years.

We sold our home in the San Fernando Valley, our home at Lake Almanor and built another—right on the lake. The fleet "must" be anchored off Cec's front window so he could check on his gray ladies and the USS BICENTENNIAL. Content to seek semi-retirement and do an occasional boat show, I relished the time I had never enjoyed where I could work in a garden, practice my piano and enjoy lunch with friends. This euphoric state of mind was soon punctured. We had been retired four years and it was 1983.

The next thing I heard was, "I think our fleet is too warlike. I'm going to dilute that thought and build the RMS TITANIC!"

"WHAT?" This time I really did a double-take, fell to the ground in a feinted faint and threw up a lot of static. "You want to build a replica of that poor ship?" I exclaimed. Little good my negative comments had on the builder. I could see the sparkle in his eyes, the drawings on the yellow 8x14 legal sheets of paper and decided all was a lost cause. I'd gone along this far, why not expand? Our corporation board of directors enthusiastically backed the President, and off he went under the pine trees and began to build the hull. How? What else?—upside down. I should have known.

All summer long friends and directors dropped by to watch the huge hull of the doomed vessel take shape. She was 23 feet long and had a six-foot beam. One day a United Airline pilot friend came over and Cec decided the keel was ready to do the flip-flop thing. With several of us watching four men turned her over and "voila!"—there was the hull of the TITANIC. She was unmistakably correct. "HOW does he get the shape right?" everyone asked. But Cecil always seemed to have the eye for detail, and from numerous drawings, sketching, overhead projectors, he seemed to be able to scale all down to a reputable facsimile of the original ships. It was amazing even to me after five other apparitions that had appeared in my backyard!

With a lot more work on the decking and superstructure on the RMS TITANIC, we launched her on Memorial Day, 1983. Our dear friend, Lu, a director on our board, gave us a beautiful red/white/blue floral bouquet which we put on the bow of the TITANIC. Replete with a British flag on her stern, we launched at a marina on Lake Almanor. It was a cold, wet, rainy day—a surprise for our area. One clown friend had constructed a plastic iceberg, and as a helicopter with TV personnel flew overhead and filmed us, our "friend" launched his iceberg right in front of our bow. Cec, being equal to his position as captain, loudly told everyone to abandon ship. We plowed right through the plastic dome floating in front of us. Trailed by helicopters for an hour, we went around the shoreline of the lake, stopping in at marinas where watchers stood stunned at the shoreline. "Is THAT the TITANIC?" they would ask. We pointed to the stern where her letters were emblazoned. It truly was a gala day.

Six ships in our fleet, entered under the Friendship Fleet, Inc. name—now to buy a trailer. And, WHAT were we to do with her? The calls began to come in to do boat shows. Again, we were hired to be "the hook." We trailered all over the West, working for old friends from south to north. We even tinkered with an idea to take her to Russia, but receiving a "*Nyet!*" loud and clear from the Kremlin we deleted that idea. Then we thought of touring England's canals. We were sure we would receive a marvelous reception from the Brits. But after some negotiating and airmails back and forth, the trip never did hatch. So much for grandiose ideas. Perhaps it was time to have our friends drive our six ships on the lake, do an occasional TV show, a boat show or two, then back off. That was not to be. There was more on the horizon that I could not have imagined.

The TV, radio, newspaper interviews and invitations to do boat shows poured in. Being retired, we had more time to participate without so much pressure of daily teaching in the classroom. "Two On The Town" from Los Angeles, *P.M. Magazine*, boat shows in Sacramento, San Diego, back to the Los Angeles Convention Center—this time the RMS TITANIC was popular and was "the hook." Countless wonderful contacts and publicity emanated from all these activities. It was gratifying to pick up our mountain phone and hear of another invitation to show one of our ships. Working boat shows is no easy job, but the perks that went with them were well worth it. Trailering all over the West, we were put up in motels, hotels, given food/beverage expense accounts and treated royally. In exchange we fielded numerous press interviews, launched our boats in precarious, unnerving places, sometimes did the impossible for the good people for whom we worked. Friendships and trust were built, and we were asked to return with different segments of our fleet. They knew they could count on us to honor our commitments and we knew we would be given the red carpet treatment. We have always, always appreciated the wonderful public relations firms for whom we worked.

The BIG launch on

MEMORIAL DAY, 1983

Lu's beautiful red/white/blue flowers
grace the bow.

By this time it was 1984, and taking care of six ships plus trailers was a full-time job. Friendship Fleet, Inc. board meetings were a once-a-year must, and communication went out to our great directors continually. Their enthusiasm and support and advice has been cherished.

Another alteration in our retirement life was soon to intrude its camel head into our tent. A friend of ours had a steamboat reunion of friends. Fifteen boats, powered by wood, were meeting at Lake Almanor, and we were invited to join in—ONLY if we came in one of our six ships. We elected to come in the USS BICENTENNIAL. Being invited to join these boat builders at an end-of-the-day BBQ was interesting. There we met a man who was to change our lifestyle for the next seven years with a gift.

Being enamored with boats and owning his own hand-made steam engine ship, this man, on an impulse, had purchased two halves of an empty hull from 20th Century Fox. These two halves were each 18 feet in length, 3/8 inch thick in chopper fiberglass and were now surplus, unused/never-to-be-used hulls. They were made on the 20th Century lot by skilled employees who were building boat halves for the filming of *Tora! Tora! Tora!* The two halves were exact duplicates of two sister ships—the USS PENNSYLVANIA and the USS ARIZONA. They were supposed to be built to a scale of 20:1 and were beautifully crafted. However, Cec's newfound friend described them as two empty peapods, left in an unused shed in Pasadena, California. Would Cecil be interested in having them as a gift?

This first mate person was not privy to that conversation, and that night I noticed the Admiral (dubbed this by friends) approached me with some bit of caution. Having gone through a logistical boating life with me for eleven years, I suspect he felt any additions, particularly one of this immensity, would be met with immediate resistance. Slowly, he unfolded the idea of the gift as a plan to somehow fiberglass the two hulls together and build the eulogized USS ARIZONA. As I listened, he waxed quite poetic about having been on the slopes of Kaimoki as a teenager and of watching the USS ARIZONA burn and how it changed his life. He continued his persuasive and increasingly impassioned pitch by drawing a silhouette of the ARIZONA and how stable she would be, how grand, and how she would reach out to a patriotic nation. Hmm-m-m, really? As I evaluated this latest turn of events, gigantic and expensive a proposition as it seemed, I thought, *Oh, heck* (or words to that effect). *Why not? I'm in so deep now, why not?*

THE USS ARIZONA IS CHRISTENED

With summer still ahead of us, I found myself headed 750 miles down south to Southern California with empty trailer behind the truck. *Déjà vu* again! We found the empty black-widowed shed with the two dejected-looking hulls—empty shells. I looked askance at them. Having previously been through ship- building, fiber-glassing, frustration, etc., I had reservations. I could see beautiful hull lines and the compound curve of a perfect dreadnaught hull bow. But I could also see two parts! Knowing quite a bit about assembling boat parts by now, I immediately questioned HOW you put two parts together and still keep the integrity strong enough to go through heavy seas.

Feeling semi-enthusiastic, I helped Cec and an old Pasadena friend load one half of the hull onto the trailer. Working in the early spring heat, we found it impossible to put both pieces on one trailer. We tried, they swore, nothing would fit. Solution? Of course! Make two trips—doesn't everyone drive 3000 total miles in one week in order to add a humongous, yet undeveloped, untried ship to an already large enough logistical problem? We were already well-acquainted with the Dept. of Motor Vehicles with six ships and six trailers. What was one more? Here is what it was. Drive, drive, drive and Los Angeles traffic. We did get the usual "what is that?" from gas station attendants. The remarks were, "Boy, that's going to be a lot of work." (I knew that.) In one week we got both parts back to Lake Almanor.

Cecil began to lay-up the ship. First he blocked up the two parts on the garage floor. By this time I was not surprised that the whole mating process had to be done upside-down. Using a lubber line (string from bow to stern) and a plumb bob from the lubber line to the bottom of the keel he trued up the two hulls. Then he had to bevel both hull joints back two inches in preparation for fiberglass hand lay-up. Next came glassing and sanding. Glass, sand, glass, sand—until the V joint was filled. After the two parts were joined, he bought four steel plates which were one-quarter inch thick and five inches wide by eighteen inches in length. He bolted the two hulls together to reinforce this, and now they were permanently married. This proved to be a big step, and neighbors and curious onlookers visited frequently.

Now it was possible to turn the hull over, and willing friends helped. What next? Two bulkheads were added. Three-quarter inch plywood and some foam flotation was put in the voids. Stringers, ribs and frame took shape. A month of work, morning til night, covered this assemblage. When this hardly-seen interior work was completed, the hull seemed strong and sturdy. Three hundred pounds of concrete ballast were poured in the bottom. Her ¾-inch fiberglass hull was decked with ½-inch marine plywood, then glassed over. Now it was time to think about the ARIZONA's superstructure. Here is where a pragmatic, inartistic wife has to insert something about a creative, artistic spouse. With what he called artist's license, he drew and built a magnificent superstructure that copied exactly the original ARIZONA. The superstructure was a mass of turrets and cannons simulating the 14-inch guns of the original. Next came the tripod mast, gantry cranes and cutout windows so the pilot could see. There was positioning for signal flags and two liberty boats that were hand-crafted (carved out of foam). Gadgets from old machine parts were made to look like boat parts, then everything was painted battleship gray.

We haunted craft stores and bought several OC2U planes which were perched on the stern launch ramps—gradually a really big battleship began to take shape. After looking over our almost completed boat, we had long-distance discussions with our former sponsor, Johnson Motors. Just how does one power a 36-foot battleship? What great engineers this good company has. Pictures were sent back to Waukegan, and much yak-yak went across the wires between Cecil and the engineering department. It was decided that two OMC sail drive engines would power the twin screws. They were each 25 hp detuned down to 15 hp and proved to be an ideal choice. Maneuverability was great, and the USS ARIZONA proved later to be able to turn 360 degrees in her own length by turning one engine in reverse and putting one forward. The engines were delivered, and Cec began mounting the two engines in the stern, placing the controls in the superstructure and glassing over everything. It was a big challenge. With my remote speaker from the house to the garage, I would have to remind the devoted builder that it was lunch or dinner time. ("Won't You Come Home, Cecil Gates?")

As the boat took shape, I made frequent trips out under the pine trees to watch the development and could not help but get caught up in the spirit of what the ship represented. Word of our new gray lady was beginning to spread. Now that she was out of the garage and under the trees, visitors became more frequent. We were urged to have a launch—a gala one. But we had no trailer adequate for her. So off to Southern California we went, where we purchased a triple-axle trailer for "ZOE" (this was our in-house name for her that has stuck with her her whole life). Back we trundled. I was beginning to wonder if I was going to continue to go through life with a trailer behind me, always nudging me on.

A ship with the history this gray lady had (December 7, 1941) deserved a grand launch. Plans were made for TV and press to cover her at our host's resort, Big Cove at Lake Almanor. We put her flags on with the American flag on her stern. On July 3, 1984 we launched her. Standing on ZOE's deck just before she was dipped into the lake, I read my launch speech: "This ship is to honor the 1102 men entombed in the Pearl Harbor ARIZONA since December 7, 1941. May all Americans who see this ship remember the sacrifice of these men who gave their lives that we may enjoy the freedoms we have today. I christen you the image, the reflection, the likeness, the replica of the original USS ARIZONA. God speed you on your way to honor the brave men enshrined in the Pearl Harbor ARIZONA."

What a gala day! Press boats and friends boats following us, we did a grand tour of the lake. We stopped at resort docks, honked at cabin/home owners, were circled continually by those wishing to get up close and see what she really looked like. It was exhilarating to be back on the water with a loved replica. Now, with a fascinating boat like this with all the "hoopla" over her, shouldn't one have to do something with her? For her? But, what?

We began contacts. The USS ARIZONA Survivor group was behind any river/waterway trip we wanted to do. They would notify their members and they would pull out the stops with the Navy, Sea Cadets, any officials who would listen. Then one contact paid off big time. The nation was refurbishing the Statue of Liberty. We received an invitation to be in New York for the statue's unveiling on July 4, 1986. We began to think and talk as the TV show, "De Boat, De Boat!!" What a trip this could be. But where and when would we start? What would we live on? And it would take more than two of us to undertake a sea journey of any magnitude with such a large battleship in our care, plus having a ship on which to live.

The newspaper coverage on our ARIZONA made it to the *Sacramento Bee*. Soon we had a call from NBC's KCRA channel, Sacramento. Their helicopter pilot, Dann Shively, would be flying a crew up to cover the whole fleet from the air. He had been here once before. "Now, Pat, I'll be flying right up the Feather River Canyon with the camera crew. I know where your house is, and the lake is low. I think I can put this bird down in the cove right by your house."

Surprised that he would land by our home rather than the Chester Airport, I asked him if we should stand outside and wave flags or flash a mirror at him. "No, the only thing I need is for you to buy a 10-pound bag of flour. I want you to make a 40-foot diameter circle, then make two crossing X lines through it. I'll be able to set this bird down just great if you'll do that!"

The gala July 4, 1984 launch of the USS ARIZONA
(We call her "ZOE")

The night before he was to arrive, we trotted our bag of flour out to the cove, measured carefully and produced a huge circle complete with the bisecting lines. We were not disappointed. The next A.M., right on time, we saw the graceful helicopter approaching us from the canyon. Dann flew directly across the lake to us and did a marvelous landing in the appointed spot. After debarking the interviewer and her equipment, he flew off with the cameraman. Cecil and I scurried to Big Cove to join the rest of the crew to pilot our own ships. With seven boat pilots and seven ships out in the middle of the lake, we conversed with the cameraman on our CBs and followed Cecil's directions. "Port flank turn, execute, execute!" We did several hours of maneuvers for Channel 3 and watched in amazement as the cameraman hung out the helicopter's side door. Even though he was strapped in, it looked quite precarious. We were finally finished, all ships were tied up at Big Cove Resort, and Cecil and I did our final interviews. We hurried back to the house for the lunch I had prepared for all boat and plane crews, then we went over to the cove and watched Dann skillfully lift off, up and over the surrounding pine trees. This TV segment is one of the best we have in our files, as the seven ships look like a real Navy fleet.

We began to question our old friends Bill, Dru, and Paul about another trip, but they were either tied up at work or not well. We began to feel out our present friends at Lake Almanor and suddenly found two adventuresome souls who would agree to go with us. Ernie, on our board of directors, and spunky wife and my soul mate, Peg, would accompany us! Cec and I would buy the boat that the four of us would live on, Ernie would drive the mother ship, Peg and I would continually "fend off" the USS ARIZONA and Cecil would be general all-round battleship boat driver and fill-in person. Sounded grand, and we looked forward to sharing this newest adventure with good friends (and good sports!).

Before we were to head out for our jumping-off point, Houston, we had dates to fulfill. Renewed interest from all sorts of people surfaced, and we knew we had to get our gray lady out of the Sierras before the snows came. In November of 1984 (we pushed our weather luck), we trailered ZOE in snow and ice down to the valley floor and put her in storage in Oroville, CA. Our first date was to be with the PHSA (Pearl Harbor Survivor's Association) in San Diego. This was to be a December 7 date.

We picked up ZOE on December 4 and trailered her over the Tehachapi mountains in a terrible fog, then a severe windstorm. Battleship weather? Finally reaching our appointed spot in San Diego, we were told to place our battleship in the local Coast Guard station. On the appointed day, the Navy was alerted to the fact that our USS ARIZONA battleship would be part of the PHSA in dedicating a plaque to their group on a local bridge. We heard later that the Navy personnel had remarks such as, "Didn't the ARIZONA go down in Pearl Harbor?" We also heard that the Navy sailors went into a tail spin trying to get ready for a 600 plus foot ship with 800 men on board. They felt their tie-up was inadequate and there was quite a flurry about such a huge ship pulling into their docking area. An old chief finally cleared up the matter and told them that this was a replica of the original—a 36-foot USS ARIZONA. Relief abounded, and long electrical cables were put away. The garbage detail put all their cans back in storage. We didn't realize we had caused such Navy consternation until later.

Having to flee back to the Sierras for holiday time with family and friends, we left our battleship in the Coast Guard yard. What better place for safe-keeping? The next time we saw her would be near the end of January, 1985.

Grinding our way out of a mid-January snowstorm, we headed for San Diego to pick up ZOE and brought her to the Los Angeles Convention Center. Once again we would be working as "the hook" for our old friend, Al Franken. How graciously we were treated—wonderful hotel quarters, expense account, super publicity. Our relationship was a trusted one—they gave, we gave and neither ever disappointed the other. The upcoming ARIZONA adventure gave us a lot of fodder to give to the press. The boat show was an emotional one. Out of 65 USS ARIZONA survivors, seven came to visit our boat and be filmed alongside her. We did big publicity with one badly-burned survivor, Don Stratton, who proudly rode our battleship in the Marina Del Rey Harbor as we did pre-publicity for the show. Other survivors were invited to be filmed alongside our ship in the convention center. How grandly they were treated by Al—lunch, accolades, publicity. We began to realize that we were trailering and representing a cherished national symbol. The emotion connected with this ship began to dawn on us. We knew we were on the right track using our gray lady to bring publicity to the story of Pearl Harbor. While working the L.A. Boat Show, we saw a young boy circling our display. He turned to his father and asked, "Who sank her, Dad?" This query, though startling, was not the first time we had heard remarks from young people that indicated they had no clue as to December 7, 1941's disaster. Our crusading spirit caused us to ask ourselves: "Why not take our USS ARIZONA on a waterway trip and show her to America's youngsters to illustrate the sacrifices made that give us the freedoms our country's people enjoy?" We felt it incumbent on us to get out on the water again and exemplify what the machinations and nostalgia regarding our ship and WW II represented.

Since the Statue of Liberty invitation for July 4, 1986, we had given great thought to what river or ICW trip we should undertake. Our board felt that we should begin our trip one year ahead of the unveiling of the statue and generate publicity for the coppery lady and also give our fleet some publicity. It had been ten years since we had been up the ICW with Bill. We laid out the trip into two different years. In 1985 we would meet Peg and Ernie in Houston, buy a sea-going houseboat there, head down to Galveston, then go east along the Intracoastal Waterway. We would touch the shorelines of Louisiana, Mississippi, Alabama, and likely stop near Apalachacola, Florida. We would store ZOE somewhere and head for California for the remainder of the year.

In 1986 we would somehow get across the Gulf of Mexico, go across Lake Okeechobee, head south to Miami, then north to New York. Arriving at Miami, we would once again take the same route up the ICW we had covered with Bill ten years earlier. Big plans, big dreams—another adventure. We put in a request for a 40-foot Holiday Mansion (a sea-going houseboat) which would be delivered to a marina in Houston, TX.

Our USS ARIZONA invitations lay ahead. After the boat show, our next stop was an invitation to appear in Phoenix, AZ along with many PHSA veterans. The governor (Babbitt) was going to dedicate land for a cemetery for WWII veterans. We would be the star attraction. As we trailered along, our CB picked up all sorts of interesting remarks. Truck drivers, particularly, were vocal in their assessment of our long rig. They would pace us, then "holler" to another driver, "Damn, there goes a battleship down the road." Hoots of disbelief came from other truckers who had not seen us. "This must be a wrong day for me. I'm seein' cars goin' the wrong way, ah seen a battleship goin' down the road, ah seen a spider monkey leadin' a water buffalo down the freeway. Ah think I'll throw out all this dope and go home—if ah kin find it." Many truckers would engage us in long conversations about our ship, our waterway trips and our fleet, congratulate us, then, roaring past us, flash their lights. "Thumbs up" would greet us at rest stops, and the curious would gather round with their usual questions. By this time we had learned to carry plenty of press releases and publicity with us and distributed many at gas stations, restaurants and rest stops. It was like working a boat show! We never could go in disguise. Somehow we were always discovered, no matter where we stopped for a break.

As we trundled into Phoenix on a late Friday afternoon, the traffic was horrendous. Not knowing where we were, this navigator unintentionally gave a lot of misinformation to the distraught driver. We managed to pull a one-eighty right through a factory parking lot at quitting time. We had to do this to retrace our path. The astonished workers stood, mouths agape, as we ricocheted through their parking lot, exited at the entrance and jumped out into Friday afternoon traffic. Whump, bump, we were embarrassed as our huge rig (as long as a truck and trailer) stretched across the road as we tried to make a left. Fortunately, the name of the ship seemed to excuse us from the other driver's exasperation, and they tooted, waved and gave us the thumbs up. Landing at our Best Western destination, we were given a position of "honor" where the office could properly chaperone our boat in order that vandals would not destroy or mar her. What a relief to bring this whole rig to a halt. Houston looked far away!

The next A.M. all sorts of officials escorted us to the roundabout in the middle of Phoenix where the ceremony would take place. Poor Cec, told to put his battleship on the grass in the middle of the round-about ring, had no way to climb up over the 9-inch curb. Some resourceful servicemen, seeing his predicament, found some two by fours and made a ramp so he could climb up and over. Governor Babbitt spoke and dedicated the land to the veterans. To our surprise, we were asked to speak. By this time it was "give me the mike, I'll go first." It truly was gratifying to be a part of this ceremony.

We were told the next day there would be many government officials to view our ship in the water (we didn't KNOW we were to go in the water) and we must trailer out to Tempe and launch. What a nightmare that was. The road to the launch was a snake. How Cecil ever backed that huge rig down and launched, none of us will ever figure that out. But he did it. Many curious homeowners came to see us, but no officials showed. Oh well, win one, lose one.

Off we went for Tucson. We had been invited to make an appearance on the steps of the University of Arizona and take part in a ceremony for the PHSA. Happy to do, so we drove our huge rig through the masses of students who cheered and waved. We dropped ZOE right at the steps of the student union building for all to see. In all our boating appearances we had never encountered a negative remark. As I wiped down the USS ARIZONA (road dust), a weird looking, bearded older man approached me. His remark caught me off guard. "Whatcha doin' with somethin' so warlike? You don't stand for peace. Your ship is a disgrace."

My only answer was, "There were 1102 men who went down with this ship. Doesn't that say something about the futility of war?"

The NROTC men were furious as they overheard this exchange. Unbeknownst to us they shared guard duty all night to take care of ZOE. There was no graffiti, no vandalism to ZOE the next A.M. We were grateful! Next day, we thanked them!

The University of Arizona has become a welcome museum home for numerous USS ARIZONA artifacts gathered from various places. We were enamored with the silver service that rests behind glass. The pictures, uniforms, and mementos of the men who served on this ship reach out to all visitors. We were impressed with their exhibit and enjoyed a wonderful day with the University of Arizona officials. Lunch, presentations, all were most interesting.

Signal Flags

spell out

C—E—C—I—L

G—A—T—E—S

THE "ADMIRAL"
(Cecil)

puts his fleet

at anchor in front

of our home

ZOE is working

at the Los Angeles

Convention Center

Boat Show

Now we were off for Fredricksburg, Texas! We were to help dedicate a 50-cent stamp to Admiral Nimitz at his museum in the aforementioned town. It was a surprise to find such German background in this town. The shops, the people, all exemplified that heritage. It was a wonderful experience, and the admiral's stamp was dedicated. We also met a man who was to be larger

281

than life in our later years, J.R. Brown, president of the USS ALABAMA Crewmen's Association. We had no idea our paths would intertwine over the years as they did. J.R. found that we were headed along the ICW and would go through Mobile, AL. He invited us to the USS ALABAMA crewmen's reunion and asked that we have dinner with and speak to his association. There would be approximately 300 in attendance. We agreed that if we could tie up near Mobile, we would be glad to be a part of their March reunion.

It was on to Houston! The sky grew dark; the rain slammed down on us. We stopped at a "quick stop" to ask where we were. We were looking for storage for ZOE so we could go to the Clear Lake marina and check out the sea-going houseboat we had asked to be delivered to our slip. With tornado warnings and ugly skies surrounding us, we finally found our storage and backed ZOE into a storage unit. Unaccustomed to the violence of Southern storms, we found a motel and sat out the tempest. Then we went to the Clear Lake Marina to find the boat we had ordered. It looked beautiful and it was locked. Frustration set in. We finally got the key from the factory, and after checking her out, we pronounced our boat very livable. A cuddy up in the bow with their own head would take care of Peg and Ernie. The double bed and head in the stern would take care of me. Cec, with his long frame, would use a pull-out sofa mid-ship. There was a very adequate galley, and the swim platform was perfect for me to stand on and get Cecil into the ARIZONA. There was also a nice fly bridge, and we felt we had made a good choice. With anticipation we drove to Houston's airport and picked up Peg and Ernie. We hoped they would also like the boat and help us with a name!

THE USS ARIZONA SAILS AGAIN!!

The next three weeks were a flurry of buying supplies for the boat and installing needed equipment. The men were not happy with some of the plumbing and reinstalled water lines. The needed VHF was put in, and the small pilot wheel was exchanged for a larger one. The Volvo 225 hp gas engine seemed quite adequate, and we felt we were ready for sea trials. After much deliberation, we decided it was appropriate to name our ship the PEARL H. Pearl Harbor did match with the name USS ARIZONA just as CELEBRATION II had matched with our nation's BICENTENNIAL 200th birthday.

The local TV came to cover us, and the Navy visited us. We were finding that our 36-foot battleship was a big attraction. Everyone loved her and what she stood for. People thought that being in New York Harbor for the unveiling of the Statue of Liberty was a grand thing for our miniature replica to do. At last it was time to venture out into the busy waters of Port Houston and take a look around.

Timidly we crept out in Clear Lake. We peeked out under a bridge and looked at the Port of Houston. The usual intimidating barges, tankers and freighters looked disdainfully at us as if to indicate, "Don't mess with us!" We found our way back to the marina, determined that we would head out tomorrow for Galveston and get the first leg of our anticipated trip behind us.

We had a 40-mile run ahead of us and got off to an early start. When we emerged into the shipping channel, I clambered down to the swim platform, Cec climbed out of ZOE and we put him on board. All seemed to be going well. Passing oil wells and industrial areas, we cranked our way south, gaining confidence as we moved southward. We already had an invitation to tie up with the old sailing ship ELISSA. She was an old square-rigger being refurbished by the Galveston Historical Society, and the crew hoped to be ready to join in on the 1986 celebration in New York Harbor. They asked us to tie up alongside this lovely old sailing ship. Early afternoon and we sighted

ELISSA.

We began to go through the machinations of tying up the mother ship first, PEARL to ELISSA, then tethering Cecil and ZOE to the starboard side of PEARL H. No matter we all had to climb up onto the fly bridge, vault over the ELISSA's railing, cross her deck, and plunge down the gangplank! All this to get two grandmothers ashore! Peg and I called it swashbuckling! We didn't mind. We were secure and safe. We felt quite smug that our first foray out had been successful and we had the first notch in our gun belt. Our only problem that night was a deluge of rain, a violent windstorm and a lot of sloshing about next to ELISSA. We might not have been so self-satisfied had we known what the next two days were to bring.

Galveston Bay is big—30 miles northeast to southwest, and 17 miles at its widest. It is shallow with an overall depth only eight feet. The shores look flat and marshy without much on them. Galveston is also the oldest deep water Gulf port west of New Orleans and carries a tremendous volume of ship trade. For the visitor Galveston has numerous attractions. There are 32 miles of beaches, excellent hotels and restaurants, old Victorian homes to visit and a museum which described in detail the devastation from an earlier hurricane that killed 6000 people.

We had a call from CBS that they would send out a TV cameraman who would like to film our ZOE in the harbor. We agreed to meet him early in the morning. We got Cecil and the cameraman off in the ARIZONA (they always like close-up shots!) and he covered the first part of Cec's departure. As the cameraman climbed off ZOE, he threw a line on top of her deck. Cec made a grab for the line; it fell into the water and wound tight around two props. Peg, Ernie and I were inside PEARL and we heard an excited voice erupt over the VHS. "I've lost power and I'm drifting in under the pilings. If someone doesn't catch me I'm going to wipe out the superstructure."

At that moment Ernie discovered our starboard battery was dead. Cursing the Murphy law which is multiplied by 17 when one is on the water, all three of us leaped up and over the ELISSA to rescue the ARIZONA. Before we could reach him, Cec, in one last desperate moment, shouted to a well-dressed lady above him on a dock to "please catch this line and hang on to it." She caught the line on the first throw and just saved ZOE and Cec from a most untimely crash into the barnacle-encrusted pilings. The cameraman kept insisting he wanted more shots. He came on board PEARL, climbed up on the fly bridge, and after a new battery in PEARL H, we towed ZOE all over Galveston Bay in front of oil tankers and shipyards. It was not an auspicious beginning for the day, but the sun shone bright, we bade the cameraman goodbye, put our crippled ZOE under tow, and headed for what we hoped would be a great marina where we could untangle the line from ZOE's two props. We could not possibly reach the snarled lines in the harbor.

This part of the ICW was similar to the East Coast in that it was a series of canals, rivers and sounds which is dredged and maintained by the Corps of Engineers. The waterway begins in Brownsville, TX and we knew it could be followed all the way to Boston. We just wanted to get across the wide bay and into a safe harbor for the night. As we headed out across the bay we found that the barges left "gopher holes" behind them which were two feet deep as they sucked the water out at their stern. We tried to avoid these.

We found our marker at Mile 350 and our logbook said it was now March 22. We chugged along all afternoon, meeting a lot of barge traffic and tows. We had many comments and a lot of admiration from the tugboat skippers. We figured their job, though full of responsibility, also must be monotonous, and we gave them something to talk about. One conversation that came over Channel 12 was, "That's somethin' cute you got thar. Cute little feller. Got sunk in Pearl Harbor, didn't it? Ah couldn't figure out what river it could be in. Does the state of Arizona have an outlet to the 'guff' (Gulf) anywhere?

No? Ah didn't think so. How about Colorado? Guess not, couldn't get around the dam." We wondered where the confusion as to history and geography had begun in his life.

As the afternoon waned and a marina was a long ways off, we began to search for a side channel where we could tie up for the night. It looked impossible to find anything that led off from the ICW. Around 5 P.M. we saw a small opening where we felt we could get back in far enough to be away from the wakes of the passing ships. There were creosote pilings, gravel slid down the incline and it was not a welcoming slough. After we pulled ZOE ashore and anchored PEARL, Peg and I stood around wringing our hands and discussing the loneliness of our night's tie-up. No creature comforts tonight! We hoped our batteries in PEARL were adequate! As Ernie and Cec beached ZOE, they crawled under her stern and tried to cut the terribly tight ropes from around the props. They cut one loose when we heard a weird buzzing. The sound was ominous, but we had no idea what it was. The four of us checked out the sky. It wasn't loud enough for an airplane and it wasn't bees. Good Grief! A swarm of mosquitoes were out looking for dinner and we were IT. The attack was so fast and violent that the four of us ran for PEARL's sliding screen and glass door. We tore the screen off its track, everyone jumped into the boat, we slammed the slider shut and watched. The mosquitoes were furious that we had escaped. They lined the windows and we knew they would not be leaving. We had had our one and only time to work on ZOE.

Trapped inside for the night, we made the best of it. We named this awful stop "The High Island Massacre." Peg and I served dinner, our one light went out, and we were bedded down before 8 P.M. That night Ernie must have heard what I heard. It was the deep-throated chug-chug of a huge freighter. We both met in the cabin at 3 A.M., wondering if we were having another gigantic mosquito attack. Then we saw "it." A fast moving, LONG tanker was going by us from west to east. It was lit up with "Christmas" lights and was huge. It came by and came by, and we stood in astonished silence. It was like a snake, slithering along, foot by foot. We were overawed and said no one would believe us in the morning. Ships slip by like ghosts in the night.

Waking early, we looked out through the windows. There was not one mosquito in sight. After breakfast, Ernie and Cecil got ZOE taken care of. We were glad to leave this awful place and hoped for a good marina that night. We had made over 30 miles yesterday; today we hoped to cover 46 miles. We were enroute to Port Arthur!

Considering some of its other great dimensions, Texas has a relatively short coastline. Over half the length of the Gulf Intracoastal lies in Texas. It follows a long curve from Louisiana to Mexico along a route that is not very scenic. It is highly commercial territory broken at long intervals by plush yachting oasis. We found they were very welcome because they were so far apart. The waterway skirts Lake Sabine to the mouth of the Neches River. Then it follows the Sabine-Neches Canal along the edge of the lake to Port Arthur, which is a big oil refinery center where much of the heavy ship and barge traffic on the Waterway in this area begins. We were headed for a marina off the Waterway.

The chatter on the VHF was heavy this morning. The tugboat and barge captains were full of conversation…mostly about our battlewagon. "Ah swear, she's got to be at least 40 feet. Ah heered about them in Houston. Wisht ah knew more 'bout them. Sure lak to know all 'bout it." I answered politely about our ARIZONA's dimensions and where we were going. The silence lengthened. A woman was talking to them on the sacred channel! After the shock wore off over hearing a woman's voice, the airwaves were full of questions…and my answers. Since boating protocol is not to fill up the airwaves with unnecessary chitchat, we signed off and remained silent. The conversations did not end between the captains. "Where they at? Tell 'em to get their cannons ready. Ahm westbound. They gonna shoot me?"

Our "fame" sped up and down along the "ditch" for days. "Where the %#$% is it? Comin' eastbound? Sure would like to have a job drivin' that. Just putt, putt, putt along. He's comin' up on the salt ditch. Ya'll cain't miss him. See him at the bridge. Those people proud of it. They proud—sure would be proud to drive it."

Gaps in the conversations happened when the captains were at full alert with the tremendous responsibility they had in front and behind them. As they resumed their talk, we heard " How'd they get that thing from Californy here?"

Answer: "To hell with the battleship. I want to see the lady on it. Her voice sounded like it might belong to a good body. Don't allow no women on ships in the Navy. Well, if he built it guess he can put anyone on he wants. I cain't get in love with no boat, but a woman would be a different story."

As the distance between us widened, the conversation began to fade and we would encounter a new flotilla nearby. The last words we heard were, "See ya on the two. I'll be in the intersection before you know it. This captain's comin' out of that northdraw and ahm headin' in where y'all just been." The pilots were always a source of amazement for their skills and our amusement at their conversations.

We had one "minor" problem that day. Our starboard engine quit. Ernie found there was air in the fuel tank. Out went the anchor, and Ernie threw up the hatch in the stern, which happened to have my bed over it. Down into the engine compartment he went. This grew to be an almost daily occurrence. "Go secure your bed, Pat. I'm coming back!" Well! Our motto became "It's GOT to get better!"

As we headed into Sabine Lake, we tuned in Channel 16 and raised the marina where we hoped to have two slips waiting for us. We told them that we wanted to gas up two ships, one a battleship. "Ya'll can't come in hyar!" said a shocked marina owner. "We ain't got no room for a battleship." After a lengthy explanation, we were told to come on in. It was a grand welcome. We had power, water, two TV stations, and adults and youngsters wandering down. There was tremendous warmth expressed, and we had our Statue of Liberty magazines given to us by Lee Iacocca's committee to pass out to all, telling where we would be the next year.

Our usual logistical nightmare of hopping the truck and trailer forward was always with us. Usually Cec and I would catch a ride or take the Greyhound bus to the last place where the rig had been left. Peg and I would go on a big shopping spree whenever we had wheels and plan ahead for at least five nights of dinners.

Leaving from this marina, we had Cec out in ZOE, Peg and I were untying our lines for PEARL's takeoff. Peg's line had a hook on the end of it as it was also used for the starboard hookup for ZOE. As we were taking off, the hook caught on the pilings and jerked PEARL H around. We almost crushed ZOE and a frantically waving Cec against a wall. (Scratch one new boat hook lost on this cute maneuver.) We began drifting sideways into other boats. There was much yelling and shouting. I leaped for the dock, got the jammed hook out, threw it to Peg and leaped back on. Another ten feet and we would have been slamming into other pleasure boats. Somehow one achieves miraculous jumps, Superman style, when trying to save boats. Our hearts were beating much too rapidly, and Cec was on the VHF asking, "What's going on? Why are you trying to back out?" (Be quiet, Cecil.)

We mothered up, caught ZOE, and Cec came on board. Soon a lockmaster told us to hurry up and go through, as the lock was going to be temporarily closed in the morning. He painted pictures of good anchorages and out-of-the-channel spots where we could go with our precious cargo. We had one problem going through. The captain of a tug going west wanted a picture and story of our boats for his daughter. He begged us to leave literature with the lockmaster, and he would pick it up on his return trip. Poor Peg had to make "the drop." She stood on top of PEARL and as we went speeding through the lock, Peg stretched as far as possible to place the papers in the long handled net held down to her from the high lock walls. With just one chance to find her target, she flung her package into the out-held bag, stumbled and nearly fell overboard. Success! Everyone clapped for acrobatic performance.

We forged on with no marina in boating vicinity—there was nothing we could reach before nightfall. We should have followed the advice of our *Waterway Guide*. As dusk grew closer and we were looking for a tie- up, "cricket" went mad. The depth sounder told us we had only 1 ½ feet of water under our hull. We traveled on and found a dreadful, snaggy, collapsing dock. It looked lethal. Rusty bolts protruded and as we approached this jumble of creosoted poles the wind treacherously threw a gust at our high profile. The jutting spikes reached out to impale PEARL. The rigid appendages found the cuddy cabin window below and triumphantly punched through. An atmosphere of dismay pervaded the crew. In addition we found that we had tied up near a bascule bridge and were entertained all night be toots, blasts and whistles every time the bridge opened or closed. At least the noise drowned out the mosquitoes that soon found the broken window. The wakes from the barges tried to pry us off our tie-up, and we were up and down all night checking lines.

The next morning our battle cry "it's got to get better" was proven wrong. As we tried to get off the impaling tentacles clutching us while we strung ZOE out, one line accidentally fell into the water and made a beeline for the starboard prop. We were immediately helpless in the river. The two boats with their harness line between them began to drift sideways and backward. We were drifting helplessly across the channel and toward the bridge. It looked as if PEARL would crush ZOE against the steel bridge. There was a shrimp boat bearing down on us as he prepared to go under the open bridge. We saw the bridge master watching our performance with binoculars, no doubt amazed at our crablike drift. Our trip must have been pre-ordained to be completed. We continued to drift, but with a side crawl. We ran aground on the sandy bank opposite where we had been. Cricket, our fathometer, loudly and insistently chirped her disapproval. After regrouping we started afresh, Peg and I swearing to be super careful with our lines.

We were less than a week out and already we had so many difficulties. The diversity of this type of boating travel leaves one anxious but eager to begin another day to find out what is around the next bend in "the ditch." Woe to the unwary boater who cuts a river bend too sharp and encounters a tug pushing a doublewide tow of barges. These skillful tugboat operators are courteous, helpful, full of questions and colorful language. Two pilots got into a squabble later on this day about who was going to pass, where and when. The remarks to one another became more rude and descriptive about each other's background. The final devastating remark by one captain apparently shocked the other into total silence: "Y'all so dumb yo' chillun gonna be born nekkid!"

The shocked captain's only response was "Nanner-nanner-nanner!" Thus ended that conversation. We slowed down so as not to get caught up in this confrontation.

Despite the bad morning's beginning, the day proved to be a beautiful one. We did our 39 miles that day through quiet bayous where birds met tugboats. We went through some rough, exposed water that only added to the problem we always encountered with the wakes from passing barges. PEARL H and ZOE would rock, snort and toss their bows as they fought off the huge wake which barges throw out. A two-foot depression would be left in the water behind these behemoths. Someone would always rush to the stern to fend off the ARIZONA or to check on a line. It was not an easy passage in this long area from Texas eastward. Pleasure boating is not the order of the day as one heads east toward New Orleans. Marinas and fuel were far apart, and heavy commercial boat traffic goes on 24 hours per day. Sophisticated radar makes it possible for these highly-skilled skippers to speed through day or night with their huge, floating hotels in front of them.

As we traversed through a quiet part of the ICW, we found ourselves over the Texas border and into Louisiana territory. White herons, pelicans and egrets squawked at us. Occasional bays with white-capped waves sloshed about us. Our spirits rose and we were lulled into thinking "things have gotten better!"

One should never think "we have conquered" when on the water. We were shocked to see our six-foot- long padded bow cushion suddenly catch a gust of wind, sail into the air and land with a splash in the water. Ernie made a huge swing with ZOE obediently trailing along. Much shouting followed as to how we could retrieve the cushion with ZOE hanging on behind. It was too far to reach down to the water with the one short boat hook we had left.

From out of nowhere, a piroque boat with two surprised fishermen came streaking across our bow, picked up the errant cushion and handed it up to us. Here was an example of true Cajun help. We shouted our thanks. We held out some cash to them as they swept by, and with a wave and a "Well, I'll be damned," they disappeared waving the cash at us. We wondered where they had come from? There wasn't another boat in sight for miles.

Onward! Our *Waterway Guide* assured us that at upcoming Mile 193 there was a marvelous marina. They called it "an oasis for the traveling boater complete with fuel and supplies." We pictured this spot as one would when contemplating a South Pacific Island in mid-winter. Wow!—showers, power, we could hardly wait. Anticipating our first really *good* marina, we journeyed eastward. That afternoon as we approached Mile 193, we were horrified to find nothing but crew boats, old tugs, rusty pilings and NO gas sign. The place looked deserted. Knowing we could not proceed further without taking on more fuel, we decided to venture into the narrow, crowded inlet. Maybe the fuel dock was hidden in the back. Cutting Cecil and ZOE loose from PEARL H, we turned in first. There were no slips, no welcoming gas dock.

The wind, determined to play havoc with this pleasure boat which had stumbled into a barge diesel fueling station, gave us the usual contrary crosswind. We had a line on the starboard bow; Ernie was cranking around on it. The wind caught PEARL broadside and we drifted, slewing around toward a huge, rusty steel eight-foot-wide extension jutting out over the water. PEARL, intent on her suicidal path, careened and spun inexplicably downwind. Ernie tried to get the bow in so I could jump ashore. Time hung suspended. I sensed PEARL coming closer to self-destruction. Calculating my chances of leaping the oily water abyss below, I climbed up on the top rail, line in hand, leaped/scrambled up and along the gravely bank and threw a hitch around a creosote pole, then turned to watch PEARL spin. Thwarted in her headstrong approach on the suicidal mission, she finally lined up her starboard side to the "dock." Peg threw out a stern fender and I hugged the dirty piling. PEARL's 12-foot-wide stern with her beautiful rear bay windows lay eight feet from the ugly protruding pile of steel. It reached out like a giant chisel at us. We were all shaken. We tethered PEARL to the shore. The men courteously named me "Superwoman." To this day I do not now how I made the jump.

The crews who were refueling barges were astonished at our visit, particularly when the gray battleship called on the VHF "Are you ready to bring me in now?" We ran to catch ZOE. The only place to bring her in was next to a too-high rusty barge. Four of us grabbed at the low-in-the-water battleship, but the wind pushed her in too rapidly. We fended her off with the remaining short boat hook. The shove proved to be a bit much. Boat hook count was now zero.

The crewmen could not have been nicer. When we asked about gasoline (after reading the description of this fabulous "marina" to them), they sprang into action, rolled over two gasoline drums and proceeded to hand-pump gas into PEARL. These delightful men could not do enough for us. As night was coming on, they invited us to fender up against an old tugboat. At this point, anything looked good to us. The local newspapers even found us. Lady reporters crawled over the rusting tug and a barge to get to us. We gave them a long interview. We told them their reporting was done "under extremely hazardous duty."

There was no place to go except climb over rusty hulks and onto dusty roads. I desperately needed a phone to call for our next press interviews, our taxman and future dates in Mobile, AL. All these conversations always seemed to be conducted from an outside telephone and by a noisy road, construction sites or tug boats gassing up. I always ended up shouting and saying "What?" As I phoned, I watched the 50- gallon drums being rolled over to refuel PEARL, all the while the other men were burning trash—open flames so near the gasoline. We figured, "This too shall pass." It did, but not before the owner came down to greet us and give us flags from his company.

We had another early to bed night for a tired foursome! Tomorrow we *knew* we would find that elusive, wonderful marina and all would be well. It HAD to get better!

"IT'S GOT TO GET BETTER!"

We left the next morning amidst shouted good wishes, noisy crew boats departing to take their group out to oilrigs, and a surprise doublewide tow waiting for us around the first bend. After all this maneuvering was over, Peg and I hooked ZOE up behind PEARL. The only way to do this was to have supreme confidence in your life jacket, hang by your toenails from the swim platform and hope that the lines and hooks did not forever ruin your hands.

The day was lovely. There were long stretches of unusual trees, occasional fishing shacks lined the shore and the birds sang their stories to us. We began to pass boats coming toward us from the east. The comments were interesting! The VHF crackled with "What's that battleship a-doin' goin' east?" Reply: "You didn't see no battleship. Shut up and talk good now and go straight." Or a polite tugboat captain came by and said "Is that y'alls?" Another said, "That's a cute lil' rascal y'all gots theah!"

Our *Waterway Guide* warned of a lock ahead. After communicating with the lockmaster, we knew we had a wait. We nosed into a bank, and Cec tied ZOE up on our port. Cec stayed in ZOE, and Peg and I threw loops over pilings. It was hard, but we did it. We had much chitchat about releasing lines at the same time—two boats/three lines! Our directions were explicit and we knew our jobs. When Ernie shouted, "GO!" we cast off our lines and all came off but the last stern line. It was our own fault. There were too many lines bunched on one cleat and they cinched up. Peg screamed, PEARL slewed violently, and we could see the ARIZONA was about to be crushed. I ran to the top and tried to help Peg undo the line from the cleat with our fingers. It was too tight, so as a last resort I took off my tennis shoe and used the rubber bottom to push off the line. It slipped off just in time. The lockmaster and all watched our performance with amazement, I am sure. Would it EVER get better?

By afternoon we were ready for Intracoastal City, which we knew to be a gathering area for shrimp boats, tugs, oil supply boats and geodesic survey boats. We cut Cec loose with the ARIZONA while PEARL H prowled the shoreline looking for the narrow opening which our chart indicated was to lead to a real marina. Cec's voice crackled over the VHF. "I've developed a terrible vibration. ZOE is really shaking." We commiserated, but were too busy trying to figure our where our turn in and landing spot was to be. We could not lend much sympathy. Later we found he had knocked a blade off his prop—probably on an oyster bed or what we termed "a submerged BAD thing."

At last we found the opening. It was a most uninviting, restricted channel which led to a so-called gas dock at the end. Lining the constricted route were sailboats on each side with spear-like anchors pointing straight out from their bow brackets. We began to thread our way down the narrow entrance. The high tides had covered the gas dock and raised the water level so that dock cleats could not be seen. Spotting some upright posts ahead which showed only two feet above water, we made for them. We slowed down when we were six feet from our goal. Our nemesis, the wind, caught PEARL's starboard side and slammed her port window into the last projecting anchor point. *MUNCH! TINKLE! CRASH!* In went the port stern window. Two windows gone now! As the ARIZONA came in behind us, the good people at the "we-can't-see-it dock" were sympathetic about our latest casualty but much more interested in the battleship. In radio contact with the vibrating Cecil and ZOE we told him to come on in. We hastened to the end of the marina to try to fend him off, followed by a group of interested, excited people asking questions about ZOE. Our hearts were heavy with anxiety over the latest mishap, and we were not really ready to deflect questions with answers for the nice people, but we did our best. Soon Southern hospitality took over, along with offers of help. Within three hours both windows were replaced, an invitation to have dinner with an oilrig captain and his crew on their geodesic survey boat was extended, and our morale began its climb up the ladder of optimism after the glass man left!

It had to "get better," and it did. We learned about PEARL and her idiosyncracies, her willfulness, her suicidal impulses to take on afternoon landings in 20 knot winds. Not our fault! It was the wind.

We were given a high tide slip, and the tie-up for the two ships was incredibly difficult. With the water so elevated we were high, high above the dock and the lawn nearby. We finally got ashore by taking the swim ladder and leaned it up against the side of PEARL. Then we jumped three feet from the bottom rung to the ground. Not the best of tie ups, but a lot better than some in our past.

The next two days we ran around repairing things. What a wonderful meal we all enjoyed aboard the geodesic survey ship. The crew had a few days off, and we were guests of the captain and his chef. The four of us felt as though we were special, elite company on board. We were given a full tour of the ship and a gourmet meal. These two men became instant friends and they fell in love with ZOE and our desire to get to NY Harbor for the unveiling of the Statue of Liberty.

We confided our fears to Capt. Tim about the locks that lay ahead of us in New Orleans. The stories sounded horrendous—two difficult locks, two crabby lockmasters. Tugs, tows were welcome. Pleasure craft were a pain! Oh dear—we were a high-profile pleasure craft with a very odd attachment behind us! As we continued our numerous conversations with the captain and the chef, a plan of their own design emerged. Capt. Tim had a few days off. If he could please bring his wife, Debbie, on board, he would take over PEARL's helm and guide us through the locks. Would that be all right with us? All right? It would be better than all right. It would be stupendous to have a real, honest-to-goodness captain confront the grumbly lockmasters, explain our strange battleship and help us into the Mississippi River.

We decided to leave ZOE in Intracoastal City at the marina and come back for her later. It would not be wise to go through the locks near New Orleans with her. We would trailer her forward later. Out of the water she came, and as we cranked her onto the trailer, one of the trailer tires went flat. Just our luck. The tire had to be replaced before we could go anywhere with ZOE, so Cec changed it right on the muddy, garbage-filled ramp. It was not easy to find a tire repair shop with our 36-foot gray lady behind us. Perseverance finally paid off and the job was completed. We arrived back at PEARL H late.

Capt. Tim brought his lovely, young wife aboard and they left their three children home with relatives. Six of us on board did not seem to matter. Cec came back with me to the stern, and the young couple took the pull out bed in the main salon. They shared our head and sang to the captain's guitar strumming. It was an ethereal time. We were so grateful for the companionship and skilled help, which we desperately needed, that we did not feel crowded but were happy to share.

We were together for two and a half days. Tim got us up early as we left Intracoastal City. We left our rig there, always mindful that somewhere along the line we would have to come back and pick it up. We had an all-day run and went through one small lock with no mishap. We tied up at a Cajun dock and a young couple came down to see us. We showed them pictures of ZOE and invited them to see a video of her on board PEARL. They fell in love with the idea that we were trying to teach children the sacrifices made by earlier Americans to give us the freedoms we enjoy. They insisted on making a Cajun dinner for us, delivered it to PEARL and ate with us. We shared another video of the rest of our fleet to them, and they seemed enthralled. They were lovely back-in-the-woods-real-Cajun people. The evening ended when we had a warning from Tim that we would be getting up early the next A.M. Our spirits lifted even though the two monster locks loomed ahead.

We cruised through the real bayous and wondered what reptilian creatures lived up the estuaries. We were told that Cajun people are fiercely protective of their fishing and hunting rights and areas. Cajuns were forced emigrants from French Canada and settled in "Evangeline Country," also called "Cajun Country." This is a corruption of Arcadia, the Canadian home of Evangeline in the Longfellow poem. French names predominate and many speak a French-derived *patois*. It was said that some Fish and Game Wardens, investigating fish and animal catches, mysteriously disappeared deep into the bayous and never returned. As we left Texas, their last words to us were, "Yall lookout fo' them Cajuns. They gonna shoot you!" We found them to be wildly independent and wonderfully friendly to our ships and us. But woe to the oilrig captain who zooms out of the ICW, leaving a huge wake to erode the shores of Cajun property. Their boats have bullet holes to prove the Cajuns want no interference with their way of life.

We approached two bascule bridges (seven feet clearance closed). The first was Algiers with two lift bridges, the second was a bascule bridge with seven-feet clearance closed. We found a lot of traffic at the Harvey Lock, the preferred one for Tim. He had taken over and was conversing with the lockmaster. We tied up next to a tug, something that was frowned upon, but we had no choice. The lockmaster told everyone that a mental patient was clinging to the bridge and was threatening to do a suicidal jump. This was great cause for conversation on the VHF among the captains, and there was all sorts of speculation, analysis and unprofessional diagnosis as to why someone would hold all of us up with this action. The consensus from the delayed captains was "Push him!"

At last we were allowed through. Were we glad we had Capt. Tim. There was nothing to tie to on the lock walls. When the tugs began to move, the lock chamber became a giant washing machine from the agitation of their huge propellers. Getting into the Mississippi River was more than we anticipated. Peg and I hit the floor with the eight-knot wind and four-foot waves. The five miles to our marina were harrowing. We crashed our way through, and the two of us spent most of our time on the floorboards trying to save dishes, plants, books, charts, anything that was not nailed down. "Mr. Toad's Wild Ride" was the title for this last five miles. And suddenly it was over; there was the marina ahead. Tim brought the boat in beautifully and we sadly said our *adieus* to this wonderful couple. As a touching goodbye to us, Deb and Tim gave us the most beautiful shell we had ever seen. They said it had been brought to the sea surface from 250 feet below. It opened and closed—a bivalve, but the spikes on it, the encrustations, made it unique. Today, it reposes on a piece of teakwood on our coffee table. What a treasure. And we were the ones who owed them!

HELD CAPTIVE IN NEW ORLEANS

After dropping off our saviors, we hunted for a marina where we could spend a day or two visiting New Orleans. We found the perfect spot for catching the streetcars and walking, but what a horror story to get into the marina. Once again, it was a very narrow channel with boats lethally pointing their various appendages at us. Poor Ernie. He was a good pilot, but we were sure he would rather pilot his own plane rather than a boat caught by capricious winds. It was a city marina and very crowded, but we managed to find a slip and breathed a big sigh of relief. We would worry about getting out later!

It was the first week of April and we had an enforced stay for four days in New Orleans. First, Cec and I rented a car and drove back to Intracoastal City to pick up the USS ARIZONA. We had decided the area next to be covered was too industrial and Lake Ponchartrain too unpredictable to risk taking our battleship eastward so drove ZOE to Gulfport, Mississippi. The gracious people at the local Ramada Inn were willing to let us leave her there until we returned by boat. People seemed to appreciate the fact that we were carrying a message to young people about the sacrifices made to give us the freedoms our country enjoys. Back we went to New Orleans, turned in the rental car and waited for small craft warnings to subside.

After the four-day stay, we crawled out of the marina and poked our bow out onto choppy Lake Ponchartrain. We continued heading east. Each day was different. Open water crossings were a challenge as the ICW ran out into the ocean off the Mississippi Coast. On one particular crossing we had found sailboat friends who suggested we go along with them. It was comforting to hear their voices on the VHF as we tried to find various buoys and markers way offshore. We did take a five-hour pounding as we crossed the Mississippi Sound on our way to Gulfport. One night we were so far out we knew we had to anchor, and we turned into the shelter of Rabbit Island. We were fairly close to the island. There was no one to greet us except the "no-see-ums."

Suddenly a man, a Cajun, came out in a small boat. He told us he was a "coon-ass" (the Cajun name for themselves) and that there was a wooden dike below us. With a two-foot tide we would be impaled. By this time we had both Danforth anchors out, bow and stern, and thought we were settled for the night. We knew we would have to move, but both anchors were caught. Cec had to cut one anchor line and tied a float on the line. Ernie gave PEARL some gas and we managed to pull up one anchor. The Danforth was bent. The prong was three inches long and made of strong steel, but it twisted. Cec had to go out in the dinghy and coax the other anchor out. We saved both anchors, but by 7:45 P.M. we were exhausted and turned in. The trains roared all night from somewhere, but we were glad that tomorrow we would find a marina and be off the open expanse of sea.

We were up at 5 A.M. and the water became rough and rougher. Ernie slowed from 3800 RPM down to 2500. We were pitching, wallowing, tossing and catching an occasional roller coaster wave. We had hoped for a 9:30 A.M. Gulfport landing. We made it just before noon. We found the marina, a fuel dock and protection from the raging (to us) waters outside in the bay. Relief! A great span of water had been conquered. We walked to our truck and trailer, launched ZOE and did our usual gyrations for TV and the local press. We continued to pass out our USS ARIZONA buttons and literature telling about the unveiling of the Statue of Liberty. Our welcome was always appreciated!

Our Gulfport pit stop enabled us to visit the seaquarium, have seafood dinners, visit Confederate president Jefferson Davis's last home, buy charts, do laundry and shopping. Then it was time to move on. We had a mid-April date with our Fredricksburg friends who were officers for the USS ALABAMA crewmen's association. They had invited us to be their guests at their Mobile reunion and to be guest speakers at their banquet.

We picked up ZOE in her trailer, left Ernie and Peg to bring PEARL H to Mobile, and off we went for the USS ALABAMA reunion. This was another warm welcome. The ALABAMA Crewmen parked us right by their big "mommy" ship, which is tied up as a museum in the 75-acre memorial park. The ALABAMA earned six battle stars in WWII and is moored as a shrine. The devoted ex-crewmen have done much to perpetuate the history of their beloved ship. We were guests on board and had a unique, special tour of the ship, then spoke at the dinner that night. The ALABAMA crewmen and families were fascinated with our waterway adventure, and we stood by ZOE almost all next day and told the story of our various boats. They encouraged us to continue on in 1986 and make it to New York Harbor.

Back we zoomed to meet PEARL and our faithful friends. We arranged to trailer ZOE and meet at Dauphin Island, just outside Mobile, AL. Dauphin Island is the closest marina/port to the ICW for pleasure boat centers. It is west of the bay's entrance to the Gulf, and we found it to be a quiet spot after the hustle-bustle of Mobile. Happy to see our friends, we picked Peg and Ernie up at the dock, took our wheels and explored the island. We were not yet ready to launch ZOE so our gray phantom trailed behind the truck. We could see hurricane damage left over from the last onslaught to this vulnerable island. It was here I met the oystermen as we walked along the dock. My curiosity as to what they were netting led to a generous offer to eat a raw oyster. Not wishing to be rude about this courteous presentation, I "glomped" it down. "Delicious," I squeamishly lied. That resulted in another bighearted handout for a second gourmet experience. This time I thanked them and moved on. I have never ordered raw oysters since that time.

Here at Dauphin Island we were to meet someone who would come into our lives and prove to be a forever faithful and loving friend. Skip was a free-spirited boating bachelor. We had no clue he was going to turn out to be our newest skipper, our lifelong friend and our savior on the water. Cecil, Ernie and Peg had gone off somewhere and I was left on PEARL to catch up on correspondence. Coming out on the dock for air, I saw a fortyish, tousled-haired young man hosing off a most interesting, unusual boat. It was salty looking, a double-ender, and looked very seaworthy. The man washing down his ship looked equally salty. I was so curious about the configuration of his ship that I walked over and said, "What a beautiful boat you have. She really looks seaworthy."

The bronzed, shorts-clad, curly-haired man smiled the most broad, friendly smile and said, "You like her? Want to see her? Come on board!"

I disappeared below for three hours. I was shown his ship, and we sat and talked and talked and talked some more. The more he talked, the more I liked him. He was single, had come close to being married a few times, but had never quite made it. He had run away from home at age 14 and had learned to be a tile setter by trade, but also had his 200 Ton license and delivered yachts sometimes for people. He was highly intelligent, self-taught, a maverick from South Haven, MI and was on an exploratory trip with his boat. He was a true "free spirit" and answered to no one but his own agenda. His pride in his boat was catching, and I told him I wanted to introduce him to Cec and our two friends. Coming topside, I saw the three approaching, and we invited Herbert (Skip) Crabtree to go to dinner with us. We all found him to be friendly, charming, full of boating adventures, and the epitome of independence. He also fell in love with our USS ARIZONA and appreciated what we were doing. Having been in the Air Force, he admired our project and our efforts to instill some history and patriotism in young people.

We had a few days with him, but soon it was time for us to leave. Our next marina stop was Bear Point. Just as we were tying up, in came Skip on his ROMAR. We were glad to see him and once again enjoyed one another's company at dinner. He seemed amused at all the phone calls I had to make ahead to people waiting to greet us in the east part of Alabama's coast.

We had to set off early from Bear Point for Pensacola, as we had a date with the mayor in that city. This time Cecil would trailer ZOE and meet us in Pensacola, a distance of approximately 40 miles. We heard later that Cecil had a harrowing time getting his huge rig on a ferry and got lost when he found the mainland. We had better luck and found our marked passage into Pensacola's harbor. Our only problem was a very strong beam wind and PEARL tried to go sideways into her slip. Peg said, "She's a headstrong lady and has a fat rear end."

Cec also reported that at a gas station a man was admiring the ARIZONA and commented, "Our children remember what we leave them." At another stop a lady came up to him and said, "My father was on the USS ARIZONA and I never knew him." We seemed to evoke emotions and memories with our gray lady.

All the dignitaries of Pensacola must have come to greet us. Two TV channels and the news came for interviews. As soon as we hit the TV and newspaper, the local Navy people all brought their children to see the USS ARIZONA and receive the big white buttons we were continually passing out. We tried giving them mainly to children, but many retired veterans shyly asked if "I could have one for my grandson!" Sure we had several thousand to give out, but wanted to save some for the 1986 trip to New York.

Pensacola was first settled in 1559 by the Spanish. They abandoned it in two years, but returned in 1698. After that the city changed hands 17 times with Spain, France, England, the Confederate States and the US contesting control. The newly-formed Gulf Islands National Seashore was a treasure of history with its Fort Pickens. Today it is homeport for the world's largest red snapper fleet. Pensacola is also a major stop for cruising boats.

We had another pleasant surprise. Skip came meandering in late one afternoon, and we were delighted to see him. Always easy, always level, always pleasant, he had become a welcome face and a friend by this time.

Most boaters have a kinship already formed before they meet. They know there will come a time when each needs the other's help in some way. We enjoyed another dinner and day together. Skip began to help us hand out our literature and the ARIZONA buttons. We liked his friendly outreach to the visitors who came in a steady stream. We all toured the Naval Air Museum and had a steady stream of information about each plane from engineer Ernie. His flight engineering background and knowledge was fascinating for us. He had been a part of that elite group at Lockheed: "Kelly's Skunkworks." Ernie gave us a real in-depth history of the many planes in the museum. We all found it fascinating. Then it was good-bye again to Skip, thinking we would never see him again.

Off we went for Ft. Walton, where we were invited to tie up in front of Liollio's Restaurant. What a gang of visitors we had here. Ernie and Cecil were invited to tour Elgin's Air Force Base and came back to PEARL and ZOE with glowing descriptions of what they had seen. Peg and I had accumulated a lot of mail so we decided to walk into town and find the post office. As we left PEARL, Peg picked up the trash and said she would put it in the dumpster behind the restaurant. As we walked along talking, she took the trash and tossed it into the empty dumpster; but it wasn't the trash. It was my mail she was also carrying! She recoiled in horror and we began to laugh. How were we to get down into the dumpster and retrieve everything! That was the problem. We were both short and neither of us could find anything to help us to climb up and in. I finally rolled a big rock over so she could claw her way in. She hung over the side with her feet up in the air, trying desperately not to go in headfirst. I glanced around to see if anyone was watching this spectacle of two middle-aged bag ladies scrounging for their lunch. Fortunately no one witnessed our plight, and Peg retrieved the mail and left the trash. We laughed so hard we hurt.

Some delightful Ft. Walton shop owners came to visit ZOE and ended up inviting us to be their guests for dinner at their private club. People were so good to us and always seemed to understand and grasp the fact that we were doing an "up with America" trip, trying to teach them some history of "the day that will live in infamy." One man who visited us told us his story of being on the USS BUNKER HILL, a carrier badly hit during WWII. He had gone off on a flight, and his ship was torpedoed. His stateroom was demolished and his roommate killed. The only thing he saved was a picture of his wife. He became so emotional in reliving this story that he could not finish and walked away. We were finding that our ships triggered many memories and uncovered long-held-in emotions. People used us as a sounding board, not only for their sense of patriotism, but for their frustration with the government and the media and a sense that their lifestyle was being eroded by a bureaucratic system.

We always listened carefully and tried to ask the right questions. At the end of a day we found that not only were we physically tired, but emotionally spent from the many visitors and their observations. That night our tie-up was unprotected from the Gulf, and a tremendous storm hit and bounced the two boats all over the place. We decided to leave and try to find a more sheltered slip.

Our next stop was to be Biloxi, and we knew we would be meeting tugs and barges although there were not as many this far east of Mobile; however, our "bible" warned us that commercial craft on the Gulf Intracoastal expect yachts to stay clear. In an emergency, the helmsman of a tanker or a shrimp boat can take evasive action; but a barge has no maneuverability, as it is dead weight and is pushed or pulled through the water by one or more towboats lashed to its stern, sides or both. The barges are big, unwieldy and one rarely meets just one. They come in strings or tandem, sometimes two or more abreast. They can be as long as 1,000 feet. Such a rig must swing wide on turns and may need a quarter mile or more to come to a stop.

We would leave the truck and trailer in the last city, Ft. Walton, and Cec would go back to trailer it forward. We had heard there was a storm expected within 24 hours and we wanted to be in a sheltered, protected marina before it hit. We read about trying to get to Choctawhatchee Bridge at the correct time so the bridge master would open up for us. The clearance was exactly what our boat height was and we knew we would have to toot for him to open for us.

The day was beautiful and there was only one big, wide tow far behind us. We were at Mile 249.8 when we began to call the bridge. We tried the usual Channel 16; no answer. Then 13, no answer, then 14, no answer. We made seven calls and received no answer and came closer and closer to the bridge. We even gave one long/one short whistle—no reply. The tug captain behind us had heard our one-way communication. He came through loud and clear on 16. "If he don't answer ya, y'all can blow him up with that cute lil rascal behind y'all."

Not wishing to irritate whoever was in the small bridge house, we said little. It is considered impolite if one calls and whistles too much; but we knew we could not go under the bridge without it opening. The chart said it was 15 feet at the center without opening. The gauge at the bridge said it was a 12-foot clearance. We were 12 feet plus our antennas. We were willing to take the latter down, but it was too close for us to take a chance. The bridge still did not open. Then we were forced to circle. We gave another long and another short.

Channel 16 crackled with the tug captain's voice. He wasn't funny this time. "Choctawhatchee Bay Bridge—ya'll gonna open that bridge for me? I cain't slow down. Ahm right behind that gunboat ahead." No answer from the bridge.

Ernie yelled, "Look, he's cranking up the bridge." Slowly, grudgingly, the bridge lifted a few feet. By this time the tow was right behind us since we had had to circle. We headed for the dead center of the bridge and slid through. The cantankerous bridge master yelled down at us, "You had plenty of clearance to go through." He also said some other unintelligible things which likely were not polite. Concerned for the barge captain, we turned to watch what was happening to the fully-loaded tug. The barge came through sideways. We figured he had slowed down because of us and the fact the bridge was not opening for either of us. It was a dangerous situation. The tugboat captain said something sarcastic to the bridge master, and Ernie had me write down the whole situation: the time, the place, the circumstances. We would turn in a complaint to the Coast Guard.

TIME TO SAY ALOHA

We continued on our way and I busily wrote up the complaint to turn in to the Coast Guard. Idly listening to Channel 16 chitchat between tug boat captains, I heard, "This wind tearin' my butt up. Ah gat three empties and ahm takin' a corner mighty fast-like." We managed to get into St. Andrews Marina in the early afternoon. We found the marina to be strangely configured. There was a protective concrete wall around the marina, but the bottom was open to the Gulf by three feet. The abutment protected the inner harbor, but the waves and wash came in and under and made jouncing around a minute-by-minute occurrence. We could see the black clouds from the predicted storm rolling in, and we tied our two ships down more securely than ever. We put extra lines on and worried about the sailboat in the slip next to us.

The TV reporters came down. We had numerous visitors, then took our wonderful friends to dinner. We were nearing the end of April and the end of our 1985 trip, and we were so grateful to them. What good sports! We walked back to PEARL in sticky, hot weather. Thunder and lightning warned us that we had better get on board before the tempest hit us. Just in time we closed sliding doors and windows. "Batten down the hatches," Cec roared over the approaching growl of the wind. Then it hit.

What a scene. Boats began to jump up and down, bow and stern alternately slicing the water. The surge from the waves came thundering in under the opening in the wall. We decided California had nothing to compare with the violent Southern storms we had seen. The uproar lasted a few hours, but during this time the sailboat next to us flopped over on its port side, slamming its mast onto our bridge. Ernie and Cecil raced out to tie the mast down on the starboard side. Fortunately the only damage done was to our railing, but it was menacing. With the storm wearing itself out, we decided we would hit the hay early, for tomorrow would be a busy day.

Morning arrived, and to our amazement we saw ROMAR coming into the marina with Skip. What a surprise. We hurried over to greet him and tie him up. What a wild tale he had to tell. He was caught out in the night storm and was badly tossed about. He had a few broken things, but his boat was a sturdy, seaworthy one. A very tired Skip gratefully came to our PEARL and had breakfast. He left to clean up his boat and later told us he slept almost all day. We had visitors all next day and had a group board meeting as to what our end-of-the-trip game plan should be. We checked out all the charts for Florida's western coastline and saw that our jumping off place for Tarpon Springs would have to be Apalachicola. This distance from Apalachicola to Tarpon Springs was 150 miles in open water. Discretion overcame valor, and we decided it would be unwise to try to run day and night with a tow, worry about weather and other boats. We had already found free winter storage for ZOE, given to us by a Mobile businessman. We would trailer the ARIZONA back to the Mobile warehouse and we would also have to do something with PEARL H. So, our mutual decision was to see that Peg and Ernie got to the nearest airport and we would take care of ZOE and PEARL. Ernie and Peg helped us make a final move to Bay Point Marina/Hotel where Cec and I would headquarter until all boats were on dry land, then we would go back and pick up our truck/trailer. Deal!

Giving our special friends one last dinner and a gift, we thanked them with heartfelt gratitude. There are not many people who would take on such a difficult trip. We faced so much together and they were such good sports about everything. We owed them a lot. We also felt that we could not ask them to do the 1986 trip with us as the next one would be longer. We well remembered the problems we had had when Bill was with us during the Bicentennial. In fact, we had problems with every trip! It would not be fair to put these nice people in such a difficult situation. Who could help us?

I had been giving Skip some thought for several days and was mentally kicking myself that I had not asked for his Michigan home address. How would I ever locate him? He seemed to be the perfect person to captain our next PEARL H and ZOE trip. He was the above-named free spirit, he had his 200 T license, he was affable, obviously boat smart and we noticed everyone liked him wherever he went. He had a boyish charm that attracted men and women. I approached Cec with the idea of asking Skip to captain our next trip. Apparently the idea had not occurred to him. He was too busy with logistical endings to this trip. Cec was skeptical that anyone, even Skip, would go with us next year. We agreed to ask him.

Skip had planned to sail over to our last marina and help in any way he could. He was a help! We found transportation to the airport for Ernie and Peg. We backtracked and brought the truck/trailer forward and took ZOE out for her trip to Mobile. We found a trucking company that would pick PEARL H up at the closest boat yard lift and take her to a marina in Tarpon Springs. It all seemed to fit together. Even Skip said he would take our trip offer under consideration over the fall and winter months in Michigan. We said a fond goodbye to him. He was headed back to Mobile, then up through the Tom Bigbee Canal, into the Mississippi, the Illinois River, then across Lake Michigan to his home in South Haven. There he would begin his tile work and do an occasional yachting delivery. His ROMAR would take him anywhere.

Pat on PEARL H
stern as seen
from inside ZOE

Handling lines

USS ARIZONA and
PEARL H
Tied up together

Bayport, Florida

ZOE in sling

Readying her to
place her on
her trailer

PEARL was left reposing on chocks in a Tarpon Springs marina and would wait for us to pick her up in February of 1986. We finally got our act together and had a June 1 last land appearance with ZOE in Mobile—this was for the opening of the Tom Bigbee Canal. We counted up water miles covered in our logbook. We had put 1100 miles under PEARL's hull since Houston.

Are we ready to do it again? we thought. *It's hard work and there are so many emergencies connected with boating.* We loved reaching out to young people and their grownup guardians and sharing the ARIZONA's sad but brave war history. We were happy to participate in the birthday party for the Statue of Liberty. Why do we do this to ourselves?

We suspect the answer lies with the quiet, elderly, frail little lady who was looking pensively at our USS ARIZONA in Bay Port, Florida. "Have you ever stopped to think," she asked, "how grateful the men on the USS ARIZONA would be that they have not been forgotten?"

This touching, heartfelt analysis spurs us on. A part of ZOE's christening message speaks for us. "May the 'new' ARIZONA's voyages travel as a miniature shrine into the ports and hearts of America"—AND, SHE DID!!

1986

Tarpon Springs, FL to New York Harbor

USS ARIZONA

Capt. Skip Crabtree
Pat and Cecil

Tarpon Springs, FL to New York Harbor—1986

STATUE OF LIBERTY—
HERE WE COME!!

Over the winter we were in touch with Skip and kept urging him to come with us! Along about February, 1986, he called and informed us "It's a go!" We were elated. Having four river trips under our belts already, we knew the pitfalls and hardships of water travel and felt we could no longer lean on friends to accompany us amidst so many unexpected trials. Skip had numerous boating trips to his credit and we felt we could ask him to share the hardships we knew were ahead.

A board member and his wife of our Friendship Fleet, Inc. (Gary and Connie Waldron) had had a golf tournament fundraiser for us the year before in Southern California! What loyalty! We had trailered our ZOE down to their Red Hill Country Club, and they and their friends surely went to bat for us. They raised enough money to partially fund the two trips with the USS ARIZONA. We were counting on those dollars for the 1986 Tarpon Springs to New York saga along with some of our own. How can we ever say an adequate thank you to so many people who believed in our history teaching/patriotic/up with America adventure!

We talked with Skip and prepared to meet the first week in February, 1986 at PEARL H's marina in Tarpon Springs. We were glad to know PEARL was still there, for a hurricane had passed nearby during the season. Off we went, a route well traveled by us—Las Vegas, Texas, Mobile,AL. We found ZOE none the worse for wintering in a cobweb- and spider-infested warehouse. Dusty and dirty, but happy to know she would soon be in the water, she let her hitch down on the truck's ball and we were no longer incognito! We were also some 3200 pounds heavier. As soon as we drove out the warehouse gate and stopped to get gas, the questions and comments began again. Out came the press releases.

We stopped for gas and both of us left the rig. When we returned there was a plump, formidable looking couple arguing and standing beside ZOE.

The lady had a camera in her hand and was gesturing to the man. "Git up thar, Henry. Climb yo'self up on that thar deck and ah'll take a pichur of ya."

Henry was saying, "NO, Mabel, ah won't do that. If ah put one foot on that ship, he'll shoot ma ass off. Now git away frum thar." They grumbled off together.

On we drove eastward, anticipating seeing Skip again. The truck drivers did their usual thing. They either paced behind us, beside us or tailed us as we talked on the CB. Questions and comments bombarded us along Highway 40. One truck driver behind us said to his buddy going the opposite direction, "Ah could use that thing to shoot squirrels with."

His buddy's reply: "You shoot with that and they ain't no squirrel left."

On February 8 we drove into the Tarpon Springs marina. There was PEARL all shined up and inside was Skip, obviously tired from his cleanup work, but happy to see us. There was much chattering and catching up as we had our shakedown. He was already into the cuddy cabin and we transferred our things into the stern bedroom and center area. We took a few days to stock up the ship—refrigerator, cleaning supplies. In my delight to see Skip, I offered to do his laundry along with mine. I ended up with fourteen machine loads just for him(!) and loudly went on record as "I'll NEVER do that again." There was a lot of talk about getting a wife who would put him on a schedule for laundries, etc., but a huge protest from Skip who had come close to marriage three times. The final commitment had never quite reached its culmination. I was to find later that it was my pleasure to introduce him to every available anchor lady or reporter who covered us on the East Coast and set them up with dates. After awhile my new title became "The Madam."

We had rain, rain, rain, but finally all was ready. PEARL and ZOE were in the water and we had a gala send-off from the marina and boat owners who had gathered to wish us *bon voyage*. We also had an offer from friends who lived near Orlando, FL. Did we want to leave our truck/trailer on their horse ranch? Did we ever! We would back track and leave it with them while we did the west and east coasts of Florida! Things looked promising.

With the local chart laid out by the pilot wheel, we carefully checked the shallow areas which we had to bypass before we could get out into the more deeply dredged Intracoastal on Florida's west coast. Three miles out and CRUNCH! A shoal had shifted and our out drive was hung up. We could not plow forward or get off in reverse. A sailboat had decided to run shotgun with us as they, too, were headed for the ICW. When they saw our problem they came back and threw a line, which Skip snubbed into our bow cleat. I helped Cecil get into ZOE and cast him loose. There was no damage to ZOE, and only a rail was broken on the battleship. It was obvious we had a problem. The sailboat people towed us back to the marina which we had left an hour previously. With our tail (rudder?) between our legs, we slunk back to the fuel dock. "WHAT happened?" was the chorus that greeted us. We told our sad tale and were immediately taken to the sling and hoisted up.

CAPTAIN SKIP (Herbert) CRABTREE

200 Ton License

We lived in the sling with a ladder up against the port side so we could climb the ten feet up to PEARL's deck. Another *déjà vu* for me! Within two days the broken yoke on the out drive was repaired, and we chose to try to sail out unnoticed with no fanfare. We were put back into the water and found the ICW with no mishap. Skip heaved a sigh of relief. There was a chop on the waters, but we felt we were able to weather it. No way did we want to return to the marina.

We had a long run down Florida's west coast from Tarpon Springs. Clearwater sounded like a potential problem. Just south of that city there is a place called The Narrows, where the ICW enters a confined passage. Shoaling is chronic (oh dear) and some parts of the passage are frequently down to five feet, even less. The 100-foot channel comes within yards of either shore. We were cautioned to reduce speed, watch our depths carefully and ease through. After what happened to us up at Tarpon Springs, we did just that. On we went through Indian Shores, then into Tampa Bay. Ahead of us was the spectacular Sunshine Skyway Bridge whose twin spans formed a 15-mile highway across lower Tampa Bay. We headed northeast for the marked St. Pete channel and then ran due north to the Municipal Pier. We were looking for our tie-up at the end of the St. Petersburg Pier. We were to be Johnson Outboard's guests for three days. Bill Au Coin, the PR man from Johnson Outboard who helped us so much with the USS BICENTENNIAL trip arranged all this. Sponsoring our visit at this prestigious spot were OMC, Harborage at Bay and Landmark United. We were to welcome visitors after interviews with the local papers and TV channels. It was with some trepidation we went in to this busy place. ZOE was to be tied up on the south side toward the west and PEARL was somehow to be perpendicular to her. We would have power, which was always a bonus!

Blessings on Bill Au Coin. He was there to help us tie up, and soon the flood of media people came for interviews. Not only did this bring an inundation of people, but we also found out the local pelicans were fed near us every afternoon! What a mess. The lady with the buckets of fish came by three afternoons in a row and fed the awkward looking birds. Pelican ploop! It was everywhere, all over both ships. Skip's greatest verbal agitation always came out with an "Oh, my Gawd." There was a lot of repetition of that short sentence for the next three days as we all battled to clean up our ships for the visiting public.

Our tie-up was a rough one—there was no protection from the wind which swept across the bay and we tossed, sloshed and were slammed by waves. It was rough and Cecil or Skip were up for two nights checking and rechecking lines. Our visitors were many—Navy personnel, a survivor from the "real" USS ARIZONA, the widow of a man who had been on the ship, people from miles away who brought their youngsters to see the copy of the real thing. It was a lovely welcome, but after three days of pelicans we did not mind leaving.

We decided to take care of the truck/trailer rig immediately and get that logistical problem off our back. Skip and I would take PEARL and ZOE down to the Harbour Villa marina, Cec would meet us there, then soon we would head for our friend's horse ranch near Lake Mary. Skip and I were enchanted to have a cotillion of dolphins escorting us for miles along the waterway. Late afternoon we met and went out to rent a car so I could bring Cec and myself back to PEARL. It was always double tracking and we would be glad to dump the rig for a long period of time. A thunderstorm hit that night and the next morning was not a good time to go boating so Cec and I left Skip and drove back to Tarpon Springs and on to the horse ranch. What a pleasant greeting we had from our friends. We were offered lunch and the invitation to leave our outfit at the ranch for as long as we wished. With that assurance we climbed into our rent car and went back to join Skip.

We stayed at this lovely marina for a few days while we rested, shopped and caught up on some much needed sleep. I found that when Cecil, builder of all ships, was gone from PEARL, I was next best. Our visitors always wanted to meet the man whose creativity brought the replicas to life. I soon learned I was always to be second best in his absence. Skip and Cecil decided it was time to leave for Ft. Myers, so we were up early and I cast Cec and ZOE loose from the swim platform. As we left the harbor, the captain and I made a port turn. Cecil had gone ahead with the ARIZONA. The two of us were so intent on watching our markers to find the ICW that we did not check on the battleship. There was a shout from Skip. "Where in the blankety-blank is Cec going?"

I looked around. No sign of a gray lady.

"Look back at our stern."

I grabbed the binoculars and searched the skyline. Way off in the distance was the low silhouette of ZOE—going the wrong way. She was fast disappearing. "What is he doing?"

Skip grabbed the VHF. "I hope he's got his radio on."

The conversation was funny. "Hey, Admiral. You ruze yo' mind? WHERE y'all goin'?"

The voice answered, "What do you mean, where am I going? I'm headed for Ft. Myers."

"No you're not," said the captain. "You are headed back to St. Petersburg."

There was a long pause. "Are you kidding?"

"NO! Now check your compass, turn around and follow us."

We watched and the ARIZONA did a one-eighty and began to churn back toward us. "Good thing you saw me," said the Admiral. "I was just dreaming along, happy as a clam. Sorry about that."

Then the fog rolled in. It dropped so suddenly we were startled. Skip told Cec to follow us and we would circle Markers 26 and 27. Fog, fog, fog. Would it never lift? We were always concerned about other boats in the area that might be running on radar. It was a weekday and not as many boats were out on the water. After two hours of uneasiness, the fog began to lift and we started south again. We didn't think crossing Tampa Bay was much by car, but by boat and with a tow it seemed to take overly long before we ducked into the protected ICW again.

We did a quick two overnights in Sarasota where two TV channels came out to interview all three of us. We hooked a ride with other boaters to the famous Ringling Circus Museum of Art. We had no concept of the scope of this beautiful palatial home with its Renaissance style palace, Baroque art, old masters and a centuries-old theater were transported from its home in Italy stone by stone and reassembled. It is the site of a two- month theater festival in mid-summer. The Museum of the Circus had a marvelous collection of "circusana," starting with ancient Roman relics to the latter-day wagons and carnival equipment. We were immensely impressed with the whole exhibit.

We passed Boca Grande, one of the world's great tarpon fishing grounds. It was also the entrance to Charlotte Harbor, but we had miles to go before we headed into the Caloosahatchee River, the entrance to the Okeechobee Waterway. As we neared Captiva, then Sanibel we knew we must begin to look for our pivot point marker to head eastward across Florida's middle to the Atlantic. Our guidebook told us that Sanibel Island is a winter habitat for 200 species of migratory birds. There were many islands in this area and their names had a Spanish origin. Jose Gaspar (aka Gasparilla) made this area his home base. Captiva apparently acquired its name because it was here Gaspar reportedly kept his female prisoners. Having captured a shipload of aristocratic maidens bound from Mexico for finishing school in Spain, he gave the homelier girls to his crew and kept the pretty ones out of harm's way and the crew's way. Skip allowed we should stop and see if there were any captive maidens. We chorused, "No way…no bad thoughts…STEER!"

As we headed eastward on the Caloosahatchee River, we made two discoveries. One, that there were the most beautiful, magnificent homes right on the water. Two, that we should never, if possible, travel on a Saturday or a Sunday on the water. The boat drivers in 1986, as opposed to 1976, seemed oblivious of the rules of the road, the danger involved with speed and the lack of courtesy when one has a huge ship under tow. The wakes from powerboats and jet skis caused us much consternation and concern. The captain said, "This is the LAST Sunday we are going to be on the water" (if possible). Cec and I were constantly on the swim platform, trying to keep ZOE from climbing onto our swim platform or whipping back and forth. We let her out a bit more, but the operators of the jet skis seemed to love to make her rock and cut much too close to our special cargo.

"ZOE" under tow along west coast of southern Florida

We passed Cape Coral, which was nine miles west of Fort Myers. Channel markers had to be observed carefully because the shore was lined with coves and lagoons carved out of the mangrove wilderness. The real estate developers had certainly made inroads into this once-isolated area.

We made our way into a terrible boat yard. It was a late afternoon and hard to read the markers as nesting birds were on top of the markers and the bird's residue had eradicated the numbers! Cec was unharnessed, and Skip and I went in first, then brought in the Admiral. Even though this marina did not have all the amenities we had hoped for, it was an oasis out of the crazy river. We decided to lay low for two days and visit Thomas Edison's winter home. Before we left to visit this fascinating place, we had two TV channels visit us. Thus, the next day we had numerous visitors.

Thomas Edison's home was astonishing. We saw his fully furnished home, laboratory and the surrounding grounds, which were noteworthy for their tropical specimens. There was a light bulb which had been burning since before Edison's death and had never been turned off. We were told it had a bamboo element! His old Victrola had teeth marks around the edge and we asked if Thomas' grandchildren might have teethed on that invention. The docent told us that Edison was deaf and the only way he could hear sound was to put his teeth on the edge of the Victrola and feel the vibration. What an inventor! We were very impressed. His friend Harvey Firestone gave Edison a banyan tree that was two inches in diameter. When we visited it had spread 200 feet. The small fig tree Henry Ford had given to Edison was immense.

It was time to face up to crossing Lake Okeechobee. We read about it in our "bible." The crossing to the St.Lucie Canal on the Atlantic side would be 156 miles with 21 more miles to St.Lucie. We would be going through primitive, unspoiled territory. Okeechobee in Seminole means "plenty big water." Few people traveling by land ever get to see this naturalist's delight. We would pass cattle empires and vast farming combines along with watery wildernesses and sleepy villages. We also learned that the Waterway had four locks and more than 20 bridges which ran from electronic to hand-operated. With all the locking we had done on our way to the St. Lawrence, we felt somewhat competent. Draft was to be no problem, and depth was well maintained. "The crossing is easy," said our guidebook, "but watch out for the actual lake crossing." We would be taking the southern Rim Crossing and we were warned about the north winds that swept across the vast stretch of water and turned the unwary boater into a basket case.

Up the river in a fog we went headed for sleepy La Belle. Causing quite a bit of commotion among the locals, we took our two boats through the first lock. We went up three feet! What an accomplishment! We found a primitive but gorgeous spot with a free tie-up. We negotiated a spot behind the gas docks. It was tight for two boats, but we made them fit. This was where we were to meet the local newspaper reporter. Hopping off PEARL to tie her up, Cecil idled out in the water, waiting his turn to be brought in. As I leaped into the grass with my line, I saw a sign nearby: "DON'T Feed The Alligators." I had faced many problems in boating but this one had to be high on the list of "scary." After tying up both boats, we checked out our whole area carefully. The dock master seemed most nonchalant about any reptile invasion and said he had not seen a 'gator' for four days. We were all careful to watch where we were walking, and I demanded help carrying the dirty laundry up to the marina laundromat.

Next day we entered the Indiantown two locks. How gracious the lockmasters were to us. They allowed "we hain't had no battleship through heah for some time." Then we ventured out past the protected area right into Lake Okeechobee. The northwest wind had rolled across the lake and was whipping directly onto our port side. It was so rough our ship's bell rang and clanged repeatedly. The three of us felt we were foolish to venture out into the afternoon wind with our tow behind us and did a one hundred and eighty degree turn. That was not easy. We took a pounding again. Where to go? We ended up at Slim's Fish Camp. These reclusive people must have thought we were aliens from outer space. We did not receive the usual accolades and visits that came when the USS ARIZONA tooled into port. There was a coolness and, we felt perhaps, a suspicion that we might not be what we represented ourselves to be. "Revenooers in disguise?" Who knows.

As I sat on a bench near the small country store, two of the town's farmers were conversing about something. One shot a well-aimed spit of tobacco at the local town mongrel and said, "Waall, he'll be a'wearin' the same pants whether he's glad or mad." We analyzed that remark later on the boat. No conclusion. Must be a Southern expression.

We bought a Florida newspaper that afternoon and secluded ourselves inside PEARL rather than mingle with the non-visitors. Strange. We were rewarded with some amazing news! Of all days to buy a newspaper, this had to be pre-ordained. We had told Skip about the uncooperative bridge master on the Chocawhatachee Bridge last year. The Coast Guard had asked for an explanation from the bridge master, who wrote a response with a telephone-size pencil, many misspelled words, grammatically amazing phrases and numerous excuses. Cec gave a shout and said, "Listen to this newspaper article!" He read the following story: It seems that the bridgemaster's demeanor did not change over the year despite our complaint. He refused to open the bridge high enough for a tug and barges to go through. The superstructure of the tug caught the bridge house, ripped it off the bridge, the outhouse size structure tumbled down onto the barges, bridge master and all (!) and off they went. There were no injuries except to dignity evidently, but the Coast Guard indicated that "there will be an investigation." We chortled and hee-hawed. "What goes around comes around." We felt vindicated.

We were up early the next A.M. to beat the afternoon winds. The Coast Guard weather report said winds should not be severe. Hah! From where were they broadcasting? We headed out onto the South Rim track and made a few good miles. Then, the enemy erupted. The wind roared at us and we pitched, tossed and rolled. We fought for each marker. Cec and I were constantly out on the swim platform, checking ZOE's tendency to run up onto it. We tried to steady her as we pounded our way through the waves. Skip's only remark was, "We'll shake all the dust off PEARL's rafters on this trip." We forged ahead to the next lock. What a beating we took that afternoon. At last—we made it into IndianTown and made a stop for much- needed supplies.

How warm and friendly the locals were to us. I was offered a ride into the local grocery and within 15 minutes had spent almost $100. I had been ordered to "hurry it up and get back here." Back to the two ships and the usual friendly crowd surrounded the men. We reluctantly bid them *adieu* as we had a date to meet the Coast Guard Auxiliary when we came out of the St. Lucie lock. Onward! As we came into the lock we were surprised to see hordes of people lined up along both sides, cheering and waving at us. We had not expected anyone to be there.

They all seemed to know we were coming through the lock, and it was a most unexpected greeting. As we grappled with lock lines for both boats the crowed shouted encouragement. Most of the words were unintelligible, but when we got on the VHF we found out that not only had these good people come out to greet us, but a large flotilla of boats with Coast Guard Auxiliary members came to escort us to our marina in Stuart. When we emerged from the lock, we counted 25 boats. There was much chit-chat on the VHF and we found that the nephew of Admiral Tidd, Capt. Isaac Kidd, was among those to greet us. The admiral was his uncle and had been the commander of the USS ARIZONA in Pearl Harbor. He had gone down with his ship. Capt. Kidd had pulled together the whole greeting and later followed us up and down Florida's east coast for quite a number of days.

We learned that the next day we were to be guests at the Sandpiper Bay Club and a dinner would be held in our honor! That sounded good after the pounding we had taken that day. Our escorts took us to the marina where we were to tie up. There was so much excitement about the battleship coming in that we found huge crowds on the dock. There was nothing to do but bring PEARL H in first, so Skip and I tied her up while everyone ignored us and applauded and cheered Cec as he maneuvered around in the small harbor. Skip motioned Cec in and as ZOE began to point toward us, Skip said, "Quick, run back to PEARL and get the boat hook. He's got a beam wind and we'll never catch him without it." Obediently I turned and ran—and slammed my face and left eye right into a protrusion on a piling on the dock. Ka-blooey— the lights almost went out; but, knowing the fragility of ZOE banging around on pilings, I dazedly staggered back to the boat and grabbed the boat hook. Skip caught Cecil and ZOE just in time and hauled him in. With crowds gathered around the ARIZONA, I quietly made my way back to PEARL H. I dared to look in the mirror. The beginnings of a black eye were already evident. My face was banged up on one side. I felt awful and looked worse!

The show must go on. I put on a pair of dark glasses and disguised myself the rest of the afternoon. When I continued to wear them into dusk, Skip asked me why I was still wearing glasses. Discovered! I took them off and displayed my shiner to the gentlemen. Both looked aghast. It was very rewarding to see they cared! The expletives were loud and clear. I felt somewhat vindicated from some of the unboatmanlike things I occasionally did under their glare.

FLORIDA'S EAST COAST

With our flotilla of friends, many pit stops were planned for us, and we would meet Sea Cadets, Coast Guard Auxiliary people, and tie up in private yacht clubs. Our welcome was most gratifying. We had offers of dinners out, lead boats guiding us into marinas and introductions to news media. After a night in Stuart we headed south to Lighthouse Point near Pompano Beach. Our goal was Miami, where we would turn around and head for New York. We were to spend one night at a marina while the Mayor met us and we were guests at dinner, then we had a lovely invitation from a Navy League commander who invited us to tie up on his quiet canal where we could make boat repairs. Things looked good. We should have known better. On all these waterway trips we would be lulled into a sense of well-being and security only to have some unknown circumstance put us down.

As we headed for Pompano Beach, it was getting late, as we had done an 80-mile run that day. The marinas we called were all full. "No room at the inn!" As we began to run into the more crowded area of southern Florida, the crazy boaters picked up speed. They began to circle us at great speeds with their jet skis or their powerboats. They seemed oblivious that Cec and I were both on the swim platform trying to save ZOE from crashing into the narrow concrete bulwarks. The echo chambers of water sloshing back and forth in the narrow channels was terrible. Waves rose and splashed against us in crazy patterns. Skip fought to keep PEARL steady as we fought to keep ZOE from climbing onto the stern or crashing against the walls. We had to find a place to tie up. At last we decided to pull into a dock which had a restaurant on the water and see if we could just stay the night. I crawled up and out of the heaving PEARL and told our sad tale to the restaurant owner. He was immediately sympathetic and said we could stay on the side of the channel that night and that he had a narrow slot for ZOE in the back of the restaurant area. That was all that was available. We were grateful!

The wakes were still severe, but at least we put ZOE out in the back slips and figured PEARL could take the upheaval as long as we tied her securely.

We figured sometime these crazy boating people have to leave and go home. They did, but that was not the end of the night. We had had to break our own rule that would never travel on weekends. It was a Saturday and the "nooo-noos" were out. We were so beat we all went to bed at 8 P.M. Sure enough, the boating people went home, but others came out for a big Saturday night at the restaurant. We were awakened just before midnight with loud, loud rock 'n roll music reverberating through our ship. Skip came up from his cuddy and demanded to know what the blankety-blank that noise was. By that time we were up and on investigating, Cec found out that a loudspeaker from inside the restaurant was blaring just above where our boat was tied. The noise was indescribable. We all went back to bed, but it was impossible to sleep. Cec muttered and muttered threats to himself about what he was going to do to the people who caused the racket. It was all I could do to dissuade him from climbing up on PEARL's bridge and keep him from yanking out the wires to the speaker. More and more irritable and short tempered, he grabbed his pillow and a blanket. Skip and I asked him where he was going. "I'm going out and sleep in ZOE!" Off he marched. That was the last we heard from him until the next A.M. Although stiff from sleeping on the ARIZONA's floorboards, he said, "It was better than listening to that so-called music all night." Our situation had to get better.

The next three days were a welcome relief from the ICW. The Navy League commander's home was on a quiet canal and we had an equally quiet tie-up. These hospitable people even insisted we use a bedroom and their showers. The whipped cream was that the man had a super workshop and Cec and Skip spent hours repairing the two ships. What a welcome relief from the nightmare of a weekend in southern Florida's waters. We swore to plan ahead so we would always be in a marina or tied up somewhere whenever a weekend came.

The commander's Sea Cadets visited us in droves. The U.S. President of the Navy League came to see us. We showed our video to them of the rest of the fleet and gave them literature and buttons. They all wanted to come to NY with us to see the unveiling of the Statue. Then it was time to leave for Lighthouse Point, and the same flotilla that escorted us from St. Lucie lock escorted us southward to Lighthouse. It was a cloudy, dark day. My eye still had all the colors of the rainbow around it. We were greeted at the beautiful yacht club, and they took us out to the lawn where the mayor welcomed us so graciously and gave us the key to the city. We all spoke our thank yous, and the mayor eventually said, "Mrs. Gates, it's so dark today. Why don't you take off your dark glasses?" Trapped! Cornered! I took them off to the astonishment of the mayor and those nearby. They gasped and expressed their sympathy. Back on went my glasses and I tried to disguise my disfigurement the rest of the night.

Saying our goodbyes and thank yous to the good commander and his wife, we ventured back out into the ICW and headed northward. We had come as far south as just north of Ft. Lauderdale. Evaluating the tremendous increase in boating traffic in the eleven years we had been gone, we all decided we had come far enough south! It was a weekday and the boat traffic had diminished considerably. On these long, more quiet stretches we had an opportunity to get to know Skip better. He had had a horse ranch in Michigan for five years, but tired of being landlocked. He had learned the tile man's trade at an early age. After tiring of being on a ranch, he decided to buy a boat. Then, he was hooked. He talked about tossing out the credit cards, selling his car and furniture and placing all his belongings on a boat. Eventually he fell in love with the water so deeply that he studied for and took the test for his 100-ton skipper's license. He passed and began to deliver yachts for others. He kept talking about his "freedom," and we did admit it sounded great.

As usual we encountered one problem (at least) on the way to Lake Worth. Men were working on a lift bridge and there was not enough clearance for us. We tried to tie up and wait for them to open it, but it was a very unfriendly bit of land. Cec and I were on the bridge and stern, fending ZOE off while Skip tried to keep both boats under control. The wind was having fun at our expense again. We were finally let through and met our guide boat, who led us into the lovely Riviera Municipal Marina. Again, our contacts brought dozens of Sea Cadets down to greet us. Poor Skip. After our Palm Beach interview the anchorperson suddenly turned on Skip. He was shocked at the spotlight, but he quickly learned to roll with the punches. The anchor people seemed to find his maverick background as interesting as our battleship. We were highly amused to watch this free-wheeling free spirit become a pro at handling the press. His genuine charm and friendliness came across loud and strong to everyone along the waterway. He was always adept at solving our numerous problems.

Northward we went, trying to adhere to the schedule laid out by the welcoming people ahead. We were very mindful of avoiding weekend runs. We kept telling Skip that "it gets better farther north. The boating traffic diminishes." Hah! We were eleven years later after the Bicentennial trip and we had a shock ahead.

Coming upon Marker 222 (Mr. Laff's Restaurant), we checked our *Waterway Guide* and saw that he still had all the amenities that a boater would need. Off Cecil and I went to the swim platform and cast the ARIZONA off to come in later. Skip and I went in and had a good tie-up to tall docks. Then we used the VHF to call Cecil in. Our coming in with PEARL caused no interest or commotion. When ZOE came in, the crowds began to run down the slender dock to greet him. Among the people was Mr. Laff himself! With a weekend coming up, he invited us to stay for three days, free of charge. All meals at his restaurant would be free and we would have power to PEARL. What an invitation. Who could resist. It was a great three days with the usual visitors, press and questions.

As we analyzed our trip on the east coast, we realized the bridges were numerous. There are 40 bridges between Stuart and Miami and many had restricted opening schedules. We found that the time for their opening continually changed. We were also very aware that we were boating in "millionaire's row." There were restaurants, shopping centers with docks, mansions with large yachts docked in front. It was quite palatial and overwhelming. Cec and I realized that in the eleven years we had not visited this area, so much had changed. The growth was obvious, not only with the mansions and homes, but with the number of boats on the water. We kept telling Skip that "it gets better as we go north."

Cec and I took MO (our transportation—moped) over to Jensen Beach where we had had such a debacle with Bill and the USS BICENTENNIAL at Marker 221. There was Mr. Evinrude's yacht, CHANTICLEER. Nothing had changed. It all looked the same. We wished at that moment that Bill could join us.

Before we left for Ft. Pierce we had a large magazine layout to do for *Florida Waterway* magazine. The photographer/writer insisted that he would stand armpit-deep in the water and Cec was to drive ZOE right at him. He wanted a good close-up shot! Poor Cec. He wanted to oblige, but caution overtook and he never did come as close as the reporter wanted him, but we found out later the shots he did get were wonderful, and we were on the front cover of the magazine.

Reluctantly we left Mr. Laff's splendid hospitality and planned to spend the next night with the Coast Guard who had invited us for an overnight tie-up. We envisioned great docks, water, power and good restaurant facilities. We made our stop and found that they put us in an old rusty sling and left us to dangle against the slimy walls. It was with difficulty that I climbed over the steel beams and shinnied down to more steel beams, then made a leap to more slimy walls, crept along a ledge and finally found land. All this was for the usual phone calls ahead. The men were wise and did not leave the boat. There were six bright klieg lights which shined in all night and we crashed and knocked around in our sling. Again, Skip and Cec were up checking on ZOE and our lines. We were up early and asked to be let out of the sling and soon were off for Vero Beach. So much for anticipating too much.

We had a difficult run to Vero Beach due to a bad southwest wind. Getting into a tight marina was an embarrassing experience for me. I found that with all my marine accomplishments I did not know how to throw a 100-ft. line correctly. My throws had all been much less, but with the wind and boats looming all around it was necessary to get a long line thrown out to waiting hands on the dock. I was alone with Skip and not helping at all with my lack of expertise in throwing against the wind. We managed a rather untidy, inexpert tie-up, and I asked Skip to teach me the correct way to throw a long line. Within minutes he had me on the lawn and with a few hints I got the hang of it. I vowed never to embarrass our captain(s) again. It was to stand me in good stead in the boating years to come.

The three of us were tired, but we had a contingent of Sea Cadets coming down the next day. When they came, all in white uniforms, they did the whole color guard routine for us. We were impressed with them and their leaders. Nice people at the marina took us to a shopping complex and again we did laundry, shopped and waited out the tornado watch. We had severe winds and rain and were glad we were not out in unprotected waters. After the Sea Cadets visited us we declared a "legal" holiday for each one of us. We needed rest badly. Skip left on MO to go to the beach and check out the local beauties. Cec abandoned me to go work on the tired and rusting ZOE. I crashed and burned on PEARL, getting caught up on thank you letters due people behind us and phone calls for contacts ahead of us. By this time the men were calling the payphones I ran for "Pat's office" (how easy a cell-phone could have made my days). I made four dinners ahead and felt quite smug that I could do that with the small refrigerator we had in the galley.

We wanted to leave after three days here because it was the middle of March and we had commitments ahead we had to meet. We took off, but during the day the VHF talked about tornado watches being in effect. With relief we pulled into Melbourne's harbor marina and it began to rain. We stayed long enough for me to walk into town, go to the post office, have lunch with Skip, go to the bank, make phone calls and talk to many, many visitors. Our next-door neighbors partied until 1 A.M. Our press coverage continued to be exemplary. It was a busy, noisy time! The USS ARIZONA evoked a lot of passion in the people who came to see her. We kept hearing stories about relatives who served in WWII and who were on other boats. We continued to serve as an outlet to people who wanted to share a story about a friend or relative or who had frustrations with the government and wanted to sound off about inequities. We could not figure what it was that made people want to confide in us. We finally decided it was our high-profile patriotic symbol which spoke for us. We were merely appendages to something much larger than individuals. We heard heart- wrenching stories, funny stories and secrets that we only revealed to each other. ZOE was turning out to be more of a magnet than our BICENTENNIAL. It was no wonder when one thinks of the 1177 that went down with her. (Historians still argue the exact number of men who went down with the USS ARIZONA.) We were continually amazed at what we were told and would compare stories over dinner at night.

We were off to Titusville for a one-night stay. We had only two bridges and one was a bascule with a clearance of 27 feet and one we would have to have opened. We had 81 long water miles to cruise. This was an unusually long jump for us. We timed our arrival at the bridge so we did not have to wait. We went through with three sailboats and two cruisers. We were the object of a lot of picture taking and waving. At dinner that night SKIP counted ahead on his chart and said, "Hey! I count only 25 more hookups to go and 25 'unhookups!' But there are a lot of bridges, some are swing and some are bascule. How about that?" We just glared at him. No answer.

Next A.M. we took off, knowing we would have to find fuel. We were headed for Marineland Marina south of St. Augustine and would have another long run of 80 miles. The main point of interest was that Marineland was the world's first ocean aquarium, plus it had free showers! What a terrible day for a "have-to" long run. It started out hot and humid, but the wind came up and shifted to the north. The weather turned cold. The rainstorm began and we grabbed for weatherproof jackets, something we had not needed for a long time. It was not easy getting Cecil off in ZOE, and I was afraid he would lose his balance on the slippery ARIZONA's decks, but he jumped in and got his engines started. Then I turned my attention to Skip, who needed all the help he could get for a safe tie-up in the marina. We managed, and this time it gave me an opportunity to throw a line out to a man who had that same "she can't throw that far" look that most seemed to have. The line ended up in his hands! I felt vindicated and even had a compliment from the captain about "your good right throwing arm."

PEARL HARBOR MEMORIAL II

We had left the first week of February and it was now near the end of March. We had thoroughly enjoyed being able to forget about the truck and trailer, but the time had come to retrieve it as we moved northward.

Back we went to Lake Mary via rented car and met our hospitable friends. After many thank yous, we drove as far north as St. Augustine, where they were blessing the fleet of fishing boats. We found our statue for Skip there as we anticipated giving him something special as we did Bill. Back to Marineland Marina and we turned in the rent car. Forward march with ZOE and PEARL H.

The windstorm finally blew itself out, and we had two long days of uneventful runs from north of Titusville, through Daytona and on to St. Augustine. Memories kept flooding back of our time with Bill along this same run. We saw many, many changes in that opulent marinas and restaurants had been built, new mansions had sprouted along the ICW's prime property, and the isolated stretches of waterway had shrunk. We kept telling Skip, "It gets better as we go farther north. Wait till you see all the birds!"

We made it to St. Augustine and said hello to our friends from eleven years ago. Several came down to the marina to see us and marveled at the USS ARIZONA. They remembered our red, white and blue BICENTENNIAL and the fun times we had together. They wanted to hear about all the other river trips we had taken and told us we were lucky to find Skip to replace Bill. We agreed. It was time to move the rig forward so Skip "boat sat" while we jumped truck and trailer forward to Savannah. It was back to the classy Thunderbolt Marina, and when we showed them the pictures of the ARIZONA, they remembered the USS BICENTENNIAL and told us to leave our outfit and they would be honored to give us free slips for both boats. In the meantime the call went out to the media, who promised to cover us as soon as we arrived.

Via phone we had asked for and received permission from the Navy to come into their port at Mayport, just north of Jacksonville. The PAO (Public

Affairs Officer) said he would have an LCM escort in to the Navy base. They would give us a tie-up near two huge aircraft carriers that were in. Sounded good and we achieved an early start thanks to the captain, who we had begun to call Capt. Bligh. Skip was always getting us up at 4:30 or 5:00 A.M. so we could get an early start and tie up before the afternoon winds started to blow. He was right, but after our exhausting days we were dragged out of our beds complaining. We had a wonderful morning and early afternoon run at eight knots. We went through residential areas, said "hi" to the St. John's River and went in with the crest of the tide.

As we neared Mayport, our chart told us we were right outside the "Don't come in" sign which indicated the Navy port was off limits to cruising boaters. There was no LCM to meet us in sight. We started to enter and suddenly a loud voice boomed out of the sky, "Be advised, you are entering a no trespassing area. Turn around and leave immediately."

We were all startled, and Skip said, "That must have been God talking to us."

We ran out on the deck and there was a Coast Guard helicopter circling us. Again the warning from the sky told us to back off and get out. We attempted to contact Mayport and remind them we had permission from the CO to enter. Getting on the proper VHF Channel, we heard the helicopter advising Mayport, "There is a miniature battleship below us. Does anyone know about this?" We heard the helicopter call the base three times. We held our breath and circled without entering the port.

Finally we heard a laconic answer. "Yeah, we know about them. Let 'em come in. They've got clearance."

In we went with no LCM or anyone to meet us. We tied up at an empty dock near a repair boat shop. Off in the distance we saw a Navy car driving rapidly toward us, leaving a huge dust cloud behind it. With no one in sight we figured it must be the military police coming down to check us out, perhaps to tell us to leave—or, as Cec said, "throw us in the lockup." The car screeched to a halt and out came two men in splendid white uniforms and covered with brass and braid. It was the CO and the XO. We were relieved to find out they knew all about us and the CO said, "Just the usual Navy SNAFU with communications."

Our welcome was quite overwhelming. We were given a Navy car so we could get to the BOQ, invited to have dinner at the Officer's Club and given the run of the base. We all got to giggling over our "reception" from the sky. The CO explained that they were on alert due to Kadafy's shenanigans in

Liberia. They thought we might be a secret missile coming in under a most unusual disguise. The thought was expressed that it was a good thing the Coast Guard plane didn't bomb the ARIZONA and sink Cecil and ZOE. Otherwise they would have to build another Pearl Harbor Memorial over that spot! The night was memorable! We wined and dined in style for a change. Thank you, Navy!

The next morning was a quiet, reflective time as we made preparations to leave the Navy port. An aircraft carrier was leaving the port for six months and was headed for the Middle East upheavals. With the binoculars we could see the Navy families on the faraway dock, waving goodbye to their sailors. We grabbed our own American flag and waved it at the carrier as they left the port. It was a nostalgic, rather heart-wrenching thing to watch as we could well imagine the feelings of those departing and those left behind.

The end of March and we were on our way to our memorable stop with Bill—Fernandina Beach. We had phoned our friend of long ago, Robin Springer, and he promised to come down to the dock and greet us. We could hardly wait to see him. We tied up at the Fernandina Beach Marina and shortly thereafter saw Robin and his grownup son coming down the dock to greet us. Robin had roses for me, which touched me deeply. We had a special reunion and a long visit. Skip had heard all about our trip eleven years previously and enjoyed meeting the man who had helped us so much and entertained us so graciously.

Fernandina Beach was discovered by the French explorer Jean Ribault in 1562, but it was settled by the Spanish in 1567 and obviously named for King Ferdinand of Spain. The area had served under eight flags and her harbor has welcomed ships from maritime nations the world over. Now more shrimpers and trawlers were harbored there along with factories to process the shrimp. We so enjoyed being back with an old friend and visiting this now-growing but still laid back port.

As we left this most northern stop in Florida, we celebrated our leaving this state and entering Georgia. Cecil and I remembered the song the three of us sang with Bill—"A Rainy Night In Georgia." We wondered what our weather would be like this trip.

The *Waterway Guide* warned us that the 244 miles from the northern border of Florida to Charleston is mileage where everyone should be at full alert. There is less "ditch" and large natural bodies of water constitute the greater part of the route. The ICW tacks and zigzags through a recurring pattern of big waters and many wide open to the sea. These natural waterways are usually deep to the banks and piloting is simplified, but, it warns, don't relax too much. Keep track of the markers and run approximate compass courses. It is not difficult to get lost on the wider stretches.

Also, the weather plays an important role in this segment. While the route is designed for maximum protection, crossing the large sounds can be a problem as they are exposed to the ocean. Tidal ranges increase and can range up to nine feet along the Georgia coastline. Currents are strong and if a swift flow runs contrary to a stiff wind the going can get very rough. My, this all sounded quite familiar.

More warnings about docking and selecting an anchorage—watch out for the tidal change and current. The country is isolated and sparsely settled. One can go ten miles without any human habitation. Salt marshes and exposed fringes of mud are interspersed with a bend in the river and well-wooded land. And beware—early spring bugs. No kidding! We remember them well. We felt properly warned and prepared, having done this eleven years previously.

We made the 40-mile jump up to Brunswick, GA and an old haunt, Golden Isle Marina, where we had had such a bad stop with CELEBRATION II. We told Skip how all the sleeping bags were drenched and the difficult crowding in the boat with five of us and two dogs. We felt right at home when we tied up because the no-see-ums had been waiting for us. Every time we opened the sliding glass door on the starboard side, the "widgums" would fly in. They sat on the ceiling, watching us, checking us over, and then would become invisible, dive and begin their evening meal. We spent three days here. We picked up mail, ate out every night, took a tour of the island and did a radio talk show which lasted 24 minutes. This brought Brunswick's locals flocking to visit us. And we found out that locals use Avon's Skin So Soft to drive away the no-see-ums. Everyone wears it!

WIND, WIND, and MORE WIND

We were glad to be in familiar territory along the ICW, but were shocked at the growth along the waterway. We had told Skip about the egrets, blue herons, the myriad forms of bird life we had seen by the hundreds in 1975. Residential and commercial expansion had driven the bird life out. It was disappointing to go through what had been isolated, swamp areas and find that civilization had wiped out so much of Mother Nature's creations. Eleven years saw a big change along the various segments of "the ditch."

Leaving Brunswick for Savannah, we picked up a strong crosswind which was most unpleasant. We had it all the way to our old haunt, Thunderbolt Marina, eight miles south of Savannah. The marina was as good as ever. Laundromats, hair driers in the showers, newspaper delivered to the boat deck, doughnuts placed along with the newspaper. Thunderbolt had expanded, but the courtesy to boaters was still outstanding.

Our next stop was to be in the middle of downtown Savannah in front of the Hilton Hotel. We had a date with schoolchildren and the media. Skip and I took PEARL and cruised ahead and Cec brought up the stern with ZOE. We had a rough time heading up the eight miles to our rendezvous. The wind had not stopped and the current runs eight knots on the Savannah River. We felt as if we were salmon swimming upstream to spawn. As we approached our high dock, I searched for someone to catch our bowline. A black man dressed all in whites and a Navy cap threw up his hands and gestured for me to throw the line to him. Happy to find someone who would help us, I threw the line and he hauled us in. Skip and I tied up and were about to motion for Cec to bring the ARIZONA in. The gentleman who had caught my line introduced himself and said, "Ah'm Capt. Sam. Ah'm the official greeter."

My shock at seeing this same gentleman still greeting boats knew no bounds. "Capt. Sam! You're still here!"

He smiled and turned to Capt. Skip. "Y'all dohn wanna fall in that river."

The unsuspecting Skip said, "Why not?"

"Cuz yo' gone die" was the same answer.

The Navy League entertained us royally, took us to dinner, hosted us at a Coast Guard band performance, brought their Sea Cadets down to see us and became instant friends. Cecil and I had to jump the truck and trailer forward to Charleston. Back we came on the Greyhound, one more logistical problem behind us.

Now enroute to Beaufort, we regaled Skip about Bill's confrontation with the "new" breed of Marines. We had rain the whole way and a lot of wind, which used up fuel faster than we anticipated. There were some nice swamp areas still untouched, but the growth of homes and golf courses was amazing. As we came into Beaufort, the rain and wind let go. Even so we had a good tie-up with both boats, although ZOE didn't quite fit and one-third of her stuck out into the channel, which unnerved us. Here was a great opportunity to do laundry, pay bills and visit the new art and craft shops that had gone in the last few years. There was a sighting of four Marines walking together, but that was the only reminder we had of our last visit.

We were up early for our 73-mile run to Charleston. Off by 6:15 A.M. and I fed the boys a hearty breakfast which seemed to cheer them up. Wind and more wind...up to 25 knots. It was a long cruise and I shoved Cec out in ZOE into a two-foot chop so Skip and I could bring PEARL H in first. We were not to be in the usual boating slip, but anchored by the aircraft carrier, USS YORKTOWN. The YORKTOWN director wanted us to tie up right by them. Patriot's Point is now a well-known shrine that many visit. We had agreed to this tie-up, but when we got there Skip and I were appalled at the lack of room. It meant going around an atomic freighter, a submarine, destroyer and a Coast Guard cutter. The YORKTOWN exhibit towered over us and we could not see where we would end up.

As Skip and I came around the freighter's bow, we had an acute 30-degree angle to cut and were confronted with the bows of three ships looking at us. There was just NO room. There was no way to do it without two people to tie up, and we have to congratulate Skip on not only piloting PEARL in in reverse, but he also took the stern starboard line as I used the starboard bowline. The cross wind did not help, and it was terror time, but we came in without a scratch. We just looked at each other when we were finished. No one saw us except Cec, then we disappeared around the bow of the tied-up exhibit ship. No one came to help. There was just no one around. We sighed and chalked this one up to luck! Then we worried about Cecil. He told us later we cautioned him three times to make a sharp left turn when he came around the bow of the atomic freighter. He did it beautifully and we brought him in with some difficulty and then made our way up over the pilings and to the USS YORKTOWN offices.

We were welcomed and given a grand tour of the old aircraft carrier. We were part of a two-day visitation by Scouts, Sea Cadets and service groups. TV coverage and newspaper interviews were slipped in between driving the rig forward to Wilmington, N.C. This was an unusually long jump, but we needed Cecil on PEARL as we had many media dates ahead and appointments with Pearl Harbor survivors and even some USS ARIZONA survivors. We treated ourselves to a motel stay at a Holiday Inn and felt strange that our floor did not rock with passing wakes. We told Skip about a future date in Wilmington in which the museum manager of the battleship USS NORTH CAROLINA wanted Cec to tool around the big ship while the TV cameras would record the miniature ship against the backdrop. He said he could hardly wait and hoped the NORTH CAROLINA was anchored alone with no impediments in the way.

Now we were enroute to Georgetown and it was mid-April. The three of us were having a pleasant run up the ICW with ZOE trailing along behind. Over the VHF we had a call from a large cruiser who asked permission to pass us. Most cruising people are very aware of the wake problems when one is under tow. Ninety-five percent of them slow down, and with the ARIZONA trundling along behind us, they usually rode on our port or starboard asking questions, carefully pacing themselves, then were off and running. This day Skip thanked them for their courtesy, and slowly they drew up on our starboard side. "My Gawd," I heard Skip exclaim. "Here Cecil, take the helm," he shouted and was out the door. I followed to see what the problem might be. No problem at all. The cruiser driver was piloting from the fly bridge and had a lady sitting beside him. The lady was topless and Skip was out getting an eyeful. He came back in laughing and got the man on the VHF. "Nice looking first mate you have there, sir," he exclaimed.

The answer came back: "Yes, she keeps me company on lonesome stretches."

With a following sea to our stern we must have made nine knots all the way to Georgetown. When we arrived we had a very difficult tie-up due to bad crosswinds. The dock master was most helpful in trying to guide us in and secure our lines. We were even taken via a little jitney to a hot dog place and returned to our slip. I was given a ride into town, and this gave me an opportunity to finish up the trophy we wanted to give Skip at the end of our trip as we had Bill. We were usually so far from a city's shopping area that I had to plan way ahead and pick up pieces of things as we went along. Georgetown had the trophy and I was also able to find an engraver.

We were zinging along as we had a lot of miles ahead before New York harbor so headed out to North Myrtle Beach. Vereen's Marina had a fish restaurant, so off we went. The marina ducks talked to each other all night long. We were there only one night and pushed on up the Mad River as it is aptly named. We had a US Navy mini-flat top following us up the river in the wind and it was right on our tail. He had a six-foot bow wave Skip spotted through the binoculars and we hurried to keep ahead of him. Catching that wave would have turned us over! We did kept ahead of him and turned into Snow's cut, thank goodness. That was a fright for almost an hour but we were now well into North Carolina. We had the usual difficult tie-up at the marina with the wind still chasing us, and Cec had to put the ARIZONA next to a visiting PT boat. The TV coverage along with the newspapers was great. The wind was terrible.

Next A.M. we headed for Wrightsville and came to Seapath Marina. We were so aware of the changes since we had tied up here eleven years ago with Bill. The condos were numerous as were the additional commercial facilities. We did recognize a bridge and the motel where the three of us had stayed. Here, an old friend of mine from USC days came down to greet us and also helped us pick up our truck and trailer. We were pleased to see that we had hit the front page of the Sunday paper.

More fish dinners were on our evening agenda, as we were all addicted by this time. Looking ahead with new boating charts, it was decided Cec and I would leapfrog the truck and trailer with ZOE forward to Elizabeth City. ZOE was in need of some work and we thought about the marina we had been in with Bill. It was a working marina and we hoped we would be welcome there. The distance was 240 miles and we did not want to take ZOE across Albemarle and Pamlico Sounds. These huge open stretches of water were exposed to the Atlantic and we knew the crossings could be treacherous. Cec and I would make our way back to Wrightsville and help Skip move the PEARL H across the broad expanses of water without a boat under tow.

It took us two full days to drive up to Elizabeth City with ZOE and return to Wilmington. It rained the whole way. Cec said the narrow two-lane roads we were on were exactly eight inches wider than the trailer we had ZOE riding on. It was a tense driving trip. We headed for the same boat yard that we had visited in 1975, and Mary Hadley remembered us and told us we could leave the truck and boat on the trailer in her boat yard. What a relief and how great it was to revisit a spot that had been welcoming eleven years earlier. Her hospitality had not changed! We treated ourselves to a Holiday Inn that night and we both enjoyed the 10,000 gallon showers that the three of us were always complaining we missed in PEARL. What luxury to have a motel room and to expand our living into that large room! We caught an early morning Greyhound and enjoyed the ride back to Wilmington. We grabbed a taxi and were soon back with Skip, regaling him with our luck in finding a welcoming, working marina.

On April 22 we had a long run of 84 miles to Morehead City, where we had met the college students in 1975. It was great fun to return to Tony's Sanitary fish market and enjoy his still-outstanding fish dinners. The same marina had not changed in any way. Next day it was on to Belhaven on the Neuse River. This was a 68-mile run. Capt. Bligh had us up at 4:30 A.M., and we took a pounding from the wind. We slammed through the waves and Skip cut PEARL's speed way down to 2300 rpm. We were glad ZOE was safely on her trailer in faraway Elizabeth City.

The old hotel at Belhaven had a golf cart available for cruisers, and I went *big* supermarket shopping. Upon our return, we toured all over the old mansion and enjoyed a delicious dinner put on for hotel and cruising guests. Skip didn't let us dawdle too long as we planned an early takeoff and the longest run we would make. We had to get across Albemarle Sound early, and the Elizabeth City marina was 107 miles away. It looked like a challenge.

It was a challenge, but we did it! As we came out of the mouth of the river and looked at the vast expanse of water we had to cross, we checked the marine weather and decided it was a "go." The run to the marina took us 13 hours and we were tired out when we finally arrived. We all agreed it was a "dinner out" night.

Our crew of three pitched in and cleaned up ZOE and PEARL H. Cec had fiber-glassing to do on the ARIZONA and we made ready for our anticipated trip through the Dismal Swamp and on to Norfolk. This, too, was familiar territory, and we told Skip water moccasins would be riding shotgun for him. We knew that the busy Chesapeake awaited us when we departed the Dismal Swamp. We also made plans about going through the lock we knew awaited us at the end of the canal run. We recalled the way we had zipped in in 1975, did a complete one-eighty and ended up facing the wrong way.

We left Elizabeth City on May Day, and what a way to celebrate! The trip through the Dismal Swamp was beautiful, and we had a Blue Heron that rode wingman with us for miles and miles. Ditto one water moccasin. ZOE obediently trailed along, happy to be tandem with us again. When we came to the lock at the end of the swamp, the lock doors were three quarters of the way open for us when the power went out. This proved to be one long wait, as the electrician had to be called and it took him several hours to fix it.

Meanwhile, some USS ARIZONA Survivors had heard about us and three of them drove over to talk. We climbed up and out of the lock onto the grass and had a most pleasant conversation with them. They were thrilled that we were going to show their ship all along the way to New York. A helicopter from one of the TV channels also flew over us and took some amazing footage. Finally the power went back on and we left the lock and began to look for a marina. We found a beautiful new one and also found out why it was so beautiful. We were charged 60 cents per foot for each boat. Our 40-foot houseboat plus our 36-foot ARIZONA added up to $46.50. We had been so spoiled by the many free tie-ups offered to us along the way that we decided this was a bit much. We would stay one night and be on our way. We were not able to go into the Navy base this time as they had too much going on with the war in the Gulf.

Déjà vu and we were off to Yorktown. We passed the magnificent U.S. Navy fleet—destroyers, carriers, frigates, tenders and the mighty USS IOWA. They looked so resplendent. We ventured out into the Chesapeake and today's run was up and over the rollers. Swells pushed us in several directions and ZOE swayed and bucked behind us. We were glad to find the York River and our same tie-up from years ago. Cec and I were programmed to go back to Elizabeth City for truck/trailer so took the bus down and brought everything back to Yorktown. It was another scary ride with narrow, narrow roads. Cec and Skip had a great time visiting with a former Navy man who was on the sister ship of the ARIZONA, the USS PENNSYLVANIA in Pearl Harbor. They spent hours together listening to his wild tale of December 7, 1941. Skip also visited the Crabtree Museum in Yorktown. He was most interested in his ancestral name being given to a museum. We went back to the Greek restaurant we had visited with Bill only this time we drove! The same Greek lady welcomed us, her husband had passed on and she insisted we be her guests for dinner. Another warm memory. We also visited the Yorktown battleground where Washington had accepted the surrender of Cornwallis. We learned a bit of history trivia. The song Cornwallis had his band play during the surrender observance was "The World Turned Upside Down!"

WE PUT OUT A PAN PAN!

The morning we were to leave Yorktown, we did our usual routine. We turned on the weather channel and stood on the dock, evaluating our route and wondering if we should depart. Hands in pockets Skip paced, Cecil kept listening to the repeated weather broadcast and I stood around wringing my hands. We had a date with 75 Sea Cadets at the Washington D.C. Navy dock in a few days. We needed to get going. We had a few spots in between where we were expected. Decision time! Destination fixation? We had eradicated that (almost). Caution? Yes, we had an abundance of that. The Coast Guard report indicated smooth sailing out in the Chesapeake main channel, but afternoon winds would be at 25 knots. They would be coming from the south. Well! That sounded good. We would have a following sea, but we were getting an early start and would be in Kilmarnock on the west side of the Chesapeake before those afternoon winds rose. After an overnight we would be close enough to the mouth of the Potomac River and could easily be able to make our turn NW, make one more marina overnight stop on the way to D.C. and be on time for our Navy League appearance. We took a vote. It was a unanimous "let's go."

Down the York River we chugged, with ZOE obediently behind us on an eighteen-foot line connected to her port/starboard harness. Out we went into the Chesapeake and in an hour Skip found our compass course in the middle of the bay. It was still early morning and the water began to have a chop. It did not stay at a chop. It began to churn and the wind whipped the chop into waves. Then the waves began to grow higher and higher and PEARL started to pitch and toss. Within minutes the waves were three to four feet high. It happened so rapidly we had little time to evaluate anything. I hurried to the stern window over my bed and looked back at ZOE. She was bucking wildly, trying to run up on our port then starboard sides and looked as though she could aim for the swim platform. I hurried up to Skip and Cecil and relayed what a problem we had at the stern. "She's going to slam into our swim platform with that following sea," I shouted. Skip said he would give the helm to Cecil and he would go back and let the ARIZONA out on a 100-foot line so she would be far away from us. I ran back to the window and saw that ZOE had already hit the swim platform and had broken the hook on her port harness. I ran shouting up to the men and told them the battleship had only one line on her. Skip shouted to Cec, "Take the helm. I'm going back and get a line on her and let her way out." He was on his way. I checked out the stern window once more and watched ZOE break her starboard hook. She smashed into the swim ladder. Even though the platform was strong, she smashed some of the boards we stood on. If it hadn't been so strong she might very well have run into the outboard and we would have been out on the wild bay with only one engine. I watched the ARIZONA break loose as Skip tried to catch her. Within four seconds she was 100 feet away from us.

Skip came rushing back in and we watched in dismay as our boat drifted farther and farther away. The orders came thick and fast. "Pat, put all the fenders out on the starboard side. We'll try to pull close to her and Cec can jump onto her deck and get in the hatch." Within minutes I had all seven fenders spaced on the railing. Skip chased the ARIZONA and tried to pull close to her side. The age-old scientific theory about boats repelling one another proved to be true. As Skip nudged PEARL toward the gray lady, Cecil was ready to jump. The battleship had a mind of her own and skittered away. We tried time after time. The wallowing around, the pitching, tossing was wild. The ARIZONA looked more seaworthy than us. She rode the waters like a seagull. Cecil ventured the opinion that ZOE did not like being tethered to the big PEARL and was happy to be set free. We had no comment. Skip said, "We're never going to catch her. We'll have to swallow our pride and call the Coast Guard." He clicked to the Coast Guard channel and said "PAN, PAN." (Personal Assistance Needed, no life endangerment.)

The Coast Guard radioman was right back to us. "Yes, Coast Guard here. What is your problem?"

I noticed a slight hesitation from Capt. Skip, who said, "We've lost our battleship. She broke loose."

There was a noticeable pause at the other end of the channel. "Really? You've lost your WHAT?"

Skip began to explain our dilemma and after some conversation at the other end of the line the young man said that the commandant of the whole East Coast had received a letter about our journey, he knew we were for real and they would be out to help us. Skip gave them our position and assured them we would keep the battleship in sight and we could expect them in about an hour plus. With relief Skip signed off.

The pitching, bucking and wild ride continued. My grapefruit and oranges were rolling back and forth from bow to stern and across the floorboards. The dishes jumped out of cupboards and we caught the small TV as it tried to commit suicide. It was a long, long wait. Then, in the distance, Skip spotted the 34-foot launch with five young Coast Guardsman aboard. We looked at their seaworthy outfit and regretted our high profile silhouette. So much for "sea-going houseboats." With much shouting and gesturing and not very good audible conversation on the VHF, it was determined that Cec would jump from PEARL onto the cutter, then they would try to place him on the battleship. At first some of the young men wanted to get onto the ARIZONA, but Cec was adamantly opposed to that. The skilled pilot of the launch came close to PEARL's starboard side and with helping hands Cec was dragged onto their boat. The launch made several passes at ZOE, but she skittered away again. Finally the Coast Guard pilot told us he would reverse into ZOE's side and Cecil could jump from the cutter's stern onto ZOE's deck. Skip and I watched with apprehension. The sea was so fierce, the waves so jumbled and the whole scene fraught with problems that it was a nightmare.

I looked away for a moment when a large wave crashed on us, and when I looked back Cec was nowhere to be seen. "Oh, Skip. I don't see him. He's disappeared."

Skip's answer was, "He's either in the sea or inside the battleship. Call him on the VHF and if he's in there let's hope he turns it on."

I put out the call letters while the Coast Guard stood by and checked on both of us. I thought I saw ZOE making a bit of headway into the waves, but was not sure.

Then we heard Cec's voice. "I made it. I'm inside. I can't believe what happened. I never turn on both engines at the same time. The battery can't take it. In my excitement I turned on both engines simultaneously and they both fired. Let's head for shore."

Skip and I looked at each other with relief. The Coast Guard had been listening and asked if we were all OK or if the PEARL needed help. My reaction was to hang on to the safety of those young men in their stable boat. I asked Skip one question. "Are we OK?"

He didn't answer immediately, but said, "Yes, the ship can handle this. Keep your life jacket on." Oh dear.

Skip thanked the Coast Guard warmly and said we would head for the west shore and find a marina and get out of the wind. They told us it would take us approximately two hours to find something over there. Skip said we would be fine and were on our way. They Coast Guard launch disappeared and I felt very vulnerable and alone.

We began to converse with Cecil. He assured us riding in ZOE was much more comfortable than being on the PEARL. His only problem was being thrown around so much that his head kept hitting the bulkhead above him. Her silhouette was so low profile and her ballast so heavy that he was riding more comfortably than we were. Then he asked, "Where are we headed?" My orders were to get out the *Waterway Guide* and find the nearest most direct approach to the closest marina. I stood at the chart table and tried to read. PEARL dove down into the trough made by the waves, then started her climb up. I wondered at the seaworthiness of the boat, and if the waves would go right up over the bow and bury us, but the foam and splash seemed to slide off around us. Our "bible" said that Horn Harbor was the only close-to-the-channel harbor of refuge for 30 long miles, so we analyzed our situation. I checked out the description with Skip and we slowly began our torturous two hour ride to safety.

The marina described a doglegged entrance channel and we could draw five feet. It promised slips, fuel, storage, transportation and hot showers. We could hardly wait. We wallowed, pitched, tossed and kept checking to see how far we were from shore. We limped back slowly, trying to make a wake for Cecil, but he was doing better than we were. The shoreline began to loom on the horizon. How beguiling it looked, but it took awhile for us to see much detail. Cec was plowing along beside us and assured us if PEARL couldn't take the rough seas, he would save us. Nice! He also told us that while he was gauging his ability to jump onto the deck of ZOE from the launch, the men questioned him repeatedly. "Did you build that? Where do you live? Where are you going? What's it made of?" One of the men said, "Oh God, mister, don't do it! Don't jump!" But he did jump, and we are grateful to this day for the help and concern!

As we neared land the seas began to calm down a little, at least enough for us to find the narrow channel that led around a spit of land and into shelter. It looked so isolated, so out in the country, that we were not sure this was the way to a marina, but by this time anything looked good. We would anchor in the channel for an overnight if we had to. We crept in and the pastoral scene was such a contrast to the fury out on the water that the difference was obvious. There were cows grazing in the pasture, a few children were flying kites in the wind. The channel wound around and around and we were concerned for the shoaling. Where was that five-foot draft we had read about? Sometimes Cricket went off loud and long, chirping over zero water under us. Instead of markers we found fragile twigs stuck vertically up in the water. I stood on the bow, checking depths for Skip. Deeper into blessed Mother Earth we drove and we could not help but talk about the crisis we had just left and the peace and tranquility we were now experiencing. Our only concern now was running aground in the shallow water. The disparity of what we had just left and the tranquility we were enjoying now was such a relief that we gave up conversation and just tried to bring the boat in to land.

The VHF crackled. "Where are we going?" said the Admiral who was following us.

"I don't know, but its title is Horn Harbor," I answered him. "We see a few buildings up ahead."

Skip slowed as we approached what looked like an old, old dock with a few disreputable buildings around. There was no sign of life, gas pumps, or buildings. It looked abandoned. Carefully he pulled PEARL up to the dilapidated dock and I jumped out and tied him up. Skip came out to help with lines, then we pulled in a tired Admiral. The three of us had a few hugs then looked around. There was one old sailboat tied up in front of us, but no sign of anyone.

Then a middle-aged man came out of an old building. "What are you doing here?" he asked. Then he caught sight of the battleship and his eyes widened. "What's that?" We were so tired and beat and so grateful to be on land, but felt we had to explain our strange presence to this stranger. We told him of the battering and pounding we had taken out on the bay, and his sympathy was evident. He explained to us that the marina was abandoned, but we could still get electricity and were welcome to stay here and rest up. There was no charge. He lived on the sailboat in front of us and if we wanted to give a few dollars for using the power that was OK, but not to worry about it. At that point we would have given him all our worldly goods. He pointed us in the direction of town, which he informed us was walkable, and then he left the scene.

It was only a little after noon, but the three of us went inside PEARL and just sat and looked at one another. After debriefing everything, it occurred to me that the men must be incredibly hungry. I managed some king-size sandwiches, fruit, and coffee, and the three of us decided to crash. We all flaked out around 1:30 P.M. and no one woke until long after the dinner hour. It had been one rough day. I fed them soup and salad, and we all went back to bed and slept the night. The Chesapeake had not been nice on this trip. We would proceed with caution!

RECOVERING

Waking refreshed from the many hours of sleep, we walked into the small town and tried to locate a ramp where we could take out the battleship. The weather report predicted more wind, and after the fright we had just been through, we decided to meet Cecil and ZOE at the Kilmarnock Marina where we had been invited to stay at their yacht club. We would go our separate ways. The two men found a grouchy old man who owned the only ramp in the small town and he refused to let us use it or pay for its use. The air was full of description of his background when Skip and Cec returned to PEARL. Cec took off to go back and pick up the trailer and Skip, who always had the facility to meet people and find help, took off again for town and found a young man who was willing to help us. For $20 he agreed to sit on ZOE's deck near the bow and guide Cecil through the curving channels of the pastureland, thickets and swamp to a ramp some five miles away.

We rendezvoused and made our plans to move. It was a strange sight to see just the top of the gray boat with a man perched on the superstructure, gliding through the pastureland. Cecil reported that maneuvering was crazy. The only markers were fragile willow sticks or twigs stuck in the water. The guide tried to line the "markers" up for Cec, but had difficulty. For five miles they navigated this way until near the end the man said to Cec, "I think you're going to hit the bottom." They did. Cec gave some gas to the ARIZONA and he said he felt them slithering through the sand—then they were off! They continued on while Skip and I drove over to the ramp to await their arrival. We had stumbled into a campground and were soon surrounded by people who could not believe the apparition that had suddenly shown up. We were continually brought to the realization that although we were accustomed to having a battleship, others were not, and they always expressed their amazement and astonishment.

We trailered up and had one more night in the quiet, abandoned marina. Next A.M. Cec took ZOE off to Kilmarnock, VA, 30 miles northward, and Skip and I brought PEARL into the Indian Creek Yacht Club by noon. It was a relaxing, wonderful time, as we were in by twelve and were guests of the man who had invited us there so long ago. There was even a piano for me to play. This stop enabled me to make the numerous phone calls ahead and to celebrate Skip's birthday. As we checked out our statistics, our logbook says we have now consumed 1468.5 gallons of fuel, we have traveled 1595 water miles, we have 231 hours on the engines and so far we have tied up in 41 marinas. Great…a ways to go.

Since we were not yet over our Chesapeake fright and there were no cities in which we were to make an appearance, Cec trailered ZOE on to the Colonial Beach Marina and Skip and I were to bring PEARL 20 miles north to the mouth of the Potomac River, then make a port turn and go 58 miles up to Colonial Beach, on the Westside of the Potomac. Our run up to the Chesapeake Bay was wonderful for two hours. We were chattering and having a great time without worrying continually about any tow behind us. We began to approach Smith Point and the chop began. Then Skip found his compass/pivot point, checked the chart and made his turn to port to begin the run up the river. WOW!! The skies clouded over, the wind blew, we began to pitch, toss and buck larger and larger waves. Not again!

PEARL was snorting and tossing her head and shaking off the water. Although I felt confident that PEARL could handle this after our previous stormy time, it was tension time. We were able to quarter the waves for a while, but then they began to hit us on the beam. We had been warned by boat owners at Kilmarnock that the current and wind mills around at the mouth of the Potomac. It did that. We were getting the current on the Chesapeake from the north, then we caught the tide and wind coming down the river. It was churning around violently and we fought it every step of the way. Could we never escape the bad weather? We had thought getting off the Chesapeake we were home free, but not so. The Potomac was much wider than I remembered and the current was against us. It seemed as though the markers were terribly far apart, yet they were only two miles, but we just crawled from one to the next. We had to brace ourselves and put our legs far apart just to be able to get around inside the boat. This went on and on and Skip slowed down from 4200 to 3100 RPM.

We fought our way up the river for almost four hours and it was most uncomfortable. At one point the captain thought if we tried to cross the river and take refuge on the other side, we might be more protected. We chopped our way across and hugged as close as possible to the Maryland shoreline and got some protection. This made our last hour much easier. Skip had a hard time seeing through the windshield due to rain and ocean spray. The first time I went out to clean his windshield he shouted at me, "DON'T go out there without your life jacket." Ah yes, I had forgotten. I did this frequently as the spray continued, then dried and the windows became salt-encrusted. Six times the windows had to be cleaned. Twice Skip would not let me out. It was rough!

The water and wind seemed to smooth out a bit, and I was able to retrieve the TV, Cec's camera and goodies I had stored on the floor. I put them back on the tables and began to put the whole boat back together. It always amazed me how much one has to tie down or put away when rough weather hits. It was a wild day for us and a no-fun one for Cecil, who was driving from Kilmarnock to Colonial Beach. He complained again about his trailer being eight feet wide and the roads being eight feet, six inches in width. We estimated he had three inches' clearance on each side! He arrived at Colonial Beach long before we did, put his boat on a ramp ready to launch and suddenly the whole town appeared. The town was lovely and the people so genuine and welcoming. He kept calling and calling us on the radio and it was awhile before we answered. We made it into hearing range contact and eventually had a wonderful reunion.

The storm continued, and we stayed in port the next day. We also worried about an area we did not know existed called Dahlgren Naval Weapon Lab. It seemed that sometimes the Navy chooses to practice their firing on the Potomac instead of out at sea. When this happens, the Potomac is closed down and no boats are allowed up or down the river. We hoped this would not be an incident we would have to confront, as we had a date with 76 Sea Cadets who would meet us when we tied up in the Washington D.C. Navy shipyard. It was still a long run into Washington D.C. and we planned one long day of towing ZOE to the Ft. Washington Marina.

This turned out to be a gorgeous day except PEARL had two planks broken in her swim platform from the Chesapeake Bay caper and it made it difficult for me to stand back there, hook and unhook ZOE, but I managed. The day was quiet, uneventful for a change and we had long stretches of good towing and met few boats of any kind. It was so good to have a day without a fright that we all rejoiced over the lack of an emergency! When we got into the marina we were rafted up next to a large houseboat and were glad that we had just eleven miles to go find Washington D.C. We needed a fish dinner fix, so the cook ate out in Ft. Washington! We suddenly found out it was Mother's Day, so the gentlemen sprang for a meal. Over dinner we talked about our upcoming Capitol City visit, the buildings we would see, the places we would visit. We wondered what the Navy shipyard would be like. Would we be alone or surrounded by Navy ships as in Mayport, FL? Where would we tie up? What kind of docks would we confront? Would the pilings be covered with creosote and be anxious to impale us? We decided we should think positive and anticipate a great tie- up. (By this time we could not help but be wary.)

YEAH, NAVY!!

The next day we left at noon and had only the eleven miles to go. We dodged the usual debris on the way up river, and our chart told us we were coming close to the shipyard. (It should be mentioned we had to sign numerous papers relieving the Navy of all responsibility for us. By this time they were also paranoid about security and rightfully so.) The tide was low and the dock was high as we pulled in next to a small destroyer. Standing on the long dock were the 76 Sea Cadets all decorated out in their white uniforms. They saluted us as we threw our lines up to Navy League waiting hands. What a greeting! Washington D.C. went all out for us. Our California Congressman Norman Shumway was there to welcome us, as were all the Navy League officers of that division. CBS was allowed in the shipyard and did extensive filming for that night's news. What a reception! We were honored. After a couple of hours of handshaking, introductions and interviews, we were suddenly alone. Our first stop was to walk over to the Navy Museum. That proved to be a wonderful visit for us. Then off we went to rent a car and be tourists like everyone else.

We had a full two days of visiting the Smithsonian, the Voice of America, the Supreme Court, and the FBI. Mrs. Shumway gave us a private tour of the White House. Then-Congressman John McCain called us into his office to thank us for what we were doing for children with our USS ARIZONA. We treasure the picture today of us shaking hands with him in his office. He said he would soon run for Senator Barry Goldwater's senate seat. We also visited Congressman Molinari's office to thank him for cutting some cumbersome red tape for the ARIZONA's participation in the unveiling of the statue in NY's harbor. His intervention would allow us to tie up on Staten Island for only the expense of ZOE's dockage in a slip. Other boats were paying $1500 for the privilege of being anywhere near New York Harbor. Congressman Shumway asked President Reagan to come down to greet us, but reported the President's schedule was too full for the time we would be in port. We would love to have met him. *USA Today* came to interview us, Cec put on his usual USS ARIZONA show for all, we visited Mt. Vernon, the Navy Leaguers took us to an elegant dinner at the Officers' Club. It was a busy time. On one occasion the Marine Honor Guard came to the Navy Ship Yard and astonished us with a three-gun salute over the top of our USS ARIZONA. We were totally surprised and again quite honored.

We had one surprise visit from Vice Admiral Stansfield Turner (Ret.) USN. We were shocked to look out PEARL's door and see him standing there. He asked permission to come on board and we hurriedly invited him down and into our "salon." He perched on Skip's pilot stool and we had a very special visit with him. Within 15 minutes a Navy lieutenant came scurrying toward us and knocked on the bridge of PEARL. Skip asked what she wanted. The lieutenant was breathless and apologized to Adm. Turner about the fact that no one had greeted him or saluted him at the entrance to the base. How had they missed him? The Admiral laughed and said, "I purposely sneaked in the back gate to avoid that. Don't worry about it." The lieutenant was mortified that he should get in without the proper Navy greeting, but the admiral didn't seem to care. The lieutenant finally left, much relieved. So much for Navy etiquette. Flag rank officers receive great respect from their troops.

The three of us did a quick analyzing of our next few days and it was decided that Skip would take PEARL alone down the Potomac and make his way to Annapolis. Cec and I would truck ZOE to that city. There would be no city harbor stops on the way to show off ZOE, so this seemed wiser rather than to do the Chesapeake Bay again.

We drove to Annapolis where we left our boat at a Holiday Inn and went to the marina to see if Skip had made it from Washington D.C. He was there and told us it took him eleven and one-half hours to do the full trip in one day. He was tied up at a combination condo/marina facility. With his help we picked up the trailer, found a ramp and launched ZOE again. Cec went out into the harbor, then made his way into downtown Annapolis where he once again confounded all the viewers with the battleship. He threaded his way through the narrow slot as he had done eleven years before and received a gala welcome from the tourists who were there for the Navy's June grad week. He reported that turning the 36-foot battleship around at the end of the quay was not as easy as when the 18-foot USS BICENTENNIAL was turning around in 1975. This stopover gave me a chance to make the usual phone calls ahead and I found that we were to have a gala reception in Baltimore.

What a week it was in Annapolis. The ARIZONA caused quite a stir among the whole Academy and many cadets and their parents came to visit us. We were guests at the graduation and had the privilege of watching the Blue Angels fly high over the graduating seniors. We did have a rather surprising request in Annapolis. We were approached by a Rock 'n Roll band who had just written a new song and wanted a picture of our battleship USS ARIZONA on the front jacket of their album. They assured us they would pay us well. We were flattered until we found out the song had words that said, "My baby has me tied up in battleship chains." We could just picture what the USS ARIZONA Survivor's group would say to us should we allow a picture of their beloved ship to be used in this manner. We were meeting them all along the ICW and their love and respect for their sunken ship was something they carried in their hearts and on their sleeves. We graciously declined the request.

ANOTHER DÉJÀ VU

After a few days in Annapolis we put ZOE under tow and headed up the Chesapeake, into the Patapsco River which leads to Baltimore. Although our experience there eleven years ago had left an indelible memory, we read in our guide book that Baltimore Harbor had been remodeled, refurbished and offered fuel (thank goodness!) and facilities. We decided to take a chance as the city officials said they had a reserved a spot for us in the harbor. We wondered where it could possibly be. On our way up the river, we regaled Skip about our trauma the last time we visited Baltimore with our robbery, no fuel, return of the camera and the sinking of our USS BICENTENNIAL. As we were talking with him, we saw a fireboat unexpectedly loom into sight through our port window. It came closer and closer. Radio contact told us they had come to escort us into the harbor. My, what a switch from the last time we timidly crept in. We accepted the escort with alacrity.

A few miles out, I stood on the swim platform, got Cecil into ZOE, cut him loose and off he went with the fireboats trying to douse him with their high-reaching streams of water. It was a wonderful sight to watch. We found ourselves overwhelmed with the change in the harbor and the reception we were given. Gone were the barren fields with buildings in the distance. The high bulwark walls were there, but steps and ladders were available for the visiting boatman. We were directed to tie up at the centerpiece of the new, huge mall that had been erected in the once vacant field. City officials met us, newspaper and TV crews came to see us and the mall shoppers were thick. We were able to put ZOE directly behind the PEARL H and we were placed by the centrally located steps that led up to the brick decks. What a change and what a shock to see the once-barren area filled with numerous shops and shoppers. It was very crowded. We wished Bill could see it.

We had a busy, fun-filled three days in the midst of heavy pedestrian traffic. The people swarmed to visit us, knocked on PEARL's bridge if we were not to be seen (we had to pull the curtains on the dockside for privacy). We lived in a goldfish bowl for three days. It was difficult to sleep at night as the citizens of Baltimore did a lot of walking and running during the cooler night hours. We would hear them out jogging at 2 A.M. They were approximately three feet from our heads that were on our pillows! Daytime foot traffic was incredible. We had a three-day entourage of boats that came in to visit us. Boats of all sizes and descriptions came alarmingly close, turned around, took pictures and left us sloshing and wobbling. We talked to hundreds of people, gave away our USS ARIZONA buttons and once in awhile ducked inside PEARL for a moment of privacy. We visited the aquarium, Cecil put ZOE through her tricks in front of the frigate CONSTELLATION, the skipjack MINNIE V, and the submarine TORSK (now a Sea Cadet training ship). The media coverage was full to overflowing. The scrapbook continued to grow!

Skip made some contacts for us which eventually paid off. He thought he had a buyer for the PEARL who would purchase our boat after our appearance in Philadelphia. The man said he wanted to live on her in Baltimore Harbor. This sounded good, but it also indicated we were nearing the end of this trip. How would we ever be able to part with Capt. Skip? We were so welded into a *troika* by this time that we were like a three-legged stool. If one leg is missing the whole thing collapses. We had been through this feeling before with Skipper Bill. The dock master was kind enough to loan Cec and me a car and we hurried back to Annapolis to pick up the truck and trailer. We found a spot in which to leave the rig and hurried back to Skip. That night we had the mandatory pow-wow regarding where we would dismantle our trip. It would be after one bigger stop in Philadelphia.

After thanking the Baltimore officials for their gracious welcome and help we left for Big Oak Marina. How welcome this spot was after the noise of Baltimore. We slammed and banged around as we made our way north up the ICW to this marina. We found the short length tow to be dangerous and the men let the ARIZONA far out behind us on this stretch of the Chesapeake. Next day we headed for Schaefer Canal House and tied up on the bulkhead. We found that the large ships left little wake as they slipped through the canal. It was the small high-powered craft that created problems for us. That night Skip and Cecil decided that we were facing heavy boating traffic ahead, ZOE had to be on a long tow, so Cecil would ride inside the battleship on our way to Philadelphia Navy yard. If needed he could cut loose and navigate on his own.

Our ride up the C&D Canal was again through greasy, dirty industrial areas. There were petroleum factories and tanks and we slowly made our way into the Philadelphia Navy Yard. It was a great stop for Navy ships, but dirty and unprotected for our outfit. We went past the USS WISCONSIN after having put Cecil and ZOE out on their own. Skip and I made our way in with PEARL and called the ARIZONA to come in. Just as he was ready to come in, five Navy cutters came along with Navy trainees from Annapolis. Poor Cec—after riding in ZOE all day he was ready to be brought in, but he had to "sit on his props" in the outer harbor until the cutters were all in and tied up. We strung ZOE out among the floating trash, and soon our Coast Guard Auxiliary contacts came to greet us. They had made arrangements for us to tie up at Penn's Landing, Philadelphia, our next stop, near the OLYMPIA. They told us the latter was an old battleship that Dewey had in The Battle of Manila. That night we all went to the "O" Club and had steaks! We discussed what the ARIZONA could do to promote Safety Week for the Coast Guard and the Auxiliary in Philadelphia!

BEN FRANKLIN'S "PHILADELPHIA"

We made the easy move up to Penn Landing in downtown Philadelphia, went under the Ben Franklin Bridge and were soon ensconced in a crowded harbor. Our Coast Guard friends saw to it that we had power and water. We were most grateful for the power, as the heat and humidity were severe and we had to put on the air conditioning in PEARL. We rarely used it, as running or tying up on the water gave us Mother Nature's natural air conditioning, but the combination of high heat plus humidity was too much for us. Both were 97! We had a series of media visits, as our job was to bring a high profile to the Coast Guard Auxiliary while they advertised their Safety Week. We also had the opportunity to visit the many historical places that Philadelphia offers. Our hosts saw to it that we were driven to all of them, and we filmed many to bring home. Our Coast Guard friends took as back to the "O" Club and to great fish restaurants in the area. We were surely treated in a most grandiose manner and enjoyed our contacts with the "real" Coast Guard members.

We regaled our new friends with some of our past adventures. We told them of huge cruise boats that passed us at night. The passengers were feeling no pain and shouted at us, and the ship turned her tremendous spotlight on us. We were usually so tired we fell into our bunks by 8:30 P.M. We told them of the war stories we heard over and over. Or the stories of "we know someone who..." We shared with them the generosity of the many marinas that invited both our ships to stay with them at no charge. Their reason? "We believe in what you are doing!" The invitations to lunch and dinner and aboard other boats were numerous (we always tried hard to stay awake when we were guests of these generous people). Meeting the Pearl Harbor survivors and USS ARIZONA survivors was a special experience.

Our hosts told us they were glad that three salty sailors had made it to their harbor. By this time, June 1, 1986, we had tied up in 53 marinas since Tarpon Springs. ZOE and PEARL had done 2200 water miles. We had jumped the truck and trailer forward approximately the same distance. Both ships had consumed 1800 gallons of fuel, nine thousand USS ARIZONA buttons and press releases had been distributed and "jillions" of questions had been answered. By this time we had been on 24 TV channels and had close to 60 newspapers featuring us...all from just one trip. We recapitulated our adventure for these nice people and we could begin to feel the end drawing near.

As the three of us checked the NY charts, we realized it would be better to take ZOE to Staten Island by trailer rather than try to take two ships in to the crowded harbor area. The boat traffic would be vastly multiplied from the 1976 NY Harbor visit. Congressman Molinari had already made it possible for us to tie up ZOE on Staten Island and we could not ask for more. We had heard there would be thousands of boats in NY harbor, and we were not so foolhardy as to want to tangle with boating problems while under tow. We would return the two boats to Chesapeake City. Later Cecil and I would trailer the ARIZONA to Staten Island. The three of us would take PEARL and ZOE back to the C&D Canal in Chesapeake City where we knew there was a small, working boat yard. There we would dismantle the ship and put Skip on a plane by driving him back to Philadelphia's airport. We would do the New York Harbor appearance alone without the captain. Skip had already solidified the deal on the sale of PEARL H. The buyer would pick her up in Chesapeake City and would take her back to Baltimore Harbor.

It was with reluctance that we turned and both boats went south. This meant the end of PEARL and ZOE, Cecil, Skip and Pat together in our closely-knit quintet. Cecil and I would do New York Harbor and the celebration of the statue's refurbishing without the captain. We found this difficult to face. Our *troika* was unique and special just as it had been with Bill. Our great Auxiliary friends gave us a fond farewell and just as with many others along the 2200 water miles, we promised to keep in touch.

By June 3 we were back in Chesapeake City. We sailed at almost twelve knots back down the Delaware River retracing the areas we had just passed. With the tide pushing us we zinged past the Navy docks, the industrial areas and thought we are going to be "home free." Our optimism vanished, for we had to make a sharp starboard turn to avoid a tanker and its wake. Then it was into the C&D Canal with the tide against us and it was like hitting a brick wall. Skip was down to six knots as we made our way to the Dockside Marina. Wearily we tied both boats up for the night. There was not a lot of elation about "we made it" because the end of our trip and companionship was almost over and we would go our separate ways. We would think about that tomorrow. Tonight it was an early "crash and burn" night.

CAPT. BLIGH LEAVES US SHIP SHAPE

The next day we moved to the Harbor North Marina. We put PEARL in her last resting place. Then the cleanup began. Capt. Crabtree reverted to his Bligh personality and soon had us scrubbing fenders, polishing all chrome, and washing the inside and outside of the mother ship. We carried what seemed like tons of boating equipment, linens, dishes, etc. to our pickup truck. HOW had we accumulated so much? We complained to Skip that he was heading back to Michigan with just his clothes and flight bag. How had we become so encumbered? The mementos given to us took up a lot of space. Pictures of our fleet, a teak ring carved from the deck of the USS ARIZONA, pictures of Admiral Tidd, pictures of people's boats, newspaper clippings. We were piled high with lines, one anchor, flags and life jackets. After three days of cleanup under the watchful eye of the captain, we had our last dinner together, gave Skip his trophy and took him to the Philadelphia airport. Hugs and tears preceded the depression we felt as just the two of us headed back to our last night on PEARL.

The next morning we left the keys to PEARL H with the dock master and began our trek with the ARIZONA behind us. We were headed for a marina on the east side Staten Island, a distance of 175 miles, and we had no clue as to where we were going. The freeways in this eastern area were full of chuckholes, and the traffic was heavy. As we trundled along, we talked about how we would much rather travel by water into the busy cities. As we put the miles behind us, we left Maryland then Pennsylvania behind us.

Just as we pulled onto the New Jersey Turnpike, I heard an expletive from Cecil. "What in the blankety- blank is that police car doing behind us? He's got his reds on and he's flashing me to stop."

Alarmed, I looked back over the ARIZONA's superstructure. There was the New Jersey State Police car and sure enough, he was lighting up like a Christmas tree. What had we done? Cec checked our speedometer and was within the speed limit for trailering a large rig. He wondered about his license plates or our trailer lights. Had they become inoperable due to some unplanned for dousing in the water?

We pulled over and the state trooper came to the window. With apprehension we looked at him. "Hi, Ah'm with the New Jersey Police and Ah'm gonna give youse an escort all the way across the New Jersey Turnpike and Ah'm gonna turn youse over to some Pearl Harbor survivors at the end of the turnpike and youse are gonna be taken to your marina by them. Youse falla me. OK?"

Somewhat in shock, we agreed, and the trooper pulled out in front of us. With red lights flashing and siren blaring, he started out. By the time he was up to 65 mph, Cec was having difficulty. The tension silently mounted between us because we never drove this fast with the long, heavy ship behind us. We always felt it was highly dangerous to go too fast, not only because it took a long time to stop our outfit, but because we attracted so much attention and shock that people didn't always drive safely near us. We watched in fascination as frightened drivers pulled off the freeway in droves and over to the side of the road. On we roared, Cec's hands gripping tightly on the wheel. We really were going much too fast for the weight behind us. After we had gone 15 minutes in this fashion, the trooper signaled us to pull over. We parked right behind him and wondered what was wrong now. Had we done something?

"Ah'm gonna have tuh go behind youse. Everyone thinks ah'm after dem. Ah'll ride behind youse." Great, now we would really have to do it right!

We slowed down to our own comfortable pace of 55 mph and crawled across New Jersey with our escort flashing his lights behind us. It was a bit unnerving, but it was nice, also, not to have the big trucks tailgate us due to curiosity and their desire to talk with us on the CB. In a couple of hours the trooper pulled ahead of us and led us to a service station. By this time nothing surprised us. There, waiting by three cars, was a group of men, all Pearl Harbor survivors, ready to escort us to our Staten Island Marina in mid-New York Harbor. What a pleasant surprise to have such hospitable guides as we crossed into the unknown territory of Staten Island.

We took these delightful gentlemen to lunch even though we had a dreadful time trying to find a parking place for our long rig. After lunch the PHSA escorted us all the way to our marina, helped us back ZOE into a preordained spot where security could watch her, said goodbye to us—and we were alone. It seemed so odd after all the hoop-la of the past four months. We felt odd without Skip or Bill. It was not quite mid-June and we would not be required to show up in NY Harbor until July first. What should we do? The two-legged stool feeling took over and we went to a close-by Holiday Inn to decide what we would do for two plus weeks.

By mutual agreement we found a nearby travel agency and asked what trips they offered in the East that would occupy us for two weeks. Eureka! We struck gold. In two days there was a Tauck Tour leaving from the New York Waldorf Astoria that would take us through New York, Massachusetts, New Hampshire, Maine, then into Montreal and Quebec. The trip offered history and beauty and we grabbed it. Within two days we taxied to the entrance of the Waldorf and found ourselves totally alone. Only joggers were up and we would find nothing in the hotel that was open. We had never seen New York City in this sleepy state and it was a fascinating few hours to enjoy before the city woke up.

The next two weeks were welcome and we enjoyed leaving the driving to someone else. We luxuriated in the elegant hotels and the camaraderie of more newfound friends. This helped us ease the ache and emptiness we felt from having Skip, PEARL, ZOE and the water no longer a daily part of our lives. The two weeks passed quickly and we were soon back at the Holiday Inn and the ARIZONA. We gussied her up for her appearance and found our place for the parade of ships for July 4. The local news media came out and did a nice story on us and CBS planned to find us on July 3 for a pre-parade interview.

With hopes high for a grand parade of tall ships, we climbed in the ARIZONA and took a run out into New York Harbor for a trial run on July 2. The sun shone, and the water was sparkling and dappled with a slight chop. The harbor was beginning to fill up with Navy ships and pleasure craft, all getting into position a few days ahead of the big day. We caused incredible excitement as we steamed about the different watercraft. The Navy tooted at us, and people in all kinds of boats saluted and begged us to tie up next to them. There was only one scary incident when the Staten Island Ferry crept slowly by us. The ferryboat captain must have seen us (we certainly saw him) because we heard him announce over the PA system, "Folks, look over on our starboard side and you will see the USS ARIZONA. I am not kidding you. She is right there below us." By this time the ferry loomed over us, and as the people crowded to the starboard railing, we both swore the towering boat tipped our way. We tried to ease away, but the ferryboat captain followed us for some yards until he finally veered away. We went back to the marina, happy to put the ARIZONA in a safe slip and escape to the safety of our motel room.

July 3 we had an early morning interview for a nationwide talk show right off our marina. It was dark and windy, and Cec had a difficult time holding the battleship steady for his interview. I helped bring him in and he talked about how the wind was picking up. He was glad to be off the bay.

A WINDY HAPPY BIRTHDAY
—AND HOME

The next morning, the BIG day, we discovered that the wind had not stopped but had increased in velocity. The TV anchor people were already talking about it, and the weathermen were being closely questioned. After breakfast we went to the marina and climbed in ZOE. She had full fuel tanks, and off we went into the harbor. By this time the whole harbor was full of boats. We read later there were 35,000 boats in addition to the Tall Ships. We tried to find our place in the parade. The wind was so strong Cec could hardly control ZOE. Twenty-five to thirty knot gusts of winds kept us from keeping our TV date by the USS Kennedy and Verrazano bridges. We were being swept across the bay into some old abandoned pilings. It was only with full power Cec was able to avoid a collision. We put on our VHF and heard that other ships were having severe problems. Anchors were dragging and newsmen complaining they could not get to their interviews. Even though we had wind and waves to fight, we knew ZOE was stable. It was just terribly uncomfortable inside her, and we were being thrown around violently. We did manage to watch the parade of ships, but the wind spoiled the day for many. There was to be a big dinner party aboard an aircraft carrier for all the captains, but the wind was so fierce that the captains could not get off their ships into the runabouts to join one another for this occasion.

After a few hours we gradually fought our way across the bay and into the safety and quiet of our marina. We were disappointed not to have found our position in line, but were so exhausted we were just glad to have weathered such a bad wind. By this time we had become philosophical about all kinds of weather and accepted it as just part of boating. One can never, ever have plans set up in concrete when on the water. The fireworks that night, however, were remarkable.

We found our trailer and put the ARIZONA on it preparatory to leaving for California. We spent one more night at the Staten Island Holiday Inn, and over dinner we summarized the past four months. Such a saga this trip turned out to be, and the memories would always be with us. Fifty-six marinas, 2400 water miles since Tarpon Springs, 420 hours on each of PEARL's engines and half that amount on the USS ARIZONA, 25 TV interviews, more than 60 newspaper and magazine articles. The troubles were numerous, but overcome with our teamwork. At times logistics overwhelmed us—jumping truck/trailer ahead and renting a car or hooking a ride back, then grabbing a taxi to find PEARL and Skip. We would jump on board and leave for our next date. The times out on the swim platform, hooking Cec and ZOE up, straightening her lines out, caring for lines and fenders on PEARL, then racing back to the swim platform if a bridge did not open on time and pulling the ARIZONA in close so we could circle in shoaling waters…this was a happening repeated too many times. We always seemed to be shouting at one another (especially the men!). Skip was so capable and such a help. He anticipated so much and we felt comfortable in his hands. We were a team, and many times things would go like clockwork, but always something unexpected erupted, emergencies arose and we all had to race around and patty-cake things back together. After the emergencies were over and we tied up, there was always the public to greet us, tired as we were. After long runs there was laundry to be done, changing beds, shopping, straddling MO to get somewhere, polishing ZOE. We lost track of all the black and blues we endured and the Band-Aids needed! The wonderful American people stand out with their great outreach to us and what we were trying to do. The gifts given to us—pictures, jacket patches, loans of cars, offers of rides, dinner invitations so numerous we cannot count, retired servicemen driving many miles to meet us, Navy hospitality with all its privileges in three ports, generous dock masters who gave us free tie-ups, everyone encouraging us, thanking us and giving helpful advice. What privileges we had in meeting Navy "brass." We even met the last flag officer to be left on the ARIZONA December 7, 1941 who was only an ensign at that time.

Why did we do it? The desire to share our American history and heritage and to teach the young people about the tremendous sacrifices made for our freedoms was probably the prime motive. The outreach of the people we met and their encouragement to keep going for our Statue of Liberty goal was another incentive. The public really spurred us on. It was the people who made this trip special—the young ones so interested in ZOE and her history; the good ol' boys who shyly asked if they could have a USS ARIZONA button for their caps; the servicemen from WW II who drove miles to see our ship; the Vietnam veterans who quietly thanked us for the message we were carrying. The respect shown for what our ARIZONA exemplified was evident. Special dock masters uncomplainingly played musical boats in their crowded marinas so that PEARL H could be tied up beside her 36-ft. charge. Skip, Cecil and I often talked about what mere acquaintances did for all of us. Their offers of assistance, contacts ahead, and advice about treacherous waters—all this contributed to the success of this trip.

Capt. Skip—— Getting ZOE ready for her New York appearance

USS ARIZONA greets the Statue of Liberty—July 4, 1986

On July 5 we headed west. As we threaded our way along Highway 80 we had the usual truck driver banter always with us. "Whatcha got theah behind y'all? Ya ain't gonna shoot me if I pass yuh is ya?" Or, "I saw you on TV when I had my rig in Florida. Was that you?" Or, "You going to take any more trips with that beauty? Y'all need anyone to help ah'll sure go with ya."

Then there was the flat tire in Iowa. The goodwill of our battleship was still with us, and a truck driver insisted on helping Cec change the tire on the trailer. We never did get over the charm, the mystique, the aura that our USS ARIZONA seemed to emit that pulled people in from all walks of life. We found we cut across all ages and racial barriers and touched the hearts of Americans. It was not us. It was what the ARIZONA symbolized.

ZOE continued to push us homeward on Highway 80 and we congratulated ourselves when we saw the Rockies looming ahead, for we knew our beloved West was not far ahead. One more surprise awaited us. We stayed high in the Rockies one night at a Best Western motel. The manager insisted on a picture of the ARIZONA in front of his motel. He sent it in to his company and they used it nationwide in one of their magazines. The inscription was to read, "Battleship sails over the Rockies." The manager felt sure this would be a grabber!

Our last night out was on July 13 in Reno. We elected to stay at John Ascuaga's Nugget because we knew it had ample parking for our huge outfit. As we drove around trying to find a large parking space, Security saw us trying to park our phantom and insisted we bring her to the main lobby entrance and put her right out in front so they could watch over her. She was scarred from ICW calamities and grundgy from 3000 miles of highway road dirt. No matter, Security insisted she have a place of honor. We obliged and even had enough energy to tie some American flags on her. We were given a room overlooking her and were pleased and surprised to see how many people came by and patted her rumpy-dump as she sat on the trailer—all this with few flags and her pagoda mast taken down and tied inside her. No matter where we were we understood that everyone loved what she stands for.

When we came out to pick her up the next morning, we were surprised to find that many coins had been thrown on her deck. Gamblers must have thought this would bring good luck before they entered the casino. We counted almost four dollars in change! The unexpected always seemed to accompany our boat.

What a trip, hard as it was. The joy and culmination of it out shown the obstacles we met and conquered.

If we were asked to encapsulate in one sentence what we had hoped to project it would be this:

A SMALL TRIBUTE TO A GIANT IDEA—THE FIGHT FOR LIBERTY.

1988

South Haven, MI; across Lake Michigan; to Longboat Key, FL

HELLO, DOLLY

Capt. Skip Crabtree
Cecil and Pat

South Haven, MI; across Lake Michigan;
to Longboat Key, FL—1988

WE CREW FOR CAPTAIN SKIP

Over the next few years we were busy with various segments of the fleet. Although the Bicentennial years were far behind us, the memory of the Statue of Liberty's birthday was fresh in the minds of the public. We had many invitations to be "the hook" for various boat shows in the West and did most we were asked to do. Being hired by different public relations firms in diverse parts of the West was always interesting. Invariably we worked with the most pleasant of advertising men and women. Having done six boat shows thus far we knew what they wanted and felt we should do our best when interviewed on TV and when we were on the boat show floor. The PR advisors began to trust us and gave us information to memorize and be repeated while on TV. Boat show dates, hours, times open, prices, etc., were to be reiterated along with talking about the boat that was in the boat show. We were asked back by many and had some great times with the people who had the franchises for the shows.

Inevitably the shows were always in the months of January or February. The idea was that people who endured inclement weather during those periods of time would welcome a chance to be inside a huge, heated building and think ahead to boating for the summer months. It worked! No matter where we were, the paying public streamed in to the boat shows. It was hard work, a daily long grind, particularly on the weekends, but we enjoyed it. What an opportunity to put up our pictures and signs telling of our waterway adventures and answer questions about our fleet! We were always placed in very nice hotels or motels and paid well for our work. When we finally ended the work with our fleet, we had done a total of 15 boat shows all over the country.

It was cause for celebration to have Bill drive to our northern California lake and visit us…ditto Capt. Skip. The bonding had been close and we always had a wonderful time reliving the fun and the hardships we had gone through together. We continued to do more boat shows with both the USS ARIZONA and our RMS TITANIC. The two ships seemed to hold a magnetic attraction for the public, and our pre-publicity on different TV channels in different cities proved to be a draw.

We had one rather unusual happening at Lake Almanor. We continued to come out in various magazines or tabloids. One weekly found its way to Japan. The Japanese TV people sent a crew of four all the way to our lake to interview us. Three men spoke only Japanese and the fourth man was the interpreter. In speaking via phone with the latter, he kept insisting that they wanted to film only the USS ARIZONA. I kept telling him that was not possible. Even though many years had passed since the 1941 bombing of the ships in Pearl Harbor, there was still great feeling among the men who were the survivors of the ship. Some of them found it very hard to forget—or forgive—what had happened to them and their fellow crewmates that day. Many had lost loved friends. We finally agreed that they could film all the fleet, but would concentrate on the RMS TITANIC. They would film the ARIZONA only in passing and as part of the seven ships comprising our flotilla. By this time we had worked with the USS ARIZONA survivors all over the country. They had met us in so many ports and loved our ship. Although we were dealing with an entirely new generation of Japanese nationals who had little knowledge of "the day that will live in infamy," we realized we could not hurt the men who had been part of the attack by loaning out our ship for anything less than a feeling of patriotism for our country. The young interpreter understood our position and we were grateful for his acceptance of our parameters.

An unexpected phone call from Capt. Skip came in the fall of 1988. "HELP! Listen, you guys, I've got to deliver a 34-foot trawler from South Haven, Michigan, to the east coast of Florida. I need two people to crew for me. Any chance you could take two to three weeks and help me out?" Any chance? We would forego ice cream, wine, eat spinach, be kind to the skunk who continually overturned our trash barrel, do pushups—anything to go with Skip and get back on the water. Skip was to deliver the trawler to Long Boat Key on the west coast of Florida for a couple who lived in Michigan but liked to get away from that area in the winter and live on their boat in a warmer climate. It would be a 2000 mile trip. Could we be ready to leave in five days? Could we? A resounding "YES."

On October 9, 1988 we flew from Reno to Midway Airport outside of Chicago. We anticipated this "dream trip." The ship was named HELLO DOLLY and she was tied up at the New Buffalo Marina. Skip said we would make a due west crossing across Lake Michigan from South Haven, MI, directly to the east coast of Chicago. From there we would proceed down the

Illinois River, then into the Mississippi. At St. Louis we would hang a left/ port onto the Ohio River, south onto the Tennessee River, and finally into the fairly new Tom Bigbee Canal, which empties out into Mobile Bay, AL. A short stop in Mobile was planned to check the engine and provision the HELLO DOLLY for a gulf crossing. It sounded good to us. Skip would pick us up at the airport and we would plan our trip and enjoy a pleasant evening together. What fun it would be to go to a motel, have dinner and spend the evening talking and catching up with one another's lives.

We landed and there he was! Tousled, blondish hair, tan, lean, clean blue jeans and always with that uncomfortable gait that said, "I'm-on-land-and-too-far-from-the-water." We hugged and hugged and we all began to talk excitedly. "Listen up," came the voice from the captain. "There can't be any motel or dilly-dallying. I've checked the weather and there's a storm due in late tonight from up north and it will roll right across Lake Michigan. We've got to head for the marina right now. The crossing will take about five hours, but we can make it. If we don't leave this afternoon we have to sit in port for three or four days." Oh dear! There goes our fish dinner and our motel plans. So be it. That's how it is when dealing with water and weather. We were surely accustomed to having our plans turned upside-down by this time.

He hurried us to his wagon and drove the 90 miles around the south end of the lake to his marina in South Haven. Knowing these two men well by now, I insisted he divert long enough to go into a Big Mac drive- through. I would not be able to provision this boat until we came to a marina, probably somewhere along the Illinois River. We bought hamburgers and coffee then came to the marina parking lot. Skip grabbed our two suitcases and hustled us on board. By this time it was late afternoon. Before we even had a chance to get out of our traveling/city clothes, he ordered us to untie all lines, pull in fenders and "CAST OFF!" We did as we were told. By 5:30 P.M. we were out of the marina and well into the southern part of Lake Michigan. After we checked our compass course, became familiar with the charts and located the binoculars, it was finally time to unpack suitcases and find the blue jeans. Cec and I did this one at a time, as Skip needed someone in the gathering dark to help him navigate.

It was not easy to put things away in an unfamiliar boat when no lights were allowed on. We could not use interior lights while underway, as this ruined the night vision we needed to check out all the heavy traffic in our area. I brought out the hamburgers and coffee, and the three of us munched our way through a cold meal, all the time checking out the nearby freighters.

As darkness fell we were shocked at the size of the sea-going monsters. They looked like lit-up Christmas trees lying on their side. We checked the radar to see if it was working. Skip was always suspicious of some unmarked, no-lights-boat out there somewhere.

The sea began to build as we approached the mid-point of our crossing. "Two and one-half more hours," the captain announced. With his own boat he had crossed this area many times. We began to bounce around and the waves became higher. We laughed together, remembering Chesapeake Bay. Even though we were beginning to take a pounding the trawler with her low silhouette and deep keel was a steady-as-you-go, seaworthy boat. HELLO DOLLY was a reliable craft and though we were losing our footing if we tried to move around, we knew she could take a beating. We lurched back and forth, trying to settle into HELLO DOLLY. Approximately 45 minutes out from what should be a red flasher on the east side of Chicago Skip asked me to take the binoculars and watch for the narrow harbor opening. Happy to do this as it meant the end of a jouncing, water-over-the-bow journey, I kept checking. Within 15 minutes I was sure I saw the red flasher. Skip assured me that was it and we pounded on. Cec asked, "Where are we going to tie up tonight?" Being in unfamiliar territory we had no clue as to facilities in this area. "Oh, somewhere near the Navy pier," said the captain. "Oh, OK." What did we know?

Glory be! Then it was upon us. The red flasher became far more distinguishable and we slowed down to enter the quiet, peaceful harbor. What a difference. The water had barely a ripple. We disturbed a duck family that had nested in for the night and they squawked their disapproval at us. A towering, black building which Skip later identified as the Wrigley building rose high above us. There was no one around except one Navy boat tied up along the pier across the water. "Is this it, Skip? I inquired. "Do you have permission to stay overnight here?"

"No, but it's OK. They know me."

"Oh," again from me. It was too late and I was too tired to challenge the captain. I retired to our stern head and bunk and never heard Cecil come in to his bunk. Skip crashed up in his head/cuddy cabin and at midnight we were all in la-la land. It had been one long day for all of us! I did note that 'Skip was careful to lock all hatches and entries from inside. He informed us we were in a bad area of Chicago and we had to be careful as no one was around or even near us.

Pat, Skip and Cecil
leave South Haven, MI
to deliver HELLO DOLLY

Across Lake Michigan,
down the Illinois River, into
the Mississippi, Ohio,
Tennessee Rivers, then
into the Tom Bigbee Canal

First of several dozen
bridges as we go
through the heart
of Chicago
on the Illinois River

Hanging on to lines
as we go through
a Tennessee lock

We awoke to a brilliant, cloudless, windy, cold fall day! Out came the heavy jackets. We climbed up and out onto the deck to survey our locale. What a difference the day made. We were located in the heart of Chicago with tall skyscrapers set along all the shoreline. We could see a few sailors across the water in their Navy area. The Wrigley skyscraper looked disdainfully down on us. Just how high was this building, I asked. "High enough," came the answer. Another "Oh," from me.

We did our morning ritual by turning on the weather report. Were we ever glad to be across that wide expanse of water now behind us! The marine forecast reported twenty-five to thirty knot winds and waves five to ten feet going up to six to twelve feet. We were glad to have that large body of unpredictable water behind us. I ventured a question as to "What lies ahead? Where do we go from here?"

Skip said, "Come on up to the bridge and look over our stern."

Obediently I clambered up and saw a lock! "We have to do a lock thing first off?"

Answer: "Sure do, but we don't have a tow with us and we're old pros now." It looked intriguing.

Scrounging a few fig bars and cold breakfast goodies from the larder and walking a distance to find coffee, we had a meager breakfast. Skip was anxious to get started and get south of Chicago. Cec took the bow, I took the stern, we untied lines and hauled in fenders. It felt great to be a threesome again. Around the corner we went and down we descended through a nine-foot foot lock. I looked straight ahead and saw nothing but bridges, bridges, bridges, skyscrapers on either side and the narrow river through which we were to thread. What a way to see Chicago! We had never experienced this kind of boating. Downtown Chicago as we were experiencing it was a wall of mirrored glass on the sides of many buildings, tall skyscrapers that allowed no sunlight to penetrate, concrete condos reaching to the sky. One elaborate condo setup even had Illinois River water flowing in under the buildings where there were sheltered boat slips for condo owners who obviously came down in elevators to go boating, then stepped right onto their cruisers. What a way to go to sea!

We were speechless. We went under bridges, we passed MacDonald's on our starboard side and waved at the people eating their MacMuffins; we peeked into condos where people were having breakfast. It was all so overwhelming and different. And it was cold! We didn't want to leave the bridge for fear we would miss something, but we saw the heart of Chicago. After an hour we eventually began to leave Chicago, went into the Sanitary Canal and the beginning of railroad bridges which would stop us, dead in the water. We had some long waits as trains slowly pulled across the river, then the drawbridge would lift to let us through. We began to see scrap piles of metal as we came into the industrial area, and even saw some scrub trees and brush. Nice to see some greenery. We went through three locks that day and experienced little barge traffic. Cec and I uneasily assessed the narrowness of the river and wondered how we would be able to get by the big tows we knew frequented this river. Being of a suspicious nature after all we had been through previously, we knew there were "things" lurking out there on the river.

We passed many chemical plants, slaughter yards, and towering piles of scrap metal. Skip had a rather weird (I thought) guidebook that mentioned some marinas along the way. It was not near as complete as our *Waterway Guides* along the ICW. We tied up late, 7:30 P.M. We were well south of Chicago. I cooked dinner on board as I discovered that the good captain had purchased some shrimp and goodies for our first night. We ate, then crashed and burned. It had been one long first day.

Still on the Illinois River, we wakened to windy, cold weather. After breakfast we started out, and Skip began gnashing his teeth over some steering problem. He seemed to solve it quickly, and soon we tied up next to a tug and tow and were let down through our second lock easily. While navigating this lock, Cecil and Skip were invited on board the tug and given a tour of the tugboat. They came back impressed with the engines, their power and the galley, which had a female cook who fed the crew well. They also told me that "one tow pushes 15 barges, 1200 feet long, carries 18,000 tons loaded, draws nine feet of water. It takes them one mile to stop and they take up the whole bend in the river to turn on a sharp curve." I was duly impressed. Past Joliet prison we went and tied up at Ottawa, IL. For some reason this point was called "Starved Rock Lodge."

Then it was on to Peru, where, in the early morning, I was cautioned not to carelessly walk the decks. I could see ice and gingerly climbed off the boat and walked to town to buy Cec a heavy jacket. When I came back Cecil had worked on the electrical system on HELLO DOLLY and Skip had flushed out the engine. Friends of Skip's came to visit and drove me to a shopping area where I finally stocked up on groceries. Our evening pow-wow came with a unanimous decision to really push south tomorrow hoping for warmer weather.

With 71 miles to cover to Peoria, we were up and running early. As we came into less populated areas, the birds became part of our journey. Great Blue Herons lazily flew by us and seemed not at all alarmed at our intrusion. The fall coloring was grandiose. The yellow, orange and brilliant red leaves formed a palette of indescribable colors. The maples were particularly outlandish in their apparel. They waved their almost iridescent foliage at us as if showing off their radiant attire before suddenly dropping their garments in preparation for winter's onslaught. We took yards, not feet, of film! Around every corner was another picture which we felt belonged on some calendar.

We left Peoria early, as we had to get through a lock or wait until northbound traffic got through. This could mean a wait for the turn around of three hours. We were becoming more proficient with going through locks, as we had no tow behind us. Skip was at the wheel, Cecil at the bow and I was on the stern line. We rode up and down on bollards, had lines thrown down to us that were wrapped around heavy posts at the top and were cautioned to carefully watch our lines. We went through every kind of lock tie-up there is and noticed that the height of the locks was increasing as we went south. On we went to Beardstown, a distance of 85 miles. Here I met a tugboat captain tied up near us. Capt. Dee invited me aboard and said he wanted me to know how to "make cracklin' corn bread." I found that pork rinds went into the makings. So much for cholesterol count. The hard working crew didn't care. Dee's remark about his corn bread was, "It's so good y'all want to go right back to Arkansas and slap your Grandma right in the face!" We were back in the South!

We were still on the Illinois River when we pulled into Beardstown. There was no marina, so Skip asked permission to tie up next to a barge. We rocked and rolled all night as many tows run at night. We could hear them coming with their deep-throated rumble of powerful diesel engines. The long, long searchlight's beam would find us, play momentarily over DOLLY, then look again for the mid-channel of the river. Early to bed because Capt. Bligh said we had two locks close by in the morning and we had to get through on time. We pulled off the barge by 6 A.M. and it was just daybreak. I watched, speechless, as Skip estimated his ability to pass a very large, long tow. It took us 20 minutes to get by and time seemed to crawl as I watched the massive barges slowly (too slowly) slide back behind us. We tied up at a small town which offered us the amenities of the Paradise Yacht Club. We were in by noon and I enjoyed walking to a store for supplies. A pleasant lady drove me back, as I had a full load of groceries. The next A.M. it was off for St. Louis, MO and we ran into a lot of barge traffic. The banter on the VHF was always fascinating. "Where the #$@% is yo?? Y'all gonna be at that there intersection? Yo sure y'all knows yo comin' northbound? Ah'll git to that corner afor ya. Y'all watch out. Ah got that river on my tail and ahm sailin'. Here ah cum."

Silence on the other end of the line. At last a lackadaisical voice responded, "Ah knows y'alls theah. Yo jist showin' off to that new lady cook y'all got. Y'all hush now."

WHERE'S CECIL??

At last, it was mid-October, Mile 179 and the St. Louis Arch came up on the horizon. We had just come onto the Mississippi River and was she rolling! As we tried to slow down while cruising through St. Louis, we were surprised to see a MacDonald's Arches sign on a large paddlewheel. It was right under the Arch. With no place to tie up and do a small bit of sightseeing, we journeyed on south to Hobbie's Marina and much warmer weather. We were grateful to pull in as there was a 35-knot wind and a tornado watch. Typical Southern weather, we were told.

We really made the mileage the next day—108 miles to Cape Girardeau. This was a mean tie-up. The marina was on a bend of the Mississippi with a rip-snorting current running. Skip did a great job of pulling DOLLY in, and Cec and I leaped for the dock to make a quick turn around on the cleats so Skip and DOLLY would not go careening off down Ol' Man River. Needing groceries I looked up some 150 feet to the top of the levee. There were a lot of steps to climb so I started out. Bidding the boys goodbye, I climbed…and climbed. When I was at the top they shouted, "Where are you going?"

"Searching for a grocery store," I answered. I felt like the lady moving to an early California ghost town. "Goodbye, God, I'm going to Bodie." I knew how she felt. Up and over the levee and through many boarded up shops I walked. The old river towns were losing out to the new mall, which had moved in at the outer edges of towns. It was sad to see the early history of these Southern towns so dilapidated and run down. After a two-mile walk, I found the grocery store and trudged back to learn that there was no restaurant in which I could demand to be taken for dinner. I was cooking dinner and we were taking off at 6 A.M. the next morning. OK. Roll with the punch. That had been learned long ago.

We all slept heavily and did not realize that a large cruiser had pulled in during the night and had tied up next to us. No one heard them come in, and we were quiet in the early morning hours as we got ready to leave. They must have run at night, something we did not relish doing. This time I took the bowlines. Cec was preparing the stern lines, and Skip was shouting instructions as to what we should all do due to the fast- rolling river current. Old pros by this time, we nodded and said we were ready. Skip gunned the engine in a tight pullout into the river, and I tossed my line on board and jumped on. I turned to see Cecil struggling with his line. As Skip put out full power to pull into the river, Cec had to throw the line on board and we left him back at the dock.

"Skip, Cec had trouble. He's still on the dock."

"What in the&%^^& is he doing there?"

Poor Cec—disbelieving, distraught captain. How would we ever get back into that narrow spot, go against the current and pick Cecil up? Skip made a large circle against the roiling river. DOLLY did not want to respond, but finally did. I was given instructions as to a few fenders being put out and to throw Cecil a line if he needed it. We came careening into the narrow slip we had just left. DOLLY's stern wanted to "kiss" the bow of the cruiser next to us. I managed to fend off, we skidded in, Cecil grabbed a line and a cleat and swung one leg over the railing. Skip gave full power to the engine and we got off.

"What in the blankety- blank happened? How did you end up on the dock?" demanded an irate captain.

Cecil defended himself. "Last night when those people came in, they put their line in and over ours and got them all mixed up. I thought I had everything unwound, but at the last minute a lot of our line was caught under their line." The good nature of the usually sunny captain surfaced and we congratulated him on his superior handling of a difficult situation. We went bouncing off down the "Miss-iss-sloppi," as the men named it. We were free! Another harrowing experience behind us…always unexpected. Harrowing experiences are to be anticipated on the water.

Down the Mississippi we went, all 52 miles of it left before we began to search for our pivot point for a port turn into the Ohio River. "All hands at full alert. I don't want to miss this turn," said a grim captain.

"Yes, sir. We're all at full attention." And, by golly, we found the Ohio at 11:30 A.M.

It was cloudy and chilly, but we made our port turn and felt quite proud. Milling around in the middle of the confluences of so many rivers made navigating a nightmare. Heading due east, we were now on the busy Ohio. Barge traffic was thankfully coming toward us and we felt quite smug that we were safely on our way to the Tennessee River. Just at the moment we were congratulating ourselves, Skip saw a pleasure craft in distress. He picked up their name and called them.

Their answer was, "We can't get our engine started. We need a tow."

Always mindful that the craft could have been us, we dutifully threw the cruiser a line and began to tow them. There was much discussion on the VFH as to where everyone was going. It was getting dusk and there were no close by marinas. I watched in dismay as we began to go very slowly with the large cruiser in tow behind us. There were mixed feelings expressed by all three of us, but there had been many times we were in need of a tow and grateful for it, but we were tired (every night) and where would we end up tonight?

I couldn't believe it. We were headed for Clarksville Marina!! What!? That crumby, back in the swamps, greasy, overworked boating marina. Nice people, but no creature comforts!! I KNEW, the last time we were there, we would NEVER, EVER be there again. Who in the world could have found this out-of-the-way place, anyhow?

As darkness descended I sat by the captain, complaining about everything in general. "Skip, the Clarksville Marina is awful. We tied up there eleven years ago. It's in the swamp. There's nothing there. No fuel, no facilities, NOTHING. It's AWFUL." My complaints fell on deaf ears. When a boat is in trouble the rule of the waterways is you tow and you tow GRACIOUSLY. "OK, I know, I KNOW!!" So be it. Such are the vicissitudes of life on the water. Grumble, grumble. How did I end up in this escapade? Oh well.

We pulled the pleasure craft for two and a half hours. Darkness settled in and there, and with a mini-light, Skip found the "marina." By this time it was sleeting and we could not see well. We groped our way in, Skip did a perfect job of giving an extra push to the disabled boat, and we were free. In we came. It was pitch black and we saw one small light bulb over the dock. We could barely see to make our tie-up, but with the sleet, the cold, the darkness, and getting safely into port without crunching any boats, we were glad to be in any safe harbor. We were so proud of Skip, who placed the disabled boat right in the perfect spot behind us.

We remembered the night we had tied up here with the Stewarts in 1977—good, hard-working people at this out-of-the-way marina, but not really a transient's place to stop. By this time it was 8:30 P.M., we were beat, I cooked something presentable on the propane stove, we showered and had another "crash and burn" night. *How DID I manage to get into this boating life?* I pondered, as I fell into my bunk. Surely the weather has to improve and get warmer as we go south.

The next A.M. we carefully made our way out through the dripping, mistletoe, moss-laden trees. I pushed and slashed at overhanging boughs as we reversed out of the dank channel. It was foggy and drizzly and we finally found our way out onto the Ohio. Very shortly we found our turn onto the Tennessee River and prepared for going through Ken Lake.

Onward we pushed that day for Ken Lake Marina, a state park that we heard was well-cared-for and had a great lodge restaurant. We had a three-hour wait for the Ken Lake lock, and we felt most insignificant as we stared up at an 85-foot steel wall above us. Getting through after a three-hour wait, we found a great tie-up and decided to spend two days there. Skip would clean the boat, Cec and I would rent a car and do laundry and shopping for all three of us. Friends from our 1977 trip were phoned and dutifully came down to spend an afternoon on DOLLY with us. What a great respite. The cook enjoyed two nights of lodge restaurant dinners!

A TEMPEST ON KEN LAKE

After a day or so of indolence, we felt strong enough to continue. Ahead lay Ken Lake and uncertain weather. We had an early A.M. take-off, and the thunder, lightning and rain began. It was cold, windy and it was October 23. We should have expected that fall would make her time frame known to us. The waves began to splash over our bow and douse the windows on the bridge of HELLO DOLLY; however, Skip and I had a three-year ongoing, bloody cribbage war always in operation, and we kept playing crib as we went up and over the waves. Cec, always at full alert to film, was doing yeoman service as cameraman. He was alternately filming the huge waves that threatened to inundate us or filming our equally lethal, cutthroat cribbage game, where much yelling and slamming of cards would occur. At least it made the time go faster. Skip had to slow us down. We continued to crash into Ken Lake waves and eventually found our way out of the mess.

It was late afternoon and our "guide" indicated there might be a marina in the vicinity. We found it and gratefully tied up for an overnight. Could it be that we were almost through Kentucky and ready to enter into Tennessee? WHERE was the Tombigbee Canal? We could hardly wait. Would it get warmer? What was ahead? That night the good captain cooked dinner and we offered a big thank you to the boss (AKA as "Mother Crabtree" when he did his cooking thing).

October 24 and Capt. Bligh had us leave the dock at 5 A.M. It was cold, foggy and there were two huge charter boats in the lead. Skip seemed to have known them from somewhere in the Lake Michigan area and chattered happily with his old friends. He asked permission to follow them in the fog and it was speedily granted. Groping our way through the mist, we crept along. We even passed three barges that were going slower than we were. The sun eventually burned through, and since all three of us had been at the wheel trying to peer through the fog, I left my post and made a gigantic bacon and egg breakfast for my two men. It was well-received. Good thing I fed them well. This was another full day with Pickwick Dam ahead of us. We began to have trouble with the engine. We would have to stop, Skip would throw up the floor boards and check out the engine. He was quite concerned as to the lack of power, the way the engine was beginning to act and the heat generated. Our stops began to be more and more prevalent, and I became accustomed to walking from our bunk area, doing the tight rope act around the engine compartment, floorboards up, Skip deep inside the engine's interior. Oh dear. We hated to see him have such a problem. This was slowing us down.

We finally made it to Pickwick Dam, and what a sight that was. We crept in and tied to the bollard. It was 84 feet above us, and we marveled at the height. Skip didn't really have to say, "Can you imagine the water behind that gate if it broke loose and we were down here?" No, I didn't really want to hear about that possibility. I put on my life jacket (regulations) and my gloves and clung to the wall of the lock.

We could see the lock spectators high above us and shouting to "Come on up!"

"OK, we'll be there as soon as they put some water in this darn thing!" It was obviously one of the highlights of the day for the small-town folk to come to the locks, position themselves up on the walks and watch all of us meanderers either rise or fall at the whim of the lockmaster. With relief we made it to the top, grabbed our lines and sailed out of the lock. We were about to enter the Tom Bigbee Canal.

We had been at the dedication of the Tombigbee Canal in 1985 with ZOE when it was completed in Mobile. The lovely girls in hoop skirts and vintage costumes had been pictured by our USS ARIZONA. Capt. Skip had been the number-three boat to use the canal. We were interested in just why this expensive, man-made canal had been dug when all the barges had the Mississippi River which took them down to New Orleans. The Waterway opened its lakes and locks to the public on January 14, 1985. The Tenn-Tom linked 16,000 miles of inland waters between the upper Mississippi, Ohio and Tennessee Rivers to the Gulf of Mexico and the ICW. The canal is 234 miles long, a minimum of 300 feet wide and sustains a nine-foot depth. It has ten locks 600 feet long and 110 feet wide to navigate. The waterway is in operation 24 hours a day, seven days a week. We learned that this newer route to Mobile cuts 800 miles off the journey from the north to New Orleans.

As we journeyed south, the weather gradually became warmer, and we rejoiced for the lack of ice on the decks. Even though we were losing the fall colors, our spirits were up as we began to run into balmier weather. Our only concern was the engine problem that DOLLY was beginning to have. Skip had to pull off to the side of the Tom Bigbee Canal, we would throw out an anchor and he would work on the engine. WHAT was our problem? With two good mechanics on board I felt comfortable, but their concern and inability to find out what was amiss with DOLLY's engine bothered me. I hoped it was not a "biggie"!

We began to go through locks that had the romantic labels of Lock E, Lock D, Lock C, Lock B. Capt. Bligh was on one of his marathon runs, so it was up at 5 A.M. and into Lock C by 5:30 A.M. The moon was still up as we slithered into Lock C, shivering and hoping the sun would show up and warm us. Cecil had his usual position on the bow, I was on the stern.

We had just come into Lock C, grabbed our lines and were quietly waiting for the waters to surge in and lift when I heard a yell. "MY GAWD. There's a snake. Look at that!"

I didn't dare let go of my line, as the water was rolling in and we were on a lift. Cec backed off from the cement wall.

Skip stuck his head out of the starboard door. "What's happening? What do you see?"

Cecil, hanging onto his line and probably five feet from the slimy lock walls, pointed to the ladder riveted to the walls. "Look at that. Look at that."

Skip looked and said, "My GAWD. You're right. A snake!"

The snake was coiled up on the next to top rung leading to the crest of the lock. The lockmaster, having heard the yelling, came over and looked down. "Oh, he's nothing. Just a water snake taking a rest. Let him be. When the water comes up he'll take off."

Poor Cecil. What a trauma. Later he reported the two had looked one another right in the eye. It unnerved him so much he wrote a poem which he sent to Lockmaster C. The poem read:

LOCK C

I wrote on a wall of a lock so deep
My name as a treasure for the world to keep
Oh, deck hand so low with thought sublime
To write out "Cecil" in a veil of slime.
Generations may come and man may go
But they all will see when descending below
That this infamous lock, this lock of C
Will reveal a name on the Tom Bigbee

It's Cecil, oh Cecil covered with muck
To be so slow was just my luck
So have heart dear fellows where ere you be
Things could be worse
You <u>could</u> be in LOCK C!!!!!!!

HUCK, TOM AND BECKY

The Tom Bigbee was a beautiful, quiet waterway. It was so great to cruise quietly along and enjoy the beauty of the wilderness surrounding us. We met many barges, but the canal was very wide and we felt comfortable as we passed. Our only concern was the engine which was behaving badly. A shout would come from Skip, out would go the anchor, up went the floorboards and Skip disappeared into the engine compartment. He was finding water in the engine almost every hour now. It began to be a great worry, and the two men considered quite a few possibilities as to what was wrong. We stopped at working marinas where Skip could load up on oilcans. We were not making the time or speed that Skip had hoped and our early morning rising became a habit. The morning mists were so beautiful, but as we got farther south they became less penetrable. One morning we had to go totally on radar and trust it to guide us away from the paths of the behemoths bearing down on us or coming toward us. Never having used much radar except when we crossed Lake Michigan, we trusted Skip's ability to read this confusing jigsaw puzzle of shapes. We tooted the foghorn and constantly listened for the rumbling of high-powered engines. Skip seemed able to read this maze easily and knew where the banks were, the size of the ship near us, or where a floating piece of debris was. Nevertheless this was another hairy/scary two hours before the sun shone through the fog and it dissipated.

The next few days we alternated going through locks and pulling toward shore so Skip could swear at the engine and feed and burp it with cans of oil. We had several mechanics along the way check it out. They all offered their opinion as to the problem and the solution. Skip tried them all. Water continued to seep into the engine and it was not getting any better. We were grateful to the lockmasters and the Corps of Engineers along the way. They were unfailingly courteous and helped us zap in and out of the locks with alacrity. At one stop to check the engine we tied up at a "Tote 'n Flote." It was great to find a spot close by where I could walk and buy groceries.

Near the end of October the captain had us up and out on the water by

5:45 A.M. It was still moonlight and we were headed for the Columbus Lock. There were fading fall colors, but as we were in the mid-section of Mississippi, they were not near as colorful as farther north. As the engine sputtered and slowed down, we pulled off at 3 P.M. into a tiny town called Belmont. We were loaned a truck and drove into the small town for a blackened catfish dinner. It was delicious and a welcome break from the worry daily under our noses.

We continued much too slowly, and the men felt we had a severe engine problem, as yet unanswered. A weary captain who was tired of working on the engine pulled us into Sumter State Park. We were just over the border into Alabama. As we tied up at a rickety dock, a park attendant appeared. We told him our troubles and he commiserated with us. "Y'all better be careful. Tomorrow you go through Bay Springs Lock and it's an 82-foot drop." His last words to us as he left us alone were, "Incidentally, y'all better not climb off your boat at night. There's plenty of cottonmouths out here that'll gitcha!" Oh hooray! One more problem. I checked around the whole hull to make sure no ladders for climbing critters were available.

He was right about the Bay Springs lock. It was truly overpowering to be let down into such a chasm. With Halloween just around the corner, we thought the squeaks, squawks, moans and groans of the lock machinery were just a perfect accompaniment for ghosts and witches. We had to find some levity in our daily happenings. The engine problem was becoming all-consuming.

At Gainseville we found a quiet, pleasant, uncrowded marina. Across a grassy area we saw what looked to be a raft with a blue tarp stretched over it. Curious, we went to investigate. We found two youngish in-their-twenties men who were floating down the canal in a raft. They did have a small six-cylinder engine in case it was needed, but they also had long poles and were having a difficult but fun time. They were curious about us, too, and between us we decided we were all of the Tom Sawyer vintage and the two men dubbed the three of us "Huck, Tom and Becky deliver DOLLY." This marina was going to be among our last.

By this time each day had become a nightmare with water leaking into the engine and the head gasket. Skip was making too many oil changes and putting in eleven quarts each time. He was desperate for a good mechanic, as we had a long, long way to go. We heard a tornado warning on the VHF and decided to pull into Demopolis, AL, for the night and find a really good diesel engine mechanic. We were told by the dock master, "Ya'll need a diesel doctor." We knew that! The 110 miles down to Mobile could never be navigated with the problem we had under the floorboards.

Cecil and Skip rented a car and went looking for a diesel mechanic. I tried to prepare some decent kind of dinner for two tired, unhappy men. I had few groceries and didn't know a soul in this busy, full marina. Within the hour they came back with a grizzled, friendly black man. He climbed down into the engine compartment and began to feel around in special places. Within three minutes he located the trouble. "Ya'll got a cracked block. It can't be fixed. Ya'll gotta buy a new engine." It was our worst fear which had occasionally been mentioned but the thought had been discarded right away. This great mechanic said he would try to fix the cracked block and to give him two days, but he was unsure. Skip, not wishing to tell the owner of HELLO, DOLLY that a new engine would have to go in, decided to give it a try.

Cecil and I used the rent car to tool around the area, visiting Selma, AL, and surrounding interesting areas. We always came back to the torn-up boat for the night as we did not wish to abandon Skip. By the third day it was evident there could be no repair. A new engine would have to be ordered, flown in and installed. The time frame was one we could not afford to use. We had a boat show ahead and it would take us time to get our press releases ready, trailer up the ARIZONA and head for Tacoma Dome, WA. With a lack of enthusiasm, we had to say goodbye to the captain. We had become such a team in helping one another that it did not seem right to desert him, but he certainly understood and we pledged another trip together.

With hugs and kisses all around, Cec and I left for Mobile, then a long drive to New Orleans, where we would catch a plane for Reno and home. We had a car at the Reno airport and would be there within a few days. It was interesting but nostalgic to drive along the Louisiana coastline where we had tied up on two previous trips with our friends, then with Skip. We again repeated to one another it was more fun to visit all the various cities by boat rather than by car. The problems may have been much bigger but we loved being on the water. We decided (for the umpteenth time) that "Coming ashore is a bummer."

1991

Afton, MN to Dubuque, IA

St. Croix River
Mississippi River

USS ARIZONA

Capt. Skip Crabtree
Cecil and Pat

Afton, MN to Dubuque, IA—1991

OL' MAN RIVER—AGAIN!

During the next two years we kept busy with boat shows in the West. Bill and Skip came to visit us at different times and we all wanted to take another trip. The USS ARIZONA was by far the star of our fleet of seven ships. She was much in demand for appearances—as were we—to put on a program for many civic, service organizations and schools. We always enjoyed talking of our water adventures. The trials, tribulations and the perks were fun to share. We showed our videotapes along with this.

We continued to work closely with the USS ARIZONA survivors and Pearl Harbor survivors and were happy to trailer ZOE to the latter's parades. The PHSA men usually walked honor guard around the gray lady, and the cheering parade watchers honored them with their clapping and flag waving.

We had attended some of the USS ARIZONA's survivors December 7 ceremonies which were held every year in Tucson. There was always a solemn ceremony in front of the University of Arizona where the "tolling of the bell" was a ritual honoring the lost men on the Pearl Harbor USS ARIZONA. Our ARIZONA would be on display in front of the University of Arizona's steps. We enjoyed being with these special men, and when 1990 was nearing an end, we talked with Skip about doing a Mississippi River trip with ZOE which would bring attention to the 50th anniversary of Pearl Harbor.

Our prime motivation to do one more trip in honor of December 7, 1941 was due to a proposal from Matson Navigation Shipping Co. in Oakland, California. They offered to take our USS ARIZONA to their Matson yard in Honolulu free of charge! If we would trailer her to Oakland on November 20, 1991, she would be placed on a ro-ro, a "roll on/roll off" type of ship that carried all kinds of supplies needed in the islands. We were thrilled to think we might be a small part of this ceremony. Matson had heard of our various boat trips and had been contacted by those involved in pulling together the various celebrations and memorials for the days surrounding the 50th year anniversary. We knew our USS ARIZONA survivor friends would be in Honolulu for at least a week for the memorial. They were to have a private ceremony on the ARIZONA Memorial and another at Punchbowl where many ARIZONA men were buried. When the USS ARIZONA survivors heard that we would be in Honolulu with our miniature battleship, they generously invited us to be a part of their very select group. What an honor for us! We were hearing plans for the President of the United States and an entourage of service people to be there, too.

Skip accepted the position of captain immediately and we made plans to begin our December 7, 1941 anniversary reminder trip in mid-June of 1991. We would begin way north on the St. Croix River, then head into the Mississippi. Skip would be sent ahead to purchase a boat on which the three of us could live and which would also, when needed, be able to tow the USS ARIZONA. We were excited about the prospect of one more trip! We picked up more pen pal letters from some northern California schoolchildren and from the state of Arizona. We would distribute these along they way, even though it was summer. We knew there would teachers somewhere "out there" who would visit us along the Mississippi River and hold the letters until school began in the fall. This later proved to be true.

June 12 and we were off to Beatty, Nevada, Wickenburg, AZ, then to Tucson, AZ, where the ARIZONA had been reposing since our last appearance there. She was dusty, dirty and covered with grime. We hooked her up and took off for New Mexico. The same chatter began again as our gray lady was shadowed by truckers. "What's that y'all got there behind yuh? Is it radio controlled? Where yuh goin? That thing shoot backwards? Ah thought it wuz a submarine trailin' along behind yuh. He sits in the conning tower? Well, I'll be ^%#$@. What's it running on?" The questions and our answers were passed along on the CB mile after mile. A trucker would give our mile marker location and tell his buddy miles away where he thought they could catch us. They were always polite and complimentary, and we whiled away the miles answering questions. We were warned about coming down the Mississippi. "Don't fool with that b----! That lady's a no-good muddy broad." We assured the curious ones we had been down the river once and had an experienced captain taking us. Again we were cautioned about barges and tows and we acknowledged their interest and thanked them. "Thanks for talkin'—jist wanted to know what it was. Nice little job there. Wish I could see it up close. Catch you on the next go-round." With that the trucker would pull out and soon be a small blip on the horizon.

We slowly made our way through Texas, then it was on to Oklahoma where Cecil had some relatives who owned thousands of acres of wheat, cattle and oil. We had been invited to stop by, visit them and their relatives, and meet the local farmers. By this time we had already had four newspaper interviews in the flatlands of our vast country. We would pull into a small town gasoline station and someone would inevitably ask us to wait while they called the local newspaper to "come on out and take a picture of this battleship that's on a trailer!" Overhearing some of the description about us and our battleship given to the local newsrooms, I wondered if they would even bother to come see us. As I listened it really sounded preposterous.

We had a wonderful time with the relatives who invited the farmers from miles around to come and see the high-profile oddity parked alongside their many barns. The locals were very flattering in their surprise and astonishment to see something so water-oriented on their flat lands. We were made to feel very welcome, but we had to be on our way shortly, so it was on to Kansas. We had a future date with Skip up above the head waters of the Mississippi on the St. Croix River.

Afton, MN was a very small town on the St. Croix and 18 miles south of Minneapolis/St. Paul. Skip had preceded us by a week and said he would meet us at a special restaurant on June 26. We were so glad to see him come walking in. The reunion was wonderful. With him was our first Afton benefactor, Lori Wall. She and her husband, Kevin, managed the Houseboat Vacations in St. Croix. We were glad to meet them and it was obvious Skip had already carved a niche for himself with them. What a great front man he always was for us, equal to any emergency or challenge. He would need that ability during the next few weeks.

Skip had talked on the phone with the service manager of a local Afton marina, who painted a great picture of a Chris Craft boat we were to buy and name (again) the PEARL H. He guaranteed the engines would run, so on June 17 Skip arrived at the marina to check out the boat. The first thing he inspected was the oil filter on the port engine. He took it off and it was full of water. When he checked out the starboard engine, he discovered some cracks on the manifold that had been repaired. By this time we had purchased the boat and Skip felt that there was more work on it than had been anticipated or revealed. This was about the point where we came into the picture.

The Walls had ten large houseboats all lined up along their docks. All were rentals and used mainly in the summer. They generously donated one to us so that Cecil and I could sleep on the top interior deck and be near the ARIZONA and the "new" PEARL H. We spent four days on the houseboat, then felt it was cramped and we were taking advantage of the generous owners, so we moved to a Super 8 motel a few miles away. Meanwhile, Skip and a friend he had called to come help him work on the engines had the PEARL all torn up. They rebuilt the carburetors and totally rebuilt the distributors (the distributor on the port engine was so rusted it had to be chipped out). They finally got the starboard engine started, but the port engine would not start. Carl, Skip's friend, took a compression test. They had zero compression in one cylinder—it went from 165 to zero and none of the eight cylinders was the same. All this was reported to us as we continued to journey from the motel to the marina and wonder about any progress being made. Carl decided that the operation was a success, but the patient had died.

The decision was the starboard engine was ready to go, but the port engine was no longer a part of this world. We looked for another engine, but none was to be found. Carl had left, but when Skip called him, he said he would return from his home in Michigan and rebuild the port engine. Skip prepared it as best he could by pulling the heads off. We were horrified to find that in looking through the exhaust manifolds we found three dead birds inside. A large bolt had not been put back in properly by the former "highly-skilled service manager." Had the men been able to start the engine, the whole thing would have blown apart. The men worked six days replacing all the main bearings, the camshaft, and the piston rings. They became a bit more encouraged as they worked their way up through the mess. When they checked the heads, they found the reason there was no compression the valve jobs were totally unacceptable. What a mess we were in! The heads were taken in to Napa and re-done. The Napa employees were old friends by this time!

The men finally put everything back together and had a test. The engines ran to their satisfaction and everyone rejoiced. We certainly had been the focal point of many a visit and not because of our battleship. The locals were full of sympathy and advice, and there was rejoicing when the engines were pronounced "well." The good townspeople wanted us to head out for our journey to remind America's citizens, particularly the young people, about December 7, 1941. We were ready at last!!

We decided that a short run north would be a good test run before we headed down the St. Croix for the Mississippi. Since it was almost July 4, we were invited to stay an extra two days and participate in the small- town parade. With all the support we had had from the Afton people and the Walls, we were happy to join in. The parade was small but mighty in enthusiasm, with red, white, blue decorations and the many American flags being waved. We had a wonderful time, and Cecil and Skip rode in the jeep pulling ZOE and accepting accolades from the crowd.

On July 5 we launched Zoe, then PEARL H, and made a test run seven miles up river to the small town of Hudson. There was an odd "marina" type tie-up which was really a rickety bridge between the town of Hudson and an island called Beer Can Island. We wondered about that name, but we didn't have long to wonder.

The whole July 4 holiday was still underway. The Chamber of Commerce of Hudson welcomed us with a surprising array of gifts. They gave us a check for $110, three dinners out, one breakfast for three and $50 to spend in their town. What a wonderful gift. This certainly made up for having no water or power facilities on the fragile bridge tie-up. The three of us joined in on the small town's celebrations the whole day and made our way back to the ship. As usual there was a large crowd gathered around ZOE. The crowd was enchanted to hear that our boat was going to be in Pearl Harbor in five months!

We had long since learned that we had to string ZOE out where she was visible, but could not be climbed on or touched. There were certain attachments on the battleship that were fragile. Everyone was curious about her interior, but we always answered their questions and showed them everything upon our return to the boat. We just didn't want to have to be in the repair business constantly.

After visiting with the crowd, we went for dinner and returned to find a noisy celebration going on over on Beer Can Island. Some of the holiday participants were already well-oiled and were having numerous beer parties on their island. We went to bed early, but the partygoers had no intention of rolling up the sidewalks any time soon. The clump-clump of feet along the bridge was bad enough, but the shrill voices, the giggling, the pushing and shoving of friends became a bit noisy. July 5 was turning into a bacchanal. None of us said anything until one well-inebriated passer-by said, in hushed tones, "I'm going to loosen the lines on that gray battleship and send her down with the original." Before Cec and Skip could get their shoes on he had untied two lines, and I looked out to see ZOE beginning to move out with the current. Abruptly Cecil and Skip erupted up and out of PEARL and grabbed for the interloper. The air was full of "blue" sayings, the man's friends were trying to grab him and pull him away, and the scuffle was loud enough to attract other boaters who had been asleep. There was quite a hullabaloo, but the highly sloshed intruders staggered away as soon as possible. My two heroes tied ZOE with four lines, and Skip announced he would tie a string to a line and put it on his toe. I thought he really might do it, but it was so late that most party people had left the island, and we felt fairly secure.

We had only one other incident. We had barely gone back to sleep when from a boat down the line a highly intoxicated man and woman got into a fight. They emerged from their boat and started arguing. Fortunately, it was not about our battleship. We didn't need another altercation. Before two minutes had passed the angry man had thrown the woman into the river and the cursing from her was absolutely astonishing. Even Cecil and Skip said they learned something new. Someone fished her out as the two heroes I lived with did not volunteer any assistance. Chalk up another uneasy night!

We enjoyed one more day in Hudson and met two Navy League men who came to see our battleship. Skip spent time checking out PEARL's two engines and felt satisfied we could leave the next day. So early on July 7 we headed for Prescott, WI, twenty miles down the line. Skip and I went with PEARL and Cecil piloted ZOE the whole way. Our charts told us we would sashay back and forth between Minnesota and Wisconsin as we journeyed south. When we arrived around noon at Prescott, we found the swinging railroad bridge blocking our way down the St. Croix River. We got on the VHF to the railroad master. "Ah ain't gonna let y'all through unless yo' stops at the dock and let's me see that cute lil rascal ya gots." We were stuck between a highway and a railway bridge. The railroad master called his Coast Guard Auxiliary friends while we waited, and we ended up having lunch there with the railroad master and his buddies.

"CRUISIN' DOWN THE RIVER"

With the bridge now open, we left the St. Croix and went into the Mississippi with a strong current pushing us. There was no boat traffic. One of our new found friends told us of a quiet tie-up he would like to give us beside his big houseboat, right on the river. We gave him a ride on PEARL, his wife said she would meet us back at their houseboat home, and south we went. We ended up on the east side of the river under an overhang of large trees and had power and light that night! What a treat! We took our new friends to dinner. These good people followed us along the river for several stops and helped us pass out literature regarding the 50th anniversary of Pearl Harbor in several towns..

Arrangements had been made ahead of us to have a two-day stop at Red Wing, famous for its shoes. We were intrigued with the name and found ourselves back in Minnesota. We were welcomed by city officials and were given a tie-up right on their municipal seawall. We immediately put up our kiosk with all our pictures and the history from previous trips, and were interviewed on TV and by newspaper reporters. Then the visits began. We had many, many children and met such lovely people. We did have some Minnesota rain, but it didn't stop us. The three of us took turns meeting the public, and each of us was able to get away for shopping and a visit to the town. Again, we were doing a lot of walking.

Skip's chart showed a large body of water ahead of us called Lake Pepin. It sounded as foreboding as Albemarle and Pamlico Sound had on the eastern Intracoastal Waterway. We had best choose a good time to cross. This second PEARL did not have near as high a profile as the original one, but being under tow was always a worry. We also remembered our Chesapeake Bay antic when we lost the ARIZONA and had to be rescued by the Coast Guard. We listened carefully to the Coast Guard weather report and analyzed our chances.

Although the current was against us, Cecil and Skip managed to swing their boats out into the river and I soon had the ARIZONA tied up to our

stern and Cecil on board with us. We had a long, long run, but a quiet one.
Our guidebook recommended Lake City, a hustling, bustling marina full of
boats at the end of the lake. The dock master could not believe it when we
asked if we could spend the night with him. It's always difficult to say one
wants to tie up two boats (no one comes in that way—with two boats), one a
cruiser, the other a battleship. He insisted on giving us two slips side by side
and they were both free. When we told the dock masters what our journey
was about, their outreach to us was warm and generous. The word went out,
the media came down and once again we were inundated with visitors.
Everyone had something to say about the upcoming 50th anniversary of Pearl
Harbor. So many had a connection with a father or grandfather who had been
there. The Vietnam veterans quietly visited us and told us their stories. We
always listened with respect and thanked them for what they had done. We
seemed to evoke memories and emotion with the 36- ft. USS ARIZONA.
Our visitors respected what she represented. Anyone who had visited the
memorial in Pearl Harbor always told us about his or her experience visiting
the site. We found, again, we were sounding boards for people's frustrations
with government or their particular pent-up emotional memory. Once again
I found (in what I had learned to tell the boys was) my particular "hog heaven."
We had hit a marina with my three loves—a laundromat, grocery store and a
post office, all within walking distance! I was off! Later, on their own walks,
Skip told us he found a museum, and Cecil found a craft fair. I complained
about my female role, but no one was impressed with my lack of fun things
to visit. I also made noises about "women's slavery" but there was no
sympathy.

THE USS ARIZONA IS ATTACKED!!

The next morning we woke to the most horrifying sight I think we had ever seen. Two of us were westerners, one a Michigan person. None of us had seen such a sight. The Mayflies had invaded! Our battleship was black and so was PEARL H. I looked out the port window and gave a yell. "LOOK AT THE BATTLESHIP! LOOK AT OUR DECKS!" This got the other two sailors out of their bunks, and we gawked at the revolting spectacle. Mayflies have big, black, ugly bodies. The front pair of upright wings are much larger than the hind wings and they have two or three tails. They may look like cute little sailboats when they float alone on the water, but when thousands of them cluster in one spot, it is not a pretty picture. The men grabbed a dock hose and began to try to get them off our decks, then from all over the ARIZONA. The Mayflies were not overly endowed with brains and heedlessly flew into our faces and clung to us with passion. Yuk! The morning decision was instantly made to depart Lake City and head for Wabasha. Perhaps Mayflies had not discovered that part of Minnesota yet. Just before we left, we had a glimpse of the Mississippi Queen heading upriver. We could hear her calliope playing in the distance. What fun to see her!

Mid-July and we had an almost-horror-story day. We got off OK from the marina, but I had trouble tying up Cecil and ZOE. Wakes from barges rolled in on us, and ZOE and the new PEARL did not respond to my tightening grasp on lines. We finally got the battleship in line and Cecil on board. We had three locks to go through and made it in and out of the first two with precision. We would tie the battleship up on PEARL's free side while her other was sliding up and down in the locks. Cec would climb up, out and over ZOE and get on board with us so he and I could handle the lines or bollards while Skip managed the engines. We thought we were a meticulous, highly-trained threesome by now after the many miles behind us. We were congratulating ourselves about our dexterity after two locks. Only one more to go. Easy! Not so. The port engine had begun to die and Skip kept restarting it. We thought we were so good that we did not send Cecil in separate from us. We had him tied to the port as we knew our starboard side would be tied to the side of the lock. Just as we were coming into the lock, the port engine quit and PEARL began to swing around. We nearly crushed ZOE against the side until Cecil and I grabbed boat hooks and pushed her away from the concrete walls.

We were able to get out of the marina to the nearby small town of Alma and work on the engine. Skip discovered the trouble. The carburetor had never been put in right, and a needle valve was just floating around inside. The spark plugs were fouled. At last Skip got the engine going and we limped into the backwater marina. What a welcome from Great River Marina people. This was way back in a bayou, hard to find, but what a lovely, quiet spot. They helped us find spark plugs and the engine was fixed! We were treated like royalty, included in on the town Bar-B-Q, discovered that Alma was two blocks wide and seven miles long! What a welcome stay this was. We loved the quaint town and its people. We passed out many USS ARIZONA buttons and did local radio talk show interviews. Visitors were numerous, and we received a lot of advice for our next stop which would be Winona, MN. We kept sashaying across the river from Minnesota to Wisconsin and never could seem to remember in which state we were tied up.

Another after dinner confab was held among the three of us and we decided that we had best not venture south of St. Louis. We would concentrate on the northern, upper Mississippi, and with some niggling engine problems we would not venture overly far. We evaluated our tendency to go too far in one day, through too many locks and decided that we were suffering from "destination fixation." It was determined we would do one lock per day and go no farther than 15 miles per day. There were so many unknowns, too many unseen misfortunes that befell us. We were also experiencing terrible heat and humidity. The latter left us wrung out.

We decided to try a different technique for going through the locks. After telling the lockmasters our situation they allowed PEARL to come in first and I made her fast bow and stern. Then we brought Cecil in and tied her up on our free side. The system seemed to work better, and Cec would ride up or down in the boat rather than climb out and be on PEARL. It depended on what kind of a tie-up we had in the lock whether Cecil could stay in ZOE or not. As soon as we got out of the lock I would untie him and we would go our separate ways.

Now it was on to Winona, a place known for its gloves and knitting mills. It rained while we were there. We walked into town, ducked into a store and tried to buy an umbrella. They were all sold out, but the owners insisted we take two of the store's umbrellas. Again, such lovely people. They had read about our publicity and our ARIZONA in the local paper and were happy to meet us and give us what they could to make our stay more comfortable. When the rain was over, the heat and humidity began again and we felt wiped out. We wondered how mid-westerners stand that day-to-day barrage of heat and humidity (they probably wondered how we stand the California earthquakes).

After some great visits by the townspeople, we were off to Trempeauleau, WI. No sooner had we tied up than we found our publicity had preceded us and a newspaper lady came down to do a story on us. What a great new friend! She drove me to the laundromat in town. I had a huge load, and another nice lady doing laundry offered to drive me back to the boat. As soon as I arrived back, the men had found another volunteer who offered to take me shopping, helped me by carrying groceries and returned me to the municipal dock. We could never quite get over the outreach that people had toward us, but we always knew it was what the USS ARIZONA represented. The good, loyal American people were grateful for our "up with America" thought and were most anxious that the 50th anniversary of Pearl Harbor be memorialized and honored. They were so delighted that our ship and we would be there. We came to understand that we were symbols of their inner thoughts about their love of country.

LaCrosse, WI was our next stop, a much larger city. We were directed to the Bikini Yacht Club, which had a terrible current. We thought we had done the perfect tie-up for both boats when the dock master came out and told us of a mix-up. Tired, but grateful for a refuge, we had to move both boats so they would not be in the way of others coming in that afternoon. We had a lot of publicity ahead in this town, otherwise we would have left due to the very difficult change we had to make in a terrible current. This was one overnight pit stop and we put five lines on the boats to make sure we didn't slide out into the river during the night!

We left in the rain the next morning for Brownsville, MN. On the way we passed a messy spot by the river. We had heard of some freight railway cars overturning along the river. They were full of lumber and butter. The butter had all melted and run completely over the lumber and it was reported that the river was a mess. As we drifted by the area we could see the mix of wood anointed with grease! A boom had been thrown around the spot to contain it all. The cleanup was underway and we were glad to get by without being stopped.

Brownsville was a small city with a dilapidated dock full of holes. We were presented with another difficult tie-up for both boats, and I ended up having to do the hand-over-hand pull-in to get ZOE close to us. With Skip's help we managed to get both boats in without the always-feared "crash!" Despite the old dock area they had a very nice restaurant/bar facility. We found that this was an old logging town that had burned down in the 1800s and it looked as though they could be flooded out on occasion. The entertainment at the restaurant was darts, where I nearly became impaled.

END OF THE LINE

We had been on the water three weeks and were hoping that we could struggle to Lansing, Iowa, where we knew we had a ride back to pick up our truck/trailer in Afton, MN. We were having minor but irritating trouble with both engines. One would not start and Skip discovered it had shorted out. The humidity wore us down and we felt our energy diminishing. We made the 45-mile run to Lansing with only one lock to go through and were greeted by friends of the Walls in Afton. Nancy and Carlton Johnson welcomed us as old friends. They offered us their facilities, a bit rustic, but gratefully accepted. Here was our ride back to Afton, MN to pick up our truck and trailer. We were happy to contribute some dollars to Nancy for her help in driving us 175 miles north to Afton.

We very much enjoyed the beautiful ride through the rolling Iowa hills full of waving cornstalks. We found our rig and drove south to Lansing, then decided to run the vehicles down to our next stop of Prairie du Chien. We managed to hitch a ride back to Lansing where we thoroughly enjoyed walking into town and kicking back for a few days of rest. We bid *adieu* to our wonderfully helpful new friends and made a long run of 60 miles to the Prairie du Chien town. We found an easy-to-get-into marina, the laid-back kind full of laid-back people and dogs. The minute we tied up, the marina owner called the local radio station and we were all "on" immediately. We talked about our mission—to bring history and heritage to the young people of our country and also to have a high profile to attract their interest regarding 12/7/41 with our battleship. We were always questioned about "what powers the ship?" Skip was also interviewed and became very adept at fielding questions about our trip and his own captain's skills.

We spent four nights in this great city. We filmed their Civil War enactment, which was quite noisy and full of excitement for all viewers. We toured the Louis Villa, a grand old manor full of memorabilia of another age. The Prairie du Chien docents and townspeople were very proud of the restoration and preservation of this lovely old home. We drove around the outskirts of the city and were fascinated to find old Indian Mounds, a big part of Wisconsin history. We also had the usual logistics of going back and forth with truck, trailer, and every now and then, Skip's car. The wear and tear of doing this plus the blazing heat added to our growing need to finalize this trip. The night before we left Prairie du Chien, we had a pow-wow and decided that quality, not quantity, was the name of this trip. It was unanimously decided that Dubuque, Iowa would be our last stop. There we would mount up, try to sell PEARL H II, and each go our own way.

By this time we had had many Pearl Harbor survivors come to see us and they pleaded with us to make a one-week stop at the Marriott Hotel (Tan-Tar-A) at Lake of the Ozarks. These wonderful men were having a ceremony to honor their friends who were lost. They were so hospitable and welcoming that we felt we could take the time to visit them and make it possible for them to honor the men with whom they had served. We also found that we would be their guests at the hotel and they would take care of the TV and newspaper publicity. It sounded like a lovely area, one we had not visited, and we accepted their invitation.

Meanwhile, we began our final runs along Ol' Man River. Down to Guttenberg, Iowa, we ran. We seemed to be coming into ports that were most difficult to wind our way into the main docking area. We dodged snags and pilings and felt lucky to escape with undamaged boats. Here again it was move vehicles time and we were gone for two days. Down we journeyed to Cassville, where the docking was poor. However, the dock master moved a houseboat for us as Cec hung on his props outside the marina in the main channel. We brought him in and discussed where we should go in or near Dubuque for the final port..

Arrowhead Marina, just north of Dubuque, was recommended, and the marina men could not have been nicer. It was a difficult entry, but very protected when we got back in the bay. We had a great welcome and were told to stay there as long as needed. The locals put out the word to the newspapers and TV and we experienced people packing a picnic lunch, coming to sit on the grass by us, and just sitting there looking at ZOE. It was very flattering that they appreciated her so much. We felt safe in this area and tied ZOE out so she was visible, but too far out in the water to be tampered with. Here Skip actually painted PEARL, and when she was all gussied up, we took her downstream to two marinas to show her off and try to sell her. It seemed easy to go up and down river and through locks with only one boat to worry about.

We brought her back to Arrowhead Marina, put ads in the paper and continued to try to move off the boat and pack up all our gear. We were steered to a fine man who was one of the biggest yacht salesmen in the area. When we went into his office, he told us he had sold boats similar to PEARL in the St. Croix area when they first came out and he was familiar with the boat and its stability. We told him of our original engine problems that had been overcome and were truthful about the few problems left that erupted now and then. He seemed appreciative of our honesty, and we struck a deal that covered our original purchase of the boat and the repair work done by Skip and Carl. We were all satisfied.

ANOTHER ALOHA

Now came the difficult part where we had to say goodbye to Capt. Skip. We had one last game of cribbage, hugged and hugged, and he left for his home in South Haven, Michigan. It was the middle of August and we had ten days in which we could play and relax before heading for Lake of the Ozarks.

By this time PEARL H had been left for the new owner to pick up at the marina, and the USS ARIZONA had been placed by the Casino Belle gaming ship in Ice Harbor for one week. The owner wanted to display her, so she had been strung out by his office and the ship's gangplank. We picked up our check and Cec drove the ARIZONA over to a ramp where I picked him up. We almost lost the superstructure by failing to see a big cable strung across the river. A nearby fisherman yelled a warning and we just escaped decapitating our well-traveled lady. Would our boating problems ever end? we wondered. Probably not. There are just too many unknowns on the water.

We put ZOE in Dubuque storage and took off for northern Wisconsin. How impressed we were with the greenery, the cleanliness and the nice people. We stopped to see an old friend in Wild Rose, then drove as far as Bayfield and Cornucopia on Lake Superior. What a great way to relax. We missed Skip and ZOE, but we were ready for a rest before one more appearance. Then it was back to Dubuque, we picked up ZOE and headed south through Iowa cornfields and on down to Missouri's Lake of the Ozarks. What a welcome sight the lovely Tan-Tar-A Hotel was, and what a beautiful room we were given, looking out into the trees.

The PHSA left a message they would soon be there, for us to go ahead and launch and find our display spot which had already been chosen. We had the usual horror story of finding a ramp and it was not good. Whenever there was some grand, large marina, we always had help, but when there was some small, hidden, hardly-used ramp, we never had assistance. This was the occasion. It was just the two of us down a dusty, bumpy road, a narrow turn around, much backing and filling, and a terrible ramp with snags. Our motto by now was "been there, done that," and we knew we could survive this launch along with all the other difficult ones we had catapulted ourselves into—and overcome. Such was the case. I got Cecil and Zoe off the trailer and dragged the trailer back to a parking area, then tried to find him on the water by the hotel to bring him in. I found ZOE by seeing a large crowd of people all standing, pointing and gesturing to something in the water. I knew this was the spot. There he was and I "pardon me'd" my way through the crowd so I could fend ZOE off and tie her up. The usual questions began and we were surrounded by a welcoming, curious, amazed mob.

Then the Pearl Harbor Survivor Association men and their wives came and such a time we had with them. There were banquets, meetings, display pictures of our various trips. Osage Beach's ABC and NBC covered the event. It was capped off by a serious ceremony where the Pearl Harbor men cast a beautiful floral wreath into the waters by ZOE. The solemn observance was duly noted by the media and hotel guests. We were privileged to be a part of this ritual as it meant a great deal to the ex-servicemen as they remembered their fallen friends.

After a memorable five days, we said our thank yous and goodbyes and exited Missouri for the far west. Back over Highway 70, through Kansas City, Topeka and into Denver. At last, THE WEST, with its high mountains and low humidity! The usual truck chatter clattered around us. "Ah tell ya, ah seen a battleship goin' west. Talked with the builder. It's a twin-screw boat and he crawls inside. He runs that rascal. It's cute all right. Be cute on the lake where ah live. Got guns, too. They bin all over. Show it to kids. Big kadoo about it. Cute little devil."

Another trucker was in denial. "What yo mean, y'all saw a battleship goin' west? Y'all #$$^ing me?"

Our "fame" seemed to travel back and forth across Highway 70. Truckers going both ways kept picking us up. Compliments and questions filled the airwaves. We were being handed off back and forth. It did help pass the long driving hours between motel stops, and it was great fun to have so many interesting CB friends. The gas stops were always a challenge due to the rapidity of the questions, comments and compliments. We always had press releases with us which we passed out, and this helped unravel the mystery of the ship as people jumped into their cars and were off and running. After hearing of our seven waterway trips the *coup de gras* for our interested audience was the fact that the USS ARIZONA would soon be in Pearl Harbor. This seemed to delight everyone who took the time to hear about our goal and what we were trying to share with young people.

1991

Pearl Harbor, HI
December 7, 1991

USS ARIZONA

Cecil and Pat

Pearl Harbor, HI—1991

HONOLULU HAPPENINGS

We arrived home in time for Labor Day and some much-needed relaxation in our High Sierra mountain air. ZOE was in bad shape and needed to be repainted and refurbished for her appearance in Honolulu. We began to finalize trip plans and were delighted to find that one of the Pearl Harbor survivors who had escorted us along the Staten Island's New York roads in 1986 had made arrangements for our ship to be displayed in Honolulu. We were to be in the lobby of the Sheraton Waikiki, where many of the survivors would be staying as they memorialized the 50th anniversary. What a great event lay ahead. We had several conversations with the public relations heads of Matson Navigation. They could not have been more helpful or welcoming to us. We assured them we would have our ARIZONA dockside in Matson Navigation's Shipyard, Oakland on November 20.

The weather held as we drove the 325 miles to Oakland, and we found ourselves wandering aimlessly through the industrial area of this large shipping complex. We finally found the right gate to enter and pulled into Matson's yard. The astonishment of the workers brought them running to check us out. Press releases with pictures were passed out and this always saved us time and talking. We found the head engineer on the ro-ro, and he had us drive right up the steel runway and into the bowels of the ship. ZOE would be protected from severe wind and waves, but she would be outside under a large deck. We unhooked the trailer and saw to it that the chains were properly hooked into the deck flooring and she was tied down well in case of rough weather. We had another nice offer. Would we like to ride over with our ship on the ro-ro and use the owner's stateroom? We accepted with alacrity. Bidding *aloha* to our beloved ship, we thanked the crew and were off for Lake Almanor. Home we went to pack for our ocean voyage to Honolulu. Alas! It was not to be. We had a call that the ro-ro would be carrying pigs as cargo to the islands, and the pig handlers were going to be placed in the owner's stateroom. To our surprise we found that not enough pigs were raised on the islands for luaus, and pigs had to be imported from Iowa. We quickly made airline reservations and were ready.

Arrangements had been made for a member of Honolulu's fleet reserve to use his truck to pull ZOE to the Sheraton Waikiki Hotel. We never seemed to run out of good people to help us. Arrangements were made to stay in a condo near the hotel, and the day after we flew in we met our fleet reserve helper at the Honolulu Matson yards. As soon as we were hooked up to his truck, he took off on Honolulu's freeways, then went onto the main drag through the busiest part of town, Kalakaua Avenue! What a sensation we caused as we went ripping along the streets. This Navy town was certainly tuned into the fleet's comings and goings, and the hand waving and salutes in our direction were so welcoming. The huge hotel had a roundabout that was full of stretch limos, taxis and cars. Our driver did yeoman service in getting our 36-foot boat up and over the curb and by the portico. It was not an easy job as there were hotel guests all over the place. At last ZOE was in place; we had her masts and flags on her and she looked quite regal. We gave her one last wax polishing, and she sat on her trailer ready to greet the ex-servicemen who would soon be arriving.

Our appearance at this grand hotel was from December 1-9, 1991, and it was sensational. We were visited by PHSA men and their wives; by Japanese nationals who were so interested in the ship; by servicemen stationed in Honolulu, by retired admirals and flag officers; by schoolchildren; and by CBS and NBC. We were "on" almost all day. The hotel provided a night watchman who checked our boat and trailer on his rounds. We had no vandalism to the boat any night, but we had one mysterious thing that happened night after night. Someone came along and took the 12x16 American flag that was flying on the taff rail. We kept replacing it and we would find that it had disappeared during the night! Tired of buying replacements, we bought a plastic American flag and put it on when we left for the night. The thefts stopped. We wondered in whose room in what country our flags must be!

We have no idea how many pictures were taken of our ARIZONA— alone and with us. Everyone was getting ready for the big day, December 7. What an honor it was to be included in the USS ARIZONA Survivor group, down to approximately 50 men. Most were there for the memorial visit, although a few could not make the trip. We were included in a special visit to Punch Bowl and an observance there. The highlight was being out on the ARIZONA Memorial with these fine men for their own private remembrance. We watched as many wreaths were placed in the sea over the sunken wreckage of their ship. It was an emotional time as the men spoke of a brother or friend who went down with the ship. We will never forget all that a nation did to commemorate this day for those lost.

Senator and Mrs. John McCain—Sheraton Waikiki Lobby—Honolulu

Our only disappointment was not being allowed to launch our own ARIZONA. There were several retired Cinqpac commanders who tried to help us get permission to be on the water near the sunken ship on December

7, but we heard that the Secret Service did not want any "foreign objects" near President Bush. We suggested that anyone could search our ship to see if we had explosives of any kind, but we were given a definite "no go." We were strange, off-beat, civilians and unknown. Those protecting the president and the memorial were too afraid that something would be blown up or something untoward might happen. Our whole group was frustrated, but we understood their concerns. We were just one more headache to check out. We did participate in a wonderful parade down Kalakaua Street. Our friend Senator John McCain was at the forming up area, and we exchanged memories of our time in Washington, D.C. with him. As we moved down the parade route, he waved and saluted our ship. What a memorable time this ten days turned out to be. We felt we had reached the apex of our journeys with our ARIZONA. By this time she had 6700 water miles under her hull, and she was showing signs of wear.

When the commemorations were over and people left, we, too, packed up ZOE for her return trip to Oakland. Whumpity-bump! Our Fleet Reserve driver took us over the Sheraton Waikiki's curb and into the busy street. Back to Matson's yard we went and left ZOE in their good care. We shall always be grateful to the Matson Navigation Company for their generosity in making it possible for us to participate in our nation's 50th anniversary of this infamous day. Our pictures of this event are wonderful, but the memories in our hearts are the ones we cherish. What a privilege to be able to make a small contribution to this national event.

WE SWALLOW THE ANCHOR

We timed our departure from Honolulu for San Francisco so we could pick up the ARIZONA and trailer her back to our mountain home. We stored her away for the winter and evaluated what we should do about the logistical problem of having seven ships in our fleet. The maintenance and storage of seven ships, seven engines, seven sets of flags, seven trailers, the insurance…it was getting to be a bit much! Participating in our country's 200th birthday, the unveiling of the Statue of Liberty and the finale of the 50th anniversary of Pearl Harbor had accomplished the zenith of our trips. What more could we do? We talked this over with our supportive board of directors and we all felt we should begin to scale down the fleet. How does one go about dispersing ships of this odd configuration?

First, we decided to take all the engines out of each boat and sell them as display models rather than on-the-water craft. We were advised that we did not want liability problems. We all felt that we should never sell to an individual, but our ships must go to an organization that would honor the men who had served on the various craft. We remembered one man in Miami when we did that boat show who wanted to buy our battleship. After pursuing us with offers for several days, we asked him why he wanted the ship so badly. "Because I want my wife to be the first one to water ski behind a battleship in our marina," was his answer. Oh no! We couldn't let them go for any price if they were not to be used properly.

Our first move was in the Fall of 1992 to donate our 36-foot gray lady and her trailer to the Navy League in Phoenix, Arizona. The fine men in this organization came to our home with a truck and trailered her to that city. How hard it was to let her go. A boat comes to life under her grateful owner's hands and we had been through so much with this ship (6700 water miles and 8000 road miles) that we had difficulty in parting with her. We knew she would have tender, loving care and would be seen in parades and at veteran's programs, but is was so hard to say goodbye to her. As the men pulled out of the driveway, our vision blurred as her stern disappeared around a corner.

We did have one great finale with her. That fall Capt. Skip flew to Phoenix from Michigan, and we flew there, too, and he joined us for a ceremony in which we gave our ship to the Navy League.

It was an impressive event with the governor, Senator McCain, numerous Navy flag officers and many dignitaries in attendance. Cecil and I both spoke and thanked the Navy League for their care for our boat and told a little of where she had been. It was a memorable day and brought to a close a chapter in our lives we would never forget. We have since heard that our USS ARIZONA has been used in the Fiesta Bowl Parade and numerous veterans' events. We are grateful she has a good home in Arizona.

We began to concentrate on our RMS TITANIC and found that we were welcome with her at several West Coast boat shows. We went as far north as the Tacoma Dome show and as far south as the southern California Long Beach show. We also used our USS BICENTENNIAL for several events. We went to Farrugut, Idaho for a Navy reunion. We continued to be covered by TV when we were at these events, but our appearances began to taper off. One of our final TV features was in 1998 when an ABC station from Sacramento, CA came to our lake and did a long feature on the RMS TITANIC. This ship suddenly became a high-profile ship and in demand, due to the release of the movie *Titanic*.

Our boating activities gradually diminished, but Bill and Skip continued to visit us occasionally. We began to actively contact service organizations that might be interested in purchasing our vessels and trailers. Although there was a great deal of interest, we did not have many solid offers come through for us. There was some interest in having the ships stay in our local lake area, but this never materialized.

Then action picked up when the USS ALABAMA crewmen's association became interested in our gray battleship, the USS ALABAMA (BB 60). Thanks to old friend, J.R. Brown, he and a friend who had invited us to speak at the ALABAMA's reunion in Mobile in 1985 came up with a Ryder truck. They very much wanted to buy our 18-foot boat to be displayed by the big "mommy" ship anchored off Mobile, Alabama. That is where she reposes today, and we hear she is protected in a small building by the big lady and away from the elements and is used in parades. At the same time a man who represented the USS SOUTH DAKOTA's reunion association bought our BB 57 for his group. We understand she is being used in that state's rivers for recruiting purposes and parades. Each time we sold a boat, we had several days of nostalgia, although nothing quite compared with parting with ZOE.

A few years later, in 1999, we flew to Corpus Christi, Texas, and made a presentation about our USS BUNKER HILL (CV 17) to the USS LEXINGTON director. The latter is an angle deck carrier, but the original "LEX" was an Essex straight deck as was our carrier. The "LEX" is now a museum anchored off Corpus Christi. The directors seemed interested in purchasing her and soon sent a LEXINGTON employee from Texas to Reno where he rented a truck and drove up to pick up our BUNKER HILL. Their plan was to repaint her, change her number and rename her USS LEXINGTON (CV 16). The last we heard she had been featured in a Corpus Christi parade, and the directors were pleased to tell us they had won first prize for their entry. Our aircraft carrier reposes on the inside flight deck on the big "mommy" ship, and we are told she is the first display the children run to see. Last year, 2001, we sold our beloved red, white and blue USS BICENTENNIAL (BB 76) to the American Legion Post in Sacramento. Although we knew she was going into loving, caring hands, parting with this ship was another wrench to our hearts. Such memories went with our BICENTENNIAL lady and Bill.

Now it is the year 2002, and we have one gray battleship left, the USS MASSACHUSETTS, and the RMS TITANIC. There is interest in purchasing them from different quarters, and eventually we will be boatless! Our shop and garages are almost empty, and we feel we have lost a special part of our lives.

It is a challenge to put 28 years of adventure into one book. It truly has been almost a hobby-out-of-control. I well remember lying awake late into the night many years ago wondering what I was getting into, wondering if I should go along with this crazy idea of giving birth to battleships (there was no carrier, TITANIC or ARIZONA at this time). I evaluated. What would this wild idea involve? What would it cost? What did I know about boats? What would happen to Cecil's dream(s) if I shot down his creativity and the great imagination? What should I do? What was right? In the early morning hours I decided it was the thing to do to support him, to learn about life on the water, to go along with his out of the ordinary inventions. As I look back, it was the correct decision. The myriad experiences, the hairy-scary parts, the highs, the lows, the *people*…the many privileges extended to us. What a trip! Having a fleet of Navy boats (and a TITANIC) has lifted our lives out of the even flow of teaching, where there are few waves, and into a world of excitement, exploration, escapades, treasured friends and special privileges. By joining the exclusive world of long-term boaters and having unique crafts to sail, we were privy to experiences that would usually have been out of our realm.

As we recapitulate, we are surprised at the scope covered over the years: hired to be "the hook" for 15 boat shows all over the USA; four and one-half typed pages of TV interviews; 26 large scrapbooks full of so many newspaper stories on our Friendship Fleet, Inc. that we have lost track of the count; meeting senators, congressmen, Navy brass, CEOs, ex and enlisted service men and women; tying up in over 225 marinas all through the South, East Coast and Canada; meeting thousands of well-wishers all over our country; having the support of our Board of Directors, our two captains and our dear friends who drove our boats for us on local waters and contributed dollars to buy more buttons to give to children; the great friends who cheered us on and did all they could to promote our patriotic crusade. The children we encountered were a high point!

We reiterate that, gratefully, we cut across all ages and all racial barriers. Everyone seemed to love the little ships and the history they represented. Strangers became friends. Their shock, surprise and eventual appreciation of the craftsmanship and the concept never ceased and was so genuine. It cheered us on when events beyond our control wiped us out or Mother Nature's capricious ways threw a curve ball at us.

How does one end this narrative of events? How does one say a heartfelt "thank you" to the hundreds (thousands?) who reached out to us? They took us into their homes, invited us to their churches, loaned us their vehicles, gave us dinners, drove us anywhere they could, gave us free tie-ups, escorted us in their own boats, gave us wonderful media coverage, rescued us on the water, took us to their family events, loved our boat(s)—most of all they trusted us.

We say "thank you" to the Navy, Army, Marines and Coast Guard for their help and outreach to us. What special times we had under their gated guardianship. They allowed us to enter their off-limits areas and shared their space with us. They watched over us along the whole southern and eastern coast and rescued us.

As we review this whole happening, we wish we could reach out and send a special, heartfelt "thank you" to all those wonderful people we met along the way in eight boating trips: oyster fishermen, dock and lockmasters, TV anchor people, reporters, small town American citizens, city officials, COs and XOs, youngsters now grown…it is a happy kaleidoscope of beautiful memories. If any of those good people "out there" read this, we hope they know how they helped us. We could not have survived thousands of miles of boating without their support.

The obstacles, the humongous problems, the logistics (tired of this word?) overcome, the dollars spent, the weariness at the end of each long day—it was all worth it. We are glad we did it!

Whoever you are out there, whoever reads this and remembers what you did for us—be assured we remember you all. From deep within our hearts, Bill, Skip, Cecil and Pat, we all truly say, "THANK YOU!!!"

We are glad *"YOU CAN'T GO INCOGNITO IN A BATTLESHIP!!!"*

PREAMBLE FOR FRIENDSHIP FLEET, INC.

We believe in the fellowship of man.

We believe that the United States of America best embodies the fulfillment of man's noblest aspirations.

We believe that the heritage and history of the United States of America, particularly its long and proud naval history, can serve as an inspiration for all peoples of the world to strive for peace with freedom.

We believe that the youth of the world can benefit immeasurably from a greater familiarity with America's naval history, and through it a better understanding of the ideals and principles we hold dear.

Therefore, Friendship Fleet, Inc., a voluntary association of concerned individuals, will pursue the following goals as a service to our country and all mankind:

1. To preserve the spirit of American history, particularly American naval history, for future generations of Americans.

2. To promote a greater understanding of American naval history among American youth and the youth of the world.

3. To give freely of our time and talent to bridge the gap between our people and the people of the world.

4. To undertake educational projects in our country, and abroad, which will demonstrate—through naval history and shared technology—the willingness of Americans to share the benefits of our society with others;and...

5. To foster good will among the peoples of the world.

FRIENDSHIP FLEET, INC. TELEVISION/RADIO LOG

Date	Location of Viewing Area and Event	Station
8/73	Lake Almanor, CA (news)	NBC
10/73	Los Angeles (Echo Park) Navy Birthday	NBC, CBS, ABC
11/73	Los Angeles (Ralph Story Feature pre-publicity for Los Angeles Boat Show)	Channel 11
1/74	Burbank (Elementary News for Schoolchildren)	Channel 11
2/75	Miami, FL (pre-publicity, Miami Beach Conv. Center Boat Show—Biscayne Bay)	NBC, ABC CBS

USS BICENTENNIAL trip—Miami, FL to New York

Date	Location of Viewing Area and Event	Station
4/75	St. Augustine, FL (news) Intracoastal Waterway	2 channels
4/75	Jacksonville, FL (news-awarded key to city)	1 channel
4/75	Brunswick, FL (news) 1channel	
4/75	Charleston, South Carolina (news)	2 channels
4/75	Wilmington, North Carolina (news)	2 channels
5/75	Wrightsville, North Carolina (news)	2 channels
5/75	Swansboro, N.C. (Washington, NC-news)	1 channel
5/75	Morehead City, North Carolina (awarded key to city)	2 channels
5/75	Norfolk Navy Base, VA (news)	2 channels
5/75	Wormley Creek & Navy Weapons Depot (news)	1 channel
6/75	Baltimore, MD (news)	1 channel
6/75	Philadelphia, PA (news)	1 channel
6/75	Sea Bright (Channel Yacht Club) NJ (news)	1 channel
6/75	New York City, 79th Street Yacht Basin	ABC, NBC CBS
7/75	Lake Almanor, CA (Kent Pierce Show— Sacramento)	NBC

3/76	Gates 16mm film, Miami to NY—2 showings	Channel 58
	(Los Angeles School's station)	

USS BICENTENNIAL-New York via Hudson River to Montreal, Canada

7/76	NY Harbor (Op Sail '76—Walter Cronkite)	ABC
7/76	Albany Yacht Club, NY (news)	1 channel
7/76	Whitehall, NY (Lock #4, Albany news)	Channel 6
7/76	Shelbourne Shipyard, Burlington, NY (news)	WXAC
7/76	Montreal, Canada (Expo '76—news)	2 channels
2/77	Disney's new Mickey Mouse Club	1 channel
7/77	" " " (repeat) "	

Four ships—NASHVILLE NAVY—Nashville, TN to Paducah, KY
Cumberland River

7/77	Nashville, TN (news)	ABC
7/77	Nashville, TN (news)	NBC, ABC
7/77	Nashville, TN (radio interview—10 minutes)	WKDZ
7/77	Paducah, KY (news)	NBC
8/77	Nashville (feature spot—7 minutes)	CBS
1/78	Marina del Rey , CA (Ray Duncan show—	
	pre-publicity, Los Angeles Boat Show)	NBC
12/80	Sacramento, CA (WEEKNIGHT feature)	NBC
10/81	YOU ASKED FOR IT	Nationwide &
		28 foreign lands
2/82	Re-run of above	
2/82	Marina del Rey, CA—	
	pre-publicity, LA Boat Show	Ch. 2,4,5,7, 9,
		11, 13
3/82	Sacramento, CA, pre-publicity—	
	Cal Expo Boat Show	NBC
4/82	San Diego, CA, pre-publicity—	
	San Diego Boat Show (news)	CBS
4/82	San Diego, CA—SUNUP talk show—	
	pre-publicity—boat show	CBS
7/82	Reno, NV—PM MAGAZINE feature—7 minutes	CBS
5/83	Lake Almanor, CA—Memorial Day	2 channels

10/83	Los Angeles, CA TWO ON THE TOWN (feature—5 minutes)	CBS
3/84	Repeat of above	
7/84	Lake Almanor, CA—launch of USS ARIZONA	CBS, Reno ABC, Sacramento
8/84	No. CA, feature show, EVENING MAGAZINE (all fleet filmed from Livecopter 3—Sacramento)	NBC
12/84	Dec. 9—Pearl Harbor Survivor's Assn. and Navy—San Diego Bay	All channels
1/85	PM MAGAZINE Nationwide	All channels
1/85	Marina del Rey—Los Angeles Boat Show—publicity	NBC, CBS, ABC, Ind

USS ARIZONA—Houston, TX to Panama City, FL Intracoastal Waterway

2/85	Phoenix, AZ—Gov. Babbitt/Legislature—by flag	NBC, CBS
2/85	Tucson, AZ—Univ. of Arizona CBS, NBC	
2/85	Fredricksburg, TX—dedication of stamp toAdm. Nimitz Museum	ABC, NBC.
3/85	Galveston, TX (news)	CBS
3/85	Port Arthur, TX (news)	CBS, NBC
3/85	Intracoastal City (Lafayette), LA (news)	NBC
4/85	Gulfport, MS (news)	CBS
4/85	Gulfport, MS (follow up news item)	CBS
4/85	Pensacola, FL—meeting mayor (news)	ABC, Ch. 4
4/85	Panama City, FL (news)	ABC, Ind.

USS ARIZONA—Tarpon Springs, FL to New York—Intracoastal Waterway

2/15/86	St. Petersburg, FL	ABC, Ch 13
2/15/86	" "	NBC
2/19/86	Sarasota, FL	ABC, Ch 40
2/23/86	Ft. Myers, FL	CBS, Ch 13
2/27/86	South Florida (WINK) feature	CBS, Ch 13

2/26/86	Stuart, FL	NBC, Ch 11
2/28/86	Pompano Beach, Lighthouse Point	Cable
3/16/86	Melbourne, FL	NBC
3/16-17/86	Orlando, FL	NBC
3/30/86	Jacksonville, FL	NBC, Ch 17
4/4/86	Savannah, GA	CBS
4/10/86	Charleston, SC	ABC
4/18.86	Wilmington, NC	NBC, ABC
4/19/86	Wilmington, NC	ABC, CBS
4/28/86	Elizabeth City, NC	NBC, CBS
4/30/86	Norfolk, VA	CBS
5/13/86	Washington, DC	CBS
5/23/86	Baltimore, MD	CBS
5/30/86	Philadelphia, PA	ABC
7/3/86	New York City, NY	CBS
10/86	Cable—feature USA	
3/87	Tacoma Dome Boat Show (news)	CBS, Ind.
6/87	Japanese TV-#1 show in Japan (Lake Almanor)	
2/89	Portland, OR Boat Show—	
	EXPO CENTER	CBS, NBC, ABC, KXL Radio
9/89	Oakland/Alameda Boat Show	NBC
7/90	Lake Almanor, July 4 (2 ½ minute feature)	NBC

USS ARIZONA Sails Down the Mississippi River

6/25/91	Minn./St. Paul—KSTP evening news	ABC
7/18/91	La Crosse, WI	CBS
7/24/91	Radio WPRE, Prairie de Chien	WPRE
8/31/91	Osage Bch., Marriot Hotel-Tan-Tar-A	ABC, Ch 8
9/1/91	Osage Bch	NBC, Ch 13

USS ARIZONA Goes To Pearl Harbor for the 50th Anniversary Remembrance

12/91	Honolulu, HI, 50th ann. Pearl Harbor	CBS, NBC
9/93	Farragut, ID 50th ann.—USS BICENTENNIAL	Ind.

4/98	Long Beach Boat Show	ABC, NBC
6/98	Tacoma Dome Boat Show	NBC, CBS
7/98	Sacramento, CA (feature story)	KIXE Ch 10 (ABC affil.)

CPSIA information can be obtained at www.ICGtesting.com
Printed in the USA
BVOW031947090413

317731BV00002B/194/A